The future of U.S.–India security cooperation

Manchester University Press

The future of U.S.–India security cooperation

Edited by

Šumit Ganguly and M. Chris Mason

MANCHESTER UNIVERSITY PRESS

Copyright © Manchester University Press 2021

While copyright in the volume as a whole is vested in Manchester University Press, copyright in individual chapters belongs to their respective authors, and no chapter may be reproduced wholly or in part without the express permission in writing of both author and publisher.

Published by Manchester University Press
Altrincham Street, Manchester M1 7JA

www.manchesteruniversitypress.co.uk

British Library Cataloguing-in-Publication Data
A catalogue record for this book is available from the British Library

ISBN 978 1 5261 5514 6 hardback
ISBN 978 1 5261 5515 3 paperback

First published 2021

The publisher has no responsibility for the persistence or accuracy of URLs for any external or third-party internet websites referred to in this book, and does not guarantee that any content on such websites is, or will remain, accurate or appropriate.

Typeset by
Servis Filmsetting Ltd, Stockport, Cheshire

Šumit Ganguly dedicates this book to his daughter, Tara, in the hope that her generation might see a better world.

Chris Mason dedicates this book with love to his daughter, Hannah. It's a big world out there Treasure, and full of adventures. My favorite one is being your father.

Contents

List of figures and tables	ix
List of contributors	x
List of abbreviations	xii

Introduction: an unnatural partnership? The future of U.S.–India strategic cooperation – Šumit Ganguly and M. Chris Mason — 1

Part I Military-to-military cooperation

1 Less than meets the eye: a critical assessment of the military-to-military dimension of the U.S.–India security partnership – M. Chris Mason — 19

2 Faltering friends: U.S.–India military cooperation in the twenty-first century – Abhijnan Rej — 38

Part II Cybersecurity cooperation

3 U.S.–India relations on cybersecurity: an important moment for strategic action on collective cyberdefense – Jamil N. Jaffer — 63

4 From intention to action: challenges in cyberdefense cooperation for the U.S. and India – Bedavyasa Mohanty — 78

Part III Nuclear stability cooperation

5 Southern Asia in a decaying nuclear order: regional strategic dilemmas and U.S. policy approaches toward India – Frank O'Donnell — 95

6 Enhancing nuclear stability in South Asia: the view from New Delhi – Rajesh Rajagopalan — 115

Part IV Space cooperation

7 U.S.–India strategic partnership in space: a path toward cooperation – Victoria Samson — 135
8 U.S.–India space cooperation: an Indian view – Rajeswari Pillai Rajagopalan — 151

Part V Counterterrorism cooperation

9 The U.S.–India counterterrorism relationship: striking the balance – Tricia Bacon — 171
10 Indo-U.S. counterterrorism cooperation: a bumpy road – Manoj Joshi — 197

Part VI Intelligence cooperation

11 A vision for future U.S.–India intelligence cooperation – Carol V. Evans — 219
12 Natural alliance: enhancing India–U.S. intelligence cooperation – Saikat Datta — 242

Part VII Defense technology cooperation

13 U.S.–India defense technology sharing and manufacturing: legacies of defense organizational processes – Frank O'Donnell — 263
14 "Make in India": a problem for bilateral defense technology cooperation – Pramit Pal Chaudhuri — 287

Index — 307

Figures and tables

Figures

1.1 Indian defense spending 2011–20 as a percentage of GDP. Chart by Eurasia Review News & Analysis. "India's Defence Budget 2019–20: The Slide Continues – Analysis". *Eurasia Review News & Analysis* (February 10, 2019). Online edition: www.eurasiareview.com/10022019-indias-defence-budget-2019–20-the-slide-continues-analysis/   22

1.2 Photo taken at Exercise *Yudh Abhyas* at Joint Base Lewis-McChord in Washington State, September 2019. Source: U.S. Department of Defense   27

1.3 U.S. Navy sailors man sensor arrays in the Combat Information Center of the Ticonderoga-class guided missile cruiser USS Vincennes (CG-49). January 1, 1988. Source: U.S. Department of Defense, photo by Tim Masterson, U.S. Navy (Released)   31

1.4 USS *Kitty Hawk*, at sea, September 5, 2007. Source: U.S. Navy, photo by Mass Communication Specialist Seaman Stephen W. Rowe   32

2.1 Schematic representation of the process of military cooperation   40

2.2 Indian Navy's share of defense budget. Source: "India's Defence Budget 2019–20: The Slide Continues – Analysis," *Eurasia Review News & Analysis* (February 10, 2019). Online edition: www.eurasiareview.com/10022019-indias-defence-budget-2019–20-the-slide-continues-analysis/   45

2.3 Comparing the Indian Army's pay, allowances and pensions with India's naval modernization budget   46

Tables

2.1 U.S.–India military exercises, 2014–19   49

11.1 The U.S. and India: their vital national interests in the Indo-Pacific   224

Contributors

Tricia Bacon is an Associate Professor at American University's School of Public Affairs.

Saikat Datta is an award-winning India-based journalist and author specializing in security issues and a founding partner of DeepStrat Consulting LLP.

Carol V. Evans is Director, Strategic Studies Institute, U.S. Army War College. Her wide-ranging research areas include: geoeconomics, Indo-Pacific maritime security, and U.S./NATO critical infrastructure protection.

Šumit Ganguly is a Distinguished Professor of Political Science, holds the Tagore Chair in Indian Cultures and Civilizations at Indiana University, Bloomington and is a columnist for *Foreign Policy*.

Jamil N. Jaffer is the Founder and Executive Director of the National Security Institute at George Mason University's Antonin Scalia Law School and a Senior Vice President at IronNet Cybersecurity; among other things, he previously served as the former Chief Counsel and Senior Advisor to the U.S. Senate Foreign Relations Committee and as an Associate Counsel to President George W. Bush.

Manoj Joshi is a journalist and author. He is a Distinguished Fellow at the Observer Research Foundation, a think-tank based in New Delhi.

M. Chris Mason is a retired Foreign Service Officer and a Professor of National Security Affairs at the U.S. Army War College.

Bedavyasa Mohanty is a lawyer and technology policy professional whose research lies at the intersection of emerging technologies and national security.

Frank O'Donnell is a Postdoctoral Scholar in the Rising Power Alliances Project in the Fletcher School of Law and Diplomacy at Tufts University, and a Nonresident Fellow in the South Asia Program at the Stimson Center.

Pramit Pal Chaudhuri is Foreign editor of the *Hindustan Times*, distinguished fellow Ananta Aspen Centre and member of the Indian National Security Advisory Board (2011–15).

Rajesh Rajagopalan is Professor of International Politics at Jawaharlal Nehru University, New Delhi.

Rajeswari Pillai Rajagopalan is a Distinguished Fellow and Head of the Nuclear and Space Policy Initiative at the Observer Research Foundation, New Delhi.

Abhijnan Rej is a New Delhi-based researcher, analyst, and consultant.

Victoria Samson is the Washington Office Director for the Secure World Foundation, a private organization that promotes a global, cooperative approach to ensure the long-term sustainability of space. She has over twenty years of experience in military space and security issues.

Abbreviations

BECA	Basic Exchange and Cooperation Agreement
CCIT	Comprehensive Convention on International Terrorism
COMCASA	Communications Compatibility and Security Agreement
DRDO	Defence Research and Development Organisation (India)
DTTI	Defense Trade and Technology Initiative
FATF	Financial Action Task Force
FMS	foreign military sales
FTO	foreign terrorist organization
GSP	Generalized System of Preferences
IDEX	Innovation for Defence Excellence
IOR	Indian Ocean Region
ISI	Inter-Services Intelligence (Pakistan)
MDA	Maritime Domain Awareness
MTCR	Missile Technology Control Regime
NCTC	National Counterterrorism Center
NTM	national technical means
PLAN	People's Liberation Army Navy
PRC	People's Republic of China
SDGT	Specially Designated Global Terrorist
TNWs	tactical nuclear weapons

Introduction: an unnatural partnership? The future of U.S.–India strategic cooperation

Šumit Ganguly and M. Chris Mason

Flawed assumptions?

For many American observers assessing the political, military, and economic status quo in Southern Asia, for more than a decade India has stood out as a potential security partner. From a U.S. perspective, India's strategic position – bordering China and Pakistan and jutting out like a thumb into one of the most critical maritime shipping routes on earth – is obvious. Its democratic values and its title as the world's largest democracy, added to self-evidently shared concerns about India's neighbor Pakistan, have seemed to many in the U.S. to make increased security cooperation a natural step for both countries. America's great military power and strategic reach, the Washington calculus goes, combined with India's geostrategic position and economic potential, appear to be the two sides of a solid strategic marriage of convenience. After all, both countries are largely dependent on maritime trade for economic growth, both share concerns about apparent Chinese intentions to dominate the Indian Ocean, and both are deeply troubled by an unstable state exporter of terrorism with nuclear weapons on India's contentious western border.

Indeed, viewed from the U.S. cultural perspective – of a country long accustomed to the security of vast oceans and benign neighbors – India appears to be almost completely surrounded by potential enemies and thus in need of powerful friends. China's carefully planned and growing assertiveness in the region, in particular, suggests that New Delhi should welcome a strategic ally, or at least a partner, to counterbalance China's rising economic and military power and its seemingly boundless appetite for strategic resources. Pakistan's unstable political foundations, its "forward-deployed" nuclear weapons, and its support for international terrorist organizations like Lashkar-e-Taiba make it, and other terrorist groups, a clear and present danger to both the U.S. and India. Indeed, for many American political and military leaders, this perception of a confluence of shared interests has become almost an article of faith. Why *wouldn't* India welcome a greater strategic partnership with the U.S.? Thus, for more than a decade, the U.S. has wooed India with words and deeds as a matter of national security policy. But to what practical effect?

The calculus is not nearly so simple, or as obvious, from an Indian perspective. There are many issues and concerns within India weighing against such a strategic partnership, at least as the U.S. generally conceives one, and there are some complex obstacles in the path of greater cooperation. Certainly the political climate between the two countries has thawed considerably since the days of the Cold War and India's leadership of the Non-Aligned Movement. The relationship is cordial, and punctuated frequently by the visits of the heads of state to respective capitals. Despite that, India still remains somewhat ambivalent about a more robust strategic partnership with the U.S. When India agreed in 2020 to purchase the Russian S-400 air defense system, despite ardent entreaties from the U.S. about the negative implications this would have on the bilateral security relationship, some observers in conservative circles in Washington began to question openly whether the U.S. strategic bet on India had failed.[1] Consequently, some uncertainty about the strategic partnership now exists in particular circles in Washington, D.C.

What happened?

Certainly, flawed U.S. assumptions and American naivety about its own exaggerated appeal played a role, as did an unwillingness in Washington to take no for an answer and to see India's polite rebuffs and foot-dragging as something more than "playing hard to get." But the political realities underpinning New Delhi's refusal to commit to a long-term strategic security relationship with the U.S. are more complicated than Washington's assumptions. Both capitals do agree that some sort of increased strategic cooperation, at least in some fields, would benefit both countries. The U.S. seeks a degree of exclusivity in this relationship, when it comes to security as well as to trade. However, India is still not ready to forge such a relationship. An elevated partnership with the U.S. in the future beyond the status quo today would likely take a form quite different from that of most traditional American defense partnerships.

Indeed, for a broad spectrum of reasons, India has reservations about any deeper strategic partnership with the U.S., and concerns about the nature of such cooperation which may ultimately prove insurmountable. Questions persist in India about America's trustworthiness, reliability, and motivations. In discussions with scholars and military officers in India, subtle questions about U.S. reliability and motivations always hover near the surface.

Introduction 3

U.S. leaders naturally proceed from an assumption that the U.S. is a trustworthy long-term ally and security partner. But while most Americans take this as a matter of national pride, citizens of other countries sometimes take a longer historical view. Some Indians will privately and tactfully remind visitors from the U.S., for example, of former pledges of support which the U.S. is seen to have abandoned – including those to South Vietnam, Iraq's Kurds,[2] and more recently the Iran nuclear agreement and the Paris Climate Treaty.

There are also perceptions in India that the U.S. eventually comes to dominate, and even bully, its strategic partners. There is real resistance to a strategic commitment which might lead to unequal standing, and to any security cooperation with a potential to morph into a paternalistic "big brother, little brother" kind of relationship. While national pride in independence in India takes a subtly different form from that found in some other parts of the world, it is nevertheless as strong a force there as anywhere else, and India's leaders will not countenance India as a second-tier partner to anyone. It is difficult to overstate the extent to which this concern generates an almost organic force of political resistance to the U.S. today, like two great magnets holding each other apart.

Another impediment has been India's insistence on "strategic autonomy." This stubborn policy position has roots in India's history of nonalignment, its persistent fear of any loss of its sovereign status, and its legacy as a postcolonial state. At one level, this concern may well be understandable, given the historical experience of the country. However, if India has any expectation of eliciting cooperation from the U.S. to address its extant security concerns, it will have to overcome its reservations about a putative loss to its "strategic autonomy." Another impediment to Indo-U.S. defense cooperation can be traced to a reflexive anti-American streak that still exists in India's political culture. Fortunately, with generational change in India this may dissipate over time.

How did we get here?

The history of the bilateral relationship is a field plowed frequently enough to require little additional tillage here. In brief, the Obama administration inherited a mixed hand from the Bush administration, which dramatically improved relations with India. At the same time, however, the Bush administration was completely taken in by ardent professions of cooperation for the War on Terrorism from Pakistan, which from 2001 to 2008 successfully played its favorite "double game" with a deeply credulous White House. The deceit began in late November, 2001, when Pakistan used the offer from President Bush for a face-saving exodus for the dozens of Pakistani military officers and Inter-Services Intelligence agents advising the Taliban and who were trapped in the Kunduz pocket in northern Afghanistan, to extract not only their personnel but also hundreds of senior Taliban and al Qaeda figures in blacked-out Pakistani cargo aircraft in what was dubbed "Operation Evil Airlift" by appalled American personnel on the hills outside the city.[3] Despite a steadily increasing body of evidence that Pakistan was gleefully double-crossing a naive American administration – receiving billions of dollars in U.S. military aid and actively supporting and arming the Taliban and other terrorist groups – the Bush administration was never one to be distracted from its beliefs by facts.[4] Working-level military and intelligence personnel repeatedly saw their reports of hard proof of Pakistani support to terrorists pushed back or down-played by upper levels of the Bush administration. One of the two editors, Chris Mason, saw this repeated multiple times while at the State Department prior to 2006. U.S. personnel on the ground in Pakistan cynically dubbed the ubiquitous Pakistani ploy of "arresting" a senior Taliban official 24 hours before the arrival of a high-level U.S. visit to Islamabad, only to let him go as soon as the official had flown home, Pakistan's "catch and release program."[5]

The Bush administration, to a substantial degree, accepted Pakistan's rationalizations for its seeming inability to forthrightly crack down on terrorists operating from its soil. There were also many senior and mid-level U.S. political appointees in the policy apparatus at the State Department and elsewhere who accepted Pakistan's posturing as a loyal ally "hook, line and sinker."[6] Colin Powell, George W. Bush's first Secretary of State, was openly pro-Pakistan and anti-India.[7] There were plenty of mid-level pro-Pakistan bureaucrats in important positions already, like Robin Raphel, who worked for Cassidy & Associates, a lobbyist for Pakistan, before returning to the State Department. Raphel eventually had her security clearance revoked during a federal investigation into evidence of espionage for Pakistan. She was cleared and left government service, but it would be naive to think Pakistan's influence on the U.S. bureaucracy ended there.[8] Generations of U.S. military personnel have been showered with warmth and gracious "hospitality" by their Pakistani military counterparts and treated like beloved comrades in arms, something India almost assiduously avoids. Pakistan also actively targets inexperienced U.S. diplomatic and aid personnel on their first tours with a slick propaganda campaign.[9]

Despite the penetration of so many Pakistani apologists into the system, however, in 2006 the Bush administration did achieve one game-changing, even historic policy success: the so-called "123 Agreement" (the U.S.–India Nuclear Cooperation Approval and Non-proliferation Enhancement Act), which formally became law in the waning days of the administration. The agreement effectively normalized and recognized India as a nuclear power. The signing of the accord on October 10, 2008 by then Indian External Affairs Minister Pranab Mukherjee and then Secretary of State Condoleezza Rice capped a three-year-long effort to put U.S.–Indian relations on a solid foundation. President George W. Bush became enormously popular in India as a result. Prime Minister Singh said at the time that "the people of India deeply love you, President Bush."[10]

Nevertheless, despite this popularity, the Obama administration inherited in January 2009 a vast South Asia policy apparatus which, like a giant supertanker on the high seas, would be slow to turn, even if there were a captain at the helm rapidly spinning the wheel. In fact, President Obama was not the type of leader to dramatically spin the wheel toward India in his first years in office. The pro-Pakistan personnel in various parts of the Departments of State and Defense during the Obama administration collectively had a similar effect on U.S. government efforts to improve ties and transfer technology to India as the anti-American bureaucrats in various parts of the Indian government have had on slow-rolling enhanced security from the Indian side: they could significantly slow it and partially dilute it, but not entirely stop it.

But the Obama administration was far less prone to the politicization of intelligence than was its predecessor, and, as evidence of Pakistan's duplicity piled up, the realization grew within the U.S. national policy apparatus that Pakistan was paying lip-service to cooperation in the War on Terror while actively promoting and exporting it.[11] The bin Laden raid which assassinated the al Qaeda leader in 2011 was a kind of watershed in U.S. policy in South Asia – a de facto de-hyphenating of India–Pakistan policy – and it marked a tectonic shift away from a Pakistan whose emperor now had few clothes left and towards an India whose importance against a rising Pakistan–China axis came into sharper focus. After Abbottabad, the scales fell from most American bureaucratic eyes, and the pivot towards India noticeably accelerated. Pakistan's gamble in hosting and protecting bin Laden backfired. President Obama now moved more assertively to "spin the wheel of the supertanker," to turn the ship of state towards India, and to advance U.S.–India strategic cooperation. The Obama administration first reached out to India on important environmental issues, and then named India a "Major Defense Partner." India agreed to buy six nuclear reactors from the U.S. in 2017. The capstone of U.S.–India rapprochement was President Obama's attendance as Chief Guest at India's Republic Day celebrations in January 2015, the first U.S. President ever so honored.[12] The *New York Times* described the enhanced relationship as "one of Mr. Obama's most important foreign policy achievements."[13]

Equally significantly for the U.S.– India strategic relationship, the U.S. turned away from Pakistan in seemingly irreversible ways. The Pakistan lobby with the U.S. government was mostly discredited and marginalized. President Obama, still hopeful that Pakistan would come to its senses and stop sponsoring terrorists as a matter of state policy, gradually reduced military aid to Pakistan in the last four years of his administration by two-thirds while pressing diplomatically for a change in Pakistani behavior.[14] The stage was set for a new U.S. President.

The Trump administration inherited strong momentum from the Obama administration as far as the security partnership with India was concerned. Despite continuing disagreements about how best to deal with Pakistan's ongoing involvement with a variety of terrorist groups, the two sides made significant progress on other fronts. India contracted to purchase a range of military equipment from the U.S. After myriad delays, it signed the Logistics Exchange Memorandum of Agreement. Many of these developments came to fruition thanks to the efforts of then Secretary of Defense Ashton Carter. Though not publicized, it can be inferred that Carter devoted a significant amount of time and effort to courting India because of the many uncertainties associated with the dramatic rise of the People's Republic of China (PRC) in Asia. India, in turn, responded well to these overtures because of its own misgivings about the PRC's interests and goals in South Asia and beyond.

The Trump administration, to its credit, early on sent then-Secretary of Defense James Mattis to India. Even though his visit did not yield any substantive results, it was important from a symbolic standpoint.[15] He did, however, urge India to step up its role in Afghanistan with a view toward stabilizing the country. The most important development involved India's trying neighbor, Pakistan. In January 2018, following a tweet from President Trump, the U.S. government suspended a further $2 billion of assistance to Pakistan.[16] The rationale for the U.S. cutoff of remaining aid was straightforward: Pakistan had failed, despite multiple entreaties on the part of the U.S., to end its support for terror, especially in Afghanistan.

Pakistan's use of terrorist proxies and the U.S.'s inability or unwillingness to impose sufficient costs on the country to effect significant change remain as a long-standing Indian complaint. The Trump administration's decision to take a harder line has been received with approval in New Delhi, if accompanied by a sense of "it's about time." Previous U.S. administrations privately – and on the rare occasion publicly – upbraided Pakistan. However, in the end each chose not to proceed far down this path. Of course, skeptics in New Delhi continue to express doubts about the U.S. willingness to sustain this new approach as Pakistan withdraws various forms of ongoing cooperation.[17] The Trump administration has thus far followed an inclination to continue to build gradually upon the ongoing security partnership with India.

This was evident from the steps taken before and during Trump's visit to India in late February 2020. Shortly before his visit India announced that it would purchase 24 MH-60R Apache attack helicopters for its navy as well six others for its army.[18] Furthermore, the two sides agreed to enhance counterterrorism cooperation, create a new Counter Narcotics Working Group, and boost space cooperation, and reaffirmed their commitment to conclude another enabling agreement, notably the Basic Exchange and Cooperation Agreement, which would facilitate the exchange of sensitive targeting information.[19]

India, for its part, especially under Prime Minister Modi, also appears to be willing to invest in the partnership and is especially keen on acquiring a range of weapon technologies from the U.S. Indeed, India is fast becoming a major importer of military equipment from the U.S. It is important to underscore that, as of 2014, the U.S. surpassed Russia as India's principal weapons supplier.[20] The agreement reached with the U.S. in the fall of 2018, after much deliberation, on the Communications Compatibility and Security Agreement facilitates military interoperability. Under its aegis, India has also started discussions with the U.S. to acquire twenty-two armed Sea Guardian drones. However, India's 2020 agreement to acquire and deploy the Russian S-400 air defense system is definitely problematic. The U.S. will not transfer any technology or weapon system vulnerable to compromise via the S-400 system. Another matter which further complicates the U.S.–India strategic partnership is India's policy of "Make in India," announced in 2013. This is basically at odds with the Trump administration's own focus on boosting domestic manufacturing.[21] Many view this emphasis on enhancing India's indigenous manufacturing capacity as a throwback to an earlier era in India's economic policymaking, one that failed to contribute much to the country's economic growth and well-being. How a U.S. administration not known for its flexibility and moderation in trade policy deals will square this circle with India remains to be seen. Yet this issue could, in considerable measure, shape the future of the strategic partnership. Overall in the relationship over recent years, it must be said, there is in all this a prevailing sense of "one step forward, one step back."

The China factor

Looming over the region is the "China Factor." China's economic aggressiveness and military expansionism cast a long shadow over the future of South Asia. U.S. policymaking with regard to China is seen in Delhi with suspicion. In the view from Delhi, U.S. policy has oscillated on a number of occasions, sometimes even within the span of a single administration. Indian concerns about the fickleness of American policy are not chimerical. However, given the sheer significance of the PRC to the U.S., it is unclear how Washington can adequately address this Indian concern.[22] Indian elites, for the most part, recognize that the PRC is the country's principal long-term threat. However, they do not have a clear-cut consensus on how best to cope with the challenge, and several perspectives exist on how to deal with the PRC. One segment of the strategic community leans towards accommodation based on the assumption that India does not have the strategic wherewithal to mount a credible defense. Another argues for a policy of self-help and the mobilization of its domestic resources to cope with the challenge. This group would clearly eschew any reliance on the U.S. to protect India's security interests. A third strand contends that India does need to balance against the PRC, but lacks sufficient domestic capabilities to that end and so should elicit the assistance of the U.S. in this endeavor. However, even within this line of thought there is disagreement about the extent to which India should firmly place its bets on the U.S.

Obviously, the U.S.–China relationship is far more involved and complex than is the relationship with India. The Trump administration's trade sanctions and tariff regime have only added to this complexity. There are compelling national security reasons for the U.S. to concern itself with the growing assertiveness of the PRC in Asia.[23] Given India's own fears and misgivings about the PRC, the gradual but perceptible decline in its reflexive anti-Americanism creates the potential for India to begin to push back against further Chinese assertive behavior. To that end, the U.S. has already made suitable overtures, even as China has cast a wary eye on them.[24] Consequently, regardless of the likely reactions of the PRC, it makes eminent sense for the U.S. to continue with its efforts to engage India on a range of strategic issues.

What is next?

What, then, does the future hold? Going beyond the usual bromides and clichés about the "world's two largest democracies,"[25] and "shared concerns" about both China's hegemonic economic intentions[26] and Pakistan's terrorists,[27] the U.S. and India may yet find meaningful strategic grounds for cooperation. The U.S. has stated repeatedly that it wants India to "play a greater role in regional security" and to act as a regional power which will "counter China."[28] The U.S. takes for granted the assumption, based on its own strategic philosophy of acting aggressively on the world stage, that because India is also a large, populous democracy with similar economic needs, it too would naturally desire to project its interests beyond its borders and to exert its influence, at least over its own neighborhood. Despite India's continued hesitation to play such a role it may find that it has little or no alternative if it hopes to counter growing Chinese influence in the region.

Are the U.S. and India still unnatural partners? Can they forge a meaningful strategic partnership that goes beyond rhetoric, bonhomie, and handshakes? Given the progress that has occurred in Indo-U.S. relations since the turn of the century, it is now at least possible to envisage circumstances under which the partnership might gain real strength. For its part, the U.S. would have to accept that one size does not fit all in security partnerships, avoid condescension, recognize the continuing importance of the sovereignty issue for India, stress genuine equality in the relationship, and make concessions in trade policy. On the other side of the equation, India would have to move away from its residual attachment to nonalignment and its patchwork-quilt approach to defense acquisitions. Even so, there is no obvious or simple path forward, nor any easy answers to difficult questions. Some strategic and political gaps remain. Much depends on how developments at global, regional, and national levels beyond the bilateral equation evolve. If, for example, the perceived threat from the PRC becomes sufficiently acute and India's own capacity to cope with the emergent threat is found wanting, a willingness to work more closely with the U.S. may prove to be the only viable option for any Indian government. Indo-U.S. strategic ties today are at an inflection point. It is certainly possible that, with deft diplomacy, the two sides can further distance themselves from the baggage of the past and commit to a true strategic partnership and to seize the possibility of forming an enduring strategic partnership – natural or not.

A word about structure

This volume, like many academic projects, began as a scholarly collaboration between two people pursuing answers to similar questions. We, as the editors and originators of this project, share an interest in looking beyond the rhetoric about the security partnership between India and the U.S. coming from both capitals and to maintaining an unvarnished assessment of the actual state of defense affairs between the two countries. To interest scholars and practitioners in both countries to join in this analysis, we published a monograph expressing some skepticism across seven different segments of the relationship.[29] We then decided to pursue a wider collaborative venture that involved inviting both American and Indian academics and analysts to write paired chapters on the subjects which comprise the seven parts of this volume.

I   Military-to-military cooperation
II Intelligence sharing and cooperation
III Cybersecurity coordination and cooperation
IV Nuclear security
V   Space cooperation
VI Counterterrorism cooperation
VII Defense technology sharing

Each of the chapters in the present volume requires a brief synopsis. In Chapter 1 on military-to-military cooperation Chris Mason argues that while considerable progress has been made to boost such efforts, a great deal more needs to be accomplished to make this a more robust linkage. Mason argues that while three branches of the U.S. military have established working relationships with their Indian counterparts, India's limitations on the purpose of military maneuvers and its unwillingness to ruffle China's feathers prevent the forging of substantial joint military capabilities. He argues that significant political impediments remain, that the military establishments of the two countries have vastly different strategic orientations, and that India's defense acquisition process leaves much to be desired. All these factors have conspired to hobble the growth of the military-to-military dimensions of the strategic partnership. Since several of these barriers are structural and cannot be easily overcome, Mason suggests some limited but feasible steps that might be taken to incrementally boost the relationship.

Chapter 2, by Abhijnan Rej, is the counterpart to Mason's chapter. In this chapter Rej argues that a viable strategic partnership has steadily evolved between India and the U.S. since the year 2000. This has resulted not only in substantial weapons sales but also in a series of military exercises and recognition of a common threat in the Indo-Pacific from the PRC. While Rej takes a more sanguine view of the Indo-U.S. strategic partnership than Mason he nevertheless highlights areas of continuing discord. These, he argues, are myriad, and range from India's continuing insistence on multi-alignment, its dependence on Russia for weaponry, and the inherent, structural limits of its military capabilities. In his concluding section Rej spells out three specific issues that could help boost the relationship, including assuaging India's fears of abandonment in the event of a crisis with the PRC, and the needs to avoid sanctioning India on the issue of Russian arms sales and to find a way to incorporate India's strategic concerns in American grand strategy.

In Chapter 3 Jamil Jaffer provides a survey of U.S.–Indian cooperation in the field of cybersecurity. Among other matters he carefully highlights a series of critical turning points in the relationship as it pertains to cybersecurity cooperation. These include important agreements that were forged in 2001, 2011, and, most recently, in 2016, which culminated in the Agreed Framework for cybersecurity cooperation. Jaffer argues that the two sides share a substantial basis for cooperation because they face common threats from state actors especially China, Russia, North Korea, and Iran. Despite the progress that has been made since 2011, Jaffer underscores the need for and spells out a series of confidence-building measures that need to be undertaken to promote and sustain cooperation.

Chapter 4, Bedavasya Mohany's counterpart to Jaffer's chapter, argues that the U.S. and India face common threats and have fashioned various institutional arrangements for cooperation. However, he also cautions that stated intentions need to be converted into tangible actions if cooperative ventures are likely to come to fruition. At the outset he highlights the common cybersecurity threats that the two states face from the PRC. More recently, he argues, they are now confronting a new threat from North Korea. Given the existence of common threats, he argues that the U.S. and India need to focus on three distinct areas. These include enhancing law-enforcement cooperation, countering influence operations, and bolstering strategic command and control. The last of these, obviously, is of far greater significance for India, which has only an nascent nuclear force.

Frank O'Donnell's Chapter 5 deals with significant changes that are underway in the global nuclear order as well as in South Asia. In that context he discusses the ramifications of these changes for strategic stability in the region. In terms of American policy toward the region he proffers three distinct policy initiatives that the U.S. might pursue. The first involves an expansion of the missile flight-test pre-notification protocol with Pakistan. The second calls for a joint threat assessment of the Chinese conventional missile threat to India, with an eye toward improving India's resilience. Third and finally, he argues for American assistance to India to boost its cyberdefenses against possible Chinese efforts to interfere with military command and control systems relevant to India's nuclear forces. Adopted in concert, he argues, these policy initiatives could reduce the likelihood of nuclear instability in the region.

Rajesh Rajagopalan's Chapter 6 is the Indian counterpart on the question of nuclear stability in the region. Unlike O'Donnell, he argues that the prospects of cooperation are more limited. In the recent past, he contends, possibilities of cooperation have most coalesced around two issues. The first has dealt with the dangers of "loose nukes" in the region and the second with Pakistan's reliance on tactical nuclear weapons and its early escalation strategy. However, he expresses much doubt about the likelihood of bilateral cooperation in these arenas, largely because India and the U.S.

have long differed about the sources of these problems. On the other hand, he believes that the two parties might be able to cooperate in promoting nuclear security in the cyber realm as well as in nuclear crisis management. He nevertheless believes that there still remain important differences that will need to be bridged before such cooperation can ensue.

Chapter 7 by Victoria Samson, on U.S.–India space cooperation, argues that while the two parties have had a long history of civilian space cooperation they have pursued few efforts in the realm of space security. To that end, she argues that the two states can cooperate in the important realm of space situational awareness. This arena deals with spaceflight safety and involves improving transparency of activities in orbit. Thus far, she underscores, India and the U.S. are not partners in this endeavor. The two sides, while they have pursued discussions to forge such an agreement, have yet to arrive at one. Currently, India mostly relies on the U.S. to ensure such situational awareness. Given India's own growing capabilities, Samson believes that significant cooperation can be pursued to mutual benefit.

Rajeswari Rajagopalan's companion Chapter 8 carefully outlines the substantial history of U.S.–India civilian space cooperation. She also argues that security cooperation in space had mostly been hobbled in the past owing to a range of political differences. However, she believes that a shift may now be in the offing, largely because of an improved strategic relationship and shared concerns about the rise of the PRC. As a consequence not only have the two sides enhanced civilian space cooperation but they have also boosted the space security dialogue. In Rajagopalan's view, the two sides may well be poised to enhance cooperation in both arenas in the foreseeable future.

Tricia Bacon's Chapter 9 forthrightly states that U.S.–India counterterrorism cooperation has been constrained because their values and interests have not dovetailed. Nowhere has this been more evident than in the U.S. dealings with Pakistan. However, since 2014 the two sides have made incremental progress, largely because of shared concerns. These efforts have been institutionalized through a range of dialogues and exchanges. The chapter also explores how the two parties may cooperate as they face new challenges, most notably from the Islamic State. It concludes with a discussion of the remaining hurdles to counterterrorism cooperation and emphasizes the need for setting realistic expectations in the relationship.

In Chapter 10 Manoj Joshi provides an Indian perspective on the question of counterterrorism cooperation. Joshi's chapter offers a detailed account of past attempts at cooperation and their limits. At the outset he highlights that counterterrorism cooperation has been constrained because of the asymmetric features of the bilateral relationship. The U.S. has seen

Introduction 13

terrorism largely as a global problem, while India has been most concerned with terrorist attacks emanating from its own neighborhood. Joshi then outlines the promises and limits of early Indo-American counterterrorism cooperation, discusses a key turning point and then outlines the fitful elements of cooperation after the September 11, 2001 attacks on the U.S. His chapter ends with a discussion of possible arenas of cooperation in the future and continuing areas of discord.

Carol Evans' Chapter 11 focuses on the possibilities of enhanced intelligence cooperation between India and the U.S. Evans notes that during the Cold War intelligence cooperation was hobbled for a variety of reasons, including India's culture of prickly independence in the foreign and security policy arenas. She also notes that recent intelligence cooperation has mostly dealt with issues of counterterrorism. However, with the rise of the PRC, its heightened threat to India, and its growing influence in Asia, she envisages a new era of far wider Indo-U.S. intelligence cooperation. To that end she outlines the possibilities of cooperation in areas ranging from the maritime domain to India's troubled borders.

Saikat Datta's companion Chapter 12 provides a detailed historical overview of the evolution of India's intelligence apparatus. It then devotes a substantial section to the early record of Indo-U.S. cooperation, especially after India's disastrous military defeat at the hands of the PRC in 1962. However, this experience of cooperation mostly drew to a close owing to the exigencies of the Cold War and its impact on South Asia. It was only after the Cold War's end and a change in regional dynamics that intelligence cooperation between the two states became more feasible. Nevertheless, Datta shows that conflicting U.S. policy priorities in the region placed limits on such cooperation. He concludes his chapter with a discussion of several changes that need to be undertaken both at bilateral and domestic levels to boost intelligence cooperation.

In Chapter 13 Frank O' Donnell carefully outlines that since about 2008 the Indo-U.S. defense technology cooperation has gathered considerable pace. However, he also cautions that it has reached a stage where significant hurdles that remain in the interbureaucratic process could prevent the relationship from evolving to a higher phase. Specifically, he argues that the organizational processes of the two states are markedly different and reflect conflicting priorities. Under these circumstances, O'Donnell argues that any breakthrough in the defense technology cooperation arena will require high-level political discussions if the partnership is to reach a new level.

In Chapter 14, the counterpart to O'Donnell's chapter, Pramit Pal Chaudhuri argues that the Modi government has placed a premium on the indigenization of defense technology. This, he argues, places the U.S. at a distinct disadvantage in terms of defense-technology cooperation. Despite this obvious disjuncture, he contends that the U.S. will remain an important source of defense technology for two compelling reasons. First, it can supply certain critical technologies such as drones. Second, geopolitical considerations, especially India's misgivings about the PRC, will also induce it to turn toward the U.S.

As these chapter summaries have demonstrated, the purpose of this volume is to outline the differing perceptions, assess the assumptions and expectations of both countries, and examine the obstacles in the path of greater cooperation as seen from both sides of the equation in each of these seven key sectors.

Notes

1 Arif Rafiq, "The U.S. Bet on India Has Failed," *The National Interest*, February 2, 2020. Accessed here: https://nationalinterest.org/feature/america-making-bad-bet-india-119316.
2 Bryan Gibson, *Sold Out? U.S. Foreign Policy, Iraq, the Kurds, and the Cold War* (New York: Palgrave Macmillan, 2015), 26–7.
3 Michael Moran, "The Airlift of Evil," *NBC News*, November 29, 2001. Accessed here: www.nbcnews.com/id/3340165/ns/world_news-brave_new_world/t/airlift-evil/.
4 Fred Kaplan, "The Freedom Agenda Fizzles: How George Bush and Condoleezza Rice Made a Mess of Pakistan." *Slate*, November 5, 2007. Accessed here: www.slate.com/articles/news_and_politics/war_stories/2007/11/the_freedom_agenda_fizzles.html.
5 For a full consideration of this period, see Steve Coll, *Directorate S: The C.I.A. and America's Secret Wars in Afghanistan and Pakistan, 2001–2016* (New York: Penguin, 2018).
6 Christine Fair, "How Pakistan Beguiles the Americans: A Guide for Foreign Officials," *War on the Rocks*, June 15, 2015 Accessed here: https://warontherocks.com/2015/06/how-pakistan-beguiles-the-americans-a-guide-for-foreign-officials/.
7 Hari Sud, "Welcome Condoleezza Rice, Bye Colin Powell – Indian Perspective," *Ivarta*, February 15, 2005. Accessed here: www.ivarta.com/columns/OL_050215.htm.
8 "U.S. Diplomat and Longtime Pakistan Expert is under Federal Investigation," *The Washington Post*, November 6, 2014. Accessed here: www.washingtonpost.com/world/national-security/us-diplomat-and-longtime-pakistan-expert-under-federal-investigation/2014/11/06/f7fd3240-65f1-11e4-9fdc-d43b053ecb4d_story.html.
9 Fair, "How Pakistan Beguiles the Americans."
10 Shashi Thardoor, "Why India Loves Bush," *The Daily Beast*, October 7, 2008. Accessed here: www.thedailybeast.com/why-india-loves-bush.

11 "Obama Says bin Laden Had 'Support Network' in Pakistan," *CNN*, May 11, 2009. Accessed here: www.cnn.com/2011/POLITICS/05/08/pakistan.us.relations/index.html.
12 Suhasini Haidar, "Obama to Be Chief Guest at Republic Day Celebrations," *The Hindu*, September 23, 2016. Accessed here: www.thehindu.com/news/international/Obama-to-be-chief-guest-at-Republic-Day-celebrations/article14021221.ece.
13 "A Deepening Partnership with India," *The New York Times*, June 14, 2016. Accessed here: www.nytimes.com/2016/06/14/opinion/a-deepening-partnership-with-india.html.
14 Michael Hughes, "Pakistan Counter-strike on Trump Threatens U.S. Anti-terror Efforts in Afghanistan," *The Defense Post*, January 10, 2018. Accessed here: https://thedefensepost.com/2018/01/10/pakistan-us-anti-terror-efforts-afghanistan/.
15 "PTI, Mattis India Visit Aimed at Taking Indo-U.S. Ties to Next Level," *The Hindu*, September 24, 2017.
16 Katrina Manson and Farhan Bokhari, "U.S. Suspends $2bn in Aid to Pakistan," *Financial Times*, January 5, 2018.
17 Farhan Bokhari, Katrina Manson, and Kiran Stacey, "Pakistan Halts Intelligence-sharing with U.S. after Aid Suspension," *Financial Times*, January 11, 2018.
18 Rahul Bedi, "U.S. Signs Deals with India for MH-60R, Apache Helicopters," *Jane's Defence Weekly*, February 25, 2020.
19 For details see: www.whitehouse.gov/briefings-statements/joint-statement-vision-principles-united-states-india-comprehensive-global-strategic-partnership/.
20 Rajat Pandit, "U.S. Pips Russia as Top Arms Supplier to India," *The Times of India*, August 13, 2014.
21 PTI, "Make in India: Government Gives Shape to Five Industrial Corridors," *The Economic Times*, May 11, 2015.
22 Thomas J. Christiansen, *The China Challenge: Shaping the Choices of Rising Power* (New York: W.W. Norton and Company, 2016).
23 For a particularly forthright statement see Aaron Friedberg, *A Contest for Supremacy: China, America, and the Struggle for Mastery in Asia* (New York: W.W. Norton and Company, 2012).
24 Dan Lamonthe, "The U.S. and India Are Deepening Military Ties – and China Is Watching," *The Washington Post*, March 2, 2016.
25 "U.S.: Tillerson Calls for India Ties to Counter China," *BBC News*, October 19, 2017. Accessed here: www.bbc.com/news/world-asia-41675796.
26 "Tillerson Seeks Stronger Ties with India, Chides China," *Associated Press*, October 18, 2017. Accessed here: http://abcnews.go.com/amp/Politics/wireStory/tillerson-seeks-stronger-ties-india-chides-china-50560303.
27 "Stronger Indo-U.S. Ties for a Stronger India," *The Economic Times*, October 25, 2017. Accessed here: https://blogs.economictimes.indiatimes.com/et-editorials/stronger-indo-us-ties-for-a-stronger-india/.
28 "U.S.: Tillerson Calls for India Ties to Counter China," *BBC News*, October 19, 2017. Accessed here: www.bbc.com/news/world-asia-41675796.

29 Sumit Ganguly and Chris Mason, *An Unnatural Partnership? The Future of U.S.–India Strategic Cooperation* (Carlisle, PA: U.S. Army War College Press, 2019). Accessed here: https://bookstore.gpo.gov/products/unnatural-partnership-future-us-india-strategic-cooperation.

Part I

Military-to-military cooperation

1

Less than meets the eye: a critical assessment of the military-to-military dimension of the U.S.–India security partnership

M. Chris Mason

Introduction

Strictly speaking, "military to military" cooperation refers specifically to those forms of security engagement in which uniformed armed forces personnel of both countries interact with one another. Other chapters of this volume address other forms of military cooperation, such as arms sales, defense technology sharing, counter-terrorism operations in which uniformed military personnel play a role and so on. The great majority of this "mil-to-mil" activity, in the argot of the military, has been and remains in the form of joint maneuvers and training exercises, which until very recently were limited to service-specific training (e.g., army-with-army or navy-with-navy). In addition to training exercises, the U.S. and India also regularly exchange individual mid-career officers to attend training schools and courses in each other's military education systems. For example, one U.S. officer and one Indian officer typically attend each other's Army War College for one academic year. The same is true for the Navy and Air Force War Colleges and commissioning sources such as West Point. In addition, small numbers of officers and senior enlisted personnel attend each other's professional training courses for various military specialties. All told, however, the number on each side which participate in such individual exchanges each year is not more than a hundred or so, so this additional aspect, which is confined primarily to company and field-grade officers (those in the ranks from lieutenant to colonel), is quite limited in comparison to the numbers participating in annual joint exercises and maneuvers.

The U.S. is an eager participant in the joint training exercises which comprise the bulk of the military-to-military segment of the security relationship with India. This sector is likely one of the seven sectors in this volume which the uniformed U.S. military itself would most like to see expanded. It would be fair to assert, however, that this relatively small sector of the overall security partnership is paradoxically also, perhaps, the sector with the least potential for meaningful future growth. There are a number of reasons for this, both civil and military, which will be touched on in this chapter. Many of them are not unique to military-to-military cooperation and are shared with other sectors of the security relationship.

Three of the four major branches of the U.S. military – the Army, the Navy and the Air Force – all have established relationships with their counterparts in the Indian armed forces. The fourth major U.S. military branch, the Marine Corps, does not have a direct counterpart in the Indian armed forces, as India does not maintain a force of naval infantry under the overall aegis of the Indian Navy for the purpose of amphibious operations. Thus the Marine Corps plays a relatively small role in the "mil-to-mil" relationship. All three major branches of the two countries' armed forces have conducted joint exercises in the past. Two of them, the army and the navy, have a regular, established schedule of annual exercises which have long and largely positive, if modest, track records. Currently, military-to-military cooperation is planned by a bilateral military cooperation group, and each of the three primary services for both countries has an Executive Steering Group to coordinate service specific training. The three Executive Steering Groups meet annually to discuss joint training exercises and other, smaller forms of military-to-military cooperation. Of the three services, by far the most training exercises have been conducted by the two navies, and naturally occur out at sea and far from the public eye.

In general, the military-to-military sector is a case in the relationship where there is *less* than meets the eye. A cynic could say that the public relations component of these joint exercises is one of their most prominent features. This is not a reflection on the military and naval professionals of both nations who participate in them, but, rather, a reflection of the limitations placed on the exercises, for the most part by the government of India. Yet the obstacles to more and better military-to-military linkages and training are by no means all political, at least not in the sense of the normal flow of political parties and election cycles. There are also fundamental structural and technical impediments which run all the way from the highest strategic levels of force design and purpose down to the day-to-day tactical communications of the officers in both militaries who are tasked with maintaining routine dialog and the managing of mundane logistics and scheduling.

The political impediments are nevertheless a good place to begin, as much is often made of the fact that both nations are vibrant democracies with many common interests and shared security concerns in Asia.[1] Few analysts would dispute the suggestion that the U.S. would like to embrace India as a military security partner in a more traditional sense, and that it is India which is taking the "go slow" approach to the courtship. As has been frequently written upon, India cherishes its strategic independence and maintains many of the legacy paradigms inherited from its well-known past of nonalignment. This is a field which has been plowed often enough in the literature of South Asian security to require little additional tillage here. The U.S. for the most part understands that India places a great deal of national pride and considerable importance on its traditional strategic stance of standing in no one's shadow, and on being beholden to none for its independence and security. This is far more true of India than of the countries of Western Europe, for example, who understand that their individual security is dependent on the collective defense structure of the NATO alliance, and in particular upon the shield and sword of the U.S. In contrast, a security relationship seen in India as either too close to any other single country or out of balance in favor of any one particular country is considered by many in India's political ranks as a kind of metaphorical electrified third rail, to be avoided at all costs, given the depth of national attachment to the stance of strategic independence. For American defense officials, this reluctance on India's part to "choose sides" in the new superpower competition between the U.S. and China is a common source of frustration. This point of friction came out into the open in a now-famous discussion at a conference in 2019, when former U.S. CIA Director David Petraeus stated that it was time for India to "take a side in this competition." India's Minister of External Affairs Subrahmanyam Jaishankar replied tartly: "India will take a side – India's side."[2] At the least, this Indian "go slow, remain neutral" approach has resulted, over the past decade, in limiting the size and scope of joint U.S.–India military and naval exercises, to the quiet disappointment of the U.S. military establishment.[3]

This dimension of the bilateral military-to-military relationship, which might be dubbed the "political limitations factor," however, is not necessarily permanent or immutable. Future Indian governments might, for example, wish to steer defense policy closer to alignment with the U.S. for any number of reasons. New generations of voters in India may gradually distance themselves from the legacies of the past, for example, and eventually come to view India's future security requirements through a more collective lens, as the nations of Western Europe do today. Or India's strategic calculus may in the future be affected by powerful external forces. China, for example, might become much more territorially and economically aggressive than it already is today, causing India to reconsider its "go it alone" or "stand alone" approach to its national security. Since the 1980s, China has been mostly active in very adept pinprick military harassment of India – making tiny military investitures of effort and money along their shared border which provoke much larger and more costly responses from India – but this could change. The point is simply that while the "political limitations factor" *today* inhibits the growth of the U.S.–India military-to-military relationship, it will not necessarily always be so.

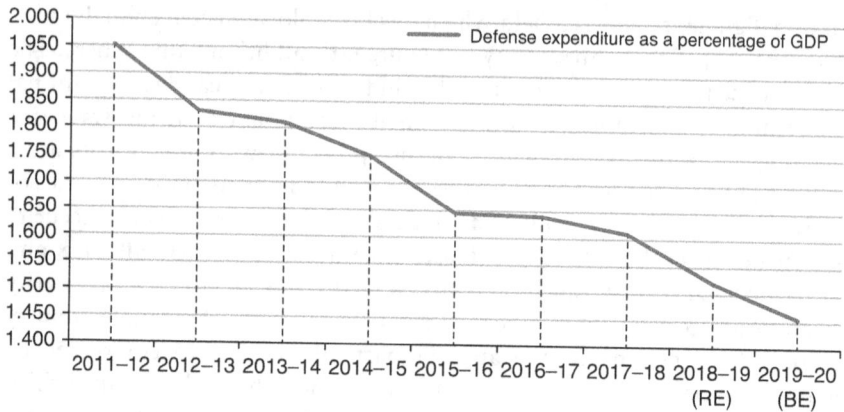

Figure 1.1 Indian defense spending 2011–20 as a percentage of GDP.

This being said, however, it would be remiss not to point out that the U.S. is alone among the nations of the world in committing such a vast proportion of its resources to military expenditures, and even if India should in the future desire a more robust relationship with the U.S. and seek to increase military spending to do so, it remains a developing nation working to provide for the basic needs of a large segment of its population with limited budgetary resources.[4] Furthermore, those expenditures as a proportion of Gross Domestic Product (GDP) have been in decline for some time (Figure 1.1). In 2019, India devoted the lowest percentage of its budget to defense spending since 1962, the year of the disastrous China–India War.[5] Thus, any hypothetical future closer military-to-military cooperation would still face financial impediments.

The strategic military dimension

As daunting as the civil limitations are, the structural military impediments to meaningful growth in the military-to-military sector of the relationship run deeper still. Perhaps the best way to enumerate these obstacles is from the strategic level down through operational factors and finally to some examples of the tactical minutiae which create stumbling blocks to real cooperation. At the macro level of strategic consideration, the first structural impediment to "mil-to-mil" cooperation is the obvious observation that the U.S. and Indian militaries could hardly be more different from one another in structure and purpose. In fact, it is not an exaggeration to say that they are almost diametrically opposed. The Indian armed forces are designed, one might fairly say *exclusively* designed, for the defense of the realm. The defense of India's borders is the *raison d'être*, indeed the entire *raison d'être*, for the Indian Army, Navy and Air Force. It is said in the U.S. military that the best defense is a good offense, and the Indian Army could, if attacked by a neighbor, certainly mount counteroffensives at the operational level of war. By this it is meant that the Indian Army, supported by its Air Force, could respond to an incursion into its territory with a combined arms counterattack, and possibly pursue an invader's forces back across the original border in order to inflict damage on the retreating enemy, or to temporarily seize terrain features more readily defensible than the international boundary lines.

But this type of operational-level response beyond India's borders is not what India's armed forces are primarily designed, trained and equipped for. India's military is a self-defense force, and this is manifested in many ways. An army on the offensive outside its home territory, for example, requires a large and sophisticated logistics network to move fuel, ammunition, sustenance and medical supplies up to ever-advancing front lines while moving casualties and broken equipment back to the rear areas where they are best taken care of. India lacks this kind of offensive logistical combat support in depth for operations far from its borders. It can sustain its army on the ground perhaps twenty or thirty miles beyond India's boundaries, but not 200 or 300 miles. And this is in respect to contiguous territory. India has virtually no capacity to project military force to non-contiguous territory. Indeed, India's lack of ability to project military power any distance from its own borders has been conspicuous on numerous occasions. For example, Operation RAHAT, the evacuation of Indian citizens from Yemen in 2015, required a fully permissive (i.e., non-hostile) environment for the operation, the full cooperation of the Saudi government, the aircraft of the Indian national commercial airline and a number of civilian cargo vessels. The Indian Army, Navy and Air Force simply lack the capability to protect or extract any significant number of Indian citizens from a combat zone in a non-permissive environment, much less seize territory. When it comes to protecting its people or its interests abroad, India remains, in the words of Tennessee Williams, almost entirely dependent on the "kindness of strangers."[6]

In contrast, the U.S. military is almost diametrically opposite in design. Ignoring President Trump's deployment of a few military personnel to the border with Mexico in 2019 as a political stunt, the last time U.S. military forces were deployed to protect America's borders was General John "Blackjack" Pershing's expedition to the badlands between Texas and Mexico shortly before World War I in an (unsuccessful) effort to kill or capture Mexican revolutionary Pancho Villa. Prior to that, the last internal use of the U.S. Army was the genocidal suppression of Native Americans in the Great Plains, California and the Great Northwest after the American Civil War.[7] In part because the U.S. faces no conceivable threat to its territorial integrity from its neighbors, in part because the U.S. Coast Guard exists to patrol home waters and in part because of the existence of powerful National Guard units in all fifty states available to perform many of the missions often assigned to the military in other countries, for more than a century the U.S. military has been focused entirely on the projection of national power across the oceans which separate it from Europe and Asia. As a result, American researchers and scholars visiting security institutions in India, when broaching the topic of greater military-to-military cooperation between the two countries, are often asked rhetorically "on what would we cooperate?"[8] Thus India's military will not only not engage itself in conflict zones outside the auspices of the United Nations, it *cannot*. The only mission which the Indian Army and the U.S. military really have in common is disaster relief, and indeed, this is the premise for most of the "mil-to-mil" exercises which take place annually. The government of India simply does not conceive of the potential projection of military power beyond its own national boundaries as an element of its foreign policy, and does not have any significant ability to do so even in the highly unlikely event that that should ever change.

A strategic hardware hodge-podge

Further complicating a potential deepening of the military-to-military relationship is India's arsenal of random weapons systems, which is frequently described as a hodge-podge.[9] By following its nonalignment paradigm into weapons acquisition, India has perhaps satisfied its political need for not becoming dependent on a single country for its supply of military hardware, but in doing so it has created a haphazard arsenal of random, disconnected systems not originally designed to communicate with each other, let alone with the systems of the U.S. When, for example, India purchases one batch of fighter planes from France (e.g., the Dassault Mirage 2000), another from Russia (e.g., the Mikoyan MiG-29) and a third from Great Britain (e.g., the SEPECAT Jaguar), it creates not just a problem of combat interoperability in its own fighter command, it also creates a serious logistics and training burden for its Air Force. Instead of one training pipeline for fighter pilots after basic flight training, for example, it needs three, one for each fighter type. Instead of stocking its replacement parts shelves with, for example, a single landing gear hydraulic pump, it must stock three different pumps from three different suppliers. Its mechanics must be trained not to repair one aircraft, but three different ones. This is costly, and the negative effect this has on "up time" (the percentage of the air fleet which is fully operational and ready to fly) is significant. This hodge-podge also has serious ramifications for joint exercises and joint warfighting as well, as U.S. military equipment is not designed to communicate with any of these weapons systems.

The operational level: a consideration of joint exercises by service component

Because bilateral and multilateral military exercises and maneuvers comprise the great bulk of the U.S.–India military-to-military sector of cooperation, an appreciation of the actual state of these joint military operations today is important to the consideration of where the relationship might go from here. What follows is a service-specific discussion of each branch's history of "mil-to-mil" joint training, with an emphasis on the most recent developments as the most pertinent. These are ordered in ascending rank by the potential for genuine future security prospects. As will be seen, each of the branches' joint exercises is hobbled by a strategic-level Achilles heel, in addition to minor problems at lower levels of military organization. The U.S. Marine Corps is not included in this appraisal, as India has no comparable force.

Air force-to-air force exercises

The branch of service with the least potential for real future security cooperation is the Air Force. U.S.–India joint air force training exercises are named *Cope India*, and the last such exercise (somewhat confusingly named *Cope India 2019* although it was held in 2018) took place from December 3 to 14, 2018 at Air Station Kalaikunda and Air Station Arjan Singh in West Bengal. The resumption of *Cope India* in late 2018 marked the end of an eight-year hiatus in the exercises, the last previous joint air maneuvers having been held in 2010.[10] To give a sense of the (small) scope of the exercises, about 100 American Airmen and approximately fifteen American aircraft took part in 2019. Air Force joint training exercises are not only hampered by the lack of a common tactical operating picture among the aircraft, they also suffer acutely from the equipment incompatibility problem mentioned earlier. Much of the Indian Air Force is comprised of Russian-built and sourced aircraft, and Russian and American airplanes cannot be interlinked in a classified communications system which is not then susceptible to electronic espionage. Neither the U.S. Air Force nor the Indian Air Force is keen to reveal classified capabilities in either the top-end performance of their aircraft (i.e., what kind of speeds and maneuverability they are actually capable of) or their very highly classified combat systems capabilities (i.e., "dog-fighting" ability). In fact, to protect this sensitive kind of information, neither side even turns on its airborne electronic warfare suites during *Cope India* for fear both of revealing too much to each other and of potential surveillance by third-party observers and surveillance. The prospects for future resolution of these problems were dramatically worsened in 2019 by India's acquisition of the Russian S-400 anti-aircraft system. As analyst Benjamin Schwartz observes:

> The S-400 is a giant radar and locating a Russian radar (and Russian technicians) in close proximity to advanced American stealth aircraft is a great way to compromise that stealth. As one Pentagon official put it, "The S-400 is a computer. The F-35 is a computer. You don't hook your computer to your adversary's computer and that's basically what we would be doing."[11]

In reality the resulting maneuvers of *Cope India* amount to flying airplanes at the same time rather than practicing for joint combat against a potential enemy, and this is not the way aerial combat of the twenty-first century will be conducted. Indeed it is not the way aerial combat has been conducted since World War I, when pilots waved hand signals to each other from open cockpits. *Cope India* remains, and for many years will remain, essentially a "good will and photo op" exercise. It is useful at a limited and basic level for familiarization with routine unclassified procedures like take-off and landing clearances, such as might be helpful in the initial stages of a humanitarian crisis requiring military aircraft to bring in supplies or evacuate injured civilians. However, if one imagines a potential future scenario in which another regional power in Asia becomes hostile to the U.S. or India, and its air force were to be deployed against India or the U.S., even if some future hypothetical agreement were to exist for the two countries to act together, the two air forces have virtually no capability to fight together in any modern sense, and *Cope India* does nothing to remedy that problem.

Army-to-army joint exercises

The branch of service with the next-most potential for real future defense cooperation is the army. The joint army exercises conducted by the U.S. and India beginning in 2001 are named *Yudh Abhyas*, which ironically means "training for war" in Hindi. The most recent iteration of *Yudh Abhyas* began on September 8, 2019.[12] The Indian Army press release emphasized that "In the end a joint exercise will be undertaken by both countries in an operational setting *under a UN mandate*"[13] (italics added), a clear reflection of the political sensitivity of the optics of joint army training with the U.S. and the necessity to legitimize even a small training exercise as being under a hypothetical UN mandate. The exercises alternate each year between the two countries, with the 2019 iteration occurring at Joint Base Lewis-McChord in Washington State (Figure 1.2). In 2018, U.S. soldiers went to Chaubattia, a remote military station in Almora district (state of Uttarakhand) in the foothills of the Himalayas. In fact Chaubattia is about as remote a location, and as far from the public eye, as it is possible to get in India, as there is not even a village in the vicinity. This is another reflection of the extreme political sensitivity of the presence of even 350 U.S. Army soldiers on India soil. *Yudh Abhyas* is indeed good joint training. The problem is the relatively minute size of the annual exercises – about 700 men in all in 2019.[14] Roughly 350 men from each country represent a company-sized maneuver element plus a battalion- or brigade-level headquarters (which moves largely imaginary troops around on maps). The soldiers do genuinely enjoy the opportunity to meet and learn from soldiers of another country. But the U.S. Army has approximately 1.3 million active-duty troops, with another 865,000 in reserve, and the Indian Army is almost exactly the same size, with 1.2 million active duty personnel and 990,000 reservists – and 350 men from each army training together for a week once a year is not really going to prepare them to fight jointly in any kind of serious conflict.

Figure 1.2 This photo, taken at Exercise *Yudh Abhyas* at Joint Base Lewis-McChord in Washington State, September 2019, shows most of the soldiers of both countries who actually participated in the exercise.

Navy-to-navy exercises

The service branch with the greatest potential for meaningful as opposed to symbolic cooperation in the future is the navy. Here too, however, there are real impediments to the kind of joint interoperability which is critical to modern warfare above, on and under the world's oceans. India has made strides since 2010 towards the development of a blue-water navy with future potential to project maritime force across the Indian Ocean. In particular, the commissioning of the first Indian aircraft carrier, the *INS Vikrant* (IAC-1), and the first Indian-built nuclear-powered submarine, the 6,000-ton *INS Arihant* (SSBN 80), are noteworthy milestones in the development of ocean-going naval power beyond strictly coastal defense. The Indian Navy is also operating the Russian-built, nuclear-powered submarine *INS Chakra* (S71), leased since 2012 from the Russian government. However, as Abhijnan Rej notes in Chapter 2 of this volume, India's Navy is known within the Indian defense community as the "Cinderella service" because its share of the annual defense budget is so paltry.

The primary manifestation of U.S.–India naval security cooperation is *Exercise Malabar*. *Exercise Malabar* began in 1992 as a bilateral maritime training maneuver between the U.S. and India, making it by far the oldest joint exercise between the two countries. In 2015, Japan became a permanent partner of *Exercise Malabar*, expanding the annual drills into a trilateral joint program. Singapore and Australia have also participated in the past. Indian objections, however, have prevented Australia from becoming a permanent partner and participant. *Exercise Malabar* is now in its twenty-seventh year, the most recent iteration taking place in Japanese waters from September 26 to October 4, 2019.[15]

To give a sense of the scope and scale of a typical Malabar exercise, for the 2019 maneuvers, the U.S. Navy deployed a destroyer, the *U.S.S McCampbell* (DDG-85), and one land-based P-8A Poseidon aircraft. The Japanese Navy sent two destroyers, the *JS Samidare* (DD106, a *Murasame*-class destroyer with a hull design nearly identical to that of the U.S. *Spruance*-class destroyers) and the *JS Choukai* (DDG-176, a *Kongō*-class destroyer), as well as a helicopter carrier, the *JS Kaga* (DDH-184) and a P-1 aircraft. The Indian Navy sent the *INS Sahyadri* (F49, a *Shivalik*-class frigate[16]), the corvette *INS Kiltan* (P30, a new *Kamorta*-class vessel which was, significantly, sourced 90 percent in India[17]) and a Boeing P-8I Neptune patrol aircraft. True naval power is generated primarily by aircraft carriers and submarines, and, as none of these was present in the *Exercise Malabar* 2019 joint force, it can be seen that, in terms of displaying deterrent maritime combat power, it was a modest exercise. The vessels involved would typically be engaged in patrolling and escort duties, such as anti-piracy and maritime interdiction operations, and indeed this is India's seemingly permanent vision for the annual drills.

With respect to China as a potential future maritime adversary, it should be noted that China is in almost the exact same place developmentally with its own first aircraft carrier, the *Liaoning*, a conversion and refit of the former Russian aircraft carrier *Varyag*. Both the *Vikrant* and the *Liaoning* are jump-ramp design carriers, as opposed to the operationally superior flat-deck design operated by the U.S. Navy. An aircraft carrier alone in the ocean is a very big target, and cannot operate safely or successfully outside the sphere of an integrated Carrier Battle Group (CBG). A CBG is a cluster of ships and submarines which form a series of concentric defensive rings around the aircraft carrier itself. The function of the carrier is twofold – first to provide the defensive air cover for the entire Carrier Battle Group, and second to provide much of the offensive striking power necessary to attack an enemy's ships. Operating a CBG is an enormously complex kind of high-speed, three-dimensional chess game, and the learning curve for the successful operation of a CBG is long and steep. All vessels in a CBG must be fully linked into a common electronic operating picture and be able to function as one integrated organism simultaneously in offense and defense. Neither China nor India has any operational experience with a full peace-time CBG, much less with the intense choreography of combat operations, and both are at the very beginning of a learning curve which the U.S. Navy had largely mastered by the Battle of Midway in June 1942 and has been perfecting ever since.

This brief discussion of the specifics of *Exercise Malabar* and the basics of modern naval warfare may perhaps seem too detailed, but is necessary to illuminate the real problems facing both enhanced U.S.–India maritime security cooperation and increasing the value of future joint naval exercises. The primary U.S. strategy in the Indo-Pacific region for countering China's aggressive "string of pearls" strategy is well understood to be the "Quadrilateral Security Dialogue," or Quad, comprised of the U.S., India, Japan and Australia. The U.S. envisions strategic cooperation between these maritime powers acting as a counterbalance to the "string of pearls."[18] After a somewhat fitful period of stops and starts, including a period in which it was held in abeyance during Australian Prime Minister Kevin Rudd's tenure, the Quad was formally resumed in 2017 at the ASEAN summit. However, for much of its existence, India steadfastly and rather petulantly refused to allow Australia to participate in *Exercise Malabar*, out of typically Indian concerns about the perception of the "militarization" of the Quad, which India sees entirely differently from the U.S. perspective. India views the Quad as a kind of local maritime police and humanitarian force, limited to "illegal fishing, piracy, and humanitarian assistance and disaster relief," while the U.S. has hopes that it will grow into a naval bulwark against growing Chinese naval power in the region.[19] India, fearing the mere ire of China, wants to avoid the perception of the militarization of *Exercise Malabar* which might result from linking it to the Quad. Even the hint of a mutual defense relationship is anathema to India today. So, for example, while on a positive note India indicated in July 2020 that it "may" finally relent and agree to allow Australia to participate again in *Exercise Malabar*,[20] it then went to great public pains to stress to everyone that *Exercise Malabar* is in no way a military exercise.[21] Moreover, the absence of any real naval combat power in *Exercise Malabar* in the form of aircraft carriers and their associated CBGs – while maintaining its *raison d'être* as a maritime police force – is an Indian way of not annoying China while maintaining its strategic independence. India's maritime strategy against being bullied by China is essentially to not provoke the bully.

The structural problems are, in fact, even deeper. Indian security concerns prevent even the modest forces in *Exercise Malabar* from gaining any real practical naval integration and interoperability, due to a steadfast refusal by the Indian government to link Indian vessels into the electronic combat systems network which enables a shared and simultaneous operating picture among all the participating naval assets. The U.S. and Japan have their combat systems computers, radars, sonars and other sensors linked together, so that sailors on board their vessels, and naval aviators in their aircraft, see the exact same real-time electronic displays and share the same "track numbers" assigned to all surface, air and subsurface contacts in the operating region (Figure 1.3). Thus, for example, when a Japanese reconnaissance pilot reports to the surface ships on "Surface Track 3201," all personnel on all ships and aircraft recognize this as a reference to a particular vessel appearing on their radar screens as "S3201." All, that is, except the Indian assets in the exercise. India refuses to link its combat systems electronics to those of the U.S. and Japanese vessels, even with stand-alone portable suitcase devices not connected to the ship itself, and, as a result, Indian sailors and naval aviators have no idea which vessel hypothetical "S3201" is. Thus Indian vessels are physically present in the exercise but effectively not in the exercise, because they do not share in the common operating picture.

India also remains unwilling to link its communications systems into the shared U.S. and Japanese secure radio channels, which permit course and speed changes to be transmitted securely, so that routine adversary radio interception does not permit them to know what the friendly vessels are going to do in advance. During *Exercise Malabar*, India has such difficulty in operating even the old hand-held encryption devices used by the U.S. in World War II, despite the attachment of U.S. Navy officer observers to the

Less than meets the eye 31

Figure 1.3 The Combat Information Center (CIC) in the USS Vincennes (CG-49).

Indian surface vessels for the purpose, that course and speed changes in *Exercise Malabar* have to be transmitted in plain English via the universal international ship-to-ship ("bridge-to-bridge") radios on every ship's bridge. In terms of operational sophistication with the Indian assets, *Exercise Malabar* remains virtually at the level of the Battle of Trafalgar, which suits India perfectly, as nothing about the exercise, from their point of view, goes beyond dealing with illegal fishing operations and humanitarian assistance. To point out that this level of cooperation and coordination is far too primitive to be of use in joint, modern naval warfare is an understatement. *Exercise Malabar*, behind the public affairs and press releases, is "more about cultural familiarization than drills for joint combat."[22] (Figure 1.4)

Special forces-to-special forces training

Joint training between the special operating forces of India and the U.S. does take place, but this generally falls under the rubric of counterterrorism cooperation discussed in other chapters of this volume and thus

Figure 1.4 USS *Kitty Hawk*, at sea, September 5, 2007. Naval ships from India, Australia, Japan, Singapore, and the U.S. steam in formation in the Bay of Bengal during Exercise *Malabar* 07–2 on September 5. The formation included USS *Kitty Hawk*, USS *Nimitz*, INS *Viraat*, JS *Yuudachi*, JS *Ohnami*, RSS *Formidable*, HMAS *Adelaide*, INS *Ranvijay*, INS *Brahmaputra*, INS *Ranjit*, USS *Chicago*, and USS *Higgins*.

little will be said of it here. As noted elsewhere in this volume, U.S.–India counterterrorism cooperation is broad and deep.[23] Like disaster relief and humanitarian aid-delivery training, counterterrorism activities have broad popularity in India, and there is little opposition to the joint training of commandos, which is largely classified and kept out of the public eye in any case. The major obstacle to interoperability in this niche sector of "mil-to-mil" cooperation is the wide disparity in advanced high-tech capabilities of the two country's forces. U.S. special operating forces have extraordinarily advanced weapons systems linked to highly classified surveillance capabilities, as the raid to kill ISIS (Islamic State of Iraq and Syria) founder Abu Bakr al-Baghdadi in October, 2019 suggested even in the public realm. These capabilities are usually an integral part of how U.S. commandos plan and carry out their operations. Although the capabilities of India's special operating forces are also largely cloaked in secrecy, it has been suggested that they are less technologically advanced than their U.S. counterparts, and rely more heavily on old-school commando tactics, limited by what they can actually carry with them.

Exercise Tiger Triumph

A significant new joint exercise took place in 2019 between India and the U.S. called *Exercise Tiger Triumph*. It was the first joint exercise which involved all three services (and, unusually, some U.S. Marines from the 3D Marine Division). *Tiger Triumph* was conducted in Visakhapatnam and Kakinada in the southern Indian state of Andhra Pradesh from November 13 to 20, 2019. *Tiger Triumph* was archetypical of U.S.–India joint military training in the sense that it was a humanitarian assistance and disaster preparedness exercise, focused exclusively on civilian relief efforts.[24]

There could scarcely be a better metaphor for the state of U.S.–India military-to-military cooperation and its future than *Exercise Tiger Triumph*. The government of India is happy to welcome the assistance of the U.S. military to supplement its capabilities in alleviating humanitarian suffering from typhoons, tsunamis and monsoonal flooding. No political party in India protests about the government preparing for future humanitarian emergencies by exercising with the U.S. Indeed, such efforts have a broad popular constituency. Reports on *Tiger Triumph* across the spectrum of the Indian press, including the (center-right) *Times of India*, the (online, foreign-policy oriented) *Diplomat*, the (left-leaning and anti-BJP) *Hindu Times*[25] and the (English language, business-oriented) *Economic Times* were uniformly positive. On the American side, only reporter Tom Rogan at the conservative *Washington Observer* somewhat cynically noted that the amphibious ship-to-shore maneuvers conducted by the Marine Corps as part of *Tiger Triumph* to support "disaster relief" were in fact quite similar to what they would look like if they were a combat assault.[26] However, because humanitarian relief exercises like *Tiger Triumph* are conducted entirely with unencrypted communications and do not require integration into a common operating picture, they generate goodwill, but still do little to prepare the forces of the two countries to operate jointly in combat.

Conclusion

The two countries put up a good publicity front, but the military-to-military sector of the U.S.– India strategic partnership is one in which the whole is considerably less than the sum of the parts. The primary purpose of the military is to deter other countries from attacking, and the primary purpose of military-to-military engagement and training between two countries is to build and demonstrate a synergy of defensive strength through joint interoperability in any hypothetical international conflict. It is a fundamental military maxim that forces train together in order to be able to fight together. The time when it becomes a matter of life and death to be able to fight together, share vital real-time information and operate jointly is not the moment to begin doing it. Without doubt, there is some elementary usefulness to the U.S.–India "mil-to-mil" exercises held each year, and genuine good has come from preparation for disaster relief and planning for national emergencies. But, in terms of preparing both countries to operate their military and naval forces jointly in the event of a war, the reality is that the past and current interactions of the two uniformed militaries do little to advance that ability. In addition to extensive joint training and repetition of difficult maneuvers, in modern multidimensional warfare, the ability to share a common operating picture and to employ compatible encryption methods and equipment, and the interoperability of weapon systems, are the *sine qua non* of success in combat. To be blunt, these simply do not exist between the U.S. and India today.

The deeper reality in this sector of the partnership, however, is that the two armed forces are diametrically opposed in structure and purpose. As noted, India's military establishment is focused virtually exclusively on the defense of India's borders, while its foreign policy is based on neutrality, aversion to formal defense alliances and avoiding anything that might provoke China. It has virtually no capability to project hard power beyond its immediate neighbors. In contrast, the U.S. military effectively has no imaginable role in defense of America's borders, President Trump's symbolic deployment of some troops to the U.S.–Mexico border as a political stunt notwithstanding. U.S. foreign policy is (or was, until the Trump administration foreign policy reversals) anchored in a network of formal defense alliances, and the sole real purpose of its military establishment is to project hard power beyond its borders. In terms of their respective military policies, strategies and capabilities for the defense of their national interests, the two countries could hardly be more different.

In practical terms, the U.S. could do little to come to India's aid in the event of a Pakistani or Chinese territorial incursion. In the absence of pre-positioned forces, such as exist in Korea, Europe and Japan, the length of time (a full year) which was required for the uncontested and unopposed build-up in Saudi Arabia of sufficient land power to liberate tiny Kuwait from a third-rate Iraqi military suggests the virtual impossibility of an *ex post facto* U.S. military intervention in the event of territorial aggression against India. Even if India were to request such assistance *in extremis*, it would simply take too long to get a meaningful force on the ground. And forward basing of even limited, symbolic U.S. forces on the ground in India is unimaginable in India's current strategic thinking and current political consensus. No training has ever taken place to rehearse for such a wildly improbable scenario in any case. With mid-air refueling, the U.S. Air Force could conceivably operate from facilities on Diego Garcia island, 4,000 kilometers from New Delhi, but would experience the exact difficulties coordinating such action with Indian air defenses which cripple *Cope India* exercises today. The U.S. Navy might do more, but not in cooperation with the Indian Navy beyond staying out of each other's way. In strictly military terms, then, India is on its own, for better or worse – according to its wishes. Nor is India likely to provide troops to a foreign military adventure outside its borders any time soon. If, as Arzan Tarapore has phrased the U.S. calculus,[27] the "strategic bet" that in former Secretary of State Hillary Clinton's words, "India's greater role on the world stage will enhance peace and security"[28] is going to pay off, that payoff will likely not be in the sector of joint military operations. At present, in the military-to-military cooperation sector, the political issues and strategic-level military structural gaps are simply beyond the capabilities of either country's armed forces to remedy. And they appear to be getting worse, as India hems and haws in the tepid bathwater of nonalignment, strategic independence and declining defense spending.

Notes

1 See, for example, Sally Chung, "Deepening a Natural Partnership? Assessing the State of U.S.–India Counterterrorism Cooperation," *Asia Dispatches*, The Wilson Center, July 12, 2018. www.wilsoncenter.org/blog-post/deepening-natural-partnership-assessing-the-state-us-india-counterterrorism-cooperation.
2 Benjamin Schwartz, "From Inertia to Integration: Getting Serious About U.S.–India Defense Cooperation," *The National Interest* (June 24, 2019). Online edition: www.the-american-interest.com/2019/06/24/from-inertia-to-integration-getting-serious-about-u-s-india-defense-cooperation/. See also Government of India press release, "General Petraeus says 'Indo-Pacific Command Not Just Symbolic, Very Very Substantive'" (July 23, 2019). www.indiainnewyork.gov.in/pressevent?id=V09XeDVJUUdadml4VXRJc3ZydzdqZz09&page=2&pagecount=%208.
3 Sameer Lalwani and Heather Byrne, "The Elephant in the Room: Auditing the Past and Future of the U.S.–India Partnership," *War on the Rocks* (June 26, 2019). https://warontherocks.com/2019/06/the-elephant-in-the-room-auditing-the-past-and-future-of-the-u-s-india-partnership/.
4 Anil Jai Singh, "Budget 2019: Optimising the Defence Budget and the Need for Organisational Reform," *Financial Express* (July 12, 2019). Online edition: www.financialexpress.com/budget/budget-2019-optimising-the-defence-budget-and-the-need-for-organisational-reform/1641772/.
5 Schwartz, "From Inertia to Integration."

6 Tennessee Williams, *A Streetcar Named Desire* (Oxford: Heinemann Educational Publishers, 1947).
7 The use of the term genocide is contentious among historians of the American West, but it is becoming more commonly accepted and used. See, for example: Benjamin Madley, *An American Genocide: The United States and the California Indian Catastrophe* (New Haven, CT: Yale University Press, 2017) and David Stannard, *American Holocaust: The Conquest of the New World*. (New York: Oxford University Press, 1993).
8 The author, for example, has been asked this question on any number of occasions in meetings and conversations in India.
9 See, for example: Chris Dougherty, "Force Development Options for India by 2030," *Center for a New American Security* (October 23, 2019). Online edition: www.cnas.org/publications/reports/force-development-options-for-india-by-2030.
10 "Air forces of the U.S. and India to Hold Joint Exercise 'Cope India 2019,'" *The Economic Times* (November 29, 2018). Online edition: https://economictimes.indiatimes.com/news/defence/air-forces-of-the-us-and-india-to-hold-joint-exercise-cope-india-2019/articleshow/66868769.cms.
11 Schwartz, "From Inertia to Integration."
12 Ankit Panda, "U.S., India Begin 2019 Yudh Abhyas Army Exercises," *The Diplomat* (September 8, 2019). Online edition: https://thediplomat.com/2019/09/us-india-begin-2019-yudh-abhyas-army-exercises/.
13 *Ibid.*
14 *Ibid.*
15 "Malabar 2019 to Start Later this Month," *Aninews* (September 7, 2019). Online edition: www.aninews.in.
16 A *frigate* is a naval combatant vessel which is distinguished in design terms by having a single propeller and propeller shaft as opposed to the two propellers and shafts found on destroyers and cruisers. A frigate is a smaller vessel, generally shorter in length, more lightly armed, and less robust and capable due to its smaller size and less robust propulsion system.
17 A *corvette* is a naval surface combatant notionally smaller than a frigate (although there is often little difference between them) tasked primarily with anti-submarine defense.
18 Sumit Ganguly and Chris Mason, *An Unnatural Partnership? The Future of U.S.–India Strategic Cooperation* (Carlisle: U.S. Army War College Press, 2019), p. 48.
19 "India Keeps Australia Out of the Malabar Exercise – Again," *The Diplomat* (May 8, 2018). Online edition: https://thediplomat.com/2018/05/india-keeps-australia-out-of-the-malabar-exercise-again/.
20 "India May Invite Australia For Crucial Multilateral Malabar Naval Exercise Despite Chinese Objection," *Swarajya* (January 29, 2020). https://swarajyamag.com/insta/india-may-invite-australia-for-crucial-multilateral-malabar-naval-exercise-despite-chinese-objection.

21 Dipanjan Roy Chaudhury, "Malabar Exercise with Australian Participation Is not Quadrilateral Military Alliance: Envoy," *The Economic Times* (February 3, 2020). https://economictimes.indiatimes.com/news/defence/malabar-exercise-with-australian-participation-is-not-quadrilateral-military-alliance-envoy/articleshow/73892801.cms.
22 Sanjeev Miglani, "Indian Navy the Odd Man Out in Asia's 'Quad' Alliance," *Reuters* (November 22, 2017). Online edition: www.reuters.com/article/us-india-usa-quad/indian-navy-the-odd-man-out-in-asias-quad-alliance-idU.S.KBN1DM0UB.
23 For a summary of U.S.–India counterterrorism cooperation, see Prithvi Iyer and Kashish Parpiani, "Towards an India–U.S. Consensus on Counterterrorism Cooperation," Observer Research Foundation (April 8, 2020). www.orfonline.org/research/towards-an-india-us-consensus-on-counterterrorism-cooperation-64261/.
24 Rajeswari Pillai Rajagopalan, "Tiger Triumph: U.S.–India Military Relations Get More Complex," *The Diplomat* (November 15, 2019). Online edition: https://thediplomat.com/2019/11/tiger-triumph-us-india-military-relations-get-more-complex/.
25 In much of India, *The Hindu* is somewhat pro-Communist Party of India (CPI), although in Tamil Nadu it is more mainstream and pro-DMK. In any event, it is solidly anti-BJP, and the absence of anything negative to say about "Tiger Triumph" is a hermeneutic reflection of the lack of political resistance to humanitarian training.
26 Tom Rogan, "U.S. and India Conduct Amphibious Assault Training," *Washington Examiner* (November 15, 2019). Online edition: www.washingtonexaminer.com/opinion/us-and-india-conduct-amphibious-assault-training.
27 Arzan Tarapore, "A More Focused and Resilient U.S.–India Strategic Partnership," *Center for a New American Security* (October 23, 2019). Online edition: www.cnas.org/publications/reports/a-more-focused-and-resilient-u-s-india-strategic-partnership.
28 Hillary Clinton, "America's Pacific Century," *Foreign Policy* (October 11, 2011).

2

Faltering friends: U.S.–India military cooperation in the twenty-first century

Abhijnan Rej

Introduction

In September 2000, during a trip to New York, then Indian Prime Minister Atal Bihari Vajpayee reiterated the U.S. and India as "natural allies," a proposition he first advanced months after India's 1998 nuclear tests.[1] Vajpayee's remark was at once a signal that India was willing to put the ebbs and flows of the Cold War relationship between the two countries firmly behind, as well as an assertion of the proposition that shared natural interests and values in the international system could – and should – lead to a much deeper relationship between the two.

One of the permanent features of Indian strategic policy since the turn of the millennium has been a commitment to maintain the upswing in ties with the U.S. Most concretely, this has meant a deepening defense relationship between the two even when other differences, mostly on the economic side, have marked the background. The U.S. is now India's second-largest arms source. Bilateral and multilateral military exercises involving the two countries' armed forces have not only proliferated but also acquired substance in terms of their technical complexity. At a political level, both India and the U.S. express their commitment to a "free and open Indo-Pacific"; indeed, New Delhi finds much to rejoice at the "Indo"-suffix to the hyphenated moniker signifying, as it does, the importance of India in U.S. grand strategy. Driving this apparent convergence in the bilateral relationship is a rising China that seeks to push the U.S. out of the Western Pacific, and keep India boxed in in the South Asian subcontinent as a regional and not pan-Asian actor.

That said, significant challenges remain in the military relationship between the two countries, both at a practical quotidian level of *how* the two may further cooperate militarily and also at the grand-strategic level of *why* they may do so, given the palpable differences in the perception of their often (though not always) overlapping theatres of interest and conception of shared responses in order to meet challenges there. Geopolitically, India is a per-capita poor regional continental power whose maritime ambitions are directed towards making it a marquee pan-Asian actor – something Beijing is loath to allow. On the other hand, the global military and economic hegemon U.S. is a maritime power redoubling on its Asian identity in order to prevent Chinese spheres of influence in the continent. The resulting U.S.–India dynamic simultaneously points to further areas of strategic cooperation as well as limits of the same. While India and the U.S. are rhetorically natural allies, when it comes to their defense relationship they often come across as faltering friends.

This chapter examines the current state of the U.S.–India military relationship as well as the structural impediments that have stood in the way of its maturing to its full potential. It proceeds in the following way. In the rest of this section I present a conceptual schema about the means and ends of the relationship which will be fleshed out in the rest of the chapter. In the second section I examine the current state of the U.S.–India military relationship by looking at questions around political congruence, shared political-military objectives, as well as military interoperability. I find that Indian domestic factors – both ideational elements as well as structural/capabilities limitations – significantly and adversely affect all three. Given that these factors are most likely to persist in the near future, in the third section I look at possible alternative pathways for U.S.–India defense cooperation. I conclude, in the final section, with observations about additional steps the U.S. needs to take so as to deepen military ties with India.

A schema

In order to map the current state of U.S.–Indian military cooperation and identify bottlenecks to further enhancing the relationship in the future, one must conceptually untangle how – at least in an ideal world – military cooperation between two states comes about.

The first step in this scheme is identifying whether two states in question *converge politically* on common threats and challenges (Figure 2.1). This, in turn, may be driven by common dissatisfaction with a third power, as well as a shared vision of the structure of the international or regional system. Once this is achieved, such a vision must translate to *shared political-military objectives*. This should include not only (1) identification of common political-military goals, (2) theatres of interest where the two states' armed forces would cooperate to meet shared goals, but also (3) concrete military objectives to be met in peacetime and war. Finally, once such political-military congruence has been achieved, it should translate to *interoperability* between the armed forces of the two states. While

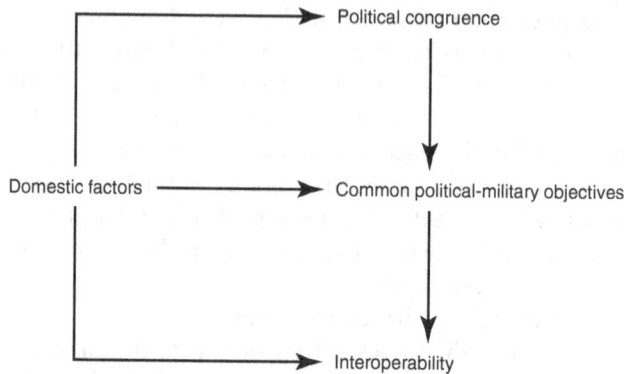

Figure 2.1 Schematic representation of the process of military cooperation.

the "base" of interoperability is (1) legal frameworks that allow for greater integration of the two sovereign forces, it comes about through (2) usage of common weapon systems and platforms (3) extensive military exercises and (4) doctrinal convergence.

Unit-level domestic structural conditions can both further and inhibit this process. Questions around capabilities of (and, therefore, defense spending by) both states, the state of military jointness and defense equipment procurement processes can all drive the process of military cooperation in both directions; so does bureaucratic politics (such as inter-service rivalry, when it comes to resource allocation) when it comes to enhancing interoperability between the militaries of the two states. At the same time, other domestic drivers of foreign policy such as ideology as well as domestic audience cost affect the achievement of political congruence.

U.S.–India military cooperation: state of play

Political congruence

If political convergence is defined as shared understanding of common threats and challenges, driven by the common dissatisfaction with a third power, as well as a shared vision of the structure of the international or regional system, do the U.S. and India converge politically? The answer is a much-qualified yes. Unlike the U.S., India does not have a public National Security Strategy (NSS) document which could be used to compare the two countries' strategic orientations.[2] Absent such a document, one must make do with other ancillary Indian documents such as military doctrines, Ministry of Defence reports, as well as public statements as one embarks on identifying points on which the two countries converge.

The 2017 U.S. NSS marked a decisive shift in the American strategic outlook as it emphasized great-power competition (with China and Russia) as the predominant challenge to be met by that country, away from counterterrorism objectives that had driven much of U.S. strategic thinking since the terrorist attacks on New York and Washington in September, 2001.[3] Both this document as well as the National Defense Strategy that flowed from it introduced the moniker of the "Indo-Pacific" in American strategic lexicon, as a key theatre (along with the Middle East and Europe) where the U.S. Department of Defense (DoD) would seek to maintain a "favorable regional balance of power."[4] In 2019, the DoD published an "Indo-Pacific Strategy Report" (IPSR), which spelled out threats the U.S. sought to mitigate in that theatre (whose definition is the region covered by the erstwhile U.S. Pacific Command, now renamed as the *Indo*-Pacific Command), principally China and Russia, in line with the emerging emphasis on great-power competition in Washington.[5]

When it comes to India, the 2017 NSS welcomed its "emergence as a leading global power and stronger strategic and defense partner" and also sought to increase "quadrilateral cooperation" with New Delhi alongside Tokyo and Canberra. It also noted that the U.S. would expand "defense and security cooperation with India, a Major Defense Partner of the U.S., and support India's growing relationships throughout the region."[6] Between this document and the 2019 IPSR, it became clear that the U.S. considered India as a major regional actor supporting its goal of a "free and open Indo-Pacific." That said, a careful parsing of the IPSR points to very mixed implications for the country.

To begin with, the IPSR flagged Russia as a one of the four key threats to peace in the Indo-Pacific that stands to affect U.S.–India relations the most. It notes – as part of its threat perception – that "Moscow seeks to alleviate some of the effects of sanctions imposed, following its aggressive actions in Ukraine, by *diplomatically appealing to select states in Asia and seeking economic opportunities for energy exports. Russia also seeks to increase defense and trade relations through arms sales in the region*"[7] (emphasis added). It is not unreasonable to expect that the Pentagon considered India as one of the "select states" Russia is interested in as part of its regional strategy.[8] The U.S. could very well note that a $24 billion India–Russia natural gas deal was operationalized in June, 2018 as part of New Delhi's effort to balance its ties with Moscow following Prime Minister Narendra Modi's vigorous outreach to Washington.

More significantly, despite direct multiple warnings that the decision would attract U.S. secondary sanctions, India went ahead in 2019 with an agreement to purchase S-400 *Triumf* anti-aircraft missile batteries from Russia. At the time, then-Defense Minister Nirmala Sitharaman justified the decision, noting that "CAATSA [Countering America's Adversaries Through Sanctions Act] ... is not a UN act, it's a U.S. act."[9] (Russian S-400 sales are a subject of serious concern to the Trump administration.[10] In fact, the IPSR notes Moscow's sale of this weapon system to Beijing as part of its bad behavior.) This defiant stance was ultimately rooted in the belief that the U.S. will never consider measures that will weaken India militarily and undermine gains since 2000. That belief stands challenged. On May 31, 2019 – a day before U.S. then-Acting Secretary of Defense Patrick Shanahan's Shangri-La Dialogue speech unveiling the IPSR – a State Department official noted that, should India stick with the S-400 deal with Russia, it would "'preclude' a deep and broad defence relationship with the U.S."[11]

But India's quest for a multipolar international architecture through political partnerships with Russia and China is also likely to irritate an administration whose stated strategic policy is maintaining American military and economic (and therefore, by implication, political) primacy. The IPSR notes, as part of its Russia threat assessment, that both Moscow's and Beijing's "preference for a multipolar world order in which the U.S. is weaker and less influential."[12] The fact of the matter is that that has also been New Delhi's unstated preference; do recall its active participation in the BRICS (Brazil, Russia, India, China and South Africa), which repeatedly seeks a "representative multipolar international order."[13] In fact, India has often gone out of its way to express solidarity with Russia and China in this quest, by participating in avenues explicitly created to advance a multipolar international system.

Most noticeably, New Delhi held a ministerial-level Russia–India–China (RIC) meeting in 2017 exactly a month *after* its participation in the first meeting of revived U.S.–Australia–Japan–India quadrilateral dialogue (which was then at mid-senior official level).[14] Publicly and privately, Indian officials equated India's participation in both at that time.[15] But what makes India's notional participation in RIC potentially irksome for the U.S. (the grouping is yet to deliver anything concrete despite multiple sporadic meetings over the years) is its history. The idea of a RIC triangle was first floated in 1998 by then Russian foreign minister Yevgeny Primakov; Moscow's mouthpieces argue that in his conception RIC would be the key to establishing a multipolar world.[16] This little bit of history is surely not lost to the current U.S. administration. For India, participation in fora such as the RIC or BRICS forms a crucial symbolic assertion of its belief in strategic autonomy.

In turn, ideology plays a crucial role in consolidating India's quest for strategic autonomy, whether that was in the guise of "nonalignment" during the Cold War or "multi-alignment" – the current driving force in Indian foreign policy which takes engagement with all major powers along specific issues.[17] The worldview of the Rashtriya Swamsevak Sangh (RSS) – parent organization of the ruling Bharatiya Janata Party (BJP) – remains deeply rooted in the suspicion of the West, especially on cultural influences emanating from it, even as RSS thinkers have prescribed seeking Western help in checking Chinese power.[18] Therefore the foreign-policy prescription that flows from this worldview has a necessarily instrumental view of the West in general, and the U.S. in particular. Fora like BRICS and RIC which continue to push for a multipolar world may be "talk shops" producing few concrete deliverables, as some Indian experts have suggested. But it is highly unlikely that an assertive nationalist Indian Right will have any interest in pushing the project of maintaining American primacy in Asia – which is what the current U.S. national security strategy seeks to achieve.

Shared political–military objectives

This dissonance when it comes to converging on a common political vision is reflected in the Indian inability to share the core strategic objectives of the U.S. as outlined in the current U.S. administration's strategy documents. Indian domestic constraints also continue to support a default strategic vision that remains occupied with continental threats. Absent the ability of both countries to come to a common set of political-military objectives – here defined as shared theatres of interest where the two states' armed forces would cooperate to meet shared goals and common political-military objectives – Rear Admiral (Retd.) Raja Menon's question about the "political military context" behind joint military exercises will remain unanswered.[19]

Consider India's vision of the Indo-Pacific. It is both politically and geographically expansive. At a political level, India continues to push for an "inclusive" Indo-Pacific. In 2018, Prime Minister Narendra Modi laid out his vision of the theatre, noting that "India does not see the Indo-Pacific Region as a strategy or as a club of limited members. Nor as a grouping that seeks to dominate. And by no means do we consider it as directed against any country."[20] Operationally, that has meant that India has actively sought to bring Russia in as a stakeholder in the region even when Moscow has firmly rejected the notion, calling it "artificially imposed."[21]

For example, in September, 2019, speaking at the 5th Eastern Economic Forum in Russia, Modi proposed a Chennai–Vladivostok maritime route, going on to remark that Indian–Russian partnership in Russia's Far East will make it a "confluence of open, free and inclusive Indo-Pacific."[22] India has also sought to expand naval cooperation with Russia, and a naval-logistics support agreement along the line of the one India has with the U.S. is in the works.[23] Even if one were to argue that the India–Russia relationship has lost most of its sentimental value of the past in New Delhi, India will continue to note the ease with which it can procure highly sophisticated military hardware from Moscow – such as nuclear-powered submarines. (U.S. defense export-control laws prevent the sale or lease of such platforms even to treaty allies.)

Geographically, India's conception of the Indo-Pacific is like Japan's as presented in Tokyo's "Two Oceans, Two Continents" strategy: it stretches from the eastern Pacific Ocean to the eastern coastline of Africa. Until January, 2019, the U.S. and Indian definitions of the maritime theatre didn't match, the former's being simply the area of responsibility of the U.S. INDOPACOM (India-Pacific Command), ending on the western shores of India. In the past, Indian analysts have tried to manage this incongruity with the American definition by essentially truncating India's Indo-Pacific to its east, to bring the country's Indo-Pacific vision into line with Modi's South-East Asia-focused "Act East" policy.[24] Even in this narrower frame, India has struggled to project military power or to politically engage with the most pressing regional challenges emanating from Chinese intransigence there. While the Trump administration's Deputy National Security Advisor expanded the U.S. definition of the Indo-Pacific to match India's at a New Delhi event in January, 2019,[25] it is unclear – at the time of writing this chapter – what that means in terms of greater coordination within the U.S. CENTCOM (Central Command), INDOPACOM, and AFRICOM (Africa Command) in terms of advancing this expansive vision.

The principal obstacles to a greater Indian engagement in the Pacific (even in its western sector, including the South and East China Seas) are strategic, normative and lack of capabilities.[26] The absence of a well-defined Indian national security strategy has meant that the strategic establishment's default position has been to overemphasize continental threats. Nowhere is this more clearly visible than in the 2017 Joint Doctrine of the Indian Armed Forces – the first-ever such public document – which was notable for its near-absent discussion of force projection and perfunctory attention to naval power.[27] At a normative level, India's position on freedom of navigation is, ironically, closer to that of China than the U.S., in that New Delhi, like Beijing, does not allow for the right of innocent passage for foreign navies in its exclusive economic zones. Because of this reason India worries that, should it participate in freedom of navigation operations with the U.S. in the South China Sea, for example, it may open up to the possibility of the Chinese reciprocating with the same in the Andaman Sea.[28] (The detection of a Chinese "research vessel" by the Indian Navy there in September 2019 means that the possibility of more frequent Chinese intrusions into Indian Exclusive Economic Zones cannot be ruled out.[29]) The Indian Navy's doctrine also considers the South and the East China Seas as part of its

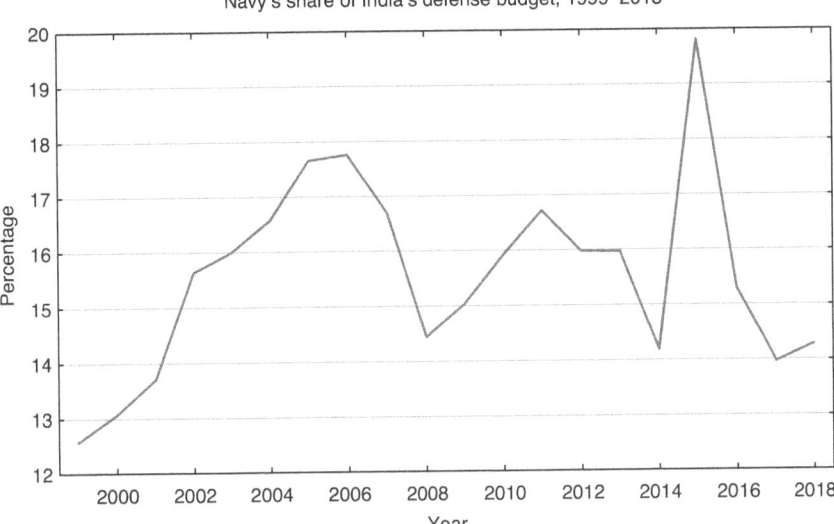

Figure 2.2 Indian Navy's share of defense budget.

"secondary" area of responsibility (AOR), while the western Indian Ocean forms part of its primary AOR, effectively robbing those maritime areas of immediate strategic salience.[30]

However, it is India's naval capabilities that constrain what the Indian Navy can or cannot do in terms of force projection, including in the Western Pacific. The Indian Navy has been panned as the "Cinderella service," reflecting its share in the country's defense budget, which stood at little more than 14 percent in 2018–19.

But the issue simply is not the navy's share of the defense budget alone, but the overwhelming preponderance of army revenue expenditure (the bulk of which are salaries and allowances and pensions) in the overall defense budget, which crowds out the modernization budget in general, and the naval modernization budget in particular. As an example, in 2018–19 India spent approximately nine times on pay, allowances and pensions for the army than on modernizing its navy (Figure 2.3). Even within India's military modernization budget, the navy's share was only 27 percent in 2018–19, with the bulk of the rest going into the Indian Air Force, whose squadron strength as well as vintage are causes of great alarm in New Delhi. The net result of these budgetary issues is that the India–China naval balance has steadily worsened since 2010, even in the Indian Ocean Region (IOR).[31] This implies that the Indian Navy's budgetary priorities will revolve around keeping the naval balance there decisively in its favor, which concomitantly implies that it will lack the array of force-projecting

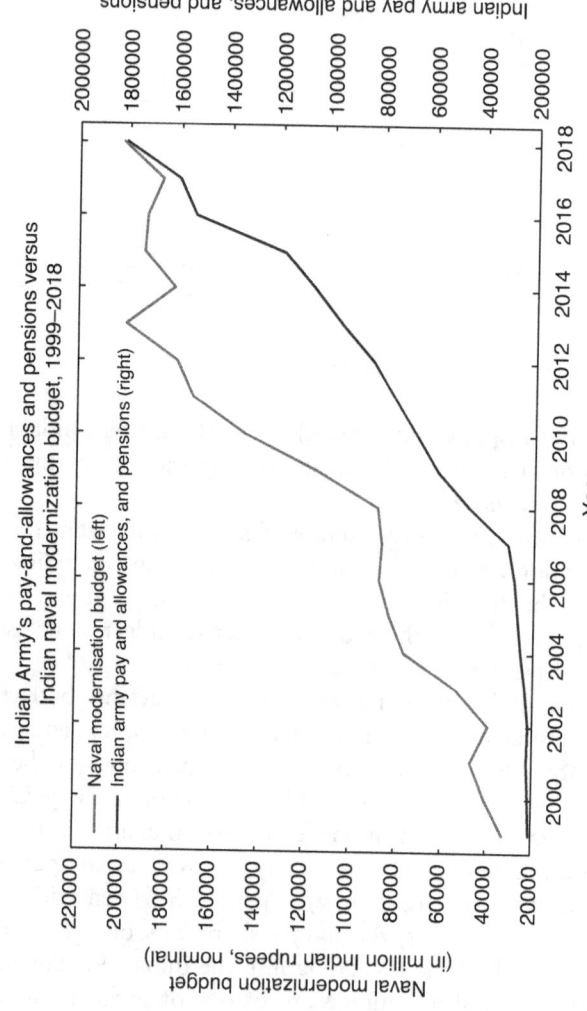

Figure 2.3 Comparing the Indian Army's pay, allowances and pensions with India's naval modernization budget. For data and computation details, see: https://abhirej.files.wordpress.com/2019/03/methodology.pdf.

capabilities required to play a meaningful role in the South China Sea, a key ask of the U.S. for India in the past.[32]

Military interoperability

In the ideal scheme outlined in Figure 2.1, once two states have political congruence they should identify common political-military objectives to be met together. The means of this end is military interoperability between the two forces. Such interoperability is provided by a set of *legal instruments* which allow for greater integration of two armed forces, which is then furthered through regular and technically complex *joint exercises*. Further interoperability is advanced using *common weapon-systems and platforms*, as well as through *shared doctrinal precepts*. Domestic variables affect all four factors.

Legal agreements

Perhaps the brightest spot when it comes to the state of U.S.–India military cooperation has been the ability of the two countries to enter into the discussions for – and sign all but one – "foundational agreements" which allow for greater interoperability between the militaries of the two countries. The first (and the most basic of the set) is the General Security of Military Information Agreement, which was signed in 2002. This agreement was the result of intense negotiations that started in 1987, and "enabled the United States to compete for the sales of military equipment either through commercial channels (U.S. defense firms to the Indian government) or government-to-government sales (what the U.S. terms Foreign Military Sales or FMS)."[33]

In 2016, India and the U.S. signed the Logistics Exchange Memorandum of Agreement (LEMOA), which became operational two years later, in 2018.[34] LEMOA is essentially an agreement that allows for the two countries' forces, navies in particular, to systematize logistics support – such as refueling and port visits – provided to each other. As such, it is a routine agreement which the U.S. has with many other countries. The fact that it took more than a decade's negotiation – and conclusion with great fanfare involving the U.S. Secretary of Defense and the Indian Defence Minister – suggests that a U.S.–India LEMOA was far from being uncontroversial in New Delhi and required significant commitment of political capital on part of the Narendra Modi government. Influential analysts – confusing LEMOA for an agreement that allows U.S. forces basing rights in India or a "Status of Forces Agreement," which the U.S. has with treaty allies such as Japan, Germany and Australia – decried LEMOA as a step in making India a "client state" of the U.S.[35] The fact that India considers even this routine agreement – which is tantamount to formalizing ad hoc logistics support arrangements of the past – as a political signal became clear in 2020 when New Delhi proposed a similar agreement with Russia, as a way to perhaps balance the perception that it was tilting towards the American side when it came to military cooperation.[36] (The strategic value of a mutual logistics support agreement for India with Russia is unclear; unlike the U.S., the Russian Navy's Indian Ocean footprint is quite small.)

If ideology provided for one set of obstruction when it came to formalizing the foundational agreements with the U.S., India's continental military preoccupations with Pakistan provided the other. In 2018, again after a long period of negotiations, India and the U.S. signed a Communications Compatibility and Security Agreement (COMCASA) which would allow the armed forces of both countries to securely communicate with each other through dedicated data links using a CENTRIXS-type communication system.[37] India's worry in the run-up to signing the COMCASA (an India-specific variant of Communications Interoperability and Security Memorandum of Agreement) was that Pakistan's status as a CENTCOM partner could mean that in the event of an India–Pakistan military confrontation, the CENTCOM CENRTIXS arrangement could be used by Pakistan to tap into secure Indian communications. A related worry was that in event of an India–Pakistan contingency, the U.S. might terminate the secure data exchange facility by way of putting pressure on India.[38]

India and the U.S. continue to negotiate the final foundational agreement that would allow both countries to share geospatial information. The Basic Exchange and Cooperation Agreement (BECA) will, according to one news report, allow India to use U.S. geospatial databanks for accurate targeting with cruise and ballistic missiles.[39] As such, BECA will greatly facilitate creation of denial complexes in the Indian Ocean that India could build to negate Chinese naval build-up there in war time (see below for more on this). BECA is also considered to be a prerequisite if India were to purchase (and use) the armed Predator-B drones for the U.S.[40]

Military exercises

The militaries of India and the U.S. have jointly exercised extensively, averaging more than two exercises in the five years since 2014 (Table 2.1). The joint naval exercise *Malabar* started in 1992 (which has, since 2009, included the Japanese Maritime Self-Defence Forces) and grew out of a 1991 proposal made by the then commander of U.S. Army Pacific Command Lieutenant General Claude M. Kicklighter to greatly expand U.S.–India military cooperation, including but not limited to the naval

Faltering friends 49

Table 2.1 U.S.–India military exercises, 2014–19

Year	Number of exercises
2014–15	1 (Army) + 2 (Navy) = 3
2015–16	1 (Army) + 1 (Navy) = 2
2016–17	1 (Army/Special Forces) + 2 (Navy) = 3
2017–18	2 (Army) + 1 (Navy) = 3[a]
2018–19	1 (Army) + 1 (Navy) + 1 (Air Force) = 3

Note: [a] The 2018–19 Ministry of Defence report does not mention the U.S.–India Airforce–Airforce *Cope* exercise.
Source: Data compiled from Indian Ministry of Defence Annual Reports.

domain.[41] The two navies also exercise together in multilateral foras such as the U.S.-organized RIMPAC and India-led Milan series. The armies of two states regularly exercise through the *Yudh Abhyas* series. However, air force exercises are relatively uncommon. The U.S.–India *Cope* series was first held in 2002. The last edition before the 2018 *Cope* exercise was in 2009.[42] India also hosted the first U.S.–India tri-service military exercise *Tiger Triumph* in November 2019.[43]

Technically, the *Malabar* exercise has grown to become quite sophisticated, involving a range of advanced platforms and concepts, including anti-submarine warfare "emphasizing high-end war fighting skills, maritime superiority, and power projection."[44] As one Indian naval strategist put it, "exercising at the higher end of the spectrum," the "interoperability [between the U.S. and Indian navies] at Malabar is very good."[45]

The saga of the two air forces' *Cope Exercise*, however, brings out how politically sensitive air force–air force exercises can be, appearing as it does as a venue where Russian platforms deployed by the Indian Air Force (IAF) are pitted against American ones. The 2004 exercise led to the U.S. Air Force being squarely defeated, "losing more than 90 percent of the engagements – eventually leading to an outcry in the Congress."[46] Similarly, one can infer that, should such exercises point to deficiencies in the IAF's Russian-supplied capabilities, there would be growing calls in India to diversify its Air Force away from its Russian suppliers – which, in turn, would clash with India's position on strategic autonomy expressed through a longstanding steady defense trade relationship with Russia. Therefore, there is a real risk that every IAF–USAF exercise could become an ersatz competition between Russia and the U.S. That said, without enough joint exercises the ad hoc nature of U.S.–India air force cooperation is unlikely to be remedied.[47]

Even at a pure "bean-count" level, the number of U.S.–India military exercises hardly stands out. As noted in Table 2.1, between 2014–15 and

2018–19 the militaries of both countries exercised, in total, fourteen times. In the same time period, India and Russia exercised together twelve times.[48]

But more fundamentally, joint military exercises should have concrete strategic objectives beyond the goals of socialization and learning about each other's best practices. Given that it is highly unlikely that U.S.–India exercises are about developing capabilities to jointly fight wars – as non-treaty partners and not allies, there is no mutual defense clause that would force such an arrangement – joint military exercises are best viewed as signaling political intent to a third state.[49] However, India's large number of military exercises partners – including China – stands to dilute this goal. To wit, if New Delhi considers many states as its military partners, the signaling value of joint exercises vastly diminishes.

Common platforms

While common platforms and weapon-systems are not a prerequisite for deeper military cooperation – even among allies, as NATO notes[50] – operating with diverse and often rival sets of platforms creates its own problems. A persistent theme when it comes to the limits of U.S.–India military cooperation has been India's use of Russian equipment. Despite direct American threats of sanctions, New Delhi has not reduced its dependence on Russian weaponry. In 2018, for example, India not only went ahead with the purchase of S-400 anti-aircraft missile batteries but also placed an additional order of two more *Krivak*-class stealth frigates.[51] As one former U.S. Navy official noted, "Indian ships obtained from the prior Soviet Union retain damage control systems/infrastructure that by U.S. standards would be inadequate."[52] While he added that this is not a "stopper" to interoperability, it remains an issue of concern.

Beyond this lies the question of security of systems supplied by both Russia and the U.S. For example, the U.S. would be reluctant to supply platforms to India whose integration with Russian-supplied weaponry might not only be technically infeasible but might also compromise the security of U.S. equipment. It is also unclear whether India can afford to retrofit all its Russian equipment with the secure communications equipment needed for the implementation of COMCASA. At this stage, it is known only that the U.S. has activated the pre-existing Selective Availability Anti-Spoofing Module GPS system in some of U.S.-supplied C-130 and C-17 transport aircraft after the agreement was signed.[53] Even when the U.S. and India use common platforms – such as the P-8I aircraft crucial for anti-submarine warfare, which could be seamlessly linked after the secure communications agreement was signed – Indian defense budgetary limitations indicate India is unlikely to increase the purchase of such platforms in the near future;

the Navy's request to purchase an additional ten P-8I aircraft was cut by half by the Ministry of Defence in 2019.[54] Meanwhile, the proposal to co-manufacture the F-16 Block 70 medium multirole combat aircraft in India – which would have greatly benefited the grand Indian goal of military technology transfer from the U.S. as well as the Modi government's "Make in India" goals – remains stalemated for a variety of reasons.[55]

Doctrinal convergence

The final point when it comes to the inhibition of further U.S.–India military cooperation is the lack of common doctrinal objectives. India was considerably influenced by the U.S. AirLand Doctrine of the 1980s as it sought to develop a deterrence-by-punishment strategy directed at Pakistan (and echoes of this doctrine can be found in the 2017 Joint Doctrine of the Indian Armed Forces[56]). An influential Indian military strategist also drew considerable doctrinal lessons from the U.S. campaign in Iraq in 2003 – on the need for greater synergy in AirLand Battle, the need for dedicated air–ground strike platforms as well as the tailored utilization of special forces – in designing a vision document for the Indian Army in 2020.[57] That said, India and the U.S. do not share many more doctrinal precepts or common strategies, especially for theaters where the latter may want the former to play a much larger role. Take, for example, any joint patrol of the South China Sea by the U.S. and India in the future. Even if the formidable political problems on the Indian side when it comes to agreeing to such joint missions were to be resolved – currently, India carries out *coordinated* patrols only with its maritime neighbors, such as Indonesia – there is no publicly available evidence that it has a maritime strategy to defeat Chinese anti-access/area denial complexes akin to the U.S. Air–Sea Battle Doctrine in the event of a kinetic engagement in the process.[58] Jointness in the Indian military architecture has considerably hampered the development of such precepts. In sum, the lack of doctrinal convergence is likely to prove to be very costly when it comes to substantive U.S.–India military cooperation.

The future of U.S.–India military cooperation: three pathways

In the previous section I have described the many structural factors that limit what the U.S. and India can do to further military cooperation. In particular, two sets of issues stood out:

1. India's enduring commitment to strategic autonomy implies that the country will hardly reduce its dependence on Russian weapons. At the

same time, it also means that India is unlikely to take steps politically that would signal a deeper defense relationship with the U.S. involving joint operations and war-fighting postures publicly.
2. India's defense budgetary travails – and the overwhelming dominance of revenue expenditure over military modernization commitments – means that it is unlikely to acquire significant power projection capabilities in the near future, especially in theaters such as the Western Pacific where the U.S. would like to see India share its burden.

In light of both, it is an imperative that the U.S. and the India radically reimagine the future of the defense relationship. There are essentially three (overlapping) pathways for the future.

The "Net Security Provider" proposition revisited

The first pathway for the U.S. would be to help India emerge as a soft-security provider in the IOR, reducing U.S. burden in the areas of counterterrorism and humanitarian assistance and disaster relief (HA/DR) and as a military first-responder to crises in the smaller IOR littorals. India's strategic preoccupation remains Islamist terrorism, as can be seen through multiple reports of the Ministry of Defence and statements by Indian officials. For the U.S., the IOR littorals are both countries where China seeks to make economic and political (and therefore, strategic) inroads, as well as potential bases for Islamist radicals as they seek to regroup from their military defeat in West Asia. The Easter Day bombings in 2019 in Sri Lanka serve as an example of how some states with limited capabilities face both challenges. In this direction, a 2+1 model of counterterrorism exercises – India and the U.S., plus a third state – could leverage India's considerable counterterrorism experience. Already, India and the U.S.'s special forces exercise together, as part of the two armies' *Yudha Abhyas* series.[59] Both countries have a decade-old framework – the U.S.–India Counterterrorism Initiative[60] – that could be expanded with renewed focus on maritime terrorism threats as well as third-country contingencies in collaboration with other partners as well. The 2019 U.S.–Australia–Japan–India quadrilateral counterterrorism simulation exercise is a first welcome step in that direction.[61] Politically as well as technically, HA/DR collaboration in third countries is a low-hanging fruit that must be plucked.

Furthering Fortress India

When it comes to balancing China, it is now clear – due to India's budgetary constraints – that a blue-water navy for the country is some time distance away. The U.S. must collaborate with India on a different model, where India's location can be leveraged to build sophisticated denial complexes capable of interdicting Chinese sea-lines of communication in the Indian Ocean.⁶² For example, off-record, U.S. officials have shown great interest in propositions advanced by Indian scholars around developing the Andaman and Nicobar Islands as bases from which precision strikes could be launched against the Chinese Navy as it ingresses into the Indian Ocean from the Malacca, Sunda and Lumbok Straits.

With the signing of BECA, a major capability has been provided to India which would enable its armed forces with targeting information for such precision strikes. In collaboration with a third country (with greater access in the southwestern Indian Ocean, such as France) a robust pan-IOR denial complex could be created; it goes without saying that purchasing or producing precision-guided munitions is, by a significant fraction, cheaper than acquiring naval platforms such as destroyers and frigates. Now that COMCASA is operational, intelligence for anti-submarine warfare, especially using the P-8 platforms both countries operate, can be more readily shared between the U.S. and India. It is noteworthy that such development of a reconnaissance-strike complex can be carried out away from the public eye – therefore the domestic-audience cost of such an effort for New Delhi would be much smaller than, say, shedding its decade-long aversion to joint military operations. Such an effort would also naturally leverage Indian air superiority in the Indian Ocean.

Co-developing asymmetric offsets

The third pathway is the most ambitious, involving joint research and development efforts between India and the U.S. to build asymmetric high-technology solutions to offset China's numerical military superiority. This would involve building common civilian–military facilities to research advances in offensive cyber capabilities whose outright transfer from the U.S. may be prohibited by American law, though India's entry into the multilateral Wassenaar Arrangement in 2017 allows in-principle transfer of offensive cyber weapons from the U.S.⁶³ India has a significant base of engineers and technologists; the U.S. has first-mover advantage in many of the technologies required for such asymmetric offsets, including those in artificial intelligence and machine learning. The two could be fused together in the form of an international collaboration between India's Defence Research and Development Organization and the U.S.'s Defense Advanced Research Projects Agency, as well as academic institutions between the two countries.

The U.S.–India Defense Trade and Technology Initiative (DTTI) has been widely decried in Delhi as more "trade" and less "technology"; in any event, India can hardly afford to buy prohibitively expensive platforms and equipment from the U.S. such as the electromagnetic-launch catapults for the next generation of indigenously manufactured Indian carriers, a key item on the Indian Navy's wish list. Reorienting DTTI for next-generation asymmetric technology development – including for electronic and cyber-warfare – would be a first step in this direction. Low highly skilled manpower costs in India stand to defray the costs of such future initiatives. In December 2019, the U.S. and India signed the Industrial Security Annex, which is a necessary step for private sector defense-manufacturing deals between both countries.[64] With this, technology co-development between both countries could receive a fillip.

Conclusion

The U.S.–India defense relationship is, in many ways, *sui generis*. Erstwhile antagonists united by a common challenge, both countries have managed to keep their often-deep political differences aside to emerge as formidable partners in the Indo-Pacific. That said, as I have explored in the previous sections, these differences – along with significant material constraints on India's part – have meant that, more often than not, the U.S.–India strategic relationship has suffered from bouts of inflated expectations arising out of not understanding them well enough or, worse, ignoring them and hoping they will disappear with time.[65]

Beyond the issues that I have highlighted in the previous sections, the fact of the matter remains that there is considerable skepticism in New Delhi – often not visible from commentaries in the Indian English-language press – about the U.S.'s long-term staying power in Asia, the possibility of a U.S.–China grand bargain or the creation of a "G2," and, finally, about U.S. interest in coming to India's aid in event of a military confrontation with China. The latter became explicit when then Indian navy chief Admiral Sunil Lanba noted in a May 2018 speech: "India is the only country in the quad with a land border with China. In case of conflict, nobody will hold our hand."[66] India also continues to worry about the presence of "extra-regional *powers*" (emphasis added) in waters such as the Bay of Bengal which it considers part of its natural sphere of influence; the plural indicates that India is not worried about China alone.[67]

What might the U.S. do to assuage India's concerns?

First, at a political level it must assure the Indian public that the U.S. will not abandon India during a contingency on land with China. While it is clear that there are limitations to what the U.S. can do in this regard, experience with the 2017 India–China Doklam crisis shows that the U.S. was indeed confronted with this question in the recent past.[68] More public signaling during future land-based India–China contingencies will reduce the pressure on the Indian government from its political opposition, should New Delhi and Washington decide to move closer in terms of military ties.

Second, any American sanctions on India following its Russian arms imports – whether that is due to the S-400 sales or others – is likely to do grave damage to the defense relationship. While India remains cognizant of the fact that a waiver from the S-400 sanctions is a complex, contentious issue in Washington and involves significant Congressional maneuverings, the U.S. must very carefully calculate the long-term costs of its actions vis-à-vis its benefits. Russian arms imports are a fact of Indian strategic life; the sooner the U.S. finds a creative modus vivendi to deal with it, the better. Direct threats from the Trump administration on the matter have hardly helped the situation. Irrespective of who assumes the American presidency in January 2021, India–Russia relations will continue to cast a long shadow on U.S.–India defense relations.

Third and finally, the U.S. needs to very clearly and publicly spell out India's position in American grand strategy. Designations such as "Major Defense Partner," while having a placating impact on India's strategic community, are hard to decipher in terms of their concrete operational content (beyond issues of export control).

Notes

1 Address by Shri Atal Bihari Vajpayee, Asia Society, September 7, 2000, https://asiasociety.org/address-shri-atal-bihari-vajpayee.
2 At the time of writing, a classified Indian National Security Strategy document is in the works that is intended to provide guidance to military doctrines and conditions under which India will employ force, making it more similar to the U.S. National Defense Strategy or the erstwhile Quadrennial Defense Review. A news report notes that part of this document is likely to be made public after review by the apex security establishment; see: S. Gupta, "National Security Adviser Ajit Doval Ready with India's New Military Doctrine," *Hindustan Times* (September 19, 2019), www.hindustantimes.com/india-news/new-military-doctrine-to-be-submitted-in-october/story-S0payhw9CgFs5FfeMqAMyI.html.
3 National Security Strategy of the United States of America, The White House, December, 2017, www.whitehouse.gov/wp-content/uploads/2017/12/NSS-Final-12-18-2017-0905.pdf.
4 Summary of the 2018 National Defense Strategy of the United States of America: Sharpening the American Military's Competitive Edge, U.S. Department of

Defense, January 19, 2018, www.defense.gov/Portals/1/Documents/pubs/2018-National-Defense-Strategy-Summary.pdf.
5 Indo-Pacific Strategy Report, U.S. Department of Defense, June 1, 2019, https://media.defense.gov/2019/Jul/01/2002152311/-1/-1/1/DEPARTMENT-OF-DEFENSE-INDO-PACIFIC-STRATEGY-REPORT-2019.PDF.
6 National Security Strategy of the United States of America, pp. 46–7.
7 Indo-Pacific Strategy Report, p. 11.
8 A senior visiting U.S. State Department official at a closed-door meeting for selected Indian analysts evaded a question from the author on whether India is indeed one of "select states" referred to the IPSR. Interaction, U.S. Embassy, New Delhi, June 5, 2019.
9 M. Pubby, "Will not Bow to U.S. Pressure on Russian Sanctions: MOD," *Economic Times* (July 14, 2018), https://economictimes.indiatimes.com/news/defence/will-not-bow-to-us-pressure-on-russian-sanctions-mod/articleshow/64977895.cms.
10 A. Tellis, "How Can U.S.–India Relations Survive the S-400 Deal?" Carnegie Endowment for International Peace, August 29, 2018, https://carnegieendowment.org/2018/08/29/how-can-U.S.–India-relations-survive-s-400-deal-pub-77131.
11 M. Abi-Habib, "India Is Close to Buying a Russian Missile System, Despite U.S. Sanctions," *New York Times* (April 5, 2018), www.nytimes.com/2018/04/05/world/asia/india-russia-s-400-missiles.html.
12 Indo-Pacific Strategy Report, p. 12.
13 10th BRICS Summit Johannesburg Declaration, Indian Ministry of External Affairs, July 26, 2018.
14 E. Roche, "RIC meet: Foreign Ministers of Russia, India, China Meet Today to Boost Asia-Pacific Relations," *Livemint* (December 11, 2017), www.livemint.com/Politics/i3GWpbkjjX4QL2snEEbAIL/RIC-meet-Foreign-ministers-of-Russia-India-China-meet-tod.html.
15 "India not Rigid: MEA on Japanese Push for Quadrilateral along with U.S., Australia," *Indian Express* (October 27, 2017), http://indianexpress.com/article/india/india-not-rigid-mea-on-japanese-push-for-quadrilateral-along-with-us-australia/. Off-record comments by senior Indian foreign ministry officials have echoed the same proposition.
16 R. K. Simha, "Primakov: The man Who Created Multipolarity," *Russia Beyond the Headline* (June 27, 2015), www.rbth.com/blogs/2015/06/27/primakov_the_man_who_created_multipolarity_43919.
17 V. K. George, "Modi Meets the World," *The Hindu* (November 6, 2014); A. Rej and R. Sagar, "The BJP and Indian Grand Strategy," in M. Vaishnav (ed.), *The BJP in Power: Indian Democracy and Religious Nationalism* (Washington, DC: Carnegie Endowment for International Peace, 2019). For a recent statement of the philosophy of multi-alignment by the current Indian Foreign Minister, see: S. Jaishankar, External Affairs Minister's speech at the 4th Ramnath Goenka Lecture, 2019, Indian Ministry of External Affairs, November 14, 2019, https://mea.gov.in/Speeches-Statements.htm?dtl/32038/External_Affairs_Ministers_speech_at_the_4th_Ramnath_Goenka_Lecture_2019.

18 For a recent account of Hindu nationalism and foreign policy, see: I. Hall, *Modi and the Reinvention of Indian Foreign Policy* (Bristol: Bristol University Press, 2019), pp. 41–59.
19 RAdm. (Retd.) R. Menon quoted in: A. C. Winner, "The U.S. Response: Naval Architecture and Plans," in R. Basrur, A. Mukherjee and T. V. Paul (eds.), *India–China Maritime Competition: The Security Dilemma at Sea* (London and New York: Routledge, 2019), p. 171.
20 Prime Minister's Keynote Address at Shangri La Dialogue (June 1, 2018), Indian Ministry of External Affairs, June 1, 2018, www.mea.gov.in/Speeches-Statements.htm?dtl/29943/Prime+Ministers+Keynote+Address+at+Shangri+La+Dialogue+June+01+2018.
21 A. Korybko, "Russia Regards the 'Indo-Pacific Region' as an 'Artificially Imposed' Pro-U.S. Concept," February 26, 2019, www.globalresearch.ca/russia-regards-indo-pacific-region-artificially-imposed-pro-us-concept/5669705.
22 "India, Russia Begin 'New Era' of Cooperation to Make Indo-Pacific 'Open, Free, Inclusive': PM Modi," *Economic Times* (September 5, 2019), https://economictimes.indiatimes.com/news/defence/india-russia-begin-new-era-of-cooperation-to-make-indo-pacific-open-free-inclusive-pm-modi/articleshow/70994445.cms?from=mdr.
23 "India to Discuss Logistics Agreement with Russia," *New Indian Express* (November 5, 2019), www.newindianexpress.com/nation/2019/nov/05/india-to-discuss-logistics-agreement-with-russia-2057397.html.
24 D. Jaishankar, *Acting East: India in the Indo-Pacific* (Washington, DC: Brookings Institution, 2019).
25 I. Bagchi, "Raisina Dialogue: 'Indo-Pacific' a Global Common, Says Foreign Secy Vijay Gokhale," *Times of India* (January 17, 2020), https://timesofindia.indiatimes.com/india/raisina-dialogue-indo-pacific-a-global-common-says-foreign-secy-vijay-gokhale/articleshow/73337528.cms.
26 This paragraph is adapted from H. V. Pant and A. Rej, "Is India Ready for the Indo-Pacific?" *Washington Quarterly* 41:2 (2018), 48–51, www.tandfonline.com/doi/abs/10.1080/0163660X.2018.1485403?journalCode=rwaq20.
27 For a detailed analysis of that document, see A. Rej and S. Joshi, *India's Joint Doctrine: A Lost Opportunity*, ORF Occasional Paper No. 139 (New Delhi: Observer Research Foundation, 2018), http://cf.orfonline.org/wp-content/uploads/2018/01/ORF_Occasional_Paper_Joint_Doctrine.pdf.
28 A. Singh, "India's Naval Interests in the Pacific," in D. Brewster (ed.), *India and China at Sea: Competition for Naval Dominance in the Indian Ocean* (New Delhi: Oxford University Press, 2018), pp. 182–3.
29 L. Zheng, "Chinese Research Vessel Expelled by Indian Warship for Operating near Andaman and Nicobar Islands," *South China Morning Post* (December 4, 2019), www.scmp.com/news/china/diplomacy/article/3040638/chinese-research-vessel-expelled-indian-warship-operating-near.
30 Ensuring Secure Seas: Indian Maritime Security Strategy, Integrated Headquarters, Ministry of Defence (Navy), 2015, p. 32, www.indiannavy.nic.in/sites/default/files/Indian_Maritime_Security_Strategy_Document_25Jan16.pdf.

31 For the evolution of India–China force ratios for crucial naval inventories, see: A. Rej, "India's Unrealized Maritime Dreams," *The Diplomat* (July, 2019), https://thediplomat.com/2019/06/indias-unrealized-maritime-dreams/.
32 The 2016 proposal by then PACCOM commander Admiral Harry Harris for India and the U.S. to jointly or in a coordinated way patrol the South China Sea was promptly shot down by then Defence Minister Manohar Parrikar. See: G. Khurana, America's Expectation Versus India's Expediency, Center for International Maritime Security, May 24, 2016, http://cimsec.org/americas-expectation-versus-indias-expediency-india-regional-net-security-provider/24471.
33 Winner, "The U.S. Response," pp. 168–9.
34 D. Peri, "LEMOA Fully Operational Now," *The Hindu* (September 8, 2018), www.thehindu.com/news/national/lemoa-already-fully-operational/article24904359.ece.
35 S. Joshi, "Why Critics of LEMOA Are Wrong," *LiveMint* (September 15, 2016), www.livemint.com/Opinion/2CaDE74d7zajrQ6e9aanSJ/Why-the-critics-of-LEMOA-are-wrong.html.
36 S. Chowdhury, "India could sign LEMOA-like logistics agreement with Russia during PM Narendra Modi's Vladivostok visit," *Times Now News*, July 15, 2019, www.timesnownews.com/india/article/india-could-sign-lemoa-like-logistics-agreement-with-russia-during-pm-narendra-modis-vladivostok-visit/454355.
37 D. Peri, "What is COMCASA?" *The Hindu* (September 6, 2018), www.thehindu.com/news/national/what-is-comcasa/article24881039.ece. For an account of how COMCASA enhances U.S.–India military interoperability and also U.S.–India–Australia–Japan political-military cooperation, see A. Rej, *Reclaiming the Indo-Pacific: A Political-Military Strategy for Quad 2.0*, ORF Occasional Paper No. 141 (New Delhi: Observer Research Foundation, 2018), pp. 19–20, www.orfonline.org/research/reclaiming-the-indo-pacific-a-political-military-strategy-for-quad-2-0/.
38 Interview with Commander Abhijit Singh (Retd.), November 15, 2017.
39 S. Gupta, "India, U.S. to Take Forward Talks for Key Military Pact," *Hindustan Times* (April 3, 3019), www.hindustantimes.com/india-news/india-us-to-take-forward-talks-for-key-military-pact/story-bi2IfgMjKtKsfA2wjTqQzM.html.
40 *Ibid.*
41 Winner, "The U.S. Response," 170.
42 U.S. and India Airforces Begin Exercise Cope India 2019, Air Force Technology, December 3, 2019, www.airforce-technology.com/news/iaf-usaf-exercise-cope-india-2019/.
43 B. Bowman and A. Gabel, U.S., "India Bolster Their Military Partnership in Tiger Triumph Exercise," *Defense News* (November 13, 2019), www.defensenews.com/opinion/commentary/2019/11/13/us-india-bolster-their-military-partnership-in-tiger-triumph-exercise/.
44 U.S., JMSDF and Indian Naval Forces Conclude Malabar 2018, United States Navy, June 19, 2018, www.public.navy.mil/surfor/cg54/Pages/U.S.-JMSDF-and-Indian-Naval-Forces-Conclude-Malabar-2018.aspx.

45 Interview with Commander Abhijit Singh (Retd.), November 15, 2017.
46 S. Roblin, "U.S. Fighter Jets Are Back in India for Wargames (The Last Two Times the Indian Air Force Won," *The National Interest* (December 7, 2018), https://nationalinterest.org/blog/buzz/us-jet-fighters-are-back-india-wargames-last-two-times-indian-air-force-won-38232.
47 Interview with academic associated with the U.S. Air Force on condition of anonymity, New Delhi, December 15, 2017.
48 Numbers compiled from various Ministry of Defence Annual Reports over the five years. The reports are available at: https://mod.gov.in/documents/annual-report.
49 Deep background conversations (details withheld) with U.S. officials confirm that this is indeed the objective behind U.S.–India exercises.
50 Interoperability: Connecting NATO Forces, North Atlantic Treaty Organization, last updated: June 6, 2017, www.nato.int/cps/en/natolive/topics_84112.htm.
51 V. Raghuvanshi, "India Signs $950 Million Contract with Russia to Buy Two Stealth Frigates," *Defense News* (October 30, 2018), www.defensenews.com/naval/2018/10/30/india-signs-950-million-contract-with-russia-to-buy-two-stealth-frigates/.
52 E-mail interview with former senior U.S. Navy officer; details withheld on the request of the interviewee.
53 P. D. Samanta, "First Secure Link between India, U.S. Navies Set Up," *Economic Times* (April 2, 2019), https://economictimes.indiatimes.com/news/defence/first-secure-link-between-india-us-navies-set-up/articleshow/68681214.cms?from=mdr.
54 India Cuts Purchase of P-8 Spy Planes from U.S. in Half, DefenceAerospace.com, November 29, 2019, www.defense-aerospace.com/article-view/release/207881/india-oks-%243.2-bn-for-more-aewc-aircraft%2C-p_8i-poseidon-and-medium-helicopters.html.
55 On this, see: B. Gopalaswamy, *India's Quest for Fighter Jets: Make in India vs. Make America Great Again* (Washington, DC: Atlantic Council, 2019), www.atlanticcouncil.org/wp-content/uploads/2019/09/India-quest-fighter-jets.pdf; on the Indian Air Force's perennial travails when it comes to replenishing its depleted fighter squadron strength, see: A. Tellis, *Troubles, They Come in Battalions: The Manifold Travails of the Indian Air Force* (Washington, DC: Carnegie Endowment for International Peace, 2016), https://carnegieendowment.org/2016/03/28/troubles-they-come-in-battalions-manifold-travails-of-indian-air-force-pub-63123.
56 Rej and Joshi, *India's Joint Doctrine*, pp. 15–20 explores this further.
57 Brigadier Gurmeet Kanwal (Retd.), *Indian Army Vision 2020* (New Delhi: HarperCollins India and the Observer Research Foundation, 2008), pp. 185–7.
58 For the U.S. concept, see: Air-Sea Battle: Service Collaboration to Address Anti-Access and Area Denial Challenges, Air-Sea Battle Office, U.S. Department of Defense, May 2013, https://dod.defense.gov/Portals/1/Documents/pubs/ASB-ConceptImplementation-Summary-May-2013.pdf. On why Air–Sea battle concept lives on despite no longer being called so, see: Sam LaGrone, Pentagon

Drops Air Sea Battle Name, Concept Lives On, United States Naval Institute, January 20, 2015, updated April 27, 2017, https://news.usni.org/2015/01/20/pentagon-drops-air-sea-battle-name-concept-lives.

59 "India, United States to Carry Out Joint Military Exercise on September 16," *Economic Times* (September 11, 2018), https://economictimes.indiatimes.com/news/defence/india-united-states-to-carry-out-joint-military-exercise-on-september-16/articleshow/65771735.cms.

60 India–U.S. Sign Counter Terrorism Cooperation Initiative, Embassy of India, Washington, DC, accessed December 1, 2019, www.indianembassyusa.gov.in/ArchivesDetails?id=1292.

61 "NIA to Host First Counterterrorism Exercise for "Quad" Countries," *Economic Times* (November 19, 2019), https://economictimes.indiatimes.com/news/defence/nia-to-host-first-counter-terrorism-cooperation-exercise-for-quad-countries/articleshow/72127071.cms?from=mdr.

62 A U.S.–India strategy of denial was also advocated in A. Tarapore, "A More Focused and Resilient U.S.–India Strategic Partnership, Center for a New American Security," October 23, 2019, www.cnas.org/publications/reports/a-more-focused-and-resilient-u-s-india-strategic-partnership.

63 I thank Saikat Datta for raising this point. For more on the Wassenaar Arrangement and cyber export controls, see: G. Hinck, Wassenaar Export Controls on Surveillance Tools: New Exemptions for Vulnerability Research, Lawfare, January 5, 2018, www.lawfareblog.com/wassenaar-export-controls-surveillance-tools-new-exemptions-vulnerability-research.

64 Y. Raj, "India, U.S. Sign Key Defence Pact, Discuss Cross-border Terror at 2+2 Meet," *Hindustan Times* (December 19, 2019), www.hindustantimes.com/india-news/india-us-sign-key-defence-pact-discuss-cross-border-terror-at-2-2-meet/story-3AvKHbw1RdvujJADEZVGKM.html.

65 On inflated expectations in the U.S.–India strategic relationship, see: S. Lalwani and H. Bryne, "Great Expectations: Asking Too Much of the U.S.–India Strategic Partnership," *Washington Quarterly* 42:3 (2019), pp. 41–64.

66 "Navy Chief Says Maldives a Challenge for India as Its Government Is More Inclined towards China," *The Scroll* (May 24, 2018), https://scroll.in/latest/880157/navy-chief-says-maldives-a-challenge-for-india-as-its-government-is-more-inclined-towards-china.

67 See, for example, S. Lanba, "Keynote Address by Admiral Sunil Lanba, PVSM, AVSM, ADC, Chief of Naval Staff," in Vice Admiral Pradeep Chauhan and Captain (Dr.) Gurpreet S. Khurana (eds.), *National Maritime Power: Concepts, Constituents, Catalysts* (New Delhi: National Maritime Foundation/Pentagon Press, 2018), p. xxxiii.

68 J. White, "Navigating Two Asias: How Washington Deals with the Indo-Pacific's Rising Powers," *India Review* 18:4 (2019), pp. 407–36.

Part II

Cybersecurity cooperation

3

U.S.–India relations on cybersecurity: an important moment for strategic action on collective cyberdefense

Jamil N. Jaffer

Introduction

This chapter argues that the U.S. and India currently face an important moment in their overall strategic relationship and, in particular, when it comes to cybersecurity issues. The chapter briefly describes the recent history of the U.S.–India strategic partnership that has blossomed in the past decade and half since 2005 and discusses the particular challenges to that partnership currently in play and the common threats facing these two nations that, taken together, argue in favor of a further deepening and strengthening of the relationship generally. The chapter then focuses specifically on the common threats that the U.S. and India face in the cyber domain and describes the recent efforts between the two nations to find common cause. The chapter places these efforts in the context of the broader strategic relationship between the two nations, as well as in the context of the common threats they face and their efforts with other partners to address these threats, both within and outside of the Indo-Pacific region. The chapter also describes the need to undertake strategic efforts in the U.S.–India cybersecurity relationship, including the critical importance of creating a collective defense capability in cyberspace. The chapter describes the need for confidence-building measures, eventually culminating in the creation of a substantive real-time threat-sharing and collective cyberdefense capability, including interoperable systems that can provide the ability for each nation to assist the other in real time or to take actions to stop a threat or limit its impact, if requested and necessary. The chapter argues that a strengthened U.S.–India relationship focused on strategic cybersecurity cooperation, including increased threat sharing and common capability development could offer a significant benefit to both nations. In the course of making this argument, the chapter offers a series of concrete, actionable recommendations which, if implemented, could help to substantially improve the two nations' joint strategic efforts on cybersecurity and provide a significant security gain to both countries, while also creating a joint bulwark against key regional-threat players, including China and North Korea, as well as external actors that are generally hostile to American interests, including India's erstwhile ally, Russia, and one of its key energy suppliers, Iran.

The burgeoning U.S.–India strategic partnership: opportunities and potential challenges

The economics of the U.S.–India relationship

There is little question that the current moment in U.S.–Indian relations is a critical one across a variety of dimensions. The world's largest democracy, India's 1.3 billion citizens form the world's third-largest economy (on a purchasing power basis),[1] and the economic and human ties between the two countries are massive and are growing significantly. In 2016 alone, bilateral trade between the U.S. and India stood at a record $115 billion, with four million Indian-Americans living in the U.S., over 160,000 Indian students studying in the U.S., and 1.2 million American visitors travelling to India annually.[2]

Today, those numbers are even higher, with the 2018 trade in goods and services exceeding $142 billion, including U.S. exports of approximately $59 billion and imports of nearly $84 billion in goods and services.[3] This makes India the U.S.'s ninth-largest goods trading partner, its tenth-largest goods supplier, and its twelfth-largest goods and services export market.[4] And the relationship is even more important to India, with the U.S. serving as India's *second*-largest export market in 2018 (after the EU) and third-largest supplier of imports (after China and the EU).[5] Indeed, in 2015 it was estimated that U.S. exports alone supported approximately 197,000 jobs in India.[6] With the Indian economy growing at a torrid pace – real GDP up an estimated 7.1 percent in 2018 alone[7] – all indications are that, in the absence of a significant external political or other disruption, these numbers are likely to grow even larger.

At the same time, however, bilateral trade tensions between India and the U.S. are quite high, with 2019 seeing tariff hikes, increases in goods duties, and concerns about compliance with intellectual property (IP) protection requirements continuing to aggravate U.S. leadership (alongside the ever-growing trade deficit).[8] At the same time, U.S. actions on steel and aluminum tariffs, and its termination of India's Generalized System of Preferences (GSP) status in 2019 based on market access concerns, as well as India's continued presence on the Special 301 priority watch list for IP protection issues, likewise continue to elicit major irritation in New Delhi.[9] Indeed, the GSP issue itself has led to significant back-and-forth action on tariffs, including major tariffs on certain U.S. exports to India.¹⁰ A related area of bilateral economic irritation comes from movement and treatment of workers, including U.S. policies on H1-B (highly skilled) worker visas (70 percent of which went to Indian nationals in 2016),¹¹ and Indian limitations on foreign ownership and requirements for local presence.¹² And this does not even account for other areas of friction, including agricultural support programs and the like.¹³

The security connection between the U.S. and India

Notwithstanding these trade tensions, the U.S.–India strategic relationship remains a matter of critical importance to both nations, particularly when it comes to national security issues. The U.S. remains firmly committed to the construct set out by former Secretary of State Rex Tillerson in 2017, when he described the U.S. administration's commitment to "building an ambitious partnership" with India and expanding the bilateral "strategic relationship," focusing specifically on the administration's "determination to dramatically deepen ways for the U.S. and India to further this partnership."¹⁴ This process of building a major defense partnership between the two nations began in earnest over a decade earlier, under President George W. Bush. Specifically, the Bush administration's revival of the India–U.S. Defense Policy Group and its subgroups, as well as with the signing of a ten-year defense framework in 2005 that "outlin[ed] planned collaboration in multilateral operations, expanded two-way defense trade, increased opportunities for technology transfers and co-production, and expanded collaboration related to missile defense"¹⁵ was at the heart of the new, expanded relationship. Since those efforts began, the bilateral defense relationship has progressed significantly, with the original framework agreement being expanded and renewed in 2015 for another decade,¹⁶ and signing of major defense contracts worth over $15 billion in the decade following 2008, including agreements for India to purchase key military equipment from American manufacturers.¹⁷

And yet even the burgeoning defense relationship between India and the U.S. is fraught with challenges. For example, India agreed in 2018 to purchase the Russian-made S-400 missile system and made a large advance payment on the purchase to assure an on-time delivery.¹⁸ This purchase could very well trigger significant sanctions from the U.S. under the Countering America's Adversaries Through Sanctions Act,¹⁹ and it raises significant questions about whether India's long-standing military and defense cooperation relationship with Russia might be resurgent, particularly coming, as it does, alongside other signs of an expanding relationship with Moscow.²⁰ This concern is to be balanced, of course, with the fact that the U.S.–India economic relationship is orders of magnitude larger than the Russia–India relationship[21] and the fact that Indian elites share a strong perception that the U.S. relationship, not one with Russia, is a key long-term strategic lever for India and its populace.[22]

At the same time, U.S. and Indian strategists and other observers continue to view the U.S.–India relationship as a key counterweight to the increasing (and unavoidable) expansion of Chinese influence in the Indo-Pacific region, not to mention globally.[23] Since 2011, when the Obama administration began to focus on a "strategic rebalancing" (or "pivot") to Asia, and then Secretary of State Hilary Clinton began describing the Asia-Pacific region (including the Indian Ocean) as a key strategic region for the U.S., the stage was set for the Trump administration's approach to a "Free and Open Indo-Pacific" with the U.S.–India bilateral relationship and the Japan–U.S.–India–Australia "Quad" relationship at its core.[24] This effort is focused at its core – at least in the U.S. – on creating a strategic bulwark against Chinese muscle flexing in the region, with India its heart. And while, as Carol V. Evans points out elsewhere, India might not view itself as playing the "bulwark" role for the U.S.,[25] the fact remains that the basic construct of this effort found its initial expression in the Obama administration-negotiated U.S.–India Joint Strategic Vision for the Asia-Pacific and Indian Ocean Region released in January 2015. That joint statement made clear, for example, that the U.S. and India intended to push back against active Chinese efforts to change the strategic situation on the ground (and in the air and on the sea in particular), calling out the need to "safeguard maritime security and ensur[e] freedom of navigation and over flight throughout the region, especially in the South China Sea."[26]

And the effort to build – or at least preparing to build – such a bulwark is likewise consistent with Indian government policy (notwithstanding protestations to the contrary), particularly given the current (and historic) challenges at play between China and India, whether they relate to tensions along the China–India border, freedom of navigation matters, concerns about the impact of the Chinese Belt-and-Road initiative on India's political and economic influence in the region, or the increasingly collaborative military and economic relationships between China and Pakistan on the one hand, and China and Russia on the other.[27] Indeed, the recent opening of a key strategic pipeline between China and Russia,[28] and ongoing military cooperation between those two nations, may very well put increased pressure on the renewal of the India–Russia relationship, and could serve to keep India more directly focused on the continued success of the strategic partnership with the U.S.

Cybersecurity and the U.S.–India relationship

The economics of technology and building a larger relationship

Technology, of course, is at the heart of much of the U.S.–India economic and political relationship. For example, the bilateral services relationship – which in 2018 was worth $25.2 billion in U.S. exports to India and $29.6 billion in imports from India – has a significant focus on IP (including computer software and various audio/visual exports) in one direction (exports from the U.S.), and telecommunications, computer and information services, and research and development work in the other (imports from India).[29] These numbers, like the overall economic relationship, grew significantly between 2017 and 2018, to more than double what they were in 2008.[30] And many of the trade and cross-border issues and tensions in play between the U.S. and India in 2019 likewise had a critical technology component – whether it relates to H1-B visa holders in the U.S., or so-called "forced localization" processes, including "in-country data storage, domestic content, [...] domestic testing requirements[,] ... restrictive localization rules for certain financial data flows ... [and] local sourcing rules."[31]

Given the huge strategic role that technology plays in the bilateral relationship between the U.S. and India, not to mention the core role it plays in the Indian economy writ large – with its 600 million internet subscribers, 650 million mobile phones (nearly half of which are smartphones), and an e-commerce base of nearly $30 billion[32] – it is no surprise that addressing regional and key global cybersecurity threats in a collective manner, in particular, is a core focus of the security relationship between the two nations. Indeed, engagement on cybersecurity issues really began in a formal sense between the U.S. and India back in 2001, with the establishment of the Indo-U.S. Cybersecurity Forum, a gathering that brought together government and private sector officials to discuss issues of mutual concern in the cyber domain.[33] While this process faced its own internal challenges,[34] the U.S.–India government-to-government relationship in cybersecurity became significantly more formalized in July 2011, with the signing of a Memorandum of Understanding (MOU) between the U.S. Department of Homeland Security (DHS) and India's Department of Information Technology,[35] and got an even more significant boost in August 2016 with the signing of the Framework for the U.S.–India Cyber Relationship.[36]

While the DHS MOU is fairly standard and reflects similar MOUs India has entered into with over four dozen countries,[37] the 2016 Framework is somewhat more unique. First, it is only one of ten such frameworks that India has signed globally[38] and, of those, it appears to be relatively detailed and focused on particular threats of mutual concern, as compared to the others, including what can be gleaned from the agreements with Russia and China.

The 2016 framework sets out the core approach to cybersecurity issues for the U.S. and India, and includes key shared principles focused on their mutual commitment to, among other things, an "open, interoperable, secure, and reliable cyberspace environment" and promoting innovation, the free flow of information, and "cooperation between and among the private sector and government authorities on cybercrime and cybersecurity."[39] In particular, the Framework highlights the

> importance of bilateral and international cooperation for combating cyber threats and promoting cybersecurity[,] ... [a] recognition of the leading role for governments in cybersecurity matters relating to national security[, a] recognition of the importance of and a shared commitment to cooperate in capacity building in cybersecurity and cybersecurity research and development[,] ... closer cooperation among law enforcement agencies to combat cybercrime between the two countries ... [and a] desire to cooperate in strengthening the security and resilience of critical information infrastructure.[40]

These precepts, in turn, inform the agreement made between the U.S. and India to cooperate in, among others, the following areas:

> sharing information on a real time or near real time basis, when practical and consistent with existing bilateral arrangements, about malicious cybersecurity threats, attacks and activities, and establishing appropriate mechanisms to improve such information sharing; ... [d]eveloping joint mechanisms for practical cooperation to mitigate cyber threats to the security of ICT [information and communications technology] infrastructure and information contained therein consistent with their respective obligations under domestic and international law; ... [c]ontinuing to promote cooperation between law enforcement agencies to combat cybercrime[;] ... [u]ndertaking skill development and capacity building programs jointly in the fields of cybersecurity, efforts to combat cybercrime, digital forensics, and legal frameworks; ... [p]romoting the applicability of international law to state conduct in cyberspace and further exploring how it applies to state conduct in cyberspace; ... and [p]romoting voluntary norms of responsible state behavior in peacetime.[41]

In particular, the Framework also calls out the commitment of the U.S. and India to abiding by and promoting voluntary norms under which, among other things, nation-states: (1) avoid intentional damage to critical infrastructure (or otherwise impair the delivery of critical services to citizens); (2) not conduct or knowingly support cyber-enabled IP theft to provide competitive advantages to companies or sectors; and (3) cooperate on telecommunications security issues, including accrediting appropriate entities.[42]

Evaluating the policy framework in the context of security threats

As noted above, many of the commitments contained in the Framework are squarely aimed at focusing the U.S.'s and India's joint work in cybersecurity on addressing some of the key cyber threats and threat actors in the Indo-Pacific region including those that Bedavyasa Mohanty correctly cites in Chapter 4 of this volume, in particular: (1) the threat posed by rampant Chinese theft of IP in order to repurpose it for economic gain; (2) efforts by key nation-state threat actors including China, Russia, North Korea, and Iran to obtain (and maintain) access to critical infrastructure entities, ostensibly for destructive attacks in the event of a crisis; (3) efforts by nation-states to gain long-term access to telecommunications infrastructure to collect intelligence and potentially engage in disruptive activities; and (4) the continuing and expanding threat of economically motivated cybercrime.

In many ways, however, while the Framework is quite specific on its goals and some of the threat trends it seeks to target, the means it provides for actual joint work are fairly limited. While the Framework routinizes the ongoing high-level dialogue and various other underlying working groups, creates a mechanism for designating points of contact for "implementing practical interaction," seeks to promote Computer Emergency Response Team (CERT)-to-CERT cooperation, and encourages the use of the U.S.–India Mutual Legal Assistance Treaty, it says precious little about how some of the key issues raised by the Framework itself are actually to be addressed.[43]

And, in fact, there is little in the public reporting to suggest that, in the three years since the MOU was signed, any effective work to share actionable threat data in real time – as the Framework specifically describes – was actually conducted between the U.S. and India. While it is certainly possible that such efforts are taking place in the classified context – given that the lead role was provided to DHS, as a CERT-to-CERT effort,[44] and the challenges that DHS has faced domestically in creating similar real-time sharing capabilities,[45] there is little basis to believe that any efforts have been successfully undertaken, even behind closed doors.

Likewise, nothing in the public record suggests that any formal mechanism for addressing threats to telecommunications infrastructure posed by particular vendors through vetting or accreditation – likewise specifically described in the Framework – has been stood up. To the contrary, senior American public officials have taken their case against certain Chinese telecommunications vendors who are seeking access to India's 5G infrastructure – like Huawei – to the public, ostensibly having been turned back in the government-to-government dialogue.[46]

And the 2019 infiltration of an Indian nuclear power plant by what appears to have been nation-state malware[47] suggests that, to the extent that there are ongoing joint efforts between the U.S. and India to focus on the protection of critical infrastructures, they are not working particularly well. While it is true that the Indian authorities investigating the attack have indicated that they do not believe anything other than an administrative system was breached, and that their systems were "air-gapped" to prevent a crossover into the operational technology, cybersecurity experts have regularly noted the general fallacy of air-gap claims.[48] Moreover, given the admitted scope of the theft in terms of the quantity and nature of the data at issue,[49] there is at least a significant possibility that this attack has, at a minimum, disclosed data that could prove highly problematic to future efforts to protect the particular plant involved, not to mention others with similar technology architectures.

Given all this, the key question that ought to be answered is how the U.S. and India might actually address some of the key strategic issues they rightly identified in the 2016 Framework.

Creating a collective cyberdefense capability between India and the U.S.

Taking advantage of the major defense partner relationship

One of the pivotal moments in the burgeoning U.S.–India strategic security relationship has been the designation, in 2016, of India as a Major Defense Partner (MDP) of the U.S. This designation, unique to India and aimed at placing India in the top tiers of U.S. partners and allies, was initially announced in a joint statement by the two nations in June 2016 and was later codified by the U.S. in the National Defense Authorization Act of 2017.[50] The MDP status, which is different than but designed to address similar issues as the Major Non-NATO Ally designation given to a number of key partners and allies (most notably in this context, Pakistan), was given some limited amount of additional structure in the Asia Reassurance Initiative Act of 2018 (ARIA). That statute, in addition to fleshing out the MDP construct for India, also highlighted the criticality of the Indo-Pacific relationship and adopted the basic structure of the administration's Free and Open Indo-Pacific policy.[51] The key purposes of providing India with MDP status, as set forth in ARIA, are to

> institutionalize[] ... progress made to facilitate defense trade and technology sharing between the U.S. and India[] ... elevate[] defense trade and technology cooperation between the U.S. and India to a level commensurate with

the closest allies and partners of the U.S.[,] ... facilitate[] technology sharing between the U.S. and India, including license-free access to a wide range of dual-use technologies, after taking into account national security concerns; and (D) facilitate[] joint exercises, coordination on defense strategy and policy, military exchanges, and port calls in support of defense cooperation between the U.S. and India.

Given these purposes for designating India a MDP, and the criticality of our cybersecurity relationship, particularly as a potential bulwark against Chinese and other key nation-state activity in the region, including from North Korea and Russia, one specific way the Executive Branch might action these goals would be to establish a cyber collective defense capability with the government of India. Such a capability would not – at least at the outset – involve any classic mutual defense agreements like Section Five of the North Atlantic Treaty, where the parties to the agreement agree to defend one another against an attack by a third party. Rather, this effort would be focused on building a capacity for the U.S. and India to share information, in real time, at machine speed, about potential cybersecurity threats. Specifically, the goal of such an effort would be to allow each nation to identify new and novel threat campaigns directed at them and their key industries, and so that each could leverage the knowledge, skills, and capabilities of the other in the course of triaging or addressing a potential threat. Such an effort would also begin the process of creating interoperable systems to allow for mutual assistance if requested by one of the parties, and begin efforts to conduct joint exercises that would allow each nation to get comfortable with the other's operating procedures and capabilities in this new domain. Similar collective defense approaches have previously been proposed within the U.S. private sector and with the U.S. government,[52] as well as between the U.S. and its NATO partners,[53] and this effort would extend this concept for the first time outside of the U.S. domestic and treaty-partner context. To be sure, the checkered history of counterterrorism cooperation between the U.S. and India that Manoj Joshi lays out in his chapter certainly may not bode well for these efforts,[54] but there is at least an argument that in an area that is so central to the U.S.–India economic relationship perhaps national security cooperation might be more readily achievable.

The need for confidence-building measures

Such a system – which might involve the sharing of highly sensitive sources and methods of intelligence collection focused on cyber threats, as well as the potential sharing of sensitive offensive and defensive cyber capabilities – would require a significant level of trust between the U.S. and India, a commodity that, at the time of writing, is in limited supply, given the heightened trade tensions. In order to rebuild trust between these nations and move forward on a cyber collective defense partnership, there are a number of steps each nation might take, some specifically focused on cyber issues and some not, to address the other's concerns. On the U.S. side, the U.S. could agree to return India to GSP status,[55] and both nations could then restore the prior levels of tariff- and duty-free trade and begin to limit the number of active matters being pursued at the World Trade Organization.[56] Such an effort might, at least at the outset, focus further trade efforts on relieving barriers related to the technology and IP industries, including local presence and ownership requirements, and then go further to undertake efforts to enhance trade in those categories. Of course, as Saikat Datta tells us in Chapter 12 of this volume, the trust issues on intelligence matters between India and the U.S. go back for decades and have faced particular key challenges in since the early 2000s.[57] Moreover, as Datta correctly points out, these issues have gotten worse when one side builds up its relationships with nations that the other perceives as strategic competitors.[58] To that end, in the cyber arena in particular, India could agree to limit its policy collaborations with Russia on cyber issues for a period of time – and strictly curtail its operational collaborations – while the U.S. and India build and test the cyberdefense capability. Under such a scenario, the U.S. might reasonably require India to undertake further collaborations only in a manner that does not interfere with any joint U.S.–India cyberdefense capability. In addition, India could likewise agree to limit its public support for various Russian cyber-related actions at the United Nations (UN), and in particular not proceeding with votes that are counter to U.S. policy, like India's recent support in the UN General Assembly's Third Committee for a Russia- and China-backed effort to push forward consideration of a highly problematic international instrument on cybercrime.[59] Indeed, if India wanted to demonstrate a serious commitment to addressing cybercrime issues alongside the U.S., it might consider joining the Budapest Convention on Cybercrime (which by 2020 had been ratified by more than a third of all the countries in the world),[60] or negotiating a final Clarifying Lawful Overseas Use of Data Act agreement with the U.S.[61] Confidence-building measures like these, particularly if they are focused on cyber-related issues, might usefully serve to set the stage – as it is being designed and built – for the actual implementation and running of a fully fledged cyber collective defense system that operates in real time between the U.S. and India.

Additional efforts to enhance cybersecurity cooperation

Another effort that the U.S. and India might consider when it comes to cybersecurity cooperation includes actioning their prior commitment to joint vet and accredit telecommunications providers. In this context, the obvious immediate concerns for countries like the U.S. and India come from providers like Huawei and ZTE.[62] In this area, adopting a methodology similar – but not identical – to that of the United Kingdom (UK) National Cybersecurity Center (NCSC) could be a useful approach. The UK NCSC, which, unlike its U.S. equivalent, the Cyber and Infrastructure Security Agency (CISA) actually sits inside of the UK's signals intelligence agency, Government Communications Headquarters,[63] has solid access to sensitive intelligence about nation-state cyber threats. Leveraging that information, NCSC oversees, through a vetted entity, fairly painstaking reviews of individual products to evaluate them for deployment in the UK telecoms infrastructure.[64] If the U.S. and India were to set up a similar agency, run jointly by their respective intelligence services, along with the right know-how and with direct private sector input, they might usefully vet entities (not just specific technologies, like NCSC) to evaluate whether the risk of putting their capabilities into core telecommunications infrastructure would be problematic. Such an agency could also recommend to their respective national legislatures how they ought to address potential risk factors, and also could be done jointly with a broader Indo-Pacific coalition. Major differences between this joint operation and the UK NCSC model are clear: first, the effort would involve multiple nation-states with differing goals, objectives, economics, and politics; second, the vetting would be of entities, not products; and third, perhaps most importantly, the vetting would be directly conducted by the joint agency, including private sector representatives, not through a vetted proxy of the manufacturer. Nonetheless, adopting a model like the UK's – one that provides some amount of transparency and direct private sector input into vetting decisions, while ensuring the right government players are at the table – might have some significant benefits both for the legitimacy of the process as well as for increasing the ability of governments to convince political and private sector actors to accept the ultimate vetting determinations. In doing so, it might prevent governments from having to reach, necessarily, for the heavy stick of regulation, at least in the first instance.

Conclusion

At the end of the day, there are a number of steps which the U.S. and India might take to improve their cooperation on cybersecurity matters. While some of these might be relatively easier than others, even taking a handful of these steps could significantly move the ball down the road. Undoubtedly, there are joint cyberdefense steps that might be taken by the U.S. and India which go well beyond those outlined in this chapter. Nonetheless, the fact remains that were the U.S. and India able to successfully execute one or more of the concepts proposed herein, particularly creating a real, sustained collective defense capability, there is the significant likelihood that there would be concrete gains for both nations' cybersecurity, as well as that of the region.

Notes

1. See K. Alan Kronstadt and Shayerah Ilias Akhtar, 'India–U.S. Relations: Issues for Congress,' *Congressional Research Service* (June 19, 2017), https://crsreports.congress.gov/product/pdf/R/R44876/6.
2. See Secretary Rex Tillerson, 'Defining Our Relationship with India for the Next Century,' U.S. State Department (October 18, 2017), www.csis.org/analysis/defining-our-relationship-india-next-century-address-us-secretary-state-rex-tillerson.
3. See Office of the U.S. Trade Representative, *U.S.–India Bilateral Trade and Investment*, Executive Office of the President (2019), https://ustr.gov/countries-regions/south-central-asia/india.
4. Ibid.
5. See Shayerah Ilias Akhtar and K. Alan Kronstadt, 'U.S.–India Trade Relations,' Congressional Research Service (October 2, 2019), https://crsreports.congress.gov/product/pdf/IF/IF10384.
6. See Office of the U.S. Trade Representative, *U.S.–India Bilateral Trade and Investment*, p. 1.
7. Ibid.
8. See Akhtar and Kronstadt, 'U.S.–India Trade Relations', pp. 1–2.
9. Ibid.
10. Ibid.
11. See Kronstadt and Akhtar, 'India–U.S. Relations'.
12. Ibid.
13. Ibid.
14. See Tillerson, 'Defining Our Relationship with India,' p. 1.
15. See Kronstadt and Akhtar, 'India–U.S. Relations,' pp. 1–15.
16. Ibid.
17. Akhtar and Kronstadt, 'U.S.–India Trade Relations.'
18. See Franz-Stefan Gady, 'India Makes $800 Million Advance Payment for Russian S-400 Air Defense Systems,' *The Diplomat* (November 20, 2019), https://thediplomat.com/2019/11/india-makes-800-million-advance-payment-for-russian-s-400-air-defense-systems/.

19 *Ibid.*; see also Akhtar and Kronstadt, 'India–U.S. Relations,' p. 15.
20 See, e.g., Amie Ferris-Rotman, 'Russia, India Agree to More Military Cooperation,' CNN (September 4, 2019), www.washingtonpost.com/world/russia-india-agree-to-more-military-cooperation/2019/09/04/81f9c20c-ce47-11e9-b29b-a528dc82154a_story.html.
21 See Government of India, *India–Russia Relations*, Ministry of External Affairs (September 2019), p. 7, https://mea.gov.in/Portal/ForeignRelation/India_Russia_Bilateral_Brief_sep_2019.pdf (showing total bilateral trade between Russia and India of approx. $10B).
22 See Richard Fontaine, 'U.S.–India Relations: The Trump Administration's Foreign Policy Bright Spot,' War on the Rocks (January 24, 2019), https://warontherocks.com/2019/01/u-s-india-relations-the-trump-administrations-foreign-policy-bright-spot/. "In a forthcoming Brookings India poll of the country's strategic elites, a full 75 percent say that their country's most important partner on global issues is the United States, with Russia a distant second at 12 percent."
23 See, e.g., Akhtar and Kronstadt, 'India–U.S. Relations', p. 1: "Many analysts view India as a potential counterweight to China's growing international clout." See also Fontaine, 'U.S.–India Relations: Foreign Policy Bright Spot', p. 1: "In identifying great power competition as the key driver of U.S. national security strategy, the administration signals a convergence in U.S. and Indian views of China. Prioritizing the China challenge also provides an underlying rationale for greater alignment with India as one element in a broad effort to balance power in the Indo-Pacific."
24 Bruce Vaughn et al., 'The Trump Administration's "Free and Open Indo-Pacific": Issues for Congress,' *Congressional Research Service* (October 3, 2018), pp. 1, 3–4, https://crsreports.congress.gov/product/pdf/R/R45396.
25 See Chapter 11 in this volume.
26 See The White House, *U.S.–India Joint Strategic Vision for the Asia-Pacific and Indian Ocean Region* (January 25, 2015), p. 1, https://obamawhitehouse.archives.gov/the-press-office/2015/01/25/us-india-joint-strategic-vision-asia-pacific-and-indian-ocean-region.
27 See Bruce Vaughn, 'China–India Rivalry in the Indian Ocean,' *Congressional Research Service* (August 16, 2017), pp. 1–2, https://crsreports.congress.gov/product/pdf/IF/IF10726. See also Vaughn et al., 'The Trump Administration's "Free and Open Indo-Pacific",' pp. 5–7.
28 See Olga Tanas and Dina Khrennikova, 'Russia Opens Giant Gas Link to China as Putin Pivots East,' Bloomberg (December 1, 2019), www.bloomberg.com/news/articles/2019-12-02/russia-s-400-billion-gas-link-to-china-set-to-begin-pumping.
29 See Office of the U.S. Trade Representative, *U.S.–India Bilateral Trade and Investment*, p. 1.
30 *Ibid.*
31 See Akhtar and Kronstadt, 'U.S.–India Trade Relations,' p. 2.
32 See Rahul Roy-Chaudary, 'India–UK Cybersecurity Cooperation: The Way Forward,' Institute of International Studies (November 22, 2019), p. 1, www.iiss.org/blogs/analysis/2019/11/sasia-india-uk-cyber-security-cooperation.

33 See Kathleen H. Hicks et al., 'U.S.–India Security Cooperation: Progress and Promise for the Next Administration,' Center for Strategic and International Studies (October 2016), p. 54, https://csis-prod.s3.amazonaws.com/s3fs-public/publication/161003_Hicks_U.S.IndiaSecurity_Web.pdf.
34 See *ibid*.
35 See *ibid*.
36 See United States Department of State, *Framework for the U.S.–India Cyber Relationship* (August 30, 2016), https://in.usembassy.gov/framework-u-s-india-cyber-relationship/.
37 See Leilah Elmokadem, 'Mapping of India's Cyber Security-Related Bilateral Agreements,' The Centre for Internet and Society, India, https://cis-india.org/internet-governance/files/CyberSecurityAgreements_Infographic_04.pdf.
38 *Ibid*.
39 See U.S. State Deptartment, *Framework for the U.S.–India Cyber Relationship*, p. 1.
40 *Ibid*.
41 *Ibid*.
42 *Ibid*.
43 *Ibid*.
44 *Ibid*.
45 See Derek B. Johnson, 'DHS Looks to Upgrade Flagging Info Sharing Program,' FCW (September 6, 2019), https://fcw.com/articles/2019/09/06/cisa-shares-ais-improve-johnson.aspx.
46 See, e.g., Andy Kazmin and Stephanie Findlay, 'Washington Warns India Over Using Huawei for 5G,' *Financial Times* (October 3, 2019), www.ft.com/content/4181ee4e-e5de-11e9-9743-db5a370481bc.
47 See Debak Das, 'An Indian Nuclear Power Plant Suffered a Cyberattack. Here's What You Need to Know,' *Washington Post* (November 3, 2019), washingtonpost.com/politics/2019/11/04/an-indian-nuclear-power-plant-suffered-cyberattack-heres-what-you-need-know/.
48 See, e.g., Hugh Taylor, 'Industrial Information Security Policy: Rethinking the "Air Gap,"' *Journal of Cyber Policy* (April 4, 2018), https://journalofcyberpolicy.com/2018/04/04/industrial-information-security-policy-rethinking-air-gap/.
49 See Das, 'An Indian Nuclear Power Plant', p. 1.
50 See Samir Saran and Richard Rahul Verma, 'Strategic Convergence: The United States and India as Major Defence Partners,' Observer Research Foundation (June 26, 2019), www.orfonline.org/research/strategic-convergence-the-united-states-and-india-as-major-defence-partners-52364/; see also National Defense Authorization Act for Fiscal Year 2017, § 1292(a)(1)(A), P.L. 114–328, 130 Stat. 2559; 22 U.S.C. 2751 note (2017).
51 See Michael F. Martin et al., 'The Asia Reassurance Initiative Act (ARIA) of 2018,' *Congressional Research Service* (April 4, 2019), p. 1, https://crsreports.congress.gov/product/pdf/IF/IF11148.
52 See Keith B. Alexander et al., 'Clear Thinking About Protecting the Nation

in the Cyber Domain,' *Cyber Defense Review* 29, 35–6 (2017), https://nation alsecurity.gmu.edu/wp-content/uploads/2017/03/CDRV2N1_Clear-Thinking_ Alexander_Jaffer_Brunet_032217–1.pdf.
53 See Keith B. Alexander and Jamil N. Jaffer, 'A Transatlantic Alliance is Crucial in an Era of Cyberwarfare,' *Financial Times* (September 4, 2018), www.ft.com/content/c01a7f94-af81-11e8-87e0-d84e0d934341.
54 See Chapter 10 in this volume.
55 See Akhtar and Kronstadt, 'U.S.–India Trade Relations,' p. 1.
56 *Ibid*. pp. 1–2.
57 See Chapter 12 in this volume.
58 *Ibid*.
59 See Keith B. Alexander and Jamil N. Jaffer, 'UN's Cybercrime "Law" Helps Dictators and Criminals, not Their Victims,' The Hill (November 26, 2019), https://thehill.com/opinion/cybersecurity/471897-uns-cybercrime-law-helps-dictators-and-criminals-not-their-victims. See also United Nations, *Vote Name: Item 107: Draft resolution A/C.3/74/L.11/Rev.1 Countering the Use of Information and Communications Technologies for Criminal Purposes* (November 18, 2019), www.un.org/en/ga/third/74/docs/voting_sheets/A.C3.74. L.11.Rev.1.pdf.
60 See Council of Europe, *Chart of Signatures and Ratifications of Treaty 185: Convention on Cybercrime*, www.coe.int/en/web/conventions/full-list/-/conven tions/treaty/185/signatures?p_auth=vTFDTqbj.
61 See Sintia Radu, 'More Countries May Dive into Data-Sharing Pacts,' U.S. News & World Report (October 18, 2019), www.usnews.com/news/best-countries/arti cles/2019–10–18/us-uk-data-pact-may-signal-more-international-cooperation.
62 See, e.g., Andy Keiser and Bryan Smith, *Chinese Telecommunications Companies Huawei and ZTE: Countering a Hostile Foreign Threat*, National Security Institute (January 24, 2019), https://nationalsecurity.gmu.edu/chinese-telecommunications/.
63 See, e.g., Robert Hannigan, 'Blanket Bans on Chinese Tech Companies Like Huawei Make No Sense,' *Financial Times* (February 12, 2019), www.ft.com/content/76e846a4–2b9f-11e9–9222–7024d72222bc; see also Huawei Cyber Security Evaluation Centre Oversight Board, *Annual Report 2019* (March 2019), https://assets.publishing.service.gov.uk/government/uploads/system/uploads/attachment_data/file/790270/HCSEC_OversightBoardReport-2019.pdf.
64 *Ibid*.

4

From intention to action: challenges in cyberdefense cooperation for the U.S. and India

Bedavyasa Mohanty

Introduction

Stripped down to its core, the internet is little more than a conglomeration of connected cables that transmit packets of data from one node to another. And yet, in the twenty-first century this interconnected network of computers acts as the backbone of the global economy. If one were to zoom out and take a panoramic view, the questions agitating cybergovernance may even appear as a simulacrum of the many unresolved challenges that nations continue to grapple with – from trade and national security to the protection of civil liberties. It is the entanglement of these multifarious challenges that makes governing cyberspace a difficult endeavor. The inextricable linkage of economic and strategic interests also makes it imperative for states to set aside political differences and pursue a cooperative framework. This, as time has proved, is easier said than done.

India and the U.S., two countries that maintain a broad strategic partnership on a range of political and economic issues, would appear to be natural partners in cyberdefense and governance. They share common democratic underpinnings, both advocate for openness in regulation of technology[1] and are bound by strong economic ties, especially in the digital realm. And yet, this is not a bilateral relationship that has been fully realized. Beyond token statements of mutual cooperation for cybersecurity and sporadic attempts at building capacity, there is little tangible evidence of serious attempts by policymakers in Washington D.C. and New Delhi to tackle the threats that emerging technologies pose.

To be fair, this is a complex and uncharted terrain to navigate, with its idiosyncratic challenges, but is also one that presents unique opportunities. A strategic bilateral partnership in cyberspace is in some ways delinked from the legacy of the larger strategic relationship and therefore can shed some of the accompanying baggage – such as India's onerous and monolithic defense procurement process.[2] This opens up the possibility of defining a new normal in how the two states cooperate in the transfer of both skills and technology. At the same time, unlike traditional military affairs, in cybersecurity there is a clear interlinking between national security, civilian technologies and market economics. For example, the Snowden disclosures about the U.S. government's intrusion into many globally used technology platforms not only created diplomatic rifts between the U.S. and its allies but may have also caused a loss of $35 billion to the U.S. cloud computing industry.[3] Given the revelations around the magnitude of U.S. spying, it comes as a surprise to no one that countries continue to remain apprehensive of cyber-intelligence sharing with the U.S.

These, and many similar concerns, will need to be addressed head on if India and the U.S. are to build a robust strategic partnership for cybersecurity. Before delving into the 'how' of the relationship, it is necessary to articulate the 'why' – especially why a new cooperative framework between India and the U.S. matters now. This chapter highlights the convergence of economic and strategic interests between India and the U.S. In doing so, it draws attention to questions around gaps of capacity and political will that have ailed cybersecurity cooperation between the two nations. It suggests modest steps that need to be taken for the full realization of the potential of this bilateral relationship.

A new normative crucible

When discussing India's importance in the larger cybersecurity conversation, the country's market size is an oft-invoked statistic. This is not without reason. Even with only 33 percent internet penetration, India boasts over 500 million internet users,[4] nearly half of whom have come online in the five years since 2014. Already, it is the largest market for some of the most important technology platforms in the world – Facebook for example has 269 million users in India, over 183 million in the U.S.[5] Moreover, with the unprecedented rollout of the Aadhaar digital-identity program, India has now created the largest biometric database in the world, which combines over a billion individuals' biometric information with demographic data such as name, age, address and contact information.

India's relevance in the cyber realm, however, goes beyond its market size or the entanglement of key economic interests. In the strategic context, India is a normative leader among emerging economies. While there are a spectrum of approaches in the regulation of technology – from the U.S.'s market centrism, to Europe's focus on individual rights and China's protectionist cybersovereignty – India is attempting to carve out a middle ground that is likely to be an attractive proposition to other democratic states, especially ones that are straddling the fence when it comes to digital diplomacy.

Despite the fact that trust in technology platforms is at an all-time low, India is adopting an approach that does not deny market access to global technology services – be they American or Chinese. Instead, it is setting down rules that these actors will have to play by that are significantly different from those of their parent jurisdictions. This approach was perhaps best captured by the Indian Secretary of Telecommunications, Aruna Sundararajan, when she said, "We don't want to build walls, but at the same time, we explicitly recognize and appreciate that data is a strategic asset."[6]

However, India realizes that approaches towards cybersecurity and the digital economy – more so than any other strategic dimension – cannot be pursued alone. It also recognizes that the U.S., the country with the most significant investments in both technology and digital policymaking, is a key partner in this endeavor. This is reflected in the fairly comprehensive Framework for the U.S.–India Cyber Relationship.[7] And yet, the laudable intention behind the framework agreement has not yet transitioned from intention to action.

This chapter analyses two things: first, the principled points of divergence that often act as a hurdle for cooperation between U.S. and India; and second, common threats that the two countries face in the period 2020–25 in the cyber realm that make it critical for them to set aside differences and work together.

Cyber espionage

On the economic front, both India and the U.S. are concerned about China's rising dominance, fueled to a large extent by its rapid technological advancement – advancement which has partly been made possible[8] by the theft of intellectual property from U.S. industry, amounting to nearly $300 billion each year.[9] China's economic espionage is both a direct and indirect threat to U.S. national security, be it in the form of stolen military technology[10] or the loss of thousands of jobs due to industrial collapse.[11]

India, similarly has long been concerned about cyber threats emanating from its eastern neighbor. The Indian market is currently flooded with Chinese smartphones – with four out of the top five most popular smartphone brands emanating from China.[12] All told, Chinese devices – whose manufacturers have come under increased scrutiny[13] globally – now make up more than half of India's smartphone market.[14] Indian policymakers have reason to be concerned about the proliferation of potentially insecure devices, given that in the past Chinese hackers have been known to have exfiltrated sensitive data from key Indian entities. In 2010, for instance, a joint investigation by Citizen Lab at the Munk School of Global Affairs and

SecDev Group found that computers at key Indian targets including: the National Security Council Secretariat; Indian Embassies in Kabul, Moscow, Dubai and Abuja; and the Military Engineer Services, among others, had been compromised by hackers based out of Chengdu, China.[15]

More recently, a common concern for both India and the U.S. has been cyberespionage activities linked with hacker groups in North Korea. The U.S. has previously been a target of intrusive hacking by the Lazarus Group – a cybercrime group believed to be linked to the North Korean government. Now designated an "Advanced Persistent Threat" by cybersecurity professionals, the Lazarus Group is believed to have been behind both the infamous Sony Hack of 2014[16] and the WannaCry ransomware attack that affected over 200,000 computer systems in 150 countries.[17]

Until 2020, Lazarus Group had been largely considered to be a syndicate dedicated to financial crimes, albeit with a view towards advancing Pyongyang's strategic interests. A confidential United Nations report found, for example, that North Korea has stolen $2 billion through cyberattacks that targeted banks and crypto-currency exchanges to fund its weapons development program.[18] While this is a serious issue in itself, it has taken on a more sinister dimension with the allegation that the same North Korean hacker group may have been behind the cyberattack targeting information systems of the nuclear power plant at Kudankulam in southern India.[19]

The hack, which was reported in early November 2019, was reportedly an attempt by North Korean hackers to access information about India's nuclear fuel yields at the Thorium-based reactor.[20] This, according to experts, would be invaluable information for a country that has successfully managed to create a nuclear deterrent against a conventionally superior adversary like the U.S.

Law enforcement data sharing

Perhaps the most significant bone of contention in cyber cooperation between India and the U.S. continues to be the current inefficient model for sharing data between the two countries' law enforcement agencies. Over the decade since 2010, access to electronic data has become critical not just for cybercrimes but for crimes in the physical realm that are planned and executed through cyber means. Much of this data is retained by popular technology platforms (such as e-mail and private messaging services) that are U.S. based. Under U.S. law, these communication service providers are barred from sharing "content"[21] data unless specifically requested to do so under a warrant by a U.S. court. Therefore, in order to pursue criminal investigations, foreign law enforcement agencies must rely on a bilateral mechanism to obtain electronic evidence.

Most analysts agree that this bilateral data sharing mechanism, called a Mutual Legal Assistance Treaty (MLAT), is broken. Even when a crime has occurred outside the U.S. and the victim and suspect are not U.S. persons, a request for data must meet the "probable cause" standard under U.S. law.[22] This often creates a conflict of laws, frustrating criminal investigation efforts.[23] The MLAT process is also fraught with delays, often taking several months for the data to materialize. According to one estimate, a request from an Indian agency to the U.S. can take up to three years and four months to return actionable intelligence.[24]

The U.S. too has acknowledged that the inefficient MLAT process has an adverse effect on its foreign relations. For example, the Review Group on Intelligence and Communication Technologies established by President Barack Obama noted that "efforts to obtain improved international cooperation on information technology" were often undermined by the U.S. Department of Justice's inability to adequately respond to legitimate investigation requests made by foreign governments.[25] The Review Group also warned that this failure was incentivizing foreign governments to adopt regressive laws forcing the storage of data within their own borders – leading to a host of privacy and security challenges. True enough, when the Indian government released a draft of its Personal Data Protection Bill in 2018, the MLAT process being "deeply flawed and overly time consuming"[26] was used as a justification for compelling technology companies to store data locally.

The abundance of inefficiencies in the MLAT process led the U.S. Congress to finally adopt the Clarifying Lawful Overseas Use of Data (CLOUD) Act in 2018, which aims to allow certain foreign governments to directly request data from U.S. technology companies, bypassing the arduous diplomatic process. For this to happen, however, a foreign government must be certified by the U.S. Attorney General to have laws and policies ensuring "substantial and procedural respect for privacy," among other things.[27] The qualifying government would then enter into an executive agreement with the U.S. This reciprocal right to request data from each other's technology platforms can ease the data-access conundrum but requires significant diplomatic effort from countries that expect to qualify. So far, the U.S. has signed an executive agreement with only the United Kingdom (UK),[28] after years of negotiation, and is said to be in talks with Australia[29] to enter into a similar arrangement.

As the country with the second-highest number of user data requests to U.S. tech companies,[30] India is a natural contender for an executive agreement under the CLOUD Act, but perhaps also one of the most controversial.³¹ Operationalizing this agreement will take significant diplomatic effort from policymakers in New Delhi and Washington D.C. If the U.S.–UK agreement is indicative of what the U.S.'s approach is likely to be, then an insistence on the First Amendment standard could be a roadblock to allowing for an India–U.S. Agreement.

The U.S.–UK Agreement states that if the U.S. feels that its essential interests in relation to freedom of speech are implicated by the UK's prosecution on the basis of data obtained, it will be able to unilaterally limit or prohibit the use of data for prosecution by UK authorities.³² This standard is well beyond the one prescribed under the CLOUD Act. Under Section 2523 of the Act, one of the conditions that a country must meet to qualify for an executive agreement is that it "adheres to applicable international human rights obligations and commitments or demonstrates respect for ... freedom of expression." It has been argued³³ that this provision refers to whether a country has ratified key international human rights instruments such as the Universal Declaration of Human Rights and the International Covenant on Civil and Political Rights.

If such an agreement were to be entered into between India and the U.S., the Indian government would be wary of the fact that the U.S. could use the provision to nullify prosecution in cases where India's laws around free expression are incompatible with that of the U.S. Take, for example, Section 295 of the Indian Penal Code – a controversial law that criminalizes insults to religions with an imprisonment for three years. While this would run contrary to the freedoms prescribed in the First Amendment, the Indian government could view the provision as necessary to maintain public order. More importantly, the fact that the U.S., through an executive agreement, is attempting to impose its domestic standards on a foreign state could be seen as an affront to India's sovereignty.

Influence operations

In the period 2016–18, both India and the U.S. have been countries that have been targets of sophisticated influence operations conducted through cyber means. In 2018, over thirty individuals were lynched by mobs in India over suspicions that they were child-abductors.³⁴ The trigger for these acts of violence was a campaign of doctored videos and images shared over WhatsApp warning people of child lifters and organ harvesters prowling in their neighborhoods. What distinguished this campaign from the rumor-mongering pervasive over the internet was its coordinated nature and the tailoring of the messages (by context and geographies) to create paranoia among certain groups of people. For example, as the messages were going viral, fact checkers noted subtle changes in the text of messages to refer to locations and neighborhoods close to where the recipient would be located – thus increasing fear and paranoia.

Similarly, in the context of the 2016 presidential election in the U.S. the Internet Research Agency (IRA) – often dubbed Russia's troll factory – is known to have targeted specific voter demographics by assuming the identity of organizations that would be meaningful to them. For instance, a brand called Black Matters, developed by the IRA, focused on the African-American community by pushing carefully curated authentic-seeming Black media content. The ultimate goal of building this online community was to expose it to messaging that emphasized a lack of trust in democratic institutions and reduce the turnout among Black voters in the 2016 presidential election.[35]

Instances such as these go on to highlight a very clear and present danger: operations that were earlier extremely expensive and required the deployment of covert intelligence operatives in foreign territories can now be conducted remotely, thanks to the internet and decentralized media networks. Combined with the reality that today more people rely on social media for their daily news than print media,[36] influence operations in cyberspace provide malicious actors with an attractive and inexpensive option to influence the psyche of their adversaries. Cyberspace also provides another key advantage that has always been sought after in traditional espionage: anonymity. Remote operators that coordinate influence-operation campaigns often use pseudonymous profiles and social media handles that appear to the target audience as their well-meaning compatriots – assuming identities that would be the most impactful for the campaign.

Both countries have recognized the seriousness of the challenge posed by social media and influence operations. As a deterrent measure, the U.S. in the aftermath of the 2016 elections declared election infrastructure as critical infrastructure,[37] prioritizing Department of Homeland Security assistance to election jurisdictions and giving the government power to issue sanctions against foreign actors that interfere with the process. Over the course of India's general election in April and May 2019, social media companies adopted a Voluntary Code of Ethics before the Election Commission of India.[38] The code obligated them to facilitate transparency in political advertisements and quick response to requests from the Election Commission for taking down content on their platforms that could adversely influence voters.

These, however, are stopgap measures. While rules against non-interference in the sovereign affairs of another state have been enshrined within Article 2(4) of the Charter of the United Nations, influence operations in cyberspace fail to meet this threshold. Influence operations even

From intention to action   85

in cases such as election interference ultimately aim to sway voters and do not directly interfere with the ballot process – the voters act of their own volition. Even the Tallinn Manual on the International Law Applicable to Cyber Warfare, which seeks to apply principles of international law to cyberspace, acknowledges that election interference does not amount to an initiation of armed conflict.[39] It is clear, therefore, that there is an absence of legal avenues to tackle influence operations. It is also clear that the threat of influence operations is unlikely to dissipate anytime soon.

Against this backdrop it is crucial for democracies like the U.S. and India that rely on the internet for commerce and communication to come together and devise rules of the road for tacking information operations. Having ceded the space to large technology platforms to arbitrate political discourse, the question before the governments of the world today is how long they are willing to wait before they act to regulate. Their challenge lies in looking past their own individual interests and framing a solution that applies globally.

Strategic command and control

Many of the threats and challenges for India discussed above are compounded by the lack of a high-level institutional architecture for cyberdefense. This gap in the ability to predict, identify and respond to threats – especially those emanating from state actors – is a glaring vulnerability for India's critical information infrastructure. It is also a significant contributing factor for why numerous serious cyberattacks against Indian infrastructure have not drawn a credible response from within the national security establishment. Instead, measures, where they have been adopted, have largely been ad hoc and piecemeal.

In 2019 the Indian government announced the establishment of a tri-services Defence Cyber Agency (DCA), drawing from the Indian Army, Navy and Air Force. The DCA is expected to coordinate both offensive and defensive cyber operations as well as to formulate a doctrine for cyberwarfare.[40] While laudable, this new agency by itself is unlikely to solve the strategic challenges posed by cyberspace. Military experts have called the establishment of the DCA at best a "half-hearted attempt" that is unlikely to be effective unless it evolves into a fully fledged cyber command in the coming years.[41]

Indeed, what the contemporary cyber-threat landscape requires is not just a specialized agency dedicated to cyberdefense but the creation of a new authority that can formulate policies around response to cyber incidents, develop the technical wherewithal necessary to operate in a highly dynamic environment, conduct proactive research into new threat vectors and, perhaps most importantly, assume authority over all branches of the armed forces to build a coordinated response plan.[42] In essence, what India needs today is an agency similar to the U.S. Cyber Command (CYBERCOM).

While some key aspects of the U.S. CYBERCOM such as its dual-hat arrangement – with the same individual serving as the commander of CYBERCOM and Director of the National Security Agency – are not replicable in the Indian context, many others are. For example, personnel arrangements such as the Cyber Mission Teams[43] established under the CYBERCOM to defend domestic networks and conduct offensive missions could serve as an organizational template for training and hiring of specialized information security professionals by the Indian defense forces. India's National Cyber Security Strategy, which envisaged hiring an additional workforce of 500,000 cybersecurity experts, has not made any significant headway and could benefit from the training methods used by the CYBERCOM. Other operational approaches such as cyber command sub-divisions[44] within the U.S. Army, Navy, Air Force and Marine Corps also provide guidance for India's nascent cyberdefense establishment in coordinating teams within various divisions of the armed forces while making them answerable to one central technically and operationally competent authority. The CYBERCOM therefore is one of the institutional mechanisms where there can be transference of key expertise from the U.S. to India through increased cooperation.

Conclusion

The entanglement of economic and security interests in cyberspace ensures that it is impossible to build a renewed strategic relationship without addressing the underlying tensions that are animating the current debate – such as privacy, antitrust and platform regulation generally. India's endorsement of data localization in its regulatory policy, for example, is already putting a strain on trade between the two countries. In 2018 the U.S. Senate's India Caucus warned that this policy posture could affect the larger economic partnership.[45] However, given the current environment where the world has been rocked by privacy and security concerns created by big U.S. technology corporations, it is unlikely that the new stance adopted by India is likely to change; at the very least, not without deliberative efforts that sincerely address India's concerns and capacity constraints.

Depending on how the 2020 general elections go, we are likely to see the U.S. take steps to repair its fraught international relations. Optimistically, this may be the best opportunity for India to negotiate a new partnership in cyberdefense cooperation. This can take many forms: exchange of information on national cyber policies, sharing knowledge on best practices, promoting regional consultations and expanding cooperation in law enforcement and international assistance for capacity building.

Concrete steps such as negotiating an agreement with India under the CLOUD Act can go a long way in addressing a long-standing thorn in the side of this bilateral relationship. Forging a mechanism where law enforcement on access to data is determined by where the subject is located rather than where the data is stored or the company incorporated can avoid triggering a conflict of laws that sours bilateral relationships and precludes any further cooperation. Given that many of the above concerns about security in the cyber domain are a result of capacity (both human and technical), efforts at capacity building must become a point of emphasis in the India–U.S. relationship going forward. Capacity-building initiatives should range from the joint training of security personnel and information security professionals to guidance and coordination on creating an institutional architecture to sustain cybersecurity. Immediate steps should be taken at a secretary/ministerial level to operationalize key aspects of the Framework Agreement on cybersecurity. At a high level, steps should be taken to script common language on key norms of cyber stability, such as responses to state-sponsored cyberattacks on critical infrastructure and the theft of intellectual property.

These efforts must aim to shed the half-heartedness of previous efforts and instead build anew a twenty-first-century cooperative framework that stands up to the test of time. The single biggest failing for India so far, perhaps, has been that its idealistic approach runs afoul of realpolitik at the international level and security considerations at the domestic level. The same can be said of America in the recent past – it is time that that changed. In the perennial tug of war between individual privacy, national security and technological innovation, a viable middle ground has so far been missing. India and the U.S. in working together have the opportunity to develop normative frameworks that are attractive to large parts of the world, while underscoring the fact that developed and developing economies can work together for the security and prosperity of a shared domain. The decade 2020–30 will either see this materialize or witness large parts of the world go increasingly out of the network.

Notes

1 'U.S.–India Strategic Dialogue Joint Statement', *U.S. Department of State*.
2 K. Lamarque, 'U.S.–German Relations Hit New Low Amid NSA Scandal: Official', *NBC News* (January 17, 2014), available at www.nbcnews.com/

storyline/nsa-snooping/u-s--german-relations-hit-new-low-amid-nsa-n11496. (Last visited on November 29, 2019).

3 Daniel Castro, 'How Much Will PRISM Cost the U.S. Cloud Computing Industry?' *The Information Technology and Innovation Platform*, August 2013, available at www2.itif.org/2013-cloud-computing-costs.pdf. (Last visited on November 29, 2019).

4 Internet and Mobile Association of India, 'India Internet 2019' (September 26, 2019), available at www.iamai.in/KnowledgeCentre. (Last visited on November 29, 2019).

5 'Leading Countries Based on Number of Facebook Users as of October 2019 (in Millions)'. Chart. October 25, 2019. Statista. Accessed November 25, 2019. www.statista.com/statistics/268136/top-15-countries-based-on-number-of-facebook-users/. (Last visited on November 29, 2019).

6 V. Goel, 'India Pushes Back Against Tech "Colonization" by Internet Giants', *New York Times* (August 31, 2018), available at www.nytimes.com/2018/08/31/technology/india-technology-american-giants.html. (Last visited on November 29, 2019).

7 Office of the Press Secretary, White House, 'FACT SHEET: Framework for the U.S.–India Cyber Relationship', June 7, 2016, available at obamawhitehouse.archives.gov/the-press-office/2016/06/07/fact-sheet-framework-us-india-cyber-relationship. (Last visited on November 29, 2019).

8 Office of the Director of National Intelligence, 'Foreign Economic Espionage in Cyberspace' (2018), available at www.dni.gov/files/NCSC/documents/news/20180724-economic-espionage-pub.pdf. (Last visited on November 29, 2019).

9 Report of the Commission on the Theft of American Intellectual Property (2013), available at ipcommission.org/report/IP_Commission_Report_052213.pdf. (Last visited on November 29, 2019).

10 E. Nakashima and P. Sonne, 'China Hacked a Navy Contractor and Secured a Trove of Highly Sensitive Data on Submarine Warfare', *Washington Post* (June 8, 2018) available at www.washingtonpost.com/world/national-security/china-hacked-a-navy-contractor-and-secured-a-trove-of-highly-sensitive-data-on-submarine-warfare/2018/06/08/6cc396fa-68e6-11e8-bea7-c8eb28bc52b1_story.html. (Last visited on November 29, 2019).

11 N. Eftimiades, 'The Impact of Chinese Espionage on the United States', *Diplomat* (December 4, 2018), available at www.thediplomat.com/2018/12/the-impact-of-chinese-espionage-on-the-united-states/. (Last visited on November 29, 2019).

12 A. Ahaskar, 'Chinese Smartphone Brands Increase India Market Share', *LiveMint* (April 27, 2019) available at www.livemint.com/technology/gadgets/chinese-smartphone-brands-increase-india-market-share-1556260390442.html. (Last visited on November 29, 2019).

13 CheckPoint Research, 'Xiaomi Vulnerability: When Security Is Not What It Seems', available at blog.checkpoint.com/2019/04/04/xiaomi-vulnerability-when-security-is-not-what-it-seems/. (Last visited on November 29, 2019).

14 BBC, 'Xiaomi: The Chinese Brand Dominating India's Smartphone Market', *BBC* (October 22, 2019), available at www.bbc.com/news/world-asia-india-50135050. (Last visited on November 29, 2019).
15 Ron Diebert, Steve Adair et al., 'Shadows in the Cloud: Investigating Cyber Espionage 2.0', Information Warfare Monitor and Shadowserver Foundation (April 5, 2010), available at www.nartv.org/mirror/shadows-in-the-cloud.pdf. (Last visited on November 29, 2019).
16 D. Cameron, 'Security Researchers Say Mysterious "Lazarus Group" hacked Sony in 2014', *Daily Dot* (February 24, 2017), available at www.dailydot.com/layer8/sony-hack-lazarus-group-operation-blockbuster-report/. (Last visited on November 29, 2019).
17 A. Liptak, 'The WannaCry Ransomware Attack Has Spread to 150 Countries', *Verge* (May 14, 2017), available at www.theverge.com/2017/5/14/15637888/authorities-wannacry-ransomware-attack-spread-150-countries. (Last visited on November 29, 2019).
18 BBC, 'North Korea "Stole $2bn for Weapons via Cyber-Attacks"', *BBC* (August 7, 2019), available at www.bbc.com/news/world-asia-49259302. (Last visited on November 29, 2019).
19 D. Das, 'An Indian Nuclear Power Plant Suffered a Cyberattack. Here's What You Need To Know', *Washington Post* (November 4, 2019), available at www.washingtonpost.com/politics/2019/11/04/an-indian-nuclear-power-plant-suffered-cyberattack-heres-what-you-need-know/. (Last visited on November 29, 2019).
20 S. Datta and A. Salmon, 'North Koreans Behind Indian Nuclear Plant Hack', *Asia Times* (November 12, 2019), available at www.asiatimes.com/2019/11/article/north-koreans-behind-indian-nuclear-plant-hack/. (Last visited on November 29, 2019).
21 The Electronic Communication Privacy Act defines content as the "substance, purport or meaning" of any wire, oral, or electronic communication. 18 U.S.C. § 2510.
22 Madhulika Srikumar, Peter Swire et al., 'India–U.S. Data Sharing for Law Enforcement: Blueprint for Reforms', Observer Research Foundation and Georgia Tech Institute for Information Security and Privacy (2019), available at www.orfonline.org/wp-content/uploads/2019/01/MLAT-Book-_v8_web-1.pdf. (Last visited on November 29, 2019).
23 Bedavyasa Mohanty and Madhulika Srikumar, 'Hitting Refresh: Making India–U.S. Data Sharing Work', Observer Research Foundation, ORF Special Report 39 (August 2017), available at www.orfonline.org/wp-content/uploads/2017/08/MLAT-Book.pdf. (Last visited on November 29, 2019).
24 "Madan Oberoi, director of cyber innovation and outreach at Interpol and a former CBI official, said at an event that an internal survey done by the Indian agency revealed that an MLAT request took three years and four months (40 months) on average to be fulfilled." economictimes.indiatimes.com/news/politics-and-nation/cbi-fbi-join-hands-to-reduce-time-required-to-fulfil-requests-on-information-and-evidence/articleshow/50069794.cms?utm_source=contentof

interest&utm_medium=text&utm_campaign=cppst. (Last visited on November 29, 2019).

25 Richard A. Clarke et al., 'Liberty and Security in a Changing World: Report and Recommendations of The President's Review Group on Intelligence and Communications Technologies' (December 12, 2013), available at obamawhitehouse.archives.gov/sites/default/files/docs/2013-12-12_rg_final_report.pdf. (Last visited on November 29, 2019).

26 Committee of Experts under the Chairmanship of Justice B. N. Srikrishna, 'A Free and Fair Digital Economy: Protecting Privacy, Empowering Indians', available at meity.gov.in/writereaddata/files/Data_Protection_Committee_Report.pdf. (Last visited on November 29, 2019).

27 The Act permits the U.S. to enter into an Executive Agreement with a foreign government only if the Attorney General and the Secretary of State certify to Congress that, among other things, the foreign government provides "robust substantive and procedural protections for privacy and civil liberties" and that it has adopted procedures to "minimize the acquisition, retention, and dissemination of information concerning United States persons".

28 Department of Justice, 'U.S. And UK Sign Landmark Cross-Border Data Access Agreement to Combat Criminals and Terrorists Online' (October 3, 2019), available at www.justice.gov/opa/pr/us-and-uk-sign-landmark-cross-border-data-access-agreement-combat-criminals-and-terrorists. (Last visited on November 29, 2019).

29 Department of Justice, 'Joint Statement Announcing United States and Australian Negotiation of a CLOUD Act Agreement by U.S. Attorney General William Barr and Minister for Home Affairs Peter Dutton' (October 7, 2019), available at www.justice.gov/opa/pr/joint-statement-announcing-united-states-and-australian-negotiation-cloud-act-agreement-us. (Last visited on November 29, 2019).

30 Y. Bhargava, 'India's Requests for Facebook User Data Increases by 37%, Second Only to U.S.', *Hindu* (November 14, 2019), available at www.thehindu.com/sci-tech/technology/internet/indias-requests-for-facebook-user-data-rising-sharply/article29975854.ece. (Last visited on November 29, 2019).

31 Alex Stamos, "The CLOUD Act deals with this by creating a process for overseas courts to issue orders for content only pursuant to a 1:1 agreement between that country and the U.S. So the U.S. DOJ gets to be a gatekeeper. UK/FR/DE/JP likely get in. CN/RU/VN do not. India will be a big test." twitter.com/alexstamos/status/1178308905891315712. (Last visited on November 29, 2019).

32 Article 8(4)(b), U.S.–UK Agreement under CLOUD Act.

33 E. Aswad, 'Outside the Beltway: An Experiment on Human Rights and Potential CLOUD Act Agreements', *Just Security* (July 15, 2019), available at www.justsecurity.org/64911/outside-the-beltway-an-experiment-on-human-rights-potential-cloud-act-agreements/. (Last visited on November 29, 2019).

34 S. Vij, 'A Single WhatsApp Rumour Has Killed 29 People in India and Nobody Cares', *Print* (July 7, 2018), available at theprint.in/opinion/a-single-whatsapp-rumour-has-killed-29-people-in-india-and-nobody-cares/77634/. (Last visited on November 29, 2019).

35 J. Parham, 'Targeting Black Americans, Russia's IRA Exploited Racial Wounds', *Wired* (December 17, 2018), available at: www.wired.com/story/russia-ira-target-black-americans/. (Last visited on November 29, 2019).
36 E. Shearer, 'Social Media Outpaces Print Newspapers in the U.S. as a News Source', *Pew Research Center* (December 10, 2018), available at: www.pewresearch.org/fact-tank/2018/12/10/social-media-outpaces-print-newspapers-in-the-u-s-as-a-news-source/. (Last visited on November 29, 2019).
37 Congressional Research Service, 'The Designation of Election Systems as Critical Infrastructure' (January 28, 2019), available at: fas.org/sgp/crs/misc/IF10677.pdf. (Last visited on November 29, 2019).
38 Press Information Bureau, 'Social Media Platforms Present "Voluntary Code of Ethics for the 2019 General Election" to Election Commission of India' (March 20, 2019), available at pib.gov.in/newsite/PrintRelease.aspx?relid=189494. (Last visited on November 29, 2019).
39 E. Nakashima, 'Russia's Apparent Meddling in U.S. Election Is Not an Act of War, Cyber Expert Says', *Washington Post* (February 7, 2017), available at www.washingtonpost.com/news/checkpoint/wp/2017/02/07/russias-apparent-meddling-in-u-s-election-is-not-an-act-of-war-cyber-expert-says/. (Last visited on November 29, 2019).
40 G. Chawla, 'India's new Defence Cyber Agency – II: Balancing Constitutional Constraints and Covert Ops?', *Centre for Communication Governance* (October 1, 2019) available at ccgnludelhi.wordpress.com/2019/10/01/indias-new-defence-cyber-agency-ii-balancing-constitutional-constraints-and-covert-ops/. (Last visited on November 29, 2019).
41 Vivekananda International Foundation, 'Credible Cyber Deterrence in Armed Forces of India' (March 2019), available at www.vifindia.org/sites/default/files/Credible-Cyber-Deterrence-in-Armed-Forces-of-India_0.pdf. (Last visited on November 29, 2019).
42 Arun Mohan Sukumar and RK Sharma, 'The Cyber Command: Upgrading India's National Security Architecture', ORF Special Report 9 (March 2016), available at www.orfonline.org/wp-content/uploads/2016/03/SR_9_Arun-Mohan-Sukumar-and-RK-sharma.pdf. (Last visited on November 29, 2019).
43 U.S. Department of Defense, 'Cyber Mission Force Achieves Full Operational Capability' (May 17, 2018), available at www.defense.gov/Explore/News/Article/Article/1524747/cyber-mission-force-achieves-full-operational-capability/. (Last visited on November 29, 2019).
44 U.S. Cyber Command, 'Components', www.cybercom.mil/Components/. (Last visited on November 29, 2019).
45 A. Kalra, 'Exclusive: U.S. Senators Urge India to Soften Data Localization Stance', *Reuters* (October 13, 2018), available at www.reuters.com/article/us-india-data-localisation-exclusive/exclusive-u-s-senators-urge-india-to-soften-data-localization-stance-idU.S.KCN1MN0CN. (Last visited on November 29, 2019).

Part III

Nuclear stability cooperation

5

Southern Asia in a decaying nuclear order: regional strategic dilemmas and U.S. policy approaches toward India

Frank O'Donnell

The global nuclear order appears to be under significant pressure as of early 2020. This order is defined as the web of international arms control agreements anchored around the Nuclear Nonproliferation Treaty (NPT), and supported by norms against use of nuclear weapons and nonproliferation. At seemingly every stage in its history, the order has featured scholarly assessments that it is in some form of crisis.[1] However, the simultaneous converging developments since 2017 are jeopardizing the system's legal and normative frameworks, to a degree arguably without precedent. The collapse of the U.S.–Russia 1987 Intermediate-Range Nuclear Forces (INF) Treaty in 2019 permits the possessors of the two largest nuclear arsenals in the world to begin constructing and fielding previously banned ground-launched ballistic and cruise missiles with ranges between 500 and 5,500 kilometers.[2] It appears unlikely at the time of writing that Washington and Moscow will agree to the single five-year extension of their 2010 bilateral New START treaty before its expiry in February 2021.[3] This outcome will not only leave U.S. and Russian nuclear forces without legal limits to arsenal growth and diversification, but will also end the comprehensive transparency and monitoring protocols that reduce potential misperception from each state regarding their mutual nuclear and missile intentions.[4] The skepticism of the Trump administration toward the value of arms control efforts in general, combined with these above developments, hinders its ability to persuade other states to retain and adopt nuclear stability measures.[5]

Simultaneously, several major nuclear weapons states are at various stages of rethinking nuclear strategies, and conventional strategies that impinge upon the former, in ways that elevate the risk of nuclear use. The 2018 U.S. Nuclear Posture Review commits to developing new nuclear submarine-launched cruise missiles, and low-yield submarine-launched ballistic missiles, in the belief that these new platforms will more directly deter Chinese and Russian policymakers from considering limited nuclear use against U.S. forces.[6] A new U.S. joint force doctrine advises geographic combatant commanders to select potential nuclear targets and strike options as part of their theater campaign planning.[7] The doctrine also calls for U.S. military training to deliver a force mentally and physically prepared "to operate in a post-nuclear detonation radiological environment" and "nuclear battlefield."[8]

Higher-level Russian military doctrine continues to affirm that nuclear use will be reserved for worst-case scenarios, and precludes limited nuclear wars. However, naval doctrines signed by Putin nevertheless permit limited nuclear use to gain advantage in a conventional conflict, an opinion shared in remarks by multiple Russian officials.[9] Military exercises since at least 2009 have involved nuclear use to prevail against an adversary fighting conventionally.[10] New delivery vehicles have even been characterized by external analysts as potentially intended for "causing terror."[11] The "Poseidon" nuclear-powered, nuclear-armed unmanned underwater vehicle is designed to "navigate autonomously with a maximum speed of 107 knots and detonate near an enemy coastal city, generating a tsunami wave."[12] Russia is also reportedly developing a similar nuclear-powered and nuclear-armed cruise missile.[13]

Pakistan is planning a seaborne nuclear force, as it continues to emphasize its first-use nuclear policy and development of Nasr nuclear artillery in official statements.[14] India's Defence Minister, Rajnath Singh, suggested in 2019 that India's previous doctrine of no-first-use (NFU) was moving toward one of greater ambiguity. In public remarks, he referred to NFU only in the past tense, and followed this deliberate phrasing with "What happens in future depends on the circumstances."[15] This is but the latest and most authoritative senior policymaker contribution to a growing debate among Indian officials and the country's strategic community regarding retaining India's NFU pledge, as opposed to moving toward an Israel-type doctrine of nuclear ambiguity and posture of flexible response.[16] In the meantime, Indian officials continue to evince interest in conventional counterforce missions, and acquiring the necessary capabilities to execute them.[17]

Among major nuclear-weapons states, China appears to have shifted the least from its previous doctrine and posture. Despite the growing nuclear threat it faces from the U.S., it has reiterated its NFU pledge, and has not been assessed by external experts to have restarted fissile material production since ending it in the 1980s.[18] Chinese officials and experts discount the real possibility of a limited nuclear war with the U.S., believing instead that any nuclear use will lead to uncontrollable escalation. These assumptions reduce the political and technical demand for nuclear war-fighting options within China's nuclear modernization program.[19]

However, other Chinese strategic activities still impinge upon the nuclear policymaking of adversaries. China's refusal to recognize India as a nuclear-weapons state currently prohibits it from initiating nuclear strategic dialogue with India.[20] This missed opportunity to clarify potential misperceptions about mutual strategic intentions elevates the risk of each state organizing its defense posture against the other around worse-case assumptions about these adversary intentions, threatening security-dilemma effects.[21] Moreover, China continues to provide technical assistance to Pakistan's nuclear weapons program, including the sale of 8 Type-041 submarines to Pakistan, some of which are highly likely to serve as part of Pakistan's emerging seaborne nuclear force.[22]

Finally, China's conventional missile armory generates concerns in each of the above states except for Pakistan. U.S. strategists grapple with the challenge of overcoming regional Chinese missile barrages that would eradicate its forces and bases as far out as Guam.[23] Russian strategists have concluded that a large, tous-azimuths cruise missile force is necessary to conventionally deter both China and the U.S.[24] The Indian Air Force reportedly views the Chinese conventional missile threat against air bases and air fields as its greatest concern.[25] As such, it is expanding its network of China-facing air bases and airfields, and investing in runway repair kits in order to ensure greater resilience against this threat.[26] China's conventional missile advantage is also partly driving discussion among Indian strategists around revising its nuclear doctrine and force to deliver a larger, more destructive force with a lower threshold of use.[27]

In this context of a decaying nuclear order and rising U.S. and Indian strategic competition with China, how can Washington best partner with New Delhi in order to arrest these trends toward greater nuclear instability? Is it possible to develop policy measures that also ensure that India is able to pose sufficient general deterrence against China and thus complicate its global rise? Finally, are there policies that achieve both ends, rather than creating tension between them?

This chapter makes arguments for three principal policies that the U.S. should pursue with India in meeting these objectives. The first line of effort is to liaise with New Delhi in expanding its bilateral missile flight-test pre-notification protocol with Islamabad to incorporate other nuclear-weapons states. In the process, this measure could salvage the important transparency measures from the U.S.–Russia New Strategic Arms Reduction Treaty (New START), through their incorporation in this new regime. The second initiative is to propose a joint threat assessment with New Delhi on the Chinese conventional missile threat to India, as a pathway toward potential U.S. assistance toward improving Indian resilience in this regard. The third policy is to assist India in developing its cyberdefenses against potential Chinese efforts to interfere with military command-and-control systems relevant to its nuclear forces. This latter cyber dialogue should also include cyberattacks intended to erode or incapacitate critical conventional forces, with their survival helping to preclude any policymaker discussions of nuclear use. Together, these three policies would build the promotion of global nuclear stability into the U.S.–India alliance; do so in a way that does not entail direct transfers of nuclear weapons or related technologies (which would constitute a violation of Article I under the NPT); and help India maintain sufficient military capabilities to better resist Chinese conventional or cyberattacks, and thus maintain a high nuclear threshold.[28]

Nuclear transparency measures[29]

The prospect of the U.S. and Russia soon fielding previously INF-banned ballistic and cruise missiles attracts much of the policy discourse around the collapse of the treaty. However, it is important to note that the treaty was foundational in establishing nuclear transparency measures. The treaty banned possession, production, and flight-testing of ground-launched ballistic and cruise missiles with a range of between 500 km and 5,500 km, with on-site verification protocols.[30] Building upon this foundation, a 1988 agreement committed Russia and the U.S. to pre-notify each other of all inter-continental ballistic missile (ICBM) and submarine-launched ballistic missile (SLBM) launches. This arrangement was then incorporated into the 1991 Strategic Arms Reduction Treaty (START). This regime required at least twenty-four hours' notice of a four-day window within which flight-tests will be conducted, with associated demarcation of the test area.[31]

New START again incorporated this 1988 agreement text of pre-notification of all ICBM and SLBM launches.[32] While important in ensuring crisis stability through prior warning of missile tests, the New START still lacks pre-launch notifications in significant missile categories, which has been exacerbated by those lost with the INF. At present, these notification gaps regard air-, ground, and sea-based cruise missiles, as well as ballistic missiles with a range of up to 5,500 km. If New START is permitted to expire, these missile flight-test pre-notifications will also cease. This elevates the risk of accidental escalation as both nuclear rivals continue to develop and test new missile platforms while reducing or even eliminating the prior warning that the other has regarding these actions.

Absent a dedicated effort to retain these protocols, both states will resort to relying upon national technical means (NTM) – primarily satellite-based monitoring – to obtain prior warning. As New START also prohibits rival interference with NTM, this is not an effective replacement system for pre-notification protocols. A recent report notes that in this scenario, NTM systems will face greater collection demands, while also being at new risk of adversary interference with their operation. The report observes that China and India could follow suit with U.S. and Russian behavior in this regard, elevating nuclear risk more generally.[33]

While India and Pakistan have not agreed to arms control measures as far reaching in ambition and verification arrangements as the INF or START treaties, their strategic competition is not entirely unregulated. Notable initiatives include a 2007 agreement on immediate notification of nuclear accidents; a 1991 accord to notify each other, and limit the geographic space, of major military exercises; a 1988 agreement to refrain from attacking nuclear installations, involving an annual exchange of details of designated facilities; and a 2005 arrangement on pre-notification of ballistic missile flight-tests.[34]

Under this latter 2005 India–Pakistan missile launch accord, Islamabad and New Delhi have committed to inform each other of a planned five-day period within which a ballistic missile test will take place, with three days' notice of the initiation of this window. The notification includes a warning of the air and naval areas to be affected by the test. India and Pakistan have also pledged that missiles will not overfly the international border and/or Line of Control, that their trajectories will remain at least 40 km away from these boundaries, and that they will similarly land at least 75 km away.[35]

However, the 2005 India–Pakistan agreement, like the others, has its own gaps. First, it entirely omits notifications of cruise missile flight-tests, leaving dangers of misinterpretation of cruise missile launches and deployments unaddressed. Second, the accord permits multiple launches within the notified window. Third, China is absent from the agreement, despite planning "arguably the world's most missile-centric approach to warfare today."[36] As Beijing continues to introduce and flight-test new missiles without any prior notification to New Delhi, a risk of Indian worst-case assumptions regarding Chinese nuclear intentions and capabilities remains unmitigated.

Moreover, isolated commitments have not yet led to further-reaching arms control or stabilization initiatives, including prospective nuclear force and infrastructural reductions. As India's nuclear force serves to deter China as well as Pakistan, India has rejected Pakistan's proposals for bilateral arms control agreements.[37] China has not participated in the above mechanisms.[38] To attenuate the intensity of the South Asian nuclear and missile rivalry, a greater Chinese commitment to confidence-building and nuclear risk-reduction initiatives is needed.

Pre-notification of missile flight-tests is one useful way to proceed. This forms a viable means to draw China into the nuclear risk-reduction measures that are now increasingly needed in this global intensifying nuclear competition. Moreover, U.S. partnership with India in proposing and developing this protocol could also ensure that this crucial nuclear stability measure is retained from the INF treaty and New START.

The partial reliance on secrecy for the survivability of the Chinese arsenal often leads its diplomats to joining nuclear transparency and confidence-building measures.[39] However, it is worth noting that China has nevertheless agreed to a bilateral accord with Moscow on pre-launch notifications. Beijing and Moscow have committed only to inform each other of flight-tests of ballistic missiles with a 2,000 km-plus range and a trajectory approaching their border.[40] This highlights that the Chinese opposition to joining such regimes is not as firm as is often assumed by policy analysts.[41]

Under the agreement proposed here, the India–Pakistan, China–Russia, and U.S.–Russia agreements would be combined, conformed, and expanded. First, all five member states would commit to pre-notify each other of any ballistic flight-test, regardless of range, at least seventy-two hours before the commencement of the launch window.[42] Second, similar notifications would be required for cruise missiles, a growing element of the nuclear-armed or nuclear-capable forces of all five states. Third, only one missile would be permitted to be launched per test window. This would assist in curtailing the scale of missile testing, including testing on a scale that could be misinterpreted as war preparations or war-fighting. Multiple missile launches could simulate major nuclear or conventional strikes, including the emerging concern of conventional missile attacks upon nuclear forces, command and population centers, and other significant strategic targets. Fourth, in addition to providing notification of the test area, states would also ban missile tests that overfly the land borders of fellow members, and prohibit trajectories and impact zones from entering areas within an agreed minimum distance from these boundaries. This distance could be initially extended to 100 km for both the flight-path and landing zone, further reducing missile threat perceptions and risks of misinterpretation of a launch.

Finally, the New START language prohibiting interference with NTM would be incorporated into this agreement. This would reduce the burden, and the related risk of missing significant missile or nuclear developments, on NTM if they are no longer the sole mechanism for states to monitor and evaluate rival strategic programs. Moreover, it would avert the potential trajectory of interference with NTM becoming a new global norm if New START is allowed to expire. Such an outcome would further heighten the risk of miscalculation in a crisis.

Washington and New Delhi could therefore make such an initiative a new element of their nuclear policy agenda, while engaging the other states toward their entry into this regime. States that remained outside the regime – for example, Beijing – would face the risk of being left to rely upon their NTM alone for understanding adversary nuclear and missile programs. Moreover, Beijing would also not benefit from the general trust-building benefits of regular data-sharing within the regime over time. Finally, this is also in the strategic interests of the U.S. and India, as these are separately determined; both would individually benefit from forming and then potentially further deepening such a multilateral protocol.

The positive effects of this initiative would be amplified by coupling it with the next policy proposal discussed, regarding a joint U.S.–Indian threat assessment of the Chinese missile threat to India. However, both would also serve effectively as stand-alone, independent efforts.

Building Indian resilience against the Chinese missile threat

Chinese, Indian, and international analysts separately assess that China would employ conventional missile strikes in a major conflict with India.[43] Indian defense experts have observed that "The PLA's large number of ballistic and cruise missiles cannot be matched by India, and are the biggest worry for the IAF (Indian Air Force)."[44]

China reportedly has assigned conventional DF-21C ballistic missiles to the regional Da Qaidam, Delingha, and Korla brigades of People's Liberation Army (PLA) Rocket Force (RF) Base 56.[45] It is furthermore probable that all three India-facing Chinese military commands independently host shorter-range missiles intended for Indian targets. The Western Theater Command likely possesses 180-kilometer-range conventional WS-1B multiple rocket launch systems (MRLS). The Tibet Military District (MD) and Xinjiang MD also probably hold 150-kilometer-range conventional PHL-03 MRLS. Moreover, there are over 100 estimated nuclear or nuclear-capable missiles stationed at facilities under PLARF Base 53 and Base 56, as the nearest missile regional control centers to India. Given that China is assessed by external experts to "store most of its nuclear warheads in its central storage facility in the Qinling mountain range, and to a lesser degree at smaller regional storage facilities," there will be relatively few missiles already mated to nuclear warheads, outside of a serious crisis in which Chinese decisionmakers judge that an Indian nuclear attack is imminent.[46] These means that a proportion of these nuclear or nuclear-capable missiles could probably serve conventional missions against India if required to do so in a crisis. Even if this supply were to be exhausted in a conflict against India, further-reaching missile forces stationed under other PLARF Bases further into China's interior could also reach Indian targets.

This is also a rapidly evolving picture. Following the 2017 Doklam crisis, China has moved to further augment its missile capabilities targeting Indian forces. It has emplaced either a WS-2 or WS-3 MRLS, incorporating twelve launcher units, at its regional Duinaxiang army facility. This grants China "sufficient range to target mountain positions of the Indian military near the original conflict zone, as well as the Indian air bases at Bagdogra, Hasimara, and Pakyong."[47]

To strengthen Indian resilience against these platforms, the IAF is constructing hardened air shelters, investing in runway repair kits and related training, constructing a network of advanced landing grounds (ALGs) to diversify possible aircraft hubs and military supply depots, and fielding Brahmos cruise missiles to pre-empt or respond to Chinese missile attacks.[48] However, there are indications that these efforts to survive and respond to a Chinese missile attack are not at the standards of U.S. protocols against a similar overwhelming Chinese missile barrage scenario. A former IAF official has calculated Chinese missile requirements needed to incapacitate the large and growing network of regional IAF base and ALG runways, and has concluded that Indian base officials can repave each runway with quick-drying concrete and ensure it is ready for use six hours after the Chinese missile attack. However, this analysis is based upon available Chinese missile inventories; assumes Chinese intentions to largely eradicate each entire runway, as opposed to only a few "cut points"; and does not provide detail on how this calculation might be affected by the width and depth of the impact craters.[49]

Nevertheless, there are signs that India is improving its resilience against this threat. The IAF is investing in fiberglass runway repair mats, similar to those used by the U.S. military.[50] Using these mats in exercises, the U.S. has been able to theoretically reduce repair times to two to three hours, compared with the six hours estimated in the Indian analysis above.[51] However, the Pentagon's view of more likely runway repair scenarios, reflected in U.S. Air Force (U.S.AF) guidance on these operations, establishes a four-hour repair deadline for crews to be certified as adequately trained.[52] U.S.AF basic runway repair equipment requirements are modelled on the ability to repair three fifty-foot diameter "large craters," with this category implying submunition damage, all within four hours.[53] The modelled repair team includes nineteen different categories of support vehicle, with multiple vehicles in each category. It is also worth noting that this is the U.S. minimum acceptable repair team size against this three-crater, four-hour scenario, and that larger team sizes are specified for repairing higher quantums of damage within four hours.[54]

As the IAF integrates fiberglass repair mats into its runway repair teams, a useful new avenue for U.S.–Indian missile resilience cooperation would be to conduct joint runway repair training exercises. This could then lead to dialogues on potential Indian technology requirements to fulfill the nineteen-vehicle checklist. Moreover, these vehicles, such as bulldozers, pavers, graders, and support trailers, are uncontroversial in terms of a potential NPT Article I violation. In such a way, the U.S. could directly enhance India's resilience against the Chinese missile threat. As such, it would help to elevate India's threshold of nuclear use, which may come under pressure in a crisis in which PLA missiles have successfully destroyed India's regional IAF presence.[55]

This potential U.S.–India cooperation will, however, be most effective if it is part of a broader joint assessment of the Chinese missile threat to India. There are signs that India's intelligence capabilities regarding identifying and evaluating Chinese nuclear and conventional missile threats are lacking. India's intelligence agencies are reportedly heavily focused upon counterterrorism, and reticent regarding interagency data sharing. With the exception of the Military Intelligence agency, Indian intelligence agency recruitment also heavily draws upon the Indian Police Service. The myriad differences between police and intelligence work contribute to the "weak analytical capabilities" identified by Indian and external experts at the Research and Analysis Wing (RAW), the premier foreign intelligence agency.[56] More definite indications of Indian intelligence abilities are provided by the fact that the U.S. had to assist India in obtaining the most accurate intelligence regarding the evolving local situation during the Doklam crisis, and that Indian missile analysts are unable to reliably identify Chinese DF-21 missile locations.[57] A more dedicated program of U.S. intelligence sharing with India regarding the positions and movements of Chinese missiles with likely India-centric missions would reduce the risk of Indian decisionmakers being surprised by an unexpected buildup or major exercise. It would also complement the transparency efforts of the multilateral missile pre-launch notification protocol recommended above.

Strengthening defenses against intelligence and cyber threats to nuclear command-and-control

The risk of cyberattacks against adversary nuclear command-and-control systems is becoming a focal concern in contemporary deterrence and escalation research.[58] Different forms of cyberattack could interfere with significant individual elements of nuclear command-and-control systems, including dual-use entities such as radars and satellites. At a lower level of interference, the adversary state could simply penetrate these or other systems to monitor secret official decisionmaking processes during a crisis, toward ensuring advance warning of crisis decisions and their potential military implications. Finally, a still lower level involves obtaining secret information on the operation – and vulnerabilities – of nuclear systems and those relevant to their protection. Of course, gaining an accurate intelligence picture at this lowest level – which Futter terms "cyber-nuclear espionage" – can open the door to penetration and interference at these higher levels.

There is also the continuing challenge of intelligence operations to acquire this information through an intermediary source, rather than directly hacking into adversary systems. Chinese intelligence activities in this regard, as directed against the U.S., have been a longstanding challenge for the integrity of U.S. nuclear and supporting systems. Recent U.S. cases that have come to public light include Chinese efforts, often through a U.S.-based intermediary, to acquire technologies and secret information, including those for nuclear weapon design; military communications equipment and National Security Agency (NSA) encryption systems; missile engine and guidance systems; "a low signature-infrared-suppressing exhaust system for cruise missiles"; missile target acquisition systems; early warning radars; the F-35 fighter; small modular reactor systems for submarines; and pressure transducers (which can be used in nuclear enrichment centrifuge cascades).[59] In addition, a case of cyber-nuclear espionage occurred in 2005, in which PLA-affiliated hackers acquired "highly sensitive information relating to missile navigation, submarines, and other strategic weapons systems" from Department of Defense systems.[60]

Chinese intelligence services tend to largely rely upon recruiting Chinese nationals, Chinese-Americans, or other individuals with Chinese backgrounds as their sources.[61] This means that there is a greater propensity of these recruits in the U.S., as compared to India, where there are only "a small number of Chinese expatriates."[62] This means that Chinese intelligence must rely more upon direct hacking, as opposed to using local sources, to obtain similar technologies and information from India.[63]

India has evidenced persistent cybersecurity vulnerabilities against such Chinese hacking efforts. In 2017, Chinese hackers accessed India's "most sophisticated and secret link" over which a "high-profile government meeting involving video chat via satellite" was being actively conducted.[64] Chinese hackers reportedly attempted to obtain classified information held at Indian Eastern Naval Command computers at the Visakhapatnam base in 2012. This same base hosts the *Arihant* nuclear-armed submarine.[65] In 2009, Chinese hackers penetrated computers within the Prime Minister's Office, which is the locus of Indian national security decisionmaking. Targets included systems used by the National Security Advisor, Deputy National Security Advisor, Cabinet Secretary, and twenty-seven other officials.[66] This followed similar successful penetrations of National Security Council and Ministry of External Affairs international communications systems in 2007.[67]

While there is little from the above incidents that indicates Chinese intentions to specifically target Indian nuclear systems in their espionage operations, this point comes with two caveats. Firstly, these are only the cases that are publicly reported, meaning there are likely more incidents that have not come to public light. Secondly, in repeatedly demonstrating their ability to access live high-level policy discussions, and reach the computer systems of senior nuclear policymakers such as the National Security Advisor, Beijing's cyber teams are proving that they could launch a nuclear-focused hacking operation if they so wished.

The difficulties that India faces regarding securing its sensitive national security – and potentially nuclear-related – systems from Chinese cyber espionage form an area of shared concern with the U.S. Indeed, New Delhi and Washington both have to continually assess the threat of a Chinese cyberattack to incapacitate their nuclear weapons systems in a crisis, and their cyber resilience in this scenario. Such a cyberattack would be termed "left-of-launch," in which the nuclear weapon and delivery vehicle are immobilized before launching, due to cyber interference.[68] As such, the third pillar of U.S.–India nuclear stability cooperation in this decaying nuclear order is to jointly study the Chinese cyber threat to critical Indian systems, and assist New Delhi in devising stronger defenses.

However, there are likely Indian concerns with this proposal that may hinder or even preclude such cooperation. Potential Indian disclosure of its areas of greatest cybersecurity need – and thus most significant cyber vulnerabilities – to the U.S. could be viewed within New Delhi as granting Washington its own cyber pathway into "left-of-launch" operations against India. This scenario of the U.S. incapacitating Indian nuclear systems could occur, for example, if a major war with Pakistan was assessed by Washington to be reaching a stage where nuclear use appeared imminent.

Nevertheless, these concerns can be addressed through careful organization of the nature of these cybersecurity dialogues. RAW and Intelligence Bureau officials regularly interact and meet with the Central Intelligence Agency for dialogues.[69] This process could be developed to include members of other related national agencies, such as the U.S. Cyber Command and NSA in the U.S., and the National Technical Research Organization, the National Cyber Coordination Centre, and the National Security Council Secretariat.[70] Cybersecurity officials from U.S. Strategic Command and the Indian Strategic Forces Command could assist in generating more focused nuclear security dialogues. To avert the Indian concern of the U.S. utilizing this interaction to aid its own potential hacking of Indian nuclear forces, U.S. officials could follow the model of the briefing on the Patriot Advanced Capability-III (PAC-III) air and missile defense system that they provided to their Indian counterparts in 2005. The U.S. team supplied a comprehensive briefing on PAC-II roles and performance, with Indian officials able to then ask questions, without necessarily being pressed by U.S. officials on how vulnerable to air and missile attacks India truly was.[71]

Following a similar approach for this context would involve a presentation by U.S. officials on the forms of Chinese cyberattacks and cyber-nuclear espionage that are persistent and relatively new threats to the U.S. U.S. procedures for detecting and blocking, and attribution of these specific cyber actions would then be covered, before opening the session to Indian questions. Such a process could lead to close U.S.–India cooperation on cybersecurity related to their nuclear systems, but it could equally end at this presentational stage. However, even if the latter were to be the case, the Indian officials would leave with a better understanding of the kinds of potential cyberdefenses against specific challenges that New Delhi is facing. They could then proceed to develop these defensive cybertools within India. If this dialogue were instead to be successful and enter additional and more detailed rounds, the conversation could potentially turn toward offensive cyberweapons against Chinese systems, and potential technology sharing or collaboration toward this end.

This third line of effort would therefore improve Indian cyber resilience against dedicated and continuing Chinese efforts to hack its most sensitive defense systems, including potentially those relevant to Indian nuclear forces. The greater integrity of these systems from Chinese penetration efforts that India would enjoy could help to improve Indian confidence in the electronic surety of its arsenal and supportive communications, logistics, and targeting systems.

This would also serve as another avenue for the U.S. and India to collaborate on nuclear stability promotion. This proposed dialogue, and the potential technical cooperation that could arise from it, would reduce the extent to which sustained Chinese cyberattacks could erode the confidence of Indian policymakers in the continuing survival of its nuclear forces. Such a loss of confidence could place Indian decisionmakers under severe pressure to threaten use of or to use nuclear weapons in order to save them, as under the classical inadvertent escalation model developed by Posen.[72]

Conclusion: building nuclear stability in a decaying nuclear order

This chapter has detailed three areas of potential bilateral cooperation to stabilize nuclear deterrence in a world where "the protocols and understandings that helped avert Armageddon during the cold war have not been renewed."[73] These consist, firstly, of a multilateral missile flight-test pre-notification agreement, including China, India, Pakistan, Russia, and the U.S. Secondly, a joint threat assessment of the Chinese missile threat to regional IAF bases and airfields, leading to potential technical cooperation toward improving India's rapid runway repair capabilities. Given the importance of this regional military air network to not just the IAF but also Indian Army operations, assuring its resilience against a Chinese conventional missile barrage is a paramount priority. If Chinese missiles succeed in overcoming runway repair operations and the air network, Indian policymakers will come under severe pressure to revisit the no-first-use pledge – even if in the form of a solely verbal retraction – in order to assure India's territorial integrity.[74] The third initiative focuses upon U.S. cooperation with India to improve its defenses against Chinese cyber-nuclear espionage and potential interference against Indian sensitive defense systems. Enhancing India's ability to ensure the cybersecurity of these systems will reduce the risk of a successful Chinese cyberattack during a crisis, which would pressure Indian decisionmakers to escalate the conflict and begin thinking about utilizing the nuclear systems that have not yet been targeted.

Each of these policy initiatives aims to bolster regional and thus global nuclear stability, and can be pursued individually or together. They are designed to form feasible pathways for the U.S. and India to work together in reducing the risk of accidental nuclear war, while still constituting forms of military nuclear cooperation that do not constitute proliferation or NPT violations. Each promotes a high Indian nuclear threshold – including through a crisis – through augmenting the trust and transparency regarding adversary nuclear and missile intentions, as well as improving the survivability of its conventional forces and defense systems. Together, these initiatives would reduce the likelihood of scenarios in which Indian policymakers are beginning to consider their nuclear options in light of what they perceive to be dangerous kinetic and/or cyber erosion, or even destruction, of India's regional conventional military posture and some elements of its nuclear systems. This scenario could in itself arise from a surprise Chinese missile attack, aided by gaps in India's NTM missile monitoring capabilities, and the inability of U.S. NTM satellites to cover these gaps for India due to a higher national demand on these satellites, and potential adversary interference against them, in a post-New START world. As New Delhi and Washington both confront this declining nuclear order, they can therefore seize these opportunities to augment Indian defenses necessary for its no-first-use policy to be retained in a crisis. Simultaneously, they can also aim to reduce the global dangers of strategic miscalculation and adversary NTM interference through leading in developing the missile flight-test pre-notification agreement.

Notes

1. See, for example, G. Perkovich, "The brittle nuclear order," Carnegie Endowment for International Peace, December 18, 2017, https://carnegieendowment.org/2017/12/18/brittle-nuclear-order-pub-75057; B. Tertrais, "Saving the NPT: Past and future non-proliferation bargains," Nonproliferation Policy Education Center, January 25, 2005, www.npolicy.org/article.php?aid=219&tid=4; and L. P. Bloomfield, "Nuclear spread and world order," *Foreign Affairs*, 53:4 (1975), 743–55.
2. U.S. State Department, "U.S. withdrawal from the INF Treaty on August 2, 2019 (Press statement)," August 2, 2019, www.state.gov/u-s-withdrawal-from-the-inf-treaty-on-august-2-2019/. For the full text and associated memoranda of the INF Treaty, see "Intermediate-range nuclear forces (INF) texts," Federation of American Scientists, April 15, 1998, https://fas.org/nuke/control/inf/text/index.html.
3. T. Balmforth, "Russia says it's already too late to replace new START treaty," *Reuters*, November 1, 2019, www.reuters.com/article/us-russia-usa-missiles/russia-says-its-already-too-late-to-replace-new-start-treaty-idU.S.KBN1XB3NR.
4. M. P. Gleason and L. H. Riesbeck, *Noninterference with national technical means: The status quo will not survive* (El Segundo, CA: Aerospace Corporation, 2020), https://aerospace.org/sites/default/files/2020–01/Gleason_NTM_20200114.pdf; P. Vaddi, "Bringing Russia's new nuclear weapons into New START," *Lawfare*, August 13, 2019, www.lawfareblog.com/bringing-russias-new-nuclear-weapons-new-start.
5. U.S. White House, *National security strategy of the United States of America*, December 2017, www.whitehouse.gov/wp-content/uploads/2017/12/NSS-Final-12–18–2017–0905.pdf, p. 31. The language on arms control in this document reads, in total: "We will consider new arms control arrangements if they contribute to strategic stability and if they are verifiable." This phrasing implies that the U.S. is willing to consider arms control initiatives proposed by other states, but will not lead in proposing its own initiatives. In addition, the brevity of this language, in the longest National Security Strategy yet produced, further strongly implies Trump administration skepticism of the value of promoting and sustaining arms control agreements to U.S. national interests and security.
6. U.S. Department of Defense, *Nuclear Posture Review 2018*, https://media.defense.gov/2018/Feb/02/2001872886/-1/-1/1/2018-NUCLEAR-POSTURE-REVIEW-FINAL-REPORT.PDF, p. xii.
7. U.S. Joint Chiefs of Staff, *Joint Publication 3-72: Nuclear Operations*, June 11, 2019, https://fas.org/irp/doddir/dod/jp3_72.pdf, viii, III-2–III-4.
8. *Ibid.*, p. x.
9. H. Kristensen and M. Korda, "Russian nuclear forces, 2019," *Bulletin of the Atomic Scientists*, 75:2 (2019), 73–84; O. Oliker, "Moscow's nuclear enigma," *Foreign Affairs*, 97:6 (2018), 52–7; K. Zysk, "Escalation and nuclear weapons in Russia's military strategy," *RUSI Journal*, 163:2 (2018), 4–15.

10 Zysk, "Escalation," 8–10.
11 Kristensen and Korda, "Russian nuclear forces," 76.
12 M. Natalucci, "Russia completes testing of 'Poseidon' thermonuclear torpedo," *Jane's Defence Weekly*, February 19, 2019.
13 M. Vranic and S. O'Connor, "Analysis: What was behind the blast near Nenoksa?" *Jane's Defence Weekly*, August 15, 2019.
14 M. Anis, "No first use of N-weapons not policy: DG ISPR," *The News International*, September 5, 2019, www.thenews.com.pk/print/522403-no-first-use-of-n-weapons-not-policy-dg-ispr; F. O'Donnell and Y. Joshi, *India and nuclear Asia: Forces, doctrine, and dangers* (Washington, D.C.: Georgetown University Press, 2018), 51–80.
15 Press Information Bureau, Government of India, "Raksha Mantri Shri Rajnath Singh Pays Homage to Former Prime Minister Atal Bihari Vajpayee in Pokhran on his First Death Anniversary," August 16, 2019, https://pib.gov.in/Pressreleaseshare.aspx?PRID=1582158.
16 For background on these developments, see F. O'Donnell, "India's nuclear counter-revolution: Nuclear learning and the future of deterrence," *Nonproliferation Review*, forthcoming, 26:5–6 (2020). I am grateful to Vipin Narang for suggesting Israel's ambiguous nuclear doctrine as a potential model for understanding India's evolving nuclear doctrine in light of the Defence Minister's 2019 statement. This Israeli doctrine has been described as "Israel would not be the first to introduce nuclear weapons into the Middle East, but neither would she be second." See A. Dowty, "Nuclear proliferation: The Israeli case," *International Studies Quarterly*, 22:1 (1978), 83.
17 See C. Clary and V. Narang, "India's counterforce temptations: Strategic dilemmas, doctrine, and capabilities," *International Security*, 43:3 (2018/19), 7–52; F. O'Donnell and D. Ghoshal, "Managing Indian deterrence: Pressures upon credible minimum deterrence and nuclear policy options," *Nonproliferation Review*, 26:1–2 (2019), 419–36.
18 For the most recent official restatement of China's NFU policy, see section II, "China's defensive national defense policy in the new era," of its 2019 defense white paper, "China's national defense in the new era," available at Lu Hui, "Full text: China's national defense in the new era," *Xinhua*, July 24, 2019, www.xinhuanet.com/english/2019-07/24/c_138253389.htm. For assessments that China ceased fissile material production in the 1980s, see Hui Zhang, *China's fissile material production and stockpile* (Princeton, NJ: International Panel on Fissile Materials, 2017), pp. 2–3; and G. Kulacki, "China's nuclear arsenal: Status and evolution," Union of Concerned Scientists, May 2011, www.ieim.uqam.ca/IMG/pdf/ucs-chinese-nuclear-modernization.pdf, p. 1.
19 F. S. Cunningham and M. T. Fravel, "Dangerous confidence? Chinese views on nuclear escalation," *International Security*, 44:2 (2019), 61–109.
20 Author interview with Chinese scholar, Beijing, January 29, 2018.
21 O'Donnell and Joshi, *India and Nuclear Asia*, pp. 110–12.
22 U. Ansari, "Pakistani naval modernization appears stalled," *Defense News*, January 15, 2016, www.defensenews.com/global/asia-pacific/2016/01/15/paki

stani-naval-modernization-appears-stalled/; "Pakistan PM approves deal to buy eight Chinese submarines: Official," *Reuters*, April 2, 2015, www.reuters.com/article/us-china-pakistan/pakistan-pm-approves-deal-to-buy-eight-chinese-submarines-official-idU.S.KBN0MT05M20150402.

23 E. Heginbotham, M. Nixon, F. E. Morgan, J. L. Heim, J. Hagen, Sheng Li, J. Engstrom, M. C. Libicki, P. DeLuca, D. A. Shlapak, D. R. Frelinger, B. Laird, K. Brady, and L. J. Morris, *The U.S.–China military scorecard: Forces, geography, and the evolving balance of power, 1996–2017* (Santa Monica, CA: RAND Corporation, 2015), p. 51.

24 A. D. Chekov, A. V. Makarycheva, A. M. Solomentseva, M. A. Suchkov, and A. A. Sushentsov, "War of the future: A view from Russia," *Survival*, 61:6 (2018), 39.

25 P. Sawhney and G. Wahab, *Dragon on our doorstep: Managing China through military power* (New Delhi: Aleph, 2017), p. 83.

26 V. Mohan, "Fiberglass mats for quick runway repairs," *Tribune*, February 3, 2019, www.tribuneindia.com/news/nation/fiberglass-mats-for-quick-runway-repairs/722957.html; R. Bedi, "Indian Air Force to build 108 new hangars," *Jane's Defence Weekly*, January 7, 2019; F. O'Donnell, *Stabilizing Sino-Indian security relations: Managing the strategic rivalry after Doklam* (Beijing: Carnegie-Tsinghua Center for Global Policy, 2018), https://carnegieendowment.org/files/CP335_ODonnell_final.pdf, pp. 6, 16.

27 B. S. Nagal, "India's nuclear doctrine and strategy," in A. K. Singh and B. S. Nagal (eds), *Military strategy for India in the 21st century* (New Delhi: Centre for Land Warfare Studies and KW Publishers, 2019), pp. 195–224.

28 As a nuclear weapon state under the terms of the NPT, Article I of the treaty commits the U.S. "not to transfer to any recipient whatsoever nuclear weapons or other nuclear explosive devices or control over such weapons or explosive devices directly, or indirectly; and not in any way to assist, encourage, or induce any non-nuclear-weapon State to manufacture or otherwise acquire nuclear weapons or other nuclear explosive devices, or control over such weapons or explosive devices." See International Atomic Energy Agency, *Information circular 140 – treaty on the non-proliferation of nuclear weapons (notification of the entry into force)*, April 22, 1970, www.iaea.org/sites/default/files/publications/documents/infcircs/1970/infcirc140.pdf, Article I.

29 This section draws significantly from and reproduces elements of F. O'Donnell, "Launch an expanded missile flight-test notification regime," in M. Krepon, T. Wheeler and L. Dowling (eds) *Off ramps from confrontation in Southern Asia* (Washington, D.C.: Stimson Center, 2019), www.stimson.org/sites/default/files/file-attachments/OffRamps_Book_R5_WEB.pdf, 14–23. The author has secured permission from the Stimson Center to reproduce and republish this essay and its elements, with appropriate attribution as above.

30 See "Intermediate-range nuclear forces (INF) texts," Federation of American Scientists, April 15, 1998, https://fas.org/nuke/control/inf/text/index.html.

31 For the text and associated protocols and memoranda of the 1991 START treaty, see "START-1 strategic arms reduction talks," Federation of American

Scientists, December 23, 1998, https://fas.org/nuke/control/start1/text/index.html. For the text of the 1998 missile launch pre-notification agreement, see U.S. State Department, *Agreement between the United States of America and Union of Soviet Socialist Republics on notifications of launches of intercontinental ballistic missiles and submarine-launched ballistic missiles (ballistic missile launch notification agreement)*, May 31, 1988, www.state.gov/t/isn/4714.htm.

32 U.S. Department of Defense, "Section IV. Notifications concerning launches of ICBMs or SLBMs, and the exchange of telemetric information, in Part four – notifications, Protocol to New START treaty," www.acq.osd.mil/tc/nst/protocol/NSTprotocolPartFour.htm.

33 Gleason and Riesbeck, *Noninterference with national technical means*, pp. 7–9.

34 Government of the Republic of India and Government of the Islamic Republic of Pakistan, *Agreement on reducing the risk from accidents relating to nuclear weapons*, February 21, 2007, www.stimson.org/agreement-on-reducing-the-risk-from-accidents-relating-to-nuclear-weap; *Agreement on pre-notification of flight testing of ballistic missiles*, October 3, 2005, http://mea.gov.in/Portal/LegalTreatiesDoc/PA05B0591.pdf; *Agreement on the prohibition of attack against nuclear installations and facilities*, December 31, 1988, https://media.nti.org/documents/india_pakistan_non_attack_agreement.pdf; and *Agreement on advance notice on military exercises, manoeuvres and troop movements*, April 6, 1991, https://treaties.un.org/doc/publication/unts/volume%201843/volume-1843-i-31420-english.pdf.

35 Government of the Republic of India and Government of the Islamic Republic of Pakistan, *Agreement on pre-notification of flight testing of ballistic missiles*.

36 A. S. Erickson, A. M. Denmark, and G. Collins, "Beijing's 'starter carrier' and future steps: Alternatives and implications", *Naval War College Review*, 65:1 (2012), 41–2.

37 Z. N. Jaspal, *Arms control: Risk reduction measures between India and Pakistan (SASSU research paper No. 1)* (Bradford, UK: South Asian Strategic Stability Unit, University of Bradford, 2005), www.files.ethz.ch/isn/99910/RP%20No%2001.pdf, p. 8.

38 Tong Zhao, "The time is ripe for a China–India nuclear dialogue," Carnegie-Tsinghua Center for Global Policy, March 17, 2016, https://carnegietsinghua.org/2016/03/17/time-is-ripe-for-china-india-nuclear-dialogue-pub-64283.

39 A. Berger, *The P-5 nuclear dialogue: Five years on* (London: Royal United Services Institute, 2014), pp. 11–12; G. Kulacki, "Chickens talking with ducks: The U.S.–Chinese nuclear dialogue," *Arms Control Today*, October 2011, www.armscontrol.org/act/2011_10/U.S._Chinese_Nuclear_Dialogue.

40 P. Podvig, "Russia and China to exchange launch notifications", October 21, 2010, http://russianforces.org/blog/2010/10/russia_and_china_to_exchange_l.shtml; L. Champlin, "China, Russia agree on launch notification," *Arms Control Today*, November 2009, www.armscontrol.org/act/2009_11/ChinaRussia.

41 See, for example, Li Bin, "Appendix 3A. China and nuclear transparency," in N. Zarimpas (ed.), *Transparency in nuclear warheads and materials: The*

political and technical dimensions (Oxford: Stockholm International Peace Research Institute and Oxford University Press, 2003), www.sipri.org/sites/default/files/files/books/SIPRI03Zarimpas/SIPRI03Zarimpas.pdf, pp. 50–7.

42 This new regime would not affect the missile bans in place under the existing U.S.–Russia arms control agreements.

43 K. McCauley, "Himalayan impasse: How China would fight an Indian border conflict," *Jamestown Foundation China Brief*, 17:2 (2017), https://jamestown.org/program/himalayan-impasse-how-china-would-fight-an-indianborder-conflict/; M. Chan, "China and India on brink of armed conflict as hopes of resolution to border dispute fade," *South China Morning Post*, August 11, 2017, www.scmp.com/news/china/diplomacy-defence/article/2106493/chinaand-india-brink-armed-conflict-hopes-resolution; D. S. Rana, "The current Chinese defence reforms and impact on India" (Manekshaw paper no. 65), Center for Land Warfare Studies, 2017, www.claws.in/images/publication_pdf/2089301056_MP65-Rana(1).pdf, pp. 30–1; O'Donnell, *Stabilizing Sino-Indian security relations*, p. 16; and author interview and correspondence with a long-time analyst of China's military, November 2017.

44 Sawhney and Wahab, *Dragon on our doorstep*, p. 83; O'Donnell, *Stabilizing Sino-Indian security relations*, p. 16.

45 This paragraph significantly draws upon O'Donnell, *Stabilizing Sino-Indian security relations*, pp. 14–16.

46 H. M. Kristensen and M. Korda, "Chinese nuclear forces, 2019," *Bulletin of the Atomic Scientists*, 75:4 (2019), 172.

47 Andy Dinville, "China and India adjust force posture in Doklam region," *Jane's Intelligence Review*, June 7, 2019.

48 Mohan, "Fiberglass mats"; Bedi, "Indian Air Force to build 108 new hangars," O'Donnell, *Stabilizing Sino-Indian security relations*, pp. 6, 16.

49 Ravinder Chhatwal, *The Chinese air threat: Understanding the reality* (New Delhi: KW Publishers, 2016), p. 186. For a description of "cut points" or "aim points," see Heginbotham et al., *U.S.–China military scorecard*, pp. 56–8.

50 Mohan, "Fiberglass mats."

51 For runway repair times using fiberglass mats in U.S. military exercises, see C. Yepez, "Afghanistan-bound seabees practice runway repair," U.S. Navy, Naval Mobile Construction Battalion 3, February 9, 2007, https://web.archive.org/web/20070213020823/www.news.navy.mil/search/display.asp?story_id=27704; and L. Walsh, "Airmen ready to rapidly repair runways," U.S. Air Force, 96th Air Base Wing Public Affairs, March 17, 2005, www.af.mil/News/Article-Display/Article/134809/airmen-ready-to-rapidly-repair-runways/.

52 U.S. Air Force, *Airfield Damage Repair Operations (Air Force Pamphlet 10–219, Vol. 4)*, May 28, 2008 (Incorporating Change 1, August 13, 2015), https://static.e-publishing.af.mil/production/1/af_a4/publication/afpam10-219v4/afpam10-219v4.pdf, p. 83.

53 Ibid., p. 55.

54 Ibid., pp. 122–4.

55 O'Donnell and Joshi, *India and Nuclear Asia*, pp. 97–103.

56 For the specific "weak analytical capabilities" quotation, see Jayshree Bajoria, "RAW: India's external intelligence agency," Council on Foreign Relations, November 7, 2008, www.cfr.org/backgrounder/raw-indias-external-intelligence-agency. See also Chapters 11 and 12 on intelligence cooperation in this volume, and Nicolas Groffman, "Indian and Chinese espionage," *Defense & Security Analysis*, 32:2 (2016), 156.
57 For the point regarding Indian DF-21 location capabilities, see Groffman, "Indian and Chinese espionage," 156. For the point regarding U.S. intelligence assistance to India during the Doklam crisis, see Chapter 11 in this volume.
58 See for example A. Futter, *Hacking the bomb: Cyber threats and nuclear weapons* (Washington, D.C.: Georgetown University Press, 2018); J. M. Acton, "Escalation through entanglement: How vulnerability of command-and-control systems raises the risks of an inadvertent nuclear war," *International Security*, 43:1 (2018), 56–99; and C. Talmadge, "Would China go nuclear? Assessing the risk of Chinese nuclear escalation in a conventional war with the United States," *International Security*, 41:4 (2017), 50–92.
59 P. Mattis and M. Brazil, *Chinese Communist espionage: An intelligence primer* (Annapolis, MD: U.S. Naval Institute Press, 2019), pp. 148, 155, 157, 159, 162–5, 168–9, 174, 192.
60 Futter, *Hacking the bomb*, p. 62.
61 W. Colson and P. Mattis, "Understanding China's intelligence services," CogitAsia podcast, Center for Strategic and International Studies, July 19, 2016, www.csis.org/podcasts/cogitasia-podcast/understanding-china's-intelligence-services; Groffman, "Indian and Chinese espionage," 148.
62 Groffman, "Indian and Chinese espionage," 148.
63 *Ibid.*, 148.
64 Yatish Yadav, "Hackers from China break into secret Indian government video chat," *The New Indian Express*, November 19, 2017, www.newindianexpress.com/nation/2017/nov/19/hackers-from-china-break-into-secret-indian-government-video-chat-1705010.html.
65 Futter, *Hacking the bomb*, 63–4.
66 Ashish Khetan, "Chinese hackers target PMO," *India Today*, January 14, 2010, www.indiatoday.in/latest-headlines/story/chinese-hackers-target-pmo-65017-2010-01-14.
67 "Chinese hack PMO's mail," *Times of India*, December 8, 2008, https://timesofindia.indiatimes.com/tech-news/Chinese-hack-PMOs-mail/articleshow/3808513.cms.
68 See A. Futter, "The dangers of using cyberattacks to counter nuclear threats," *Arms Control Today* (July/August 2016), www.armscontrol.org/act/2016-07/features/dangers-using-cyberattacks-counter-nuclear-threats.
69 See the chapter on intelligence cooperation by S. Datta in this volume.
70 M. Hathaway, C. Demchak, J. Kerban, J. McArdle, and F. Spidalieri, *India cyber readiness at a glance* (Arlington, VA: Potomac Institute for Policy Studies, 2016), www.potomacinstitute.org/images/CRI/CRI_India_Profile.pdf, 18–20.

71 H. V. Pant, "India debates missile defense," *Defence Studies*, 5:2 (2005), 233–8.
72 B. R. Posen, *Inadvertent escalation: Conventional war and nuclear risks* (Ithaca, NY: Cornell University Press, 1992).
73 M. Symonds, "The future of war," *The Economist*, January 25, 2018, www.economist.com/special-report/2018/01/25/the-future-of-war.
74 See A. Ahmed, "A consideration of Sino-Indian conflict (IDSA issue brief)," Institute for Defense Studies and Analyses, October 24, 2011, www.files.ethz.ch/isn/135486/IB_AConsiderationofSino-IndianConflict.pdf, 6–7.

6

Enhancing nuclear stability in South Asia: the view from New Delhi

Rajesh Rajagopalan

Two decades after the Indian and Pakistani nuclear tests, international concern about nuclear stability in the region has subsided significantly. Early concerns about a nuclear arms race in the region and resultant instability, as well as expectations about nuclear escalation, have largely been shown to be unfounded. Both India and Pakistan have continued to expand their nuclear arsenals, but at a measured pace. And though there is an action–reaction dynamic even in nuclear arms between the two sides, it has been fairly limited. There is also continuing military confrontation between the two sides which occasionally flares up into serious crises, but the several crises have demonstrated both strict political control and little tendency towards rapid escalation or escalation to the nuclear level. While there is always room for improvement – and the presence of nuclear weapons does introduce an irreducible measure of risk – the fear of a region on the brink of nuclear escalation is no longer a serious policy issue for most capitals in the world, and definitely not Washington. There is some continuing concern in the scholarly community about the dangerous consequences of a nuclear war in the region.[1] There has also been worry about the possibility that India's nuclear doctrine is shifting towards counterforce, though this has been disputed by Indian analysts.[2] In any case, it is unclear that the U.S. government considers this an issue to be negotiated with India. Other matters have eclipsed the nuclear instability problem: the U.S. and India are now partners, along with many other U.S. allies and partners, in managing the consequences of China's rise in Asia. This does appear to outweigh or at least mute concerns about nuclear stability in the region.

Thus, cooperation between the U.S. and India on nuclear stability in the region remains fairly low, and there is little prospect that it will improve dramatically in the near future. There is some shared anxiety about the problem of "loose nukes," specifically as it relates to Pakistan and its use of terrorism as state strategy, but little beyond. In addition, there are also some common worries about Pakistan's dependence on tactical nuclear weapons

(TNWs) and early nuclear escalation strategy. But it is unclear that these can lead to any viable cooperation between the two sides.

Current state of cooperation on nuclear stability

There has been only quite minor cooperation between the U.S. and India on enhancing nuclear stability, primarily having to do with nuclear security, and even this has reduced somewhat. In conceptual terms, "stability" between nuclear powers can be a function of three related concerns: strategic stability, crisis stability and arms-race stability. Strategic stability exists when neither side wants to start a nuclear war because both sides are confident that both have a secure second-strike capability.[3] Crisis stability is a condition where neither side has to fear pre-emptive attacks in a crisis. Arms-race stability refers to the confidence that both sides have that the other side will not develop capabilities that could threaten strategic or crisis stability. The U.S. and India disagree on how to judge the status of nuclear stability, with the U.S. worrying about strategic stability and particularly crisis stability. India, on the other hand, largely does not appear to be bothered about nuclear stability at all, reserving its concerns primarily for conventional and sub-conventional stability.

Washington and New Delhi have differed about both the intensity of nuclear instability in the region and its sources. Well before India and Pakistan became overt nuclear powers, the U.S. has worried about the possibility that the two countries could get into a conventional war that quickly escalated to the nuclear level. Such apprehensions drove the first major U.S. nuclear stability management effort, which happened during what is characterized as the 1990 Kashmir "compound" crisis.[4] This crisis also demonstrated a pattern that will recur in subsequent crises: a significant difference between the two sides about the danger of nuclear escalation in the region. The 1990 crisis was driven by the heightening tension between India and Pakistan over Kashmir. Though Kashmir was disputed between the two sides, and they had already fought two wars over the territory, the issue had more or less been quiescent since the 1971 India–Pakistan war, in which Indian intervention led to the eastern wing of Pakistan breaking away and becoming Bangladesh. But a rebellion had broken out in Indian-held Kashmir, which quickly led to Pakistani involvement in the form of support to the rebels.[5] This led to tensions between the two sides, which rapidly led to fears that the two sides would once again come to blows over the territory. What made the crisis much more serious, from Washington's perspective, was that the U.S. believed that the two sides now also had some level of rudimentary nuclear weapons capability. The U.S. feared that if the tensions escalated to open war, it could lead to further escalation and the potential use of nuclear weapons. So concerned was the U.S. that it dispatched a team of senior U.S. officials, led by National Security Advisor Robert Gates, to India and Pakistan to mediate. But neither India nor Pakistan appeared to think that nuclear escalation was a serious threat, though both sides were appreciative of American diplomacy in helping them unwind from the developing confrontation. This would change subsequently, at least in Pakistan's case, as it explicitly sought to use international, and specifically American, intervention, as a "catalytic" strategy.[6] This meant that Pakistan would explicitly use a strategy of threatening nuclear escalation both to constrain India's superior conventional military power and to garner international intervention in the Kashmir dispute. This became the unwritten Pakistani nuclear doctrine: because of the presumed Indian conventional military superiority, Pakistan was prepared to use nuclear weapons first and – it hinted – early if Indian forces entered Pakistan's territory. Indeed, early statements suggested that Pakistan will escalate to the nuclear level even without an Indian military attack, for other anti-Pakistan actions.

Pakistan's nuclear escalation threat added to existing U.S. concerns that a military confrontation between India and Pakistan could get out of hand, and it led to American efforts to enhance nuclear stability in the subcontinent. At the broadest level, New Delhi agreed with such concerns, and it was agreeable to discussing directly with Pakistan ways to ameliorate these threats. For example, at the India–Pakistan summit in Lahore in early 1999, just a few months after the two countries conducted their nuclear tests and declared themselves nuclear powers, Indian Prime Minister Atal Behari Vajpayee and Pakistan's Prime Minister Nawaz Sharif agreed to "take immediate steps for reducing the risk of accidental or unauthorized use of nuclear weapons and discuss concepts and doctrines with a view to elaborating measures for confidence building in the nuclear and conventional fields, aimed at prevention of conflict."[7] This initiative did not make any progress because the Kargil war intruded. On the other hand, India's concern about nuclear stability in the region could not become the basis of any cooperation with the U.S. because the two countries disagreed on the source of the escalation threat in the region. For New Delhi, as discussed at greater length later, this resulted primarily from Pakistan's support for terrorism as a strategy against India.[8] Terrorist attacks in India, from groups sponsored or protected by the Pakistani state, led to repeated crises between the two sides and this became a key focus of India's foreign policy. An additional source of nuclear escalation threat was Pakistan's dangerous first use nuclear doctrine, which raised the fears that these crises could escalate.[9] Thus, New Delhi repeatedly focused on these two issues and wanted international action, led by the U.S., to focus on these particular sources of threat. For Washington, on the other hand, the nuclear escalation danger came from a much more general source: the presence of nuclear weapons themselves and the unsettled state of relations between the two sides. But, on the other hand, by the early 2000s, U.S. policy was also becoming increasingly pragmatic about its own capacity to resolve the basic nuclear escalation threat in the region. This was the result of at least two developments: first, Washington's relations with the two countries, which had improved simultaneously, and were no longer hyphenated, at least from the U.S. perspective. Thus, U.S.–India relations improved as both overcame the legacy of 1998 and looked forward to strategic cooperation against China. This was to no small extent also the consequence of the Bush administration's view that proliferation per se was not bad, only proliferation to certain actors was. In addition, the Bush administration at least had much more of a 'balance of power' perspective and saw China's rise as a serious longer-term problem, one which the U.S. needed to counter in cooperation with India. Similarly, U.S.–Pakistan relations improved because Pakistan did a U-turn on its support for the Taliban regime in Afghanistan and became part of the U.S. global war on terror. Second, the U.S. also became much more pragmatic about what it could do regarding the nuclear issue. It accepted, at least de facto, that India and Pakistan were nuclear powers. Washington gave up on its 1990s focus on "cap, freeze and roll-back" of the Indian and Pakistani nuclear weapons programs and looked for ways to live with the two nuclear powers in the region.[10] The U.S. appeared now to accept that nuclear stability was much more a question of how India and Pakistan built their nuclear arsenals rather than from the presence of nuclear weapons in the region itself.[11] Thus, the focus shifted to the Indian nuclear doctrine, which in its "draft" form called for the development of a nuclear triad. Washington saw this as potentially problematic, because it appeared to suggest an open-ended and vast Indian nuclear weapons program, and sought to engage with India to moderate the weapons program. Even this American objective appeared to become less important by the early 2000s, after the Bush administration took over.

On the other hand, the Indian perspective on nuclear stability was to focus on Pakistani behavior, both its support for terrorism and its role in transferring nuclear technology to other countries, as the primary source of threat.[12] As then External Affairs Minister Pranab Mukherjee said, "the security challenges of terrorism and nuclear proliferation are inter-linked and the international community must take immediate steps to cut supply links of WMDs [weapons of mass destruction] to terrorists."[13] As for solutions, India was clearly much more comfortable dealing with larger global issues such as the Fissile Material Cut-Off Treaty and a push for global nuclear disarmament. India has repeatedly called for measures such as Global No-First Use and de-alerting of strategic weapons as a way of enhancing nuclear stability.[14] There was thus a clear gap between the U.S. and India when it came to understanding both the sources of nuclear instability in the region and what could be done about it. The only intersection between the two was on the slightly tangential issue of nuclear security, an effort undertaken under the Obama administration to gain greater control over nuclear materials so that such material does not fall into the hands of terrorists.[15] This was an issue that India and Indian analysts enthusiastically embraced because it was perceived as implicitly targeting Pakistan.[16] India was thus a keen partner in all the four nuclear security summits, and it made a number of commitments to promoting both global nuclear security as well as domestic measures to improve nuclear security.[17] This continues to remain a key area of potential cooperation between the two sides, though it is not clear how this can be carried forward, considering that the nuclear security summits themselves are no longer taking place and there does not appear to be any specific institutional mechanism by which this cooperation can be taken forward. It should also be noted that even if such cooperation should ensue, this would represent a somewhat low level of cooperation in this sector. This, by itself, is an indicator of the difference in perspective between the two sides about nuclear stability in the region.

Prospects for U.S.–India cooperation on nuclear stability

The prospects for cooperation in this sector are poor, as noted above, with two exceptions. The two exceptions are potential cooperation on nuclear security and U.S. involvement in crisis management. Though nuclear stability is an important issue, the disagreement between the two sides about both the source of the problem and its solution means that little progress can be made in moving forward. This is aided by two additional factors. The first is that the U.S. itself has become relatively less concerned about nuclear escalation and instability. This is partly a function of the different ideological orientation of U.S. administrations – and thus alterable in the future – but also possibly a function of lesser anxiety about the danger of nuclear escalation and stability in the region. The second is that improvement in U.S.–India relations, and mutual concern about and cooperation with regard to balancing China in the Indo-Pacific, have become so important that nuclear stability has become an irritant that both sides appear intent on avoiding.

Nuclear security

One potentially important area where the two sides can cooperate is on cybersecurity in India's nuclear infrastructure. The case of North Korean cyberattacks on India's Kudankulam nuclear power plant and the Indian Space Research Organization in 2019 demonstrates that India's cybersecurity practices, even in the critical nuclear sector, are far from sufficient. Part of the problem is also India's reluctance to accept flaws in its cybersecurity preparations: the Indian government initially refused to admit that an attack had even taken place.[18] Subsequently, officials dismissed concerns by minimizing the seriousness of the attack, arguing that the attack had penetrated only administrative networks, which are "isolated from the critical internal network."[19] This appeared to be a reference to "air-gapping" internal computer systems – essentially, ensuring that critical computers are not connected to the internet – but, as analysts in India have pointed out, such measures are unlikely to be sufficiently protective because there are ways of breaching such air-gaps. Indian cyberdefense capabilities could quite possibly improve with help and collaboration from the U.S. And there is a mutuality of interest here: the U.S. would want to prevent other actors, either rogue states like North Korea or terrorist groups, from acquiring information and expertise from India through such intrusions. And India has an obvious interest in securing its own systems. Moreover, New Delhi has shown greater willingness to learn from global best practices in the nuclear security arena, unlike its generally porcupine-like attitude to cooperation in other strategic sectors. Still, cooperation would not be easy. There is residual suspicion and resentment of the U.S. not only from the earlier days of U.S. technology denial policies, but also from more recent experience. In 2006, a junior officer at India's National Security Council Secretariat (NSCS) and a member of the Indo-U.S. Cybersecurity Forum, a part of the official U.S.–India Joint Working Group on terrorism, was arrested by Indian intelligence and charged with spying for the U.S.[20] The NSCS, which functions partly as an intelligence clearing house and coordinating agency, as well as the secretariat for the National Security Advisor, is a critical node in India's security apparatus. Though the episode remains murky, suspicions of U.S. attempts to penetrate or to spy on the Indian government through an official intergovernmental interaction led to significant concerns and derailed the forum.[21] Future cooperation, especially in the cyber-security aspects of strategic programs, would require greater mutual confidence.

Nuclear crisis management

The other area where cooperation is possible is U.S. intervention in crisis management between India and Pakistan. This has historically been the case, with the U.S. being an active player in resolving every major crisis between the two sides which has potentially had a nuclear angle. Even in the most recent crisis in February 2019, when India attacked what it claimed was a terrorist base at Balakot in Pakistan as retaliation for a terrorist attack on Indian paramilitary forces in Kashmir, there appeared to have been a significant U.S. role that involved both U.S. National Security Advisor John Bolton and Secretary of State Mike Pompeo.[22] But, while U.S. crisis diplomacy has helped many times, its long-term viability is in doubt because the U.S. has not been able to put much pressure on Pakistan to reduce its support for terrorist groups operating against India. Increasing Indian frustration has given way to much more robust Indian response to Pakistani provocations. Prior to the Balakot strike, in October 2016, Indian special forces had attacked a base camp in Pakistan-Occupied Kashmir after a terrorist attack killed a number of Indian troops in Uri.[23] This was apparently not the first time that India had carried out such strikes.[24] But this attack was different because India had never before publicized such attacks, in order not to provoke Pakistan into further escalation.[25] Publicizing the operation was an escalation by India which indicated its growing frustration that Pakistan was refusing to curb terrorist groups operating from its territory against India. Such new-found Indian boldness and its presumed success could lead India to engage in further retaliatory strikes in response to future terrorist attacks on India. Senior U.S. officials appear to have quickly become involved in an effort to tamp down the crisis, possibly by convincing Pakistan to release an Indian Air Force pilot who appears to have been shot down and landed in Pakistan-controlled territory. While details of the incident remain unclear, there is little doubt that the U.S. was involved in managing the crisis, in much the same way as Washington was involved in previous crises. This is a role that Washington is likely to continue playing, though, as noted below, there are likely to be greater impediments to such a role in the coming years as U.S. interest in the region changes and Pakistan leans much more on China to provide it support.

Outside of these two limited areas, it is doubtful that there is much prospect of U.S.–India cooperation in this sector. On the other hand, both are likely to continue to be important, at least in the immediate future.

Impediments to cooperation

There are at least four major impediments that limit cooperation in nuclear stability. The first and most basic is that, as mentioned above, there are significant differences between the U.S. and India about nuclear instability in the region. There are two sources of difference. First, New Delhi does not really accept the notion that there is significant nuclear instability in the region. Second, to the extent that there is any nuclear instability at all, India sees the source as Pakistan, because of its dependence on terrorism as a state strategy, its lax nuclear security and its first use nuclear doctrine.

The assumption in much of the literature that takes the threat of nuclear escalation seriously is that if India responds with military force to Pakistan's provocations, the consequences will be unpredictable.[26] Pakistan's military will fear rapid defeat at the hands of the much larger Indian forces and will then be forced to resort to nuclear weapons in order to avoid defeat.[27] In addition to such a deliberate use of nuclear weapons, there is also the additional danger that the general uncertainty in war, inadequate command and control and the growth of radicalized lower and middle ranks of the Pakistani military may all lead to the unauthorized use of nuclear weapons, i.e., use of nuclear weapons without central authorization. In other words, even if they wanted to, Pakistan's military leaders might not be able to maintain control over their nuclear weapons. Pakistan's strategy has deliberately aimed at heightening these dangers through a nuclear doctrine that warns of early resort to defensive use of TNWs to halt any Indian advance into Pakistan's territory. To remove any doubts about the seriousness of its intent, Pakistan has acquired capabilities to carry out such policies, specifically the Nasr short-range nuclear missile. In addition, the deployment of such TNWs increases other risks: the possibility of the stealing of nuclear weapons by terrorist groups; the danger of nuclear accidents; and the prospect of inadvertent or even unauthorized use of these weapons. On the other hand, it must be noted that though the Nasr appears to have been deployed, it is not clear that they are deployed to forward army units. It seems that the Nasr is still controlled by central military authorities, and they will be deployed to forward areas and command over them delegated only during a crisis. This has its own disadvantages because making any such move in the midst of a crisis could intensify the crisis, while not making it could call into question Pakistan's resolve.

Such arguments about the dangers of nuclear instability in the region are not shared in India. The general perception both in official India and among a significant proportion of the Indian strategic community is that the threat of nuclear escalation in the region is greatly exaggerated. The Indian leadership has generally dismissed concerns about nuclear escalation, even in the midst of serious crises. For example, during the Operation Parakram crisis – when India mobilized almost its entire military in response to a terrorist attack on the Indian parliament that the Indian government blamed on Pakistan – the Indian Defense Minister George Fernandes rebuked the Indian Army chief for referring to the possibility of nuclear escalation.[28] Other, Pakistani comments about nuclear escalation, such as Pakistani President General Pervez Musharraf's comment in February 2003 that India should not expect a war to remain "conventional," were also downplayed by Indian officials.[29] Indian officials have generally been uneasy about any talk of nuclear war, "unwilling to speculate on nuclear theories or doomsday scenarios," as former Prime Minister Vajpayee once put it.[30] But, to the extent that they were willing to consider the issue, Indian officials generally see this as the consequence of Pakistan's behavior and its nuclear policies and, as outlined later, they want the focus of attention on Pakistan's policies.

The second major impediment to U.S.–India cooperation on nuclear stability is the American dependence on Pakistan because of the long and seemingly endless war in Afghanistan. Any U.S.–India cooperation on nuclear security would require the U.S. to be willing to put effective pressure on Pakistan to stop cross-border terrorism, or to act against Pakistan if such attacks should take place. Indeed, the U.S. role has been critical during various India–Pakistan crises.[31] This was repeated in the most recent instance also, in 2019, when India retaliated to a terrorist attack on its forces in Pulwama by launching an air strike on what India claimed was a terrorist base in Balakot. U.S. pressure on Pakistan to reduce such support could help to remove any incentive for India to conduct such potentially escalatory attacks, but the U.S. may not currently be able to put such pressure on Pakistan. The U.S. still needs Islamabad's help in finding a solution to end the war in Afghanistan and extricate its forces, which reduces Washington's capacity to lean on Pakistan. This, in turn, reduces New Delhi's willingness to cooperate with the U.S. on nuclear stability in the region. While the U.S. may still be able to play a useful role in calming a rising crisis, as it has done in the past, this is unlikely to translate into a significant or longer-term, sustained source of U.S.–India cooperation.

An additional factor that complicates U.S. efforts (and the likelihood of U.S.–India cooperation on nuclear stability) is China's growing power, which gives Pakistan another viable and possibly a much more reliable source of foreign support and thus further reduces U.S. influence in Islamabad. U.S.–Pakistan relations have always been rocky, with periods of close strategic cooperation giving way to periods of mutual recrimination. What is different now is that China can provide Islamabad with much of what it needs, should the U.S. decide, even after it successfully withdraws its military from Afghanistan, to put pressure on Pakistan to act against terrorist groups operating in the country. China is already providing Pakistan with considerable and unprecedented support, such as in getting the UN Security Council to conduct a discussion on Kashmir after India effectively changed its status or when it repeatedly protected Masood Azhar, the leader of the Pakistan-based Jaish-e-Mohammad terrorist group, by putting a "technical hold" on the UN's effort to list him as a "global terrorist."[32] U.S. efforts in this direction have never been particularly successful, even when the U.S. was less dependent on Pakistan (as in the latter half of the 1990s), because Pakistan saw greater self-interest in pursuing its strategy than the U.S. did in countering it. With China becoming much more capable of both providing support to Pakistan and helping it counter to U.S. pressure, U.S. credibility with India is likely to suffer and make it much less likely that India will cooperate with the U.S. in any sustained effort on nuclear stability in the region.

A fourth factor that is likely to impede U.S.–India cooperation on nuclear stability in the region is that the relationship itself is now focused on more important goals for both sides, that of balancing China's growing power in the Indo-Pacific. As Alice Wells, the Acting U.S. Assistant Secretary of State put it in 2018, the U.S. has a distinct South Asia strategy and an Indo-Pacific strategy and the U.S.–India partnership is "dealing with the necessity of ensuring that the Indo-Pacific region remain free and open."[33] It is clear that where the Indo-Pacific strategy conflicts with the South Asia strategy, the former has precedence, though Ms. Wells herself did not state this in as many words. This emphasis on the changing balance of power in the Indo-Pacific was the basis of the entire transformation of the U.S. attitude towards India and the nuclear issue under the George W. Bush administration, and this transformation has continued.[34] While supporters of such a structural view of the relationship have been disappointed by India's failure to live up to the promise of the relationship, there is little doubt that the relationship is strengthening.[35] Though India has taken an inordinately long time to build the partnership with the U.S., it now has signed most of the foundational agreements (with the exception of Basic Exchange and Cooperation Agreement for Geospatial Cooperation).[36] India has also become much warmer towards the Quadrilateral security consultation group or the Quad, which has recently been upgraded to a foreign ministerial-level dialogue.[37] The growing strategic empathy between the two countries means that U.S.–India disagreements on the nuclear issue are unlikely to be given much importance by either side. The China imperative is simply far too important for either side to bring up an issue where they clearly do not agree. This is likely to impede cooperation between the two sides on nuclear stability in the region, excepting the few areas where their views and interests do coincide.

Recommendation for future cooperation on nuclear stability

The prospect for sustained U.S.–India cooperation on nuclear stability is poor. India and the U.S. see the dangers of nuclear instability and the sources of this danger differently, and the U.S. interest in the issue has also

Enhancing nuclear stability

waned somewhat. From New Delhi's perspective, this is actually positive because it removes a source of tension in the relationship. Moreover, for both countries, their emerging strategic partnership in balancing China's rise is seen as much more important, and one that could be derailed by disagreements about nuclear stability in the region. While this is not very promising from the perspective of cooperation on nuclear stability, there are at least three policy areas related to nuclear stability where the two countries can significantly improve cooperation: cybersecurity related to the nuclear sector; securing Pakistan's nuclear materials and weapons; and reducing the dangers associated with Pakistan's nuclear arsenal and policy. The prospects are best on the first issue and rather limited on the second and third recommendations.

India could definitely use more help in improving its nuclear security. Assessments by global experts on the issue have consistently ranked India near the bottom for its performance on nuclear security.[38] While Indian assessments are somewhat more positive, they also point to significant gaps in India's practices regarding nuclear security and the necessity for international cooperation, especially in learning best practices from other countries with a nuclear establishment.[39] Moreover, as referenced earlier, the 2019 cyberattacks on Indian nuclear and space establishments illustrate yet another area of weakness of Indian nuclear security. Both India and the U.S. have a common interest in strengthening India's cybersecurity capabilities, especially as they relate to India's nuclear sector. New Delhi has to worry about cybersecurity not only because rogue actors such as North Korea may be attempting to steal Indian technology – which appeared to have been the case in the 2019 intrusions – but also because Indian vulnerabilities could be exploited by adversarial actors such as Pakistan and China.[40] The close links between North Korea and China and Pakistan also suggest the possibility that these malevolent actors could coordinate or cooperate in targeting India. But also, as mentioned earlier, this does require India to have greater confidence in cooperating with the U.S., especially as it relates to U.S. intelligence activities in India.

A second area where India and the U.S. could cooperate is in securing Pakistan's nuclear materials and weapons. The fear of transfer of such materials to terrorist groups has been a persistent nightmare for Indian decisionmakers: as India's Foreign Secretary S. Jaishankar put it in 2017, "Terrorism is an international threat that should not serve national strategy. Nuclear terrorism even more so."[41] New Delhi has been obsessed with the issue because it appears to believe that Pakistan's nuclear materials and weapons could possibly be transferred to terrorist groups, either deliberately or because of Pakistan's lax controls, the presence of large numbers of terrorist groups and their close linkage to sections of the Pakistani state.

As India's foreign secretary put it in 2010, "Terrorists gaining access to WMDs has emerged as a major threat for our national security as well as globally."[42] Thus, India has repeatedly invoked the danger and has actively supported international efforts to counter the threat.[43] It is not clear how such cooperation will work in practice, but, considering the seriousness with which India invokes this threat, it is likely that New Delhi would be eager to cooperate bilaterally with the U.S. on every aspect – from detecting potential threats, to managing the consequences of any such event through nuclear forensics to trace the source of the attack, to preparing emergency personnel and first-responders to deal with such an event.

A third area of potential cooperation that New Delhi might be willing – indeed eager – to consider could be reducing the dangers associated with Pakistan's first-use nuclear doctrine and the kind of nuclear arsenal it is developing. India sees Pakistan's nuclear doctrine and its first-use doctrine as a serious danger. Shyam Saran, former Indian Foreign Secretary, typically characterized Pakistan's nuclear doctrine as based on blackmail, which "deserves equal condemnation by the international community because it is not just a threat to India but to international peace and security."[44] India has repeatedly called on Pakistan to accede to a No First Use pledge similar to India's, and Indian officials have dismissed TNWs, saying that no nuclear war can remain limited. Pakistan's development and deployment of TNWs are a particular concern that is shared by both New Delhi and Washington. It is unlikely that Pakistan will be particularly responsive to any joint U.S.–India collaboration to deal with this issue because Pakistan has very good reasons for wanting to build and deploy TNWs. Nevertheless, even if this is unlikely to be effective in changing the direction of Pakistan's nuclear weapon choices, it could still enhance U.S.–Indian cooperation in a critical area and, moreover, one of the few areas where they have a common perspective.

Conclusion

The prospects of U.S.–India cooperation on enhancing nuclear stability in South Asia is rather limited. This is a function of differing perspectives on the utility of nuclear weapons and on the nature of the nuclear danger in the region. For India, the primary source of nuclear danger and instability comes from the strategy that Pakistan has adopted, which is based on using terrorism as an asymmetrical tool to target a much stronger India, while deterring India from responding militarily by threatening nuclear escalation. This strategy, while successful for two decades since 2000 in deterring an Indian military response, may be becoming increasingly unviable. A number of Indian officials and analysts had asserted that India did have the space within the nuclear overhang to conduct conventional military operations. Under the Modi government, India has demonstrated just this: Pakistan was unable to escalate either to the Indian "surgical strike" in 2016 or to the Balakot attack in 2019, though at least in the latter case, Pakistan did attempt to match the Indian escalation. New Delhi now appears much more confident – possibly even overconfident – that it has found the answer to Pakistan's use of terrorism as a strategic tool. This makes it less likely that New Delhi will be willing to consider cooperation in this sector, except in narrow areas such as cybersecurity and nuclear counterterrorism, in addition to the traditional crisis-manager role.

At the same time, changing international political factors also appear to have made the U.S. less willing to put this issue at the forefront of U.S.–India relations. China's rise and the common challenge this poses to Washington and New Delhi make it unlikely that the U.S. will emphasize issues that could add a greater burden to the relationship. Moreover, while there is continuing scholarly concern about nuclear stability in the region, official America appears much less concerned. All of this limits the possibility of cooperation between the U.S. and India on nuclear stability in the region.

Notes

1 There is still considerable concern in the academic community about the consequences of a nuclear war in the region. See, Owen B. Toon et al., 'Rapidly expanding nuclear arsenals in Pakistan and India portend regional and global catastrophe', *Science Advances*, 2019, 5:eaay5478, October 2, 2019, DOI: 10.1126/sciadv.aay5478.
2 Christopher Clary and Vipin Narang, 'India's counterforce temptations: strategic dilemmas, doctrine and capabilities', *International Security*, 43:3 (Winter 2018/19), 7–52. For rebuttals of this thesis, see, Abhijnan Rej, 'India is not changing its policy on No First Use of nuclear weapons', *Warontherocks.com*, March 29, 2017, https://warontherocks.com/2017/03/india-is-not-changing-its-policy-on-no-first-use-of-nuclear-weapons/ (accessed on January 18, 2020); Rajesh Rajagopalan, 'India's nuclear strategy: a shift to counterforce?' *ORFonline*, March 30, 2017, www.orfonline.org/expert-speak/india-nuclear-strategy-shift-counterforce/ (accessed on January 18, 2020).
3 These definitions follow from Leon Sigal, 'Warming to the freeze', *Foreign Policy*, 48 (Autumn 1982), 56–7.
4 P. R. Chari, Pervaiz Iqbal Cheema and Stephen Philip Cohen, *Perception, politics and security in South Asia: the compound crisis of 1990* (London: RoutledgeCurzon, 2003).

5 Šumit Ganguly, 'Avoiding war in Kashmir', *Foreign Affairs*, 69:5 (Winter 1990/91), 57–73.
6 Vipin Narang, *Nuclear strategy in the modern era: regional powers and international conflict* (Princeton: Princeton University Press, 2014), especially chapter 3, pp. 55–93.
7 Ministry of External Affairs, Government of India, 'Lahore Declaration February, 1999', at www.mea.gov.in/in-focus-article.htm?18997/lahore+declaration+february+1999 (accessed January 17, 2020).
8 On Pakistan's use of terrorism as strategy, see S. Paul Kapur and Sumit Ganguly, 'The jihad paradox: Pakistan and Islamist militancy in South Asia', *International Security* 37:1 (Summer 2012), 111–41.
9 For an assessment of Pakistan's nuclear posture, see David J. Karl, 'Pakistan's evolving nuclear weapon posture: implications for deterrence stability', *Nonproliferation Review*, 21:3–4 (2014), 317–36.
10 On the changing U.S. policy, see Leonard Weiss, 'U.S.–India nuclear cooperation', *Nonproliferation Review*, 14:3 (2007), 429–57.
11 For the U.S. position and concerns, see Strobe Talbott, *Engaging India: diplomacy, democracy and the bomb* (Washington, D.C.: Brookings Institution Press, 2004).
12 See for example, Ministry of External Affairs, 'Address by Shri Shyam Saran, SEPM at the Brookings Institution', March 23, 2009, at www.mea.gov.in/Speeches-Statements.htm?dtl/980/address+by+shri+shyam+saran+sepm+at+the+brookings+institution (accessed on January 18, 2020).
13 Ministry of External Affairs, 'Field Marshal KM Cariappa Memorial Lecture 2008 delivered by Shri Pranab Mukherjee, External Affairs Minister on "Emerging India-economic and security perspectives"', September 17, 2008, www.mea.gov.in/Speeches-Statements.htm?dtl/1681/field+marshal+km+cariappa+memorial+lecture+2008+delivered+by+shri+pranab+mukherjee+external+affairs+minister+on+emerging+india++economic+and+security+perspective (accessed on January 18, 2020).
14 Rajya Sabha, Parliamentary Debates, 'Statement by (External Affairs) Minister: Non-Proliferation Treaty', 189:32, May 9, 2000, 208–11.
15 Leore Ben-Chorin and Steven Pifer, 'Takeaways from Obama's last nuclear security summit', *Brookings Institution*, April 4, 2016, www.brookings.edu/blog/order-from-chaos/2016/04/04/takeaways-from-obamas-last-nuclear-security-summit/ (accessed on January 18, 2020); and Tatsujiro Suzuki, 'Nuclear security policy of the Obama administration: Its achievements and issues left behind: An interview with Laura Holgate', *Journal of Peace and Nuclear Disarmament*, 1:2 (2018), 486–96.
16 Rajiv Nayan, 'India's nuclear security policy', *IDSA Comment*, January 5, 2012, https://idsa.in/idsacomments/IndiasNuclearSecurityPolicy_rnayan_050112 (accessed on January 18, 2020).
17 Ministry of External Affairs, 'India's National Progress Report, Nuclear Security Summit 2016', April 2, 2016, www.mea.gov.in/bilateral-documents.htm?dtl/26590/Indias+National+Progress+Report+Nuclear+Security+Summit+2016 (accessed on January 18, 2020).

18 'Kudankulam nuclear power plant denies being victim of cyber spy attack', *India Today*, October 29, 2019, www.indiatoday.in/india/story/kudankulam-nuclear-power-plant-cyber-attack-dtrack-lazarus-1613689-2019-10-29 (accessed on January 18, 2020).
19 Sushovan Sircar and Vakasha Sachdev, 'Kudankulam cyber attack did happen, says NPCIL a day after denial', *The Quint*, November 1, 2019, www.thequint.com/news/india/kudankulam-nuclear-power-plant-malware-attack-correct-confirms-npcil (accessed on January 18, 2020).
20 Sheela Bhatt, 'Techie in NSC leaked info to American woman', *Rediff.com*, June 30, 2006, www.rediff.com/news/2006/jun/30sheela.htm (accessed on January 18, 2020); Sandeep Unnithan, 'RAW in crisis with leaks outside, dissent within when India needs it most', *India Today*, August 28, 2006, www.indiatoday.in/magazine/cover-story/story/20060828-terror-in-india-research-and-analysis-wing-in-crisis-784832-2006-08-28 (accessed on January 18, 2020).
21 Manoj Joshi, 'The spies who were not', *Hindustan Times*, May 27, 2007, as reproduced in https://mjoshi.blogspot.com/2007/05/spies-who-were-not.html (accessed on January 18, 2020).
22 Sanjeev Miglani, 'India, Pakistan threatened to unleash missiles at each other: sources', *Reuters*, March 17, 2019, www.reuters.com/article/us-india-kashmir-crisis-insight/india-pakistan-threatened-to-unleash-missiles-at-each-other-sources-idU.S.KCN1QY03T (accessed on January 18, 2020).
23 Nitin A. Gokhale, 'The inside story of India's 2016 "surgical strikes"', *The Diplomat*, September 23, 2017, https://thediplomat.com/2017/09/the-inside-story-of-indias-2016-surgical-strikes/ (accessed on January 18, 2020).
24 'Surgical strikes, cross-border operations have been carried in past, say 2016 strikes "hero" DS Hooda', *The Statesman*, May 4, 2019, www.thestatesman.com/india/surgical-strikes-cross-border-operations-have-been-carried-in-past-says-2016-strikes-hero-ds-hooda-1502751835.html (accessed on January 18, 2020); 'Pak army reacts to Gen Bikram Singh's "provocative" remarks, calls them unnecessary', *Indian Express*, January 13, 2013, https://indianexpress.com/article/india/india-others/pak-army-reacts-to-gen-bikram-singhs-provocative-remarks-calls-them-unnecessary/ (accessed on January 18, 2020).
25 Snehesh Alex Philip, 'How 2016 surgical strike was different from the ones Congress is claiming under UPA', *The Print*, May 2, 2019, https://theprint.in/defence/how-2016-surgical-strike-was-different-from-the-ones-congress-is-claiming-under-upa/230409/ (accessed on January 18, 2020).
26 George Perkovich and Toby Dalton, 'Modi's strategic choice: how to respond to terrorism from Pakistan', *The Washington Quarterly*, 38:1 (Spring 2015), 23–45; S. Paul Kapur, 'Ten years of instability in nuclear South Asia', *International Security*, 33:2 (Fall 2008), 71–94.
27 Jaganath Sankaran, 'Pakistan's battlefield nuclear policy: a risky solution to an exaggerated threat', *International Security*, 39:3 (Winter 2014/15), 118–51.
28 'Uncalled for concerns: Fernandes', *The Hindu*, January 12, 2002.
29 Ministry of External Affairs, 'Q. 353-Pak stand on nuclear options against India', February 19, 2003, www.mea.gov.in/lok-sabha.htm?dtl/15124/q35

3++pak+stand+on+nuclear+options+against+india (accessed on January 18, 2020).

30 Ministry of External Affairs, 'Interview of Prime Minister of India Shri Atal Bihari Vajpayee by Ha'Aretz (Israel)', September 8, 2003, www.mea.gov.in/interviews.htm?dtl/4676/interview+of+prime+minister+of+india+shri+atal+bihari+vajpayee+by+haaretz+israel (accessed on January 18, 2020).

31 P. R. Chari, Pervaiz Iqbal Cheema and Stephen P. Cohen, *Four crises and a peace process: American engagement in South Asia* (Washington, D.C.: Brookings Institution Press, 2007); Vipin Narang, 'Posturing for peace? Pakistan's nuclear postures and South Asian stability', *International Security*, 34:3 (Winter 2009/10), 38–78.

32 On the former issue, see 'UN Security Council holds closed-door meeting on Kashmir', *NDTV.com*, August 16, 2019, www.ndtv.com/india-news/united-nations-security-councils-closed-door-meeting-on-kashmir-begins-2086134 (accessed on January 18, 2020); and on the Masood Azhar issue, see Michael Kugelman, 'Masood Azhar is China's favorite terrorist', *Foreign Policy*, March 21, 2019, https://foreignpolicy.com/2019/03/21/masood-azhar-is-chinas-favorite-terrorist/ (accessed on January 18, 2020). China did relent and remove its technical hold in May 2019.

33 U.S. Department of State, 'U.S. priorities in the South and Central Asia region', FPC Briefing, Alice G. Wells, Acting Assistant Secretary of State, September 28, 2018, www.state.gov/u-s-priorities-in-the-south-and-central-asia-region/ (accessed on January 18, 2020).

34 Ashley J. Tellis, 'The evolution of U.S.–Indian ties: missile defense in an emerging strategic relationship', *International Security*, 30:4 (Spring 2006), 113–51.

35 Robert D. Blackwill and Ashley J. Tellis, 'The India dividend: New Delhi remains Washington's best hope in Asia', *Foreign Affairs*, 98:5 (September–October 2019), 173–83.

36 Ankit Panda, 'What the recently concluded U.S.–India COMCASA means', *The Diplomat*, September 9, 2018, https://thediplomat.com/2018/09/what-the-recently-concluded-us-india-comcasa-means/ (accessed on January 18, 2020).

37 'Quad gets an upgrade as foreign ministers of India, Japan, Australia, U.S. meet', *The Wire.in*, September 27, 2019, https://thewire.in/diplomacy/quad-gets-an-upgrade-as-foreign-ministers-of-india-japan-australia-us-meet (accessed on January 18, 2020).

38 Nuclear Threat Initiative, *NTI nuclear security index: Building a framework for assurance, accountability and action,* fourth edition (Washington D.C.: Nuclear Threat Initiative/The Economist Intelligence Unit, September 2018), https://ntiindex.org/wp-content/uploads/2018/08/NTI_2018-Index_FINAL.pdf (accessed on January 18, 2020).

39 Rajeswari Pillai Rajagopalan, Rahul Krishna, Kritika Singh and Arko Biswas, *Nuclear security in India*, second edition (New Delhi: Observer Research Foundation, 2016).

40 Jay Mazoomdar, 'Not only Kudankulam, ISRO, too, was alerted of cyber security breach', *Indian Express*, November 6, 2019, https://indianexpress.

com/article/india/not-only-kudankulam-isro-too-was-alerted-of-cyber-security-breach-6105184/ (accessed on January 18, 2020).
41 Ministry of External Affairs, 'Welcome address by foreign secretary at Implementation and Assessment Group meeting Global Initiative to Combat Nuclear Terrorism (GICNT), New Delhi', February 8, 2017, www.mea.gov.in/Speeches-Statements.htm?dtl/28012/Welcome_address_by_Foreign_Secretary_at_Implementation_and_Assessment_Group_Meeting_Global_Initiative_to_Combat_Nuclear_Terrorism_GICNT_New_Delhi (accessed on January 18, 2020).
42 Ministry of External Affairs, 'Address by Foreign Secretary at NDC on "Challenges in Indian foreign policy"', November 19, 2010, https://mea.gov.in/Speeches-Statements.htm?dtl/815/Address+by+Foreign+Secretary+at+NDC+on+Challenges+in+Indias+Foreign+Policy (accessed on January 18, 2020).
43 P. R. Chari, 'India and nuclear terrorism: meeting the threat', *Institute of Peace and Conflict Studies*, March 17, 2014, www.ipcs.org/comm_select.php?articleNo=4339 (accessed on January 18, 2020).
44 Shyam Saran, 'Is India's nuclear doctrine credible?' Lecture delivered at India Habitat Centre, New Delhi, April 24, 2013. This lecture was delivered while Saran headed India's National Security Advisory Board.

Part IV

Space cooperation

7

U.S.–India strategic partnership in space: a path toward cooperation

Victoria Samson

The U.S. and India, both major space powers, have long worked together on civil space efforts but have not done much in regard to security space cooperation. This is a real missed opportunity, as each country has a lot to offer the other in terms of shoring up their national security and the stability of the space domain overall. Space has been a force multiplier for the U.S. since, arguably, the 1991 Gulf War and is now considered to be a war-fighting domain. India has not yet adopted that terminology, but is shifting its space efforts to include those with more military goals and objectives, and is increasingly giving more authority for space programs to its Defence Research and Development Organisation. The two countries have also found themselves more incentivized to work together on strategic issues in general in order to counter China's growing regional and global influence.

This chapter will discuss potential ways in which the U.S. and India can work together on strategic space issues. It will begin by providing a snapshot of current U.S. government policies related to space security in order to understand U.S. goals in space and how India might help it meet them. Next, it will discuss the U.S. space situational awareness sharing program and the value it would bring both the U.S. and India to exchange their own data. Then, it will highlight the importance of bilateral discussions and active multilateral negotiations related to space security issues, paying special attention to the challenges presented by anti-satellite tests to the security and stability of the space domain. The chapter will then examine space-based maritime domain awareness policies and priorities for the U.S. and propose ways in which the two maritime powers can use space to enhance maritime security. It will end with a plea for the Indian government to formalize a national space policy and/or strategy, as that will expedite strategic partnership in space between the two countries.

U.S. space policies and priorities

In order to truly understand the role strategic space partnership can play in the U.S.–India relationship, first one must discuss U.S. national space policy and strategy. To begin, the National Space Policy (NSP) of 2010 is still officially U.S. space policy, as it has not been replaced by one from the Donald Trump administration.[1] The 2010 NSP has a strong emphasis on international cooperation in space, an emphasis that has been fairly consistent throughout most U.S. national space policies. The 2010 NSP also indicates a willingness to consider arms control measures for space activities. Then we have the 2011 National Security Space Strategy, which includes as objectives, "Promote responsible, peaceful, and safe use of space," and "Partner with responsible nations, international organizations, and commercial firms."[2]

The Trump administration has opted to issue space presidential directives (SPDs) to demonstrate its priorities and give guidance for U.S. space policy and strategy. The first was SPD 1: *Reinvigorating America's Human Space Exploration Program*.[3] The second was SPD-2: *Streamlining Regulations on Commercial Use of Space*.[4] The third was SPD-3: *National Space Traffic Management Policy*.[5] And the fourth was SPD-4: *Establishment of the United States Space Force*.[6]

U.S. military space and the space force

There has been a recent shift in how U.S. government officials discuss space. Now, it is completely common for them to speak about space being a warfighting domain, as encapsulated in General John Raymond, Commander, U.S. Space Command's comments in August 2019: "[T]here's unprecedented alignment in our nation today that space is a warfighting domain just like air, land, sea and cyber," but to caveat that with, "our goal is to actually deter a conflict from extending into space."[7]

Any discussion of U.S. security space priorities is incomplete without addressing plans for a U.S. Space Force. First announced by Trump in June 2018, this request was made official via SPD-4 in February 2019. A Space Force would essentially reorganize how the U.S. military organizes, trains, and equips warfighters related to space. Confusingly, while Congress must authorize the creation of a Space Force and appropriate funds, the Department of Defense (DoD) can create a Space Command on its own, and the latter was stood up in August 2019. The Space Command is a combat command with an area of responsibility of 100 kilometers or higher and is intended to focus on warfighting and identifying threats to U.S. space assets and access. In theory, the Space Force would train and equip troops, who would then be turned over to Space Command to manage military operations in space and support terrestrial operations in other theaters. However, the final relationship is unclear, as the administration, House, and Senate all have different ideas as to what the Space Force will entail.[8]

SSA sharing

One good place to start for U.S.–India cooperation in space is to share space situational awareness (SSA) information. SSA is foundational to space security and stability, both in terms of spaceflight safety and for improving transparency of activities on orbit. SSA data is so crucial for safe operations in Earth orbit that the U.S. Strategic Command (STRATCOM) shares information about potential conjunctions, or close approaches, to all space owner/operators, including India. However, for certain actors, STRATCOM has signed SSA sharing agreements that give their partner more information on potential conjunctions, deorbits, launches, and reentry information. As of April 2019, STRATCOM had signed 100 SSA sharing agreements with twenty countries, two intergovernmental organizations, and seventy-eight commercial owner/operators.[9] According to Rear Adm. Richard Correll, U.S.STRATCOM director of plans and policy, "Space situational awareness agreements formalize relationships with other nations and are crucial to normalizing future space operations."[10]

India is not one of the countries who has an SSA sharing agreement with the U.S. This has been raised in discussions but not ever finalized. For example, the U.S.–India Joint Statement of September 2014 noted, "The United and India also intend to start a new dialogue on maintaining long-term security and sustainability of the outer space environment, including space situational awareness and collision avoidance in outer space."[11] And in 2015 it was mentioned by Frank Rose, then a high-ranking State Department official, during a visit to India as a potential "area of concrete collaboration."[12] It should be made a priority by STRATCOM leadership.

Indian SSA capabilities

India had forty-four active satellites as of March 2019, and it depends on the U.S. government's sharing of two-line element sets to track them.[13] But India has the potential to generate and exchange SSA data as well. India does space object proximity analysis and close approach analysis.

Furthermore, India has this year launched Project NETRA (network for space object tracking and analysis), which is a dedicated facility for SSA. The objective is to establish observation capabilities of space objects in order to evolve a mechanism to process tracking observations, make an assessment of SSA, and disseminate that information. It is estimated to cost ₹ 400 crore.[14] It will have observation facilities, three optical telescopes (a planned high-precision, long-range telescope in Leh, plus existing telescopes at Ponmudi and Mount Abu), a radar in the northeast part of the country and the Multi-Object Tracking Radar at the Satish Dhawan Space Centre in Sriharikota, and a control center for analysis in Bengaluru. Its proposed phased-array radar has multi-object tracking capabilities, with the idea that they can track space objects more than 7 cm in diameter up to 3,400 km range.[15] According to Dr. Sivan, "Even now we do collision avoidance maneuvers on our satellites. To do that we depend on data from NORAD [North American Aerospace Defense Command] and others available in the public domain but we don't get accurate [or comprehensive] information. By establishing an observation system of our own, we become part of the global network and can access precise data."[16] While Project NETRA is still in the early stages, it has the potential for providing data that would complement and enhance that being generated by STRATCOM's SSA network.

Continue bilateral discussions

Good communication is the foundation to any cooperative relationship. As such, it is important to continue already-established bilateral discussions to shore up the U.S.–India relationship in space. There is a long history of the two space actors discussing civil space issues of common interest via the U.S.–India Civil Space Joint Working Group, which consists of the National Aeronautics and Space Administration (NASA)/U.S. State Department on one side and the Indian Space Research Organisation (ISRO) on the other side.

The security space relationship is shorter in length but has the potential to be helpful in ascertaining common interests, identifying possible threats to U.S. and Indian space assets, and coordinating responses. The third round of the U.S.–India Space Dialogue was held in March 2019 and allowed the two countries to discuss "trends in space threats, respective national space priorities, and opportunities for cooperation bilaterally and in multilateral fora."[17] It was held the day before the ninth round of the U.S.–India Strategic Security Dialogue 2019, which focuses on nuclear issues.[18]

Another opportunity to inject space security issues into bilateral discussions is the U.S.–India 2+2 Dialogue, held for the first time in September 2018.[19] The second iteration of this dialogue took place in December 2019; space was mentioned as an area where the two countries could hold new cooperative efforts, particularly given the joint statement released in 2018 about the need to "strengthen defense ties further and promote better defense and security coordination and cooperation."[20] Space capabilities are an obvious part of that. Another major goal was to "Work together and in concert with other partners toward advancing a free, open, and inclusive Indo-Pacific region, based on recognition of ASEAN centrality," which also leaves it open to bringing in space security issues.[21]

Coordinate in multilateral fora in discussions on responsible behavior in space

One of the most important places where the U.S. and India could and should be strategic partners and coordinate efforts is in multilateral fora discussing space security issues. This is a difficult issue for the international community to handle. Historically, when dealing with issues that negatively impact international security, multilateral fora would ban/limit the technology or materials involved in that threat. Space security is a much more challenging issue area, as there generally is no such thing as a specific space weapon. There are technologies that provide a counterspace capability, but those technologies can also be used in a non-military way.[22] The inherent dual-use nature of space capabilities means that it is virtually impossible to define what a space weapon is: either everything is deemed a space weapon, or it is so tightly defined that nothing is a space weapon. Either way, it is not helpful to international security.

What is more useful is to focus on behavior in space and ways in which to demonstrate good intent, as that is more telling in terms of what an actor plans to do with its technology. Unfortunately, the international system is lagging in how it deals with threats to space security and stability. The time of legally binding treaties is decades in the past: the last really widely signed space-related treaty was the Registration Convention from 1974. Russia and China have been pushing for their Treaty on the Prevention of the Placement of Weapons in Outer Space, the Threat or Use of Force against Outer Space Objects Treaty (PPWT) since 2008, but it has gone nowhere, due to concerns about it allowing ground-based anti-satellite weapons (ASATs) and having no verification provisions. Meanwhile, space technologies are advancing well ahead of the governance mechanisms established to regulate them.

This means that it is more beneficial to focus on agreeing on rules of the road. Given how limited our true understanding of activities on orbit really is, it is important to try to establish what is considered to be responsible space behavior so that abnormal activities can be identified and be pointed to as being outside the norm.

The United Nations and space security discussions

The problem we run into is that the international system is not handling this well. The United Nations (UN) splits space discussions into civil and security space, with a pretty strong firewall mandated between the two. The UN Committee for the Peaceful Uses of Outer Space (COPUOS) deals with civil space; the Conference on Disarmament (CD) deals with security space. However, the CD is a consensus-driven organization and must agree on an agenda; it has not been able to do so since the mid-1990s.

Between 2017 and 2019, three different UN bodies have tried and failed to move very far on space security issues.[23] The CD, in February 2018, agreed to form four subsidiary bodies to deal with individual agenda items in the absence of an overall work plan. Subsidiary body 3 was tasked with looking at the prevention of an arms race in outer space (PAROS). It met six times over 2018 and was able to agree on a consensus report, which was forwarded on to the CD plenary. Due to political difficulties with the presidency of one member state, the CD was unable to adopt a final report to send on to the United Nations General Assembly (UNGA). The UN Disarmament Commission (UNDC), which is part of the UNGA, established working group 2 to find ways in which the recommendations of the 2013 Group of Governmental Experts (GGE) on space transparency and confidence building measures (TCBMs) may be implemented. There were disputes in spring 2019 over visa issues for Russian delegates to the UN in New York and the UNDC was unable to meet. In December 2017, the UNGA asked the Secretary-General to form a GGE on further practical measures on PAROS. The delegates met in August 2018 and spring 2019; part of their mandate was to look at elements of a legally binding treaty, using the Russian/Chinese draft PPWT as a basis for discussions, and also to look at what other elements might be introduced to make a PAROS agreement work. While it seemed for a while that a consensus document might emerge from this GGE, ultimately, the states were unable to reach consensus and so no formal document was finalized.

Even with this imperfect system, it is still important to participate in the conversations in order to find out where potential common ground lies and where the difference in priorities are for member states. India has been a participant in these conversations but not a particularly active one. For example, one of the few achievements in international space governance discussions was the agreement in June 2019 in COPUOS of twenty-one guidelines for the long-term sustainable use of outer space.[24] Given that COPUOS is also a consensus-driven organization of ninety-five countries, it is very impressive that they were able to come to agreement on these guidelines. Also, it was based on nearly a decade's worth of negotiations and was driven by the participating delegates. India is a member of COPUOS but was not a leader in the negotiations. Given how India has been active in space for over five decades and is a leading space power in many other ways – planetary exploration, launching other countries' satellites – this lack of leadership in the negotiating process is perplexing.

This has proven true for other UN fora as well. Former U.S. diplomat Rose noted regarding India, "They quite frankly have not been at the table on the diplomatic front despite talking a good game about support for norms."[25] More recently, India was a member of the recent GGE on PAROS but was not a major player in its discussions; it also was a participant in the fruitless discussions held during the informal UNDC meeting in spring 2019.

The Indian foreign ministry released a statement in September 2019 that gave its viewpoint on space security: "India remains opposed to the weaponization of outer space. India has not, and will not, resort to any arms race in outer space. India has been a consistent advocate of preserving the outer space as a common heritage of humankind, as an ever-expanding frontier for cooperative endeavors of all space faring nations."[26] It went on to say, "India supports substantive consideration of the prevention of an arms race in outer space within the multilateral framework of the UN. India is committed to negotiation of a legally binding instrument on the prevention of an arms race in outer space to be negotiated in the Conference on Disarmament, where it has been on the agenda since 1982."[27] And the statement included, "India remains committed to playing a leading and constructive role together with other partners, in deliberations and negotiations on prevention of an arms race in outer space, including legally binding measures, TCBMs and long-term sustainability guidelines."[28] It has not lived up to this role but there is hope that it can do so in the future.

Feasible efforts for multilateral negotiations

One way India can demonstrate leadership is in discussions in COPUOS about how to implement the twenty-one Long-Term Sustainability guidelines that have been agreed to thus far. The guidelines are only as successful as their implementation. There is a need for leadership in discussing how these can be implemented and in improving international capacity for carrying these out – both things in which India can prove its mettle as a leader in space governance issues.

Another arms control proposal that is slowly garnering more acceptance is the idea of KE (Kinetic Energy)-ASAT test ban. This rests on the idea that space debris can be very threatening to space assets and can have a lifespan of years, if not decades, depending on their orbit. Daniel Porras has written about this and suggested three guidelines for KE-ASAT tests: no debris; low debris; and notifications to other actors.[29] It is perceived that a common agreement not to create large amounts of debris via KE-ASAT tests would avoid some of the issues hampering other arms control proposals. It would not be legally binding and thus would avoid some of the quagmire generated by the treaty-negotiating process. It would permit missile defense testing and development, a longstanding interest of the U.S. and other countries with indigenously developed missile defense programs, including India. It would even allow the possession of KE-ASAT technology, perhaps assuaging concerns by those who would worry that it would limit countries' abilities to defend their assets (even though it is questionable how much ASATs actually do to ensure the safety and stability of the space domain and satellites in general).

Recent anti-satellite tests

Why would be it be particularly interesting for India to take a leading role in discussing this test ban? Because it held an ASAT test in March 2019, successfully intercepting its target satellite. This was not the first time an ASAT test had been held. Both the U.S. and the Soviet Union held them during the Cold War, but, over time, an unofficial test moratorium emerged after the U.S. held an ASAT test in 1985. No further testing was held until China held an ASAT test in January 2007 where it deliberately hit an aging weather satellite at an altitude of over 800 km and created over 3,000 pieces of trackable debris.[30] China, sensitive to the global criticism it received for its 2007 ASAT test, has not held another test like it since. What it has done is test the same interceptor, now calling it a missile defense interceptor, which seems to be more palatable to the international community.

Interestingly enough, in 2008, the U.S. had an unresponsive satellite that it deemed necessary to shoot down before the satellite de-orbited and leaked its toxic hydrazine; or, a year later, the U.S. used the opportunity of an unresponsive satellite to demonstrate that it too could successfully target a satellite. No matter how this action is interpreted, what is unquestioned is that the U.S. modified the software of one of its sea-based missile defense interceptors in order to target a satellite in Operation Burnt Frost. This was done at an altitude of 250 km, creating almost 200 pieces of trackable debris, most of which reentered within six months.[31] Because it was done at a lower altitude than the Chinese test, its debris was much shorter lived.

It has long been thought that India would hold an ASAT test if it felt that any sort of test ban was about to be implemented. Indian strategists have long chafed at being officially categorized a non-nuclear weapon state per the Nuclear Non-Proliferation Treaty (NPT), which categorizes the world into nuclear haves and have-nots. Many Indians believe that if their country had held its first nuclear test prior to the creation of the NPT, they would have also been grandfathered in as a nuclear weapon state, and they are probably correct. So the thinking was that if there was to be an ASAT test ban impending, India should quickly hold an ASAT test so that it could be grandfathered in as a space weapons state.

The successful March 2019 test – Mission Shakti – was announced by Indian Prime Minister Modi in a tweet.[32] An official Indian government release stated, "India has no intention of entering into an arms race in outer space. We have always maintained that space must be used only for peaceful purposes. We are against the weaponization of Outer Space and support international efforts to reinforce the safety and security of space based assets."[33] The test was done at an altitude of about 280 km, which Indian scientists said was low enough that any debris created from the test would reenter within forty-five days.[34] However, of the roughly 125 trackable pieces of debris that were created by this test, five months later, 47 pieces were still in orbit.[35]

Perhaps illustrating India's power as a strategic partner of the U.S., the U.S. government was fairly subdued about the ramifications of India's ASAT test. The U.S. State Department released a statement that said, "The issue of space debris is an important concern for the U.S. government. We took note of Indian government statements that the test was designed to address space debris issues," but that because of its "strong strategic partnership with India," the U.S. will continue "to pursue shared interests in space and scientific and technical cooperation, including collaboration on safety and security in space."[36]

In fact, the only U.S. governmental entity that was vocal about the fall-out from India's test was NASA – briefly. NASA sent a letter to ISRO on March 29, 2019, which stated it was suspending its cooperation with ISRO on human spaceflight, as "It is NASA's view that human spaceflight is simply incompatible with the purposeful creation of orbital debris generated by anti-satellite testing."[37] NASA Administrator Jim Bridenstine told a NASA Town Hall meeting on April 1, "That is a terrible, terrible thing, to create an event that sends debris in an apogee that goes above the International Space Station."[38] However, on April 4, 2019, a follow-up letter from Bridenstine to ISRO Chairperson K. Sivan said that NASA would be reinstating its cooperative efforts with India on human spaceflight.[39]

India is extremely well positioned at the present to lead the way for discussions on a KE-ASAT test ban. This would not preclude other counterspace capabilities India may or may not be anticipating working on, and, if the movement is successful, India can point to its own ASAT test as evidence that it has demonstrated this capability successfully and need not do so again. This is an arms control measure that both the U.S. and India could seek that would have minimal constraints on their national security apparatuses but would very much help to stabilize the international space domain.

Space-based maritime domain awareness

Maritime domain awareness (MDA) can be defined as effective understanding of anything associated with the maritime domain that could impact security, safety, economy, and environment. MDA relies on a layered set of terrestrial, air-borne, and space-borne systems. Satellites can play an important role in MDA, including optical and radar imaging satellites, as well as satellites that carry receivers for the Automatic Identification System (AIS) created by the International Maritime Organization, and even commercial satellites which can collect radiofrequency signals. With the rise of commercial Earth observation constellations, we are seeing much higher revisit rates with less exquisite architecture, which is allowing for an explosion of usable MDA data points. As well, many of the satellites being launched as part of the smallsat revolution are providing Earth observation capabilities that could be used to improve MDA. Space-based solutions are helping to close the gap for knowledge of what is on the oceans.

U.S. MDA policy

U.S. MDA policy is largely guided by the National Strategy for Maritime Security, which is supported by seven implementation plans: the National Maritime Domain Awareness Plan (NMDAP); the Maritime Operational Threat Response Plan; the International Outreach and Coordination Strategy; the Maritime Infrastructure Recovery Plan; the Maritime Transportation System Security Plan; the Maritime Commerce Security Plan; and the Domestic Outreach Plan. According to the NMDAP, these seven plans all together "represent a comprehensive national effort to promote global economic stability, protect legitimate activities, mitigate the effects of natural disasters, and prevent hostile and illegal acts affecting the maritime domain."[40] It has a strong international bent to it, as the NMDAP notes, "This Plan serves to unify and support efforts to enhance domain awareness, advance decision-making, and provide the best possible setting to make maritime information appropriately available to all members of the Global Maritime Community of Interest."[41]

Maritime security, particularly in the Indo-Pacific region, has been a big concern for the U.S. In its 2015 Asia-Pacific Maritime Security Strategy, DoD states, "One of the Department's top priorities is to promote greater maritime domain awareness, which is an essential capability for all coastal States ... DoD is working closely with partners in the Asia-Pacific region to encourage greater information sharing and the establishment of a regional maritime domain awareness network that could provide a common operating picture and real-time dissemination of data."[42] It goes on to say specifically regarding India, "In South Asia, the Department sees a strategic convergence between India's 'Act East' policy and the U.S. rebalance to the Asia-Pacific region, and we are seeking to reinforce India's maritime capabilities as a net provider of security in the Indian Ocean region and beyond. Given our broad shared interests in maritime security, the Department has developed a three-pronged approach to maritime cooperation with India: maintaining a shared vision on maritime security issues; upgrading the bilateral maritime security partnership; and collaborating to both build regional partner capacity and improve regional maritime domain awareness."[43]

DoD has an Indo-Pacific Maritime Security Initiative (MSI) that has expanded its reach from Southeast Asia to South Asia. Part of its responsibility is to help partner nations improve their capacity for contributing to MDA.[44] MSI funding has also been used to help increase information-sharing among participants.

Potential Indian contributions to shared MDA efforts

In December 2018, India launched its Information Fusion Centre, intended to serve as a regional hub for sharing MDA information between participating partners.[45] This is an excellent step toward enhancing Indo-Pacific MDA and should be encouraged through U.S. contributions (data, financial, logistic, a liaison officer) wherever possible.

India has many satellites which would be strong candidates for collecting and then sharing MDA information with the U.S. Through ISRO's efforts, India has the largest constellation of remote sensing satellites intended for civilian use (via its India Remote Sensing (IRS) system). November 2019 saw the launch of Cartosat-3, which grew out of the IRS system and has more sophisticated detecting capabilities, with multispectral, panchromatic, and infrared imagers.[46] With its movement toward militarizing its space capabilities, this has also led to the launch of a few imaging satellites for India's military program. Two that are planned to be launched in December 2019 are Risat-2BR1 and Risat-2BR2, both of which are Synthetic Aperture Radar satellites and thus are attractive because they are not beholden to clear skies and/or good weather to image the Earth.[47] They are also excellent candidates for collecting MDA data that could then be disseminated to strategic partners to improve the overall maritime picture of the Indo-Pacific region.

This cooperation between the U.S. and India in space-based MDA could potentially be modelled after ISRO's program of cooperating with France's space agency, CNES, on space automatic identification system (S-AIS). In August 2019, the two agencies announced joint development and operations of ten low Earth-orbit satellites. This constellation will establish the first S-AIS series to track merchant ships in real time, which will improve MDA knowledge greatly, as current S-AIS technology is affected by the limited number of satellites covering the region and thus sometimes positional data of ships can be delayed by ninety minutes.[48]

One way to deepen U.S.–India space-based MDA cooperation is the signing of enabling agreements. The Communications, Compatibility, and Security Agreement (COMCASA) of September 2018 was a good start.[49] Discussions have begun on a Basic Exchange and Cooperation Agreement but have been hung up on disagreements on what it would entail; work on that should continue until it is successfully concluded.[50] An Industrial Security Annex was signed in December 2019. All of these will strengthen the ability of the U.S. and Indian militaries to share information, which will then smooth the way for space-based MDA cooperation.

The need for a documented Indian space policy/strategy

India has been an established space player for decades, starting with participating in U.S. launches in 1962, moving on to creating its own satellites, then developing the ability to launch satellites, and then finally creating a launcher that can take up other countries' satellites. It has largely focused on civil space capabilities, looking to space to provide socioeconomic benefit and development to India. ISRO has been the primary space actor for India and, as a civil space agency, focuses on civil space capabilities and priorities.

India's shift to a more militarized use of space over the decade since 2010 reflects current trends globally in using space to shore up national security needs. India now has a handful of military satellites (used for imagery collection) and is developing its own position, navigation, and timing constellation – NavIC – which has obvious military implications. Its Defence Research and Development Organisation was the driving factor behind India's March 2019 ASAT test. None of these is inherently destabilizing. However, given that so much of space security rests on perception, intent is a key part of demonstrating one's commitment to the responsible use of space. And India, unlike many other space actors (including newly emerging ones), lacks a national space policy. It lacks a national space strategy. It lacks any documented discussion of national security space priorities. The only policy guidance that one can point to in attempting to determine

Indian priorities in space is its satellite communication policy, which dates to 1991, and a remote sensing policy from 2011. That is it.

Given that India is opening a new chapter in its space program, with a larger role given to security space priorities and the creation in 2019 of both the Defence Space Research Organisation and the Defence Space Agency, some clarity in terms of India's intent, priorities, goals, and objectives for space, both security and civil, is needed. This will also help out strategic partners like the U.S. in identifying areas of common interest and reaching out for new cooperative efforts in strategic space.

Notes

1. *National Space Policy of the United States of America*, June 28, 2010, https://obamawhitehouse.archives.gov/sites/default/files/national_space_policy_6-28-10.pdf. Accessed November 26, 2019.
2. *Fact Sheet: National Security Space Strategy*, Department of Defense, 2011, https://archive.defense.gov/home/features/2011/0111_nsss/docs/2011_01_19_NSSS_Fact_Sheet_FINAL.pdf. Accessed November 25, 2019.
3. *Space Policy Directive-1, Presidential Memorandum on Reinvigorating America's Human Space Exploration Program*, December 11, 2017, www.whitehouse.gov/presidential-actions/presidential-memorandum-reinvigorating-americas-human-space-exploration-program/. Accessed November 27, 2019.
4. *Space Policy Directive-2, Streamlining Regulations on Commercial Use of Space*, May 24, 2018, www.whitehouse.gov/presidential-actions/space-policy-directive-2-streamlining-regulations-commercial-use-space/. Accessed November 27, 2019.
5. *Space Policy Directive-3, National Space Traffic Management Policy*, June 18, 2018, www.whitehouse.gov/presidential-actions/space-policy-directive-3-national-space-traffic-management-policy/. Accessed November 27, 2019.
6. *Space Policy Directive-4: Establishment of the United States Space Force*, February 19, 2019, www.whitehouse.gov/presidential-actions/text-space-policy-directive-4-establishment-united-states-space-force/. Accessed November 27, 2019.
7. 'Media Roundtable with U.S. Space Command Commander Gen. John Raymond', Department of Defense (August 29, 2019), www.defense.gov/Newsroom/Transcripts/Transcript/Article/1949346/media-roundtable-with-us-space-command-commander-gen-john-raymond/. Accessed November 18, 2019.
8. An excellent break-down of the different iterations of the Space Force/Corps can be found in 'Space Force or Space Corps? Competing Visions for a New Military Service', K. Johnson, Center for Strategic and International Studies (June 27, 2019), www.csis.org/analysis/space-force-or-space-corps. Accessed November 19, 2019.

9 K. Singer, '100th Space Sharing Agreement Signed, Romania Space Agency Joins', STRATCOM Public Affairs (April 26, 2019), www.stratcom.mil/Media/News/News-Article-View/Article/1825882/100th-space-sharing-agreement-signed-romania-space-agency-joins/. Accessed November 20, 2019.
10 Ibid.
11 *U.S.–India Joint Statement*, The White House, September 30, 2014, https://obamawhitehouse.archives.gov/the-press-office/2014/09/30/us-india-joint-statement. Accessed November 25, 2019.
12 Remarks by Frank A. Rose, 'U.S.–India Space Security Cooperation: A Partnership for the 21st Century', given at the Observer Research Foundation, New Delhi, India, March 5, 2015, https://2009-2017.state.gov/t/avc/rls/2015/238609.htm. Accessed November 27, 2019.
13 *Union of Concerned Scientists Satellite Database*, April 1, 2019, www.ucsusa.org/resources/satellite-database. Accessed November 25, 2019.
14 D. S. Madhumathi, 'ISRO initiates "Project NETRA" to safeguard Indian space assets from debris and other harm', *The Hindu* (September 24, 2019), www.thehindu.com/sci-tech/science/isro-initiates-project-netra-to-safeguard-indian-space-assets-from-debris-and-other-harm/article29497795.ece. Accessed November 26, 2019.
15 Ibid.
16 Ibid.
17 *Joint Statement on U.S.–India Strategic Security Dialogue*, U.S. Department of State, March 13, 2019, https://translations.state.gov/2019/03/13/joint-statement-on-u-s-india-strategic-security-dialogue/. Accessed November 28, 2019.
18 T. Hitchens, 'U.S. India ASAT Test React May Backfire, Experts Say', *Breaking Defense* (April 3, 2019), https://breakingdefense.com/2019/04/u-s-india-asat-test-react-may-backfire-experts-say/. Accessed November 26, 2019.
19 S. Unnithan, 'Two to Tango: India, U.S. Embark on first 2+2 Dialogue', *India Today* (September 2, 2018), www.indiatoday.in/magazine/the-big-story/story/20180910-two-to-tango-india-us-embark-on-first-2-2-dialogue-1327248-2018-09-01. Accessed September 24, 2019.
20 'The Five Key Takeaways from India–U.S. 2+2 Dialogue', *Hindustan Times* (updated November 4, 2019), www.hindustantimes.com/india-news/the-five-key-takeaways-from-india-us-2-2-dialogue/story-Pfpj5jfsUp9Hqz0k5HQDEL.html. Accessed November 21, 2019. U.S. Department of State, *Highlights of 2019 U.S.–India 2+2 Ministerial Dialogue*, December 18, 2019, www.state.gov/highlights-of-2019-u-s-india-22-ministerial-dialogue/. Accessed September 1, 2020.
21 'The Five Key Takeaways from India–U.S. 2+2 Dialogue'.
22 For a longer discussion of counterspace capabilities around the world, please see *Global Counterspace Capabilities: An Open Source Assessment*, ed. B. Weeden and V. Samson, Secure World Foundation, April 2019, https://swfound.org/media/206408/swf_global_counterspace_april2019_web.pdf.
23 A good summary of this can be found here: D. Porras, *UNIDIR Space Security Conference 2019. Supporting Diplomacy: Clearing the Path for Dialogue*

Indian priorities in space is its satellite communication policy, which dates to 1991, and a remote sensing policy from 2011. That is it.

Given that India is opening a new chapter in its space program, with a larger role given to security space priorities and the creation in 2019 of both the Defence Space Research Organisation and the Defence Space Agency, some clarity in terms of India's intent, priorities, goals, and objectives for space, both security and civil, is needed. This will also help out strategic partners like the U.S. in identifying areas of common interest and reaching out for new cooperative efforts in strategic space.

Notes

1 *National Space Policy of the United States of America*, June 28, 2010, https://obamawhitehouse.archives.gov/sites/default/files/national_space_policy_6-28-10.pdf. Accessed November 26, 2019.
2 *Fact Sheet: National Security Space Strategy*, Department of Defense, 2011, https://archive.defense.gov/home/features/2011/0111_nsss/docs/2011_01_19_NSSS_Fact_Sheet_FINAL.pdf. Accessed November 25, 2019.
3 *Space Policy Directive-1, Presidential Memorandum on Reinvigorating America's Human Space Exploration Program*, December 11, 2017, www.whitehouse.gov/presidential-actions/presidential-memorandum-reinvigorating-americas-human-space-exploration-program/. Accessed November 27, 2019.
4 *Space Policy Directive-2, Streamlining Regulations on Commercial Use of Space*, May 24, 2018, www.whitehouse.gov/presidential-actions/space-policy-directive-2-streamlining-regulations-commercial-use-space/. Accessed November 27, 2019.
5 *Space Policy Directive-3, National Space Traffic Management Policy*, June 18, 2018, www.whitehouse.gov/presidential-actions/space-policy-directive-3-national-space-traffic-management-policy/. Accessed November 27, 2019.
6 *Space Policy Directive-4: Establishment of the United States Space Force*, February 19, 2019, www.whitehouse.gov/presidential-actions/text-space-policy-directive-4-establishment-united-states-space-force/. Accessed November 27, 2019.
7 'Media Roundtable with U.S. Space Command Commander Gen. John Raymond', Department of Defense (August 29, 2019), www.defense.gov/Newsroom/Transcripts/Transcript/Article/1949346/media-roundtable-with-us-space-command-commander-gen-john-raymond/. Accessed November 18, 2019.
8 An excellent break-down of the different iterations of the Space Force/Corps can be found in 'Space Force or Space Corps? Competing Visions for a New Military Service', K. Johnson, Center for Strategic and International Studies (June 27, 2019), www.csis.org/analysis/space-force-or-space-corps. Accessed November 19, 2019.

9 K. Singer, '100th Space Sharing Agreement Signed, Romania Space Agency Joins', STRATCOM Public Affairs (April 26, 2019), www.stratcom.mil/Media/News/News-Article-View/Article/1825882/100th-space-sharing-agreement-signed-romania-space-agency-joins/. Accessed November 20, 2019.
10 *Ibid.*
11 *U.S.–India Joint Statement*, The White House, September 30, 2014, https://obamawhitehouse.archives.gov/the-press-office/2014/09/30/us-india-joint-statement. Accessed November 25, 2019.
12 Remarks by Frank A. Rose, 'U.S.–India Space Security Cooperation: A Partnership for the 21st Century', given at the Observer Research Foundation, New Delhi, India, March 5, 2015, https://2009-2017.state.gov/t/avc/rls/2015/238609.htm. Accessed November 27, 2019.
13 *Union of Concerned Scientists Satellite Database*, April 1, 2019, www.ucsusa.org/resources/satellite-database. Accessed November 25, 2019.
14 D. S. Madhumathi, 'ISRO initiates "Project NETRA" to safeguard Indian space assets from debris and other harm', *The Hindu* (September 24, 2019), www.thehindu.com/sci-tech/science/isro-initiates-project-netra-to-safeguard-indian-space-assets-from-debris-and-other-harm/article29497795.ece. Accessed November 26, 2019.
15 *Ibid.*
16 *Ibid.*
17 *Joint Statement on U.S.–India Strategic Security Dialogue*, U.S. Department of State, March 13, 2019, https://translations.state.gov/2019/03/13/joint-statement-on-u-s-india-strategic-security-dialogue/. Accessed November 28, 2019.
18 T. Hitchens, 'U.S. India ASAT Test React May Backfire, Experts Say', *Breaking Defense* (April 3, 2019), https://breakingdefense.com/2019/04/u-s-india-asat-test-react-may-backfire-experts-say/. Accessed November 26, 2019.
19 S. Unnithan, 'Two to Tango: India, U.S. Embark on first 2+2 Dialogue', *India Today* (September 2, 2018), www.indiatoday.in/magazine/the-big-story/story/20180910-two-to-tango-india-us-embark-on-first-2-2-dialogue-1327248-2018-09-01. Accessed September 24, 2019.
20 'The Five Key Takeaways from India–U.S. 2+2 Dialogue', *Hindustan Times* (updated November 4, 2019), www.hindustantimes.com/india-news/the-five-key-takeaways-from-india-us-2-2-dialogue/story-Pfpj5jfsUp9Hqz0k5HQDEL.html. Accessed November 21, 2019. U.S. Department of State, *Highlights of 2019 U.S.–India 2+2 Ministerial Dialogue*, December 18, 2019, www.state.gov/highlights-of-2019-u-s-india-22-ministerial-dialogue/. Accessed September 1, 2020.
21 'The Five Key Takeaways from India–U.S. 2+2 Dialogue'.
22 For a longer discussion of counterspace capabilities around the world, please see *Global Counterspace Capabilities: An Open Source Assessment*, ed. B. Weeden and V. Samson, Secure World Foundation, April 2019, https://swfound.org/media/206408/swf_global_counterspace_april2019_web.pdf.
23 A good summary of this can be found here: D. Porras, *UNIDIR Space Security Conference 2019. Supporting Diplomacy: Clearing the Path for Dialogue*

(May 28–29, 2019), p. 2, https://swfound.org/media/206814/unidir-space-security-report-2019_for-publication.pdf. NB: SWF was a co-sponsor and -organizer of this conference.
24 P. Martinez, 'The UN COPUOS Guidelines for the Long-Term Sustainability of Outer Space Activities', Secure World Foundation Fact Sheet, November 2019, https://swfound.org/media/206891/swf_un_copuos_lts_guidelines_fact_sheet_november-2019–1.pdf. Accessed November 22, 2019.
25 Hitchens, 'U.S. India ASAT Test'.
26 *Permanent Mission of India to the United Nations New York Brief on India and United Nations*, India Ministry of External Affairs, September 12, 2019, pp. 5–6, www.mea.gov.in/Images/amb1/INDIA_UNITED_NATIONS_12_sept_2019.pdf. Accessed November 25, 2019.
27 *Ibid*, p. 6.
28 *Ibid*.
29 D. Porras, 'ASAT Test Guidelines: A Viable Option to Implement TCBMs', ORF *Space Tracker* (June 16, 2018), www.orfonline.org/expert-speak/asat-test-guidelines-a-viable-option-to-implement-tcbms/. Accessed November 26, 2019.
30 M. Smith, 'Debris from Chinese ASAT Test Now More than 3,000 Pieces', *SpacePolicyOnline.com*, posted October 15, 2010, and last updated December 5, 2011, https://spacepolicyonline.com/news/debris-from-chinese-asat-test-now-more-than-3–000-pieces/; B. Weeden, *2007 Chinese Anti-Satellite Test Fact Sheet*, Secure World Foundation, updated November 23, 2010, https://swfound.org/media/9550/chinese_asat_fact_sheet_updated_2012.pdf. Both accessed November 27, 2019.
31 B. Weeden, 'Through a Glass, Darkly: Chinese, American, and Russian Anti-satellite Testing in Space', *TheSpaceReview.com* (March 17, 2014), www.thespacereview.com/article/2473/2. Accessed November 19, 2019.
32 Narendra Modi, *Twitter.com*, March 27, 2019, https://twitter.com/narendramodi/status/1110800868058660864?lang=en. Accessed November 21, 2019.
33 'Frequently Asked Questions on Mission Shakti, India's Anti-Satellite Missile Test Conducted on March 27, 2019', Indian Ministry of External Affairs, March 27, 2019, https://mea.gov.in/press-releases.htm?dtl/31179/Frequently+Asked+Questions+on+Mission+Shakti+Indias+AntiSatellite+Missile+test+conducted+on+27+March+2019. Accessed November 26, 2019.
34 A. Tellis, 'India's ASAT Test: An Incomplete Success', Carnegie Endowment for International Peace, April 15, 2019, https://carnegieendowment.org/2019/04/15/india-s-asat-test-incomplete-success-pub-78884. Accessed November 26, 2019.
35 Marco Langbroek, *Twitter.com*, September 7, 2019, https://twitter.com/Marco_Langbroek/status/1170352670500110336. Accessed November 26, 2019.
36 Hitchens, 'U.S. India ASAT Test'.
37 J. Foust, 'NASA Resumes Cooperation with ISRO after ASAT Test', *SpaceNews* (April 7, 2019) https://spacenews.com/nasa-resumes-cooperation-with-isro-after-asat-test/. Accessed November 27, 2019.

38 J. Foust, 'NASA Warns Indian Anti-satellite Test Increased Debris Risk to ISS', *SpaceNews* (April 2, 2019), https://spacenews.com/nasa-warns-indian-anti-satellite-test-increased-debris-risk-to-iss/. Accessed November 27, 2019.
39 Foust, 'NASA Resumes Cooperation'.
40 *National Strategy for Maritime Security: National Maritime Domain Awareness Plan,* U.S. Department of Defense, December 2013, revised 2017, p. ii.
41 *Ibid.,* p. iv.
42 *Asia-Pacific Maritime Security Strategy,* U.S. Department of Defense, 2015, p. 28.
43 *Ibid.*
44 *The Department of Defense Indo-Pacific Strategy Report: Preparedness, Partnerships, and Promoting a Networked Region,* June 1, 2019, p. 50, https://media.defense.gov/2019/Jul/01/2002152311/-1/-1/1/DEPARTMENT-OF-DEFENSE-INDO-PACIFIC-STRATEGY-REPORT-2019.PDF. Accessed November 22, 2019.
45 *Ibid.*
46 W. Graham, 'India's PSLV Conducts Cartosat-3 Launch', *NASASpaceflight.com* (November 26, 2019), www.nasaspaceflight.com/2019/11/indias-pslv-cartosat-3-launch/. Accessed November 23, 2019.
47 D. S. Madhumathi, 'ISRO's Launch Tally Hits 5 Main Satellites This Year', *The Hindu* (November 29, 2019), www.thehindu.com/news/national/isros-launch-tally-hits-5-main-satellites-this-year/article30115143.ece. Accessed November 28, 2019.
48 G. Iyer, 'Monitoring IUU in India Using Space Technology: Prospects and Challenges', *International Symposium on Maritime-Space Cooperation in the Asia-Pacific Region,* Tokyo, Japan, October 4, 2019. NB: SWF was a co-sponsor of this conference. https://swfound.org/media/206853/iuu-gayathri-iyer-4-oct-2019.pdf.
49 A. Panda, 'What the Recently Concluded U.S.–India COMCASA Means', *The Diplomat* (September 9, 2019), https://thediplomat.com/2018/09/what-the-recently-concluded-us-india-comcasa-means/. Accessed November 29, 2019.
50 D. Peri, 'India, U.S. to Sign Industrial Security Agreement at 2+2 Dialogue', *The Hindu* (November 24, 2019), www.thehindu.com/news/national/india-us-to-sign-industrial-security-agreement-at-22-dialogue/article30063585.ece. Accessed November 29, 2019.

8

U.S.–India space cooperation: an Indian view

Rajeswari Pillai Rajagopalan

Introduction

U.S.–India relations have transformed in many ways in the two decades since 2000. This is largely being driven by their mutual concern about China's rise and the manner in which this impacts on the interests of both countries. It is also driving U.S.–India space cooperation. Indeed, cooperation in outer space has the potential to emerge as the new area that could significantly enhance strategic engagement between India and the U.S.[1] Both New Delhi and Washington need each other in an era of strategic uncertainty posed by China's rise, including in the military space domain. Further, the growing strategic partnership between Russia and China, including in the outer space sector has the potential to increase the security concerns of both India and the U.S., and this could be an additional driver in U.S.–India space cooperation.

India and the U.S. have a history of half a century of cooperation in outer space, albeit with certain gaps, especially in the 1980s and the 1990s. But since the early 2000s, both the countries have exploited opportunities for cooperation, be they around space exploration, navigation or space-launch segment. But the relationship has the potential for much greater growth, provided there is a determined and pragmatic approach to space cooperation in both countries, especially between the respective space agencies. India's successful Mars mission, a rare feat achieved by only four nations so far, has led to more streamlined cooperation between the Indian Space Research Organization (ISRO) and the National Aeronautics and Space Administration (NASA). In 2017, ISRO conducted a record-breaking launch, putting 104 satellites into space, of which 96 belonged to the U.S., a major highlight of recent Indo-U.S. space cooperation.[2] The scale of space cooperation between India and the U.S. has the potential to be multifaceted, for space safety and sustainability, space security and space global governance.

This chapter starts with a brief historical overview of India–U.S. space cooperation. The cooperative phase came to an abrupt halt in the 1970s and restarted only in the early 2000s. The chapter then lays out the state of the bilateral space cooperation as it stands today, before examining the future possibilities. The penultimate section looks at the impediments that have come in the way of building a strong and vibrant relationship and the chapter concludes with possible steps to overcome those impediments and to strengthen the space cooperation agenda between India and the U.S.

India–U.S. space cooperation: early decades

India has benefited from cooperating with the U.S. since the beginning of its space program in the 1960s. The U.S. collaborated with India in building satellites as well as in developing the Thumba Equatorial Rocket Launching Station, India's first launch station. The launch site launched hundreds of sounding rockets, mostly acquired from the U.S. In fact, India's first rocket launch was of an American-built one, the Nike-Apache rocket, carrying payload and instruments from Europe. It was launched in November 1963.[3] Similarly, two of India's successful satellite programs, the INSAT series communication satellites and the remote-sensing satellites (IRS series), both received critical technological assistance from the U.S. in the 1970s. In one of the most fruitful of such collaborations, the ISRO worked with NASA in Satellite Instructional Television Experiment in the mid-1970s, which provided a big boost to India's telecommunication sector.[4] This was considerably helped by the access and support that NASA gave to India through its ATS-6 experimental satellite, which India used for a number of experiments, including Direct-to-Home broadcasts. This early assistance helped ISRO significantly, and it went on to build its INSAT series of communication satellites, which revolutionized India's television broadcasting sector. India's first four INSAT satellites were built by the U.S. and three were launched on U.S. launch vehicles. The INSAT-series satellites are considered one of the most successful of their type, one that has impacted millions of people in rural India. These satellites have also made significant contributions to search and rescue operations in the Indian Ocean. A second area of significant U.S. assistance came in remote-sensing satellites in the 1970s. NASA's Landsat (originally called Earth Resources Technology Satellite) satellites were one of the earliest remote-sensing satellites in the world and provided a large amount of resource data from outer space. India cooperated with NASA to acquire as well as use Landsat imagery. This collaboration, and the capabilities India built through this collaboration, went on to become the foundation for India to develop its own IRS satellites.[5]

However, the U.S.–India relations soured in the 1970s owing to several factors, but particularly India's peaceful nuclear explosion (PNE) in 1974, which immediately led to the curtailing of various technological cooperative activities between the two countries. The PNE led to a number of bilateral sanctions as well as international measures that halted much of India's international space cooperation arrangements. Global technology export control regimes also accelerated. When the Missile Technology Control Regime (MTCR) was established in 1987, it had a big dampening effect on India–U.S. space cooperation. The U.S. saw even civilian rocket and space technology as potentially aiding a nuclear weapons program, and cut off most collaboration as a result. The impact of MTCR on India's efforts to procure cryogenic engines in the late 1980s and early 1990s is a case in point (this is detailed below). India was close to a deal with the Soviet Union in 1989 but the U.S. made a case against Moscow, saying that it was violating its MTCR commitments. This became a sticking point for India, with ISRO becoming suspicious of the U.S. as a reliable partner in space. This negative perception continued, and for almost two decades, through the 1990s, U.S.–India space cooperation remained fairly minimal.

Indo-U.S. space cooperation: from early 2000s to present

After more than two decades, Indo-U.S. space cooperation began to pick up momentum again. This was the consequence of renewed high-level political dialogue between India and the U.S. that followed the Indian nuclear tests in 1998. Though the U.S. imposed substantial sanctions on India for the nuclear tests, there was also realization on both sides of the need to stabilize the relationship between the two sides, leading to an extended dialogue between the U.S. Deputy Secretary of State, Strobe Talbott, and the Indian Minister of External Affairs, Jaswant Singh. The period under the George W. Bush administration also saw a push towards broader cooperation across high-end technologies. The big, bold push for a new chapter in India–U.S. relations came in the form of a common vision for a strategic partnership, which was initiated by President Bush and Prime Minister Vajpayee in November 2001.[6] This was further expanded to include specific areas of cooperation under an agreement on Next Steps in Strategic Partnership, to include civilian nuclear activities, civilian space programs, and high-technology trade.[7] The civil space cooperation eventually went on to go beyond purely civil functions to include space security engagements to enable a common understanding of the emerging space environment and the threats that are endangering safe, secure, and continued access to outer space.

One of the big highlights of Indo-U.S. space cooperation in the 2000s was India's first Moon mission (Chandrayaan-1) in October 2008. The mission carried many scientific instruments from other countries, including two from NASA – the Mini Synthetic Aperture Radar from the Johns Hopkins University's Applied Physics Laboratory and the Moon Mineralogy Mapper, an imaging spectrometer from Brown University and NASA's Jet Propulsion Laboratory (JPL), which was used to confirm the presence of water molecules on the surface of the Moon for the first time. The two countries joined again to cooperate on India's Mars mission (Mangalyaan) in 2014. NASA offered critical help in deep space communication, which was important for waking up the Mars mission from almost a year of slumber. This assistance to ISRO was provided by NASA's JPL.

Another step that is particularly prestigious is the U.S. offer to India to join the International Space Station (ISS). U.S. Assistant Secretary of State, Frank Rose made this announcement in Delhi during his trip to India for the first U.S.–India Space Security Dialogue in 2015.[8] While this could be a major boost to U.S.–India relations, it also has the potential to excite the next generation about space, and also science and STEM (science, technology, engineering, and mathematics) education more broadly. India's involvement with the ISS could also possibly lead Indian scientists and students to send climate-related Earth-observation experiments to the ISS, which has been the case for countries like Japan who have partnered with the ISS. But India did not show any great excitement about the U.S. offer to be part of the ISS, possibly because India did not attach much importance to human space missions until 2018, though another reason could also have been discomfort with collaborating as a junior partner to the U.S., especially given some of the old tensions in the space relationship.

Nevertheless, the Indian and U.S. space agencies are also working together on a research satellite. Under the Global Precipitation Measurement Mission partners, NASA, ISRO, and the National Oceanic and Atmospheric Administration (NOAA) are working in the calibration, validation, and application of ocean color observation data on ISRO's Oceansat-2 mission. NOAA additionally plans to work with ISRO in the future follow-on ocean surface vector wind missions.[9]

Civil space cooperation

NISAR

Over the decade since 2010, there are several areas of cooperation between India and the U.S. in the space domain. One of the truly important collaborative ventures is the NASA–ISRO Synthetic Aperture Radar (NISAR), in which ISRO and NASA are working on a satellite to study climate change and natural disasters by calculating changes on the Earth's surface such as variations in land vegetation, ice sheets, and land motion. Both the space agencies are working on NISAR, with plans to launch it on an Indian Polar Satellite Launch Vehicle (PSLV) in 2021. NASA Administrator Charles Bolden and Chairman of ISRO K. Radhakrishnan signed the agreement for the NISAR at the International Astronautical Congress in Toronto in September 2014. A 2007 National Academy of Science "Decadal Survey" report, *Earth Science and Applications from Space: National Imperatives for the Next Decade and Beyond*, prompted NASA to study three specific areas: ecosystems, solid earth, and cryospheric sciences. Specifically, these include ecosystem disturbances, ice-sheet collapse, and natural hazards such as earthquakes, tsunamis, volcanoes, and landslides. Thus, NASA had been exploring concepts for a Synthetic Aperture Radar (SAR) mission to understand these three specific areas. With ISRO also being interested in these mission goals, the JPL, which is implementing this mission on the U.S. side, revised the mission requirements to accommodate ISRO for a joint mission. Additionally, ISRO identified a few specific areas of special relevance to India, including monitoring of agricultural biomass over India, snow and glacier studies in the Himalayas, Indian coastal and near-shore ocean studies, and disaster monitoring and assessment.[10] As per the 2014 agreement, NASA is to provide the L-band SAR with a high-rate communication subsystem for science data, GPS (Global Positioning System) receivers, a solid-state recorder, and a payload data subsystem, whereas ISRO will provide the spacecraft bus, an S-band SAR, and the launch vehicle and associated launch services.[11]

Aiding navigation: GAGAN

The GPS Aided GEO Augmented Navigation (GAGAN) system has been developed by ISRO and the Airports Authority of India (AAI) as a Satellite Based Augmentation System (SBAS) for the India airspace. This system is aimed at establishing, deploying, and certifying SBAS for the safety-of-life civil aviation applications in India by providing additional accuracy, availability, and integrity necessary for all phases of flight, from en route through approach for all qualified airports within the GAGAN service volume. GAGAN GEO covers areas from Africa to Australia and can be expanded for seamless navigation services across the region. The system is reportedly interoperable with other international SBAS systems such as the U.S. Wide Area Augmentation System, the European Geostationary Navigation Overlay Service, and the Japanese MTSAT Satellite Augmentation System.[12] GAGAN consists of five components: (i) Indian Reference Station – at fifteen locations across India; (ii) Indian Master Control Center – two at Bangalore; (iii) Indian Land Uplink Station – three stations, two at Bangalore and one at New Delhi; (iv) geostationary satellites (GSAT8/GSAT10) in orbit and one on-orbit spare in GSAT-15 launched on November 10, 2015; and (v) a data communication subsystem – two optical-fiber communication circuits and two very small aperture terminal circuits.[13] Raytheon, which won the $82 million contract in 2009, has built the ground segment for GAGAN, which consists of fifteen reference stations spread across the country. After winning the contract, the vice president of Command and Control Systems, Raytheon Network Centric Systems, Andy Zogg stated that India's GAGAN system will be "the world's most advanced air navigation system and further reinforces India's leadership in the forefront of air navigation. GAGAN will greatly improve safety, reduce congestion and enhance communications to meet India's growing air traffic management needs."[14]

Even though GAGAN is being used primarily for aviation purposes, it will prove beneficial to many other sectors, including intelligent transportation, maritime navigation, highways, railways, surveying, geodesy, security agencies, telecom industry, and personal users of position location applications. For instance, the Indian National Centre for Ocean Information Services and the AAI worked together to launch a new satellite-based GEMINI (GAGAN Enabled Mariner's Instrument for Navigation and Information) system to alert deep-sea fishermen of any approaching weather- or nature-related dangers at sea. GEMINI can provide alerting on looming threats such as cyclones, high waves, strong winds, along with PFZ (potential fishing zones) and search and rescue mission.[15]

Involvement of U.S. private sector companies in India's space growth story is also a relatively new phenomenon. Several such companies are working with ISRO in developing key components and technologies. With India's gradual opening of the space sector to Indian private industries, the opportunities for them to collaborate with the U.S. private sector are also large. Such private sector joint ventures could change the Asian space game in terms of the capability mix that the two countries' private sectors could jointly develop, both by way of strategic impact as well as economically.

Indian satellite launch services

Since 2015, the U.S has responded positively to the possibility of using Indian launchers for its satellites, to which it was not previously open. In one of the first instances, India launched four U.S. satellites on a PSLV for the first time in September 2015. This commercial launch was done for a private U.S. company, Spire Global, contracted through Antrix, ISRO's commercial arm. Through this, India's launch services have been offered to more than fifty foreign partner countries including Austria, Germany, France, Japan, Canada, Singapore, UK, and the U.S. While the

Indian competency in providing launch services at very affordable rates ($33 million per launch) is undeniable, there have been lobbyists within the U.S. that have called for a ban on the use of the PSLV to launch U.S. satellites. This conflict will possibly be one of the bigger impediments to India–U.S. space cooperation.

India sees it as important to penetrate the global launch services market for two reasons. First, the small-satellite Earth Observation market is likely to expand, keeping in tune with the trend of large satellites being broken into small-satellite constellations. Second, and more importantly, India's launch competency lies in the small-satellite segment. India is still lagging when it comes to heavy launchers such as the Geosynchronous Satellite Launch Vehicle, whereas the PSLV, ISRO's smaller launcher, is considered its tried and tested workhorse. Hence, India worries about losing this market to other players such as China (which is also emerging as a cost-effective service provider) or to new private sector players who are emerging as potential competitors to India in the lighter segment of the launch services market. A third reason also demonstrates the Indian interest in this market. ISRO has developed a Small Satellite Launch Vehicle (SSLV), which is a derivative of the existing PSLV. The high demand and consequent unavailability of PSLV due to tight launch schedules pushed ISRO to develop a dedicated smaller vehicle to launch small satellites. Typically, these small satellites have piggybacked as additional payloads on a big PSLV mission, but the SSLV can be used instead. While the ISRO is yet to announce the rates for launching satellites using the SSLV, it is reported that it will be "at a drastically reduced price as compared to PSLV."[16] The fact that an SSLV can be assembled within a few days by a smaller team makes it an even more attractive option as compared to a PSLV. Though the SSLV is yet to be unveiled, it has already lined up customers, including a foreign one. This is possibly also the first publicly known commercial venture by the New Space India Limited, ISRO's new commercial arm created in 2019. U.S.-based launch-service organizer Spaceflight Inc. announced in August 2019 that "it will launch payloads for an undisclosed U.S. satellite constellation customer" in India's new SSLV, SSLV-D2, scheduled for "later" in the year.[17] The mission was supposed to put four small earth observation satellites in two different orbits. While, at the time of writing, there was no formal announcement of the U.S. customer, a July 25, 2019 filing with the Federal Communications Commissions by Earth imaging company BlackSky Global seeking license for four of its satellites through the SSLV in November 2019 gave a clear indication of who the customer is.[18]

Therefore, India is taking seriously the potential commercial benefits of using PSLV and SSLV to offer launch services to a large number of domestic and foreign customers. India's cost-effective and credible launch capability does make it a quite attractive option. For India, there is also the space diplomacy, in addition to the commercial gains from such launches.

Civil Space Working Group

Indo-U.S. space cooperation over the years has been driven primarily by the respective space agencies, ISRO and NASA, and over the years this has become more regular and streamlined. Giving a big push to India–U.S. strategic cooperation, Minister for External Affairs K. Natwar Singh and Secretary of State Condoleezza Rice decided to set up a Joint Working Group (JWG) on Civil Space Cooperation. The JWG had its first meeting in Bangalore in June 2005, discussing an entire range of issues that would promote greater understanding of each other's requirement and the policy framework in each other's country. This was also the forum where the two sides first discussed their cooperation on India's Chandrayaan 1 mission. Other important themes discussed include cooperation in creating a Global Navigation Satellite System (GNSS) and the progress made with regard to India's GAGAN project.[19] India has also remained an active partner along with the U.S. in the GNSS, including hosting an international meeting in December 2019.[20] The JWG has been a continuing annual initiative that adds substantially to U.S.–Indian space cooperation efforts.

The Mars Working Group

Given the success of India's Mars mission in 2014 and NASA's own Mars mission, MAVEN, the two space agencies agreed to further their collaboration exploring additional areas related to Mars exploration. Accordingly, NASA and ISRO established the ISRO–NASA Mars Working Group, and the first face-to-face meeting of the Group took place in Bangalore in January 2015. The respective Mars missions of NASA and ISRO were just days apart in 2015 as they reached the Martian orbit and therefore one of the first concrete ideas for the Working Group was to have coordinated observations and analysis between ISRO's Mangalyaan and NASA's MAVEN.[21] The Working Group has been working to develop well-coordinated exploration plans, including a possible joint ISRO–NASA Mars mission in the future.[22]

Space security dialogue

The mid-2000s saw big changes in the Indo-U.S. relationship, especially relating to strategic technologies in sectors such as nuclear and space. The U.S.–India civil nuclear agreement of 2005 was a game changer in setting the tone and tenor as well as the direction of future Indo-U.S. relations. For decades, the U.S. had attempted to impose restrictions on India's nuclear program because it worried about India building nuclear weapons. The U.S. was particularly concerned because India had not signed the Nuclear Non-Proliferation Treaty and there was little by way of cooperation between the two sides in the nuclear sector. While Indo-U.S. civil space cooperation has been forthcoming, the same cannot be said for space security conversations between the two sides. By September 2014, this approach began to change during Prime Minister Modi's maiden visit to the U.S. At this meeting, both India and the U.S. decided to incorporate space security in their bilateral agenda, resulting in the U.S.–India Joint Statement noting that both Washington and New Delhi had agreed "to start a new dialogue on maintaining long-term security and sustainability of the outer space environment, including space situational awareness (SSA) and collision avoidance in outer space." Both sides have, since then, held three rounds of space security dialogue, the inaugural round being held in New Delhi in March 2015.[23] The second round was held in February 2016 and a third one took place in Washington, DC in March 2019, but details about the nature and scope of these conversations remain sparse. The joint statement of the third meeting noted that both sides "discussed trends in space threats, respective national space priorities, and opportunities for cooperation bilaterally and in multilateral fora."[24] Space security dialogue became a reality primarily because of the growing Indian and American concerns about China's critical advancements in space, including in the military space domain. The capabilities that China has developed in the counter-space realm, including electronic and cyberwarfare in space have been important imperatives for both India and the U.S. Nevertheless, it must be highlighted that this is a platform that has the potential to include other like-minded countries such as Japan, Australia, and France in addressing the emerging space security challenges as well as in creating conversations on space security governance issues.

Prospects for the future

Though U.S.–India relations have improved dramatically, furthering cooperation in outer space will offer another avenue for a closer strategic partnership. India–U.S. space cooperation has been multifaceted, covering peaceful and civil applications of space to space security and diplomacy. If the current trend continues, the prospects for Indo-U.S. space cooperation are excellent.

As for the future, India and the U.S. are aiming higher and looking at scientific cooperation in understanding the solar system. Security analysts from both the U.S. and India have articulated the need for space to be given a more prominent role within the broader U.S.–India strategic partnership under platforms like the "2+2" dialogue between the U.S. Secretaries of State and Defense and the Indian Minister of External Affairs and Minister of Defence.[25] There is also a possible joint mission in heliophysics and such other exploration of celestial bodies being explored by the U.S.–India Civil Space Working Group.[26]

A few other tangible ideas for future India–U.S. space partnership include one relating to global governance and another that relates to joint space outreach to new and emerging space players. On global governance, both India and the U.S. can play an active role in shaping the efforts to create new rules of the road for outer-space activities. Now that India has conducted an anti-satellite (ASAT) test, in March 2019, and demonstrated its capability, it may shift from its position of ambiguity to one of pro-active engagement in shaping norms, rules, and regulations.[27] India's objectives are broadly to exercise a restraint on certain potentially dangerous activities in outer space. Having crossed the Rubicon, it is in India's interests to partner with like-minded countries and build a coalition to make fresh proposals, including one that curbs ASAT tests in future. The U.S. could be a potential partner in this venture because the two countries have a common interest in preventing further ASAT capabilities from being developed.

A second area of possible collaboration is with India–U.S. joint space outreach to new and emerging space players who have only just begun to appreciate the utility of outer space in changing their lives. From offering satellite launch services and training to providing satellite-based services could also generate significant positive goodwill for India and the U.S. The generation of such positivity could also help India and the U.S. to build a larger community of countries who can lend support to New Delhi and Washington for their global governance proposals at multilateral platforms.

A third area for possible cooperation between India and the U.S. relates to industry-to-industry partnerships. With ISRO gradually opening to the Indian domestic private sector, this may be an ideal opportunity for the U.S. space industry to open channels of communication with its Indian counterparts. Industries in both countries must engage in outreach that is not restricted to big players but that involves second-rung players who build several different system components and parts. Creating an effective supply chain between U.S. and Indian industries could be a more sustainable model.

In a fourth area, space security and space diplomacy could also be critical components as India and U.S. reach more mature levels of engagement.[28] The influence of terrestrial politics in outer space is a sad reality, but ignoring the consequences of that reality will be disastrous for both India and the U.S. China's Belt and Road Initiative and the Space Silk Road are important strategic developments for both India and the U.S. With the development of new and emerging counter-space capabilities, the need for a more effective regulatory as well as a normative framework needs to be emphasized by both sides. The growth of electronic and cyberwarfare capabilities by China should be a pertinent factor for both India and the U.S. In fact, India and the U.S. could take the lead in bringing together other like-minded countries in the Indo-Pacific including Japan, Australia, Vietnam, and Singapore. Given the great-power competition and rivalry, a number of other middle powers including India, Japan, Australia, Canada, and Switzerland could come together to generate new ideas and perspectives that may be technology aided and evidence based. While U.S. might not be part of a middle-power grouping such as this, India could keep the U.S. in the loop on the progress being made through such a grouping. Such a grouping of countries could also engage in a number of initiatives to address environmental security, disaster prevention and management, development of maritime domain awareness (MDA), and a more comprehensive SSA by connecting with the emerging regional SSA capabilities in Asia and elsewhere. Trilaterals and minilaterals such as India–U.S.–Japan, India–U.S.–Japan–Australia, and India–U.S.–France need to be pursued, especially as the Indo-Pacific navigates through strategic uncertainties. These countries could also engage in pure space exploration missions, including joint future planetary ones.

Impediments to greater cooperation

The U.S. and India have strengthened their space cooperation from the early 2000s, when India and the U.S. were once again warming up to each other. Nevertheless, close to two decades later, there appear still to be certain limitations that need to be overcome if this cooperation is to become more meaningful and effective.

Some of the historical negative experiences between India and the U.S. – such as the U.S. sabotaging India's efforts to acquire cryogenic engines in the late 1980s and early 1990s – have cast a negative perception of the U.S. In 1986, the ISRO was beginning its work in developing a one-ton cryogenic engine for India's Geosynchronous Satellite Launch Vehicle. Around 1989, the Soviet company Glavkosmos offered to sell two cryogenic engines, to give India the know-how, and to train some ISRO personnel.[29] But the U.S. government asked that the deal between New Delhi and Moscow be cancelled as it allegedly was in violation of Russian MTCR commitments.

When it became evident that India and the Soviet Union were not going to call off the deal, the U.S. imposed a two-year sanction on the ISRO in 1992 that cancelled all contracts between ISRO and the U.S. Professor U. R. Rao, writing about the episode in his book, *India's Rise as a Space Power*, notes that "While the U.S. did not object to the agreement with Glavkosmos at the time of signing, the rapid progress made by ISRO in launch vehicle technology was probably the primary cause which triggered [the sanctions after a year]."[30] This experience has made ISRO quite suspicious of the U.S. as a strategic partner in space. One of the most recent illustrations of Indian suspicions is the case of the training of Indian astronauts. Both the U.S. and Russia offered their expertise in the training of astronauts. Although the U.S. did extensive outreach to work with India on this, ISRO decided to go along with Russia instead. This was despite the fact that there have been some setbacks in India–Russia space cooperation, owing to the China factor. Yet ISRO's decision to go along with it is an indication of the greater comfort level with Russia and the organizational and cultural antipathy towards the U.S.

The lack of complementarity between the Indian and American space programs is another small but important limitation. The fact that the two space agencies have different foci as far as their programs are concerned remains an issue in their ability to broaden their scope of cooperation. But they have also worked hard to find avenues for cooperation. India's first Moon mission in 2008 is a case in point. Even though India's Chandrayaan mission was a small one with limited objectives, ISRO and NASA worked together to ensure that it was complementary in nature. The JPL's scientific payloads went on to confirm water presence on the Moon.

The fact that India and the U.S. are at different stages of space program development has sometimes slowed down the pace of cooperation between New Delhi and Washington. While it may be an impediment in certain respects, India can also leverage the situation and learn a great deal from the U.S. The U.S.'s experience with its space program offers India many lessons and pitfalls to avoid as India navigates its own encounter with outer space. But the lack of strategic convergence on space issues may be hampering significant progress.[31] Developing strategic convergence on space issues would require the two sides to place space as part of larger strategic thinking, and that conversation needs to be led by officials at the Ministry of External Affairs and the U.S. State Department, rather than by ISRO and NASA. This assumes particular importance at a time when China's rise within the military space domain is a constant reminder to India and the U.S. of the kind of strategic challenges and threats they need to address.

Even though ISRO launched its first U.S. satellites on an Indian PSLV in September 2015, there are still irritants that could impede relations in the launch services segment. Legal instruments such as the Commercial Space Launch Agreement (CSLA) could negatively impact satellite launches on the PSLV, even though the logic of cooperation could not be clearer. The CSLA that was enacted in 1984 is a U.S. federal law that sought to assist private space launches by establishing an authorization and licensing regime.[32] The Act was a clear acknowledgment of the fact that the U.S. private sector was becoming an independent actor capable of undertaking a number of activities, including development of commercial launch vehicles and orbital satellites and operation of private launch sites. While the U.S. small-satellite market is expanding, the U.S. does not have yet domestic launchers to meet such demand.[33] The same is true for the global small-satellite market. Accordingly, at present, small satellites have to wait for a rideshare arrangement on a bigger mission, but the growing demand is pushing the small-satellite companies to look to being the primary payload so that they get priority when devising timelines for launch.[34] India has a perfect solution for this problem because of its PSLV launcher. However, the U.S. has taken the stand, going back to 2006, that it will only allow U.S. small satellites to be launched on a PSLV if India signs the CSLA.[35] Senior Indian officials, including the then Joint Secretary in the Ministry of External Affairs, Dr. Jaishankar, categorically stated that "ISRO is unwilling to even discuss the issue of satellite services in this context, adding satellite launches should proceed in a 'market economy' like India's through agreements between the satellite companies."[36] U.S. Ambassador to India David Mulford summarized this in a cable in 2006 saying "The original NSSP [Next Steps in Strategic Partnership] goal to permit Indian launch of U.S. satellites and foreign satellites containing U.S. components is in danger of being stalled by the suggestion to expand the scope of a commercial launch agreement to include satellite services, which the GOI [Government of India] rejects as a unilateral change to the carefully negotiated NSSP quid-pro-quos."

The CSLA has had, and could continue to have, a negative impact on the PSLV because CSLA forbids India from offering launch services at cheaper rates than those provided by the U.S.[37] The U.S. fears that American small-satellite companies freely buying satellite launch services from foreign countries could hurt the U.S. domestic launch industry. Apparently, in a February 2016 decision, the U.S. Federal Aviation Administration noted that "it agreed with its Commercial Space Transportation Advisory Committee (COMSTAC) that Indian launch services, owned and controlled by the Indian government, threaten to 'distort the conditions of competition' in the launch-services market."[38] Analysts recognize the absence of an international regulation on launch services as a problem and that a regulation "is long overdue."[39] Analysts argue that the General Agreement on Trade in Services could possibly offer some solutions in this regard.[40]

Recommendations for overcoming the impediments

The U.S. could be concerned about security more than cost considerations on the issue of small-satellite launches. Launching through foreign organizations could also increase the risk of exposure of sensitive technology to foreign countries. Therefore, a case-by-case approval process, as is the current practice, or having different categories of countries to permit or deny satellite launch services, can possibly be maintained by the U.S. with some justification. But some broad principles are needed to remove the ad hoc nature of decision making on this issue. A second important consideration is for India to speed up the privatization of the PSLV. This is important, since the legal instruments such as the CSLA apply only to government-owned launch service providers, and India can circumvent this by privatizing the PSLV. India's decision to privatize PSLV is two decades old but there have been legal hurdles in making it happen.[41] India initially took a decision to hand it over to Larsen & Toubro, but, due to criticism from other domestic industry players, the government decided that it would hand over the PSLV program to a conglomerate of Indian industries that could together run the PSLV program. ISRO has said that it will complete the privatization of the PSLV by 2020.[42]

A second important step that both India and the U.S. need to take is to adopt a strategic vision for their cooperation in space. The absence of a strategic approach will tend to keep relations on a bare minimum tactical level, which is not what is required at a time when the Indo-Pacific is going through major strategic uncertainties. A fine balance between strategic and tactical goals in generating greater engagement between India, the U.S., and a host of other spacefaring powers is important for maintaining an open outer space domain. Countries such as Japan, Australia, France, Singapore, and Vietnam need to be engaged in a pro-active manner by India and the U.S. by building greater synergies in their approach to space, thereby ensuring better SSA. The significance of SSA and MDA cannot be emphasized enough in the Indo-Pacific context.

Conclusion

India–U.S. space cooperation has had its ups and downs. The U.S. provided significant help to India to develop its space program. But this more or less ended as a consequence of American fears about nuclear and missile proliferation. This slowdown in U.S.–India cooperation, and, indeed, active U.S. efforts to curtail the space programs through sanctions and technology denial, left a bitter legacy, especially on the Indian side. Nevertheless, India–U.S.

space cooperation did improve with the thawing of relations between the two countries, starting in the early 2000s. This was driven by shared concerns about China's rise that transformed almost all aspects of U.S.–India relations, not the space sector alone. China's growing capacities and ambitions in outer space have added some urgency to India's efforts in outer space and changed India's autarchic approach to the space program. India is now much more willing to seek partners in outer space efforts, including with the U.S. This is likely to remain an important driver of closer U.S.–India space ties, despite the lingering after-effects of Indian anger at U.S. technology-denial regimes. While there continue to be some impediments to closer cooperation, including lack of complementarity and major differences in focus, these are far outweighed by the political requirements for closer ties. Thus, the prospects for India–U.S. cooperation in space remain fairly bright.

Notes

1 Rajeswari Pillai Rajagopalan, 'U.S.–India strategic dialogue: "sky's no limit" for space,' *Commentaries*, Observer Research Foundation, July 18, 2011, www.orfonline.org/research/us-india-strategic-dialogue-skys-no-limit-for-space/.
2 'ISRO sends 104 satellites in one go, breaks Russia's record,' *Economic Times*, February 15, 2017, https://economictimes.indiatimes.com/news/science/isro-sends-104-satellites-in-one-go-breaks-russias-record/articleshow/57159365.cms.
3 APJ Abdul Kalam, *Wings of fire: an autobiography* (Hyderabad, India: Universities Press), p. 39.
4 PV Manoranjan Rao, BN Suresh and VP Balagangadharan, *Fishing hamlet to red planet: India's space journey*, 2015, e-book, www.isro.gov.in/pslv-c25-mars-orbiter-mission/fishing-hamlet-to-red-planet-download-e-book.
5 *Ibid.*
6 'Next steps in strategic partnership with India,' Statement by the President, January 12, 2004, https://2001-2009.state.gov/p/sca/rls/pr/28109.htm.
7 K Alan Kronstadt, 'India–U.S. relations,' *CRS Issue Brief for Congress*, updated February 23, 2005, https://fas.org/asmp/resources/govern/109th/CRSIB93097.pdf.
8 Remarks by Frank Rose, U.S. Assistant Secretary, Bureau of arms control, verification and compliance, 'U.S.–India space security cooperation: a partnership for the 21st century,' Observer Research Foundation, New Delhi, India, March 5, 2015, www.state.gov/t/avc/rls/2015/238609.htm.
9 Department of State, 'U.S.–India civil space and technology cooperation,' *Fact sheet*, September 30, 2014, https://2009-2017.state.gov/r/pa/prs/ps/2014/09/232336.htm.
10 'NASA partnership with the Indian Space Research Organisation (ISRO),' Jet Propulsion Laboratory, https://nisar.jpl.nasa.gov/isropartner/.

11 EO portal directory, 'NISAR (NASA-ISRO Synthetic Aperture Radar) Mission,' https://directory.eoportal.org/web/eoportal/satellite-missions/content/-/article/nisar-nasa-isro-synthetic-aperture-radar-mission.
12 Indian Space Research Organisation, 'A step towards initial Satellite based Navigation Services in India: GAGAN & IRNSS,' www.isro.gov.in/applications/step-towards-initial-satellite-based-navigation-services-india-gagan-irnss.
13 'GAGAN – India's SBAS,' *Inside GNSS*, January 18, 2016, https://insidegnss.com/gagan-indias-sbas/.
14 'Raytheon wins $82M air navigation contract from India,' July 21, 2009, *GOVCON Wire*, www.govconwire.com/2009/07/raytheon-wins-82m-air-navigation-contract-from-india/.
15 Press Information Bureau, 'Low cost device for ocean states forecast and mapping potential fishing zones launched,' October 9, 2019, https://pib.gov.in/newsite/PrintRelease.aspx?relid=193703.
16 Srishti Choudhary, 'Isro's mini satellite launcher in the works,' *LiveMint*, August 25, 2019, www.livemint.com/technology/tech-news/isro-all-set-to-spur-commercial-space-sector-with-its-newly-built-sslv-1566734694464.html.
17 DS Madhumathi, 'ISRO's mini launcher SSLV is unborn but has 2 flights booked,' *The Hindu*, August 7, 2019, www.thehindu.com/news/national/isros-mini-launcher-sslv-is-unborn-but-has-2-flights-booked/article28859854.ece; Jeff Foust, 'Spaceflight purchases first commercial flight of new Indian small launcher,' *Space News*, August 6, 2019, https://spacenews.com/spaceflight-purchases-first-commercial-flight-of-new-indian-small-launcher/.
18 Foust, 'Spaceflight purchases first commercial flight'.
19 U.S. Department of State, 'U.S.–India Joint Working Group on Civil Space Cooperation Joint Statement,' July 14, 2005, https://2001-2009.state.gov/p/sca/rls/pr/2005/49656.htm.
20 For an update on the India–U.S. cooperation on the GNSS, see U.S. Department of State, Office of space and advanced technology, 'U.S. GPS/GNSS International Activities Update,' September 17, 2019, www.gps.gov/cgsic/meetings/2019/auerbach.pdf.
21 'U.S., India to Collaborate on Mars Exploration, Earth-Observing Mission,' Solar System Exploration Research – Virtual Institute, https://sservi.nasa.gov/articles/u-s-india-to-collaborate-on-mars-exploration-earth-observing-mission/.
22 'NASA invites India to jointly explore Mars, send astronauts,' *PTI*, February 28, 2016, http://indianexpress.com/article/technology/science/nasa-invites-india-to-jointly-explore-mars-send-astronauts/.
23 Remarks by Frank Rose, U.S. Assistant Secretary, Bureau of arms control, verification and compliance, 'U.S.–India space security cooperation: a partnership for the 21st century,' Observer Research Foundation, New Delhi, India, March 5, 2015, www.state.gov/t/avc/rls/2015/238609.htm.
24 Ministry of External Affairs, Government of India, 'India–U.S. strategic security dialogue,' March 13, 2019, https://mea.gov.in/press-releases.htm?dtl/31154/IndiaU.S._Strategic_Security_Dialogue.

25 Frank A Rose and Jonathan DT Ward, 'Pompeo and Mattis should add space cooperation to the U.S.–India strategic partnership,' *Space News*, September 5, 2018, https://spacenews.com/pompeo-and-mattis-should-add-space-cooperation-to-the-u-s-india-strategic-partnership/; and Rajagopalan, 'U.S.–India strategic dialogue.'
26 Special Address by U.S. Ambassador to India Richard Verma at the ORF Kalpana Chawla Annual Space Policy Dialogue, 'Bringing U.S.–India space cooperation to the edge of the universe,' New Delhi, February 25, 2016, http://newdelhi.usembassy.gov/sr022516.html.
27 Ministry of External Affairs, 'Frequently asked questions on Mission Shakti, India's anti-satellite missile test conducted on March 27, 2019,' https://mea.gov.in/press-releases.htm?dtl/31179/Frequently+Asked+Questions+on+Mission+Shakti+Indias+AntiSatellite+Missile+test+conducted+on+27+March+2019.
28 For an appraisal on possible areas of collaboration including on space diplomacy, see Rose and Ward, 'Pompeo and Mattis should add space cooperation'.
29 Vasudevan Mukunth, 'Why haven't ISRO and the U.S. signed their commercial space launch agreement yet?,' *The Wire*, May 23, 2016, https://thewire.in/history/why-havent-isro-and-the-us-signed-their-commercial-space-launch-agreement-yet.
30 Vasudevan Mukunth, 'Why haven't ISRO and the U.S. signed their commercial space launch agreement yet?,' *The Wire*, May 23, 2016, https://thewire.in/history/why.
31 Some of these aspects are addressed in Kathleen H Hicks, Richard M Rossow, Andrew Metrick, John Schaus, Natalie Tecimer and Sarah Watson, 'U.S.–India security cooperation: progress and promise for the next administration,' Center for International and Strategic Studies, October 2016, https://csis-prod.s3.amazonaws.com/s3fs-public/publication/161003_Hicks_U.S.IndiaSecurity_Web.pdf.
32 Cody Knipfer, 'Congress and commerce in the final frontier (part 1),' *The Space Review*, December 10, 2018, www.thespacereview.com/article/3619/1.
33 Peter B de Selding, 'U.S. launch companies lobby to maintain ban on Indian rockets,' *Space News*, March 29, 2016, https://spacenews.com/u-s-space-transport-companies-lobby-to-maintain-ban-on-use-of-indian-rockets/; Aditya Madanapalle, 'Isro PSLV-C37 Mission: the U.S. private sector is threatened by cheap Indian spaceflight,' FirstPost, February 10, 2017, www.firstpost.com/tech/news-analysis/isro-pslv-c37-mission-the-us-private-sector-is-threatened-by-cheap-indian-spaceflight-3697497.html.
34 Cody Knipfer, 'Of India and ICBMs: two current concerns for American small-satellite launch,' *The Space Review*, April 25, 2016, www.thespacereview.com/article/2969/1.
35 David C Mulford, 'Expanded CSLA scope is blocking agreed progress in space,' Telegram (cable), Wikileaks, February 16, 2006, https://wikileaks.org/plusd/cables/06NEWDELHI1220_a.html.

36 David C Mulford, 'Expanded CSLA scope is blocking agreed progress in space,' Telegram (cable), Wikileaks, February 16, 2006, https://wikileaks.org/plusd/cables/06NEWDELHI1220_a.html.
37 Michael J Listner, 'India's commercial space conundrum,' SPACE THOUGHTS (July 6, 2016), https://spacethoughtsblog.wordpress.com/2016/07/06/indias-commercial-space-conundrum/, as cited in Shane Fitzmaurice, 'GATS regulation for launch services: resolving the United States-India conflict,' *Minnesota Journal of International Law*, Vol. 27 No. 1, 2018, http://minnjil.org/wp-content/uploads/2018/02/Fitzmaurice_v27_i1_283–311.pdf.
38 Peter B de Selding, 'U.S. launch companies lobby to maintain ban on Indian rockets,' *Space News*, March 29, 2016, https://spacenews.com/u-s-space-transport-companies-lobby-to-maintain-ban-on-use-of-indian-rockets/.
39 Shane Fitzmaurice, 'GATS regulation for launch services: resolving the United States–India conflict,' *Minnesota Journal of International Law*, Vol. 27 No. 1, 2018, http://minnjil.org/wp-content/uploads/2018/02/Fitzmaurice_v27_i1_283-311.pdf.
40 *Ibid.*
41 Pallava Bagla, 'ISRO's love-hate relationship with private sector – A look back at history,' *Financial Express*, 26 May 2020, www.financialexpress.com/opinion/isros-love-hate-relationship-with-private-sector-a-look-back-at-history/1970400/.
42 Anusuya Datta, 'ISRO looks at JV for PSLV manufacture; launch to be privatised by 2020,' *The Wire*, October 30, 2017, https://thewire.in/space/isro-looks-jv-pslv-manufacture-launch-privatised-2020.

Part V

Counterterrorism cooperation

9

The U.S.–India counterterrorism relationship: striking the balance

Tricia Bacon

Introduction

The U.S.–India strategic partnership is often heralded as rooted in the shared values of democracies,[1] but in practice the counterterrorism relationship is a sometimes uneasy combination of shared values and interests that do not fully align, especially when it comes to Pakistan. Despite differences, since the efforts to forge a stronger relationship between the two countries began in earnest in 2000, counterterrorism has featured prominently on the bilateral agenda. Counterterrorism was one of the main issues, arguably *the* main issue, that provided a foundation for the strategic partnership.[2]

But since about 2015, counterterrorism has been eclipsed by other issues, most notably defense, China, and economic and trade issues.[3] While there are broader strategic reasons for this change, most notably China's rise, it is also the result of shifts in counterterrorism. For the U.S., while its involvement in Afghanistan persists, the focal point for its counterterrorism efforts has shifted back from South Asia to the Middle East. In addition, both countries have made strides in their counterterrorism capabilities, especially in terms of their abilities to protect their homelands.[4] India also increased its ability to strike back quickly at Pakistan in response to terrorist attacks.[5] These developments created more space for other strategic issues to rise on the U.S.–India bilateral relationship agenda.

While the decline in focus may seem like a negative development for the two countries' counterterrorism relationship or even the strategic partnership writ large, it is not. The combination of being among the priorities without being the highest priority strikes a balance of getting enough senior attention to keep cooperation growing and expanding, but not so much emphasis that the divergences in this realm significantly hinder the relationship.

There is an important exception to the decline in emphasis on counterterrorism: during crises precipitated by terrorist attacks on India emanating from Pakistan. However, such crises are not primarily about terrorism for the U.S. They raise serious concerns about escalation and miscalculation that could lead to a nuclear confrontation between India and Pakistan.[6] These crises have produced both subsequent progress in the U.S.–India counterterrorism relationship – often leading to new initiatives and efforts to collaborate – as well as tensions, as the U.S. rarely satisfies India in its subsequent approach to Pakistan. In other words, crises caused by terrorist attacks create opportunities for cooperation *and* bring to the forefront the differences in the counterterrorism relationship caused by Pakistan with little prospect for satisfactory resolution.

Nonetheless, with some important exceptions, the U.S.–India counterterrorism relationship has been characterized by incremental progress.[7] The two countries have worked closely since 2018 to pressure Pakistan through international institutions, like the United Nations and the Financial Action Task Force.[8] Though there is still divergence, the U.S.'s view on Pakistan has grown closer to India's longstanding position, though backsliding is inevitable and full alignment is unlikely. Through the counterterrorism relationship with India, the U.S. primarily seeks to: disrupt and prevent attacks in India, which includes pressuring Pakistan; weaken groups that threaten India, albeit with limitations on what the U.S. can get Pakistan to do; increase India's ability to counter the threat; manage fallout from attacks in India emanating from Pakistan to avoid escalation between the two nuclear-armed countries; and overall to help secure India from terrorist threats so that it can focus on its rise and balance against China's rise.

The counterterrorism relationship with India has significant political support within the U.S.[9] Both improving ties with India and counterterrorism enjoy bipartisan support, even in these turbulent political times, which has helped generate political will at high levels across very different administrations.[10] While this bipartisan consensus does not make the U.S.–India counterterrorism relationship immune from the political machinations in Washington, it makes issues easier to navigate.

The U.S.–India counterterrorism relationship has been institutionalized to varying degrees through dialogues and exchanges, which has helped to connect elements of the U.S.'s and India's vast bureaucracies and tricky federal-state dynamics: no small feat. The relationship is not as warm or mature as other U.S. counterterrorism relationships, given that terrorism was a top national security concern since 2001. Perhaps more than any other area in the bilateral relationship, the longstanding suspicions and mistrust, especially over Pakistan, still permeate the counterterrorism relationship.[11]

There is ample room to improve the counterterrorism relationship without imposing unrealistic expectations. There are other areas to initiate collaboration and ways to institutionalize and make existing cooperation more substantive. While the U.S. generally seems keener for expansion in the counterterrorism relationship that India views more cautiously, the U.S. has let aspects of the relationship falter, most notably the critical link between the U.S. Department of Homeland Security and the Indian Ministry of Home Affairs. While there is recognition among India watchers in the U.S. that India balks at joining coalitions like the anti-Islamic State global coalition, there is room for greater cooperation against the Islamic State, especially in South Asia. The failure to do so to date reflects one of the constraints in the relationship: the two countries' threat perceptions and priorities differ, and they make limited shifts to accommodate one another.

Ultimately, the counterterrorism relationship's current position in the bilateral agenda and pace of cooperation is probably well suited, though far from ideal, to maintaining a productive relationship. It has produced slowly improving progress with an upward trajectory, albeit with periods of disappointment and few big breakthroughs. At times, the counterterrorism relationship is more rhetoric than substance, with regular references in major joint statements and a lot of areas of cooperation lumped under counterterrorism that are not solely or even primarily about combating terrorism.[12] Nonetheless, particularly post-2008, the counterterrorism relationship has been a qualified success story in the strategic partnership.

This chapter will proceed in five sections. First, it will examine the main challenge in the relationship: Pakistan. In so doing, it will trace how the U.S.–India relationship arrived at the current place. Second, it will then discuss how the future in Afghanistan will shape the U.S.–India counterterrorism relationship. The chapter then turns to the efforts to date to engage in counterterrorism cooperation that navigate around the issues with Pakistan. Fourth, it will assess U.S.–India cooperation on another counterterrorism challenge, namely the Islamic State. The chapter concludes by examining the remaining hurdles to counterterrorism cooperation and the need for realistic expectations in the relationship.

The elephant in the room: Pakistan

It would be difficult to deny that the U.S. and India have grown more aligned in their views on terrorism, particularly terrorism emanating from Pakistan.[13] The U.S. has shifted towards India's view of the militant landscape in the region, seeing anti-India groups as part of the same "ecosystem" as organizations that threaten the U.S. and recognizing Pakistan's persistent support for militant groups, including both anti-India organizations like Lashkar-e-Taiba, Jaish-e-Mohammed, and Hizbul Mujahidin, as well as Afghan insurgent groups that target U.S. forces in Afghanistan, namely the Afghan Taliban and its subsidiary the Haqqani Network.[14] In so doing, the U.S. has tied its perception of the terrorist threat more closely to the threat to India.

This shift has resulted in a more punitive approach to Pakistan by the U.S., perhaps most notably the Trump administration's decision in January 2018 to freeze security assistance.[15] However, barring an unforeseen event, the U.S. is unlikely to be sufficiently hardline on Pakistan to satisfy India. Instead, the U.S. will probably backslide on Pakistan periodically, in large part because there are few plausible outcomes in Afghanistan that do not require the U.S. to rely on Pakistan to some degree.[16]

Moreover, the U.S. and India still do not have the same priorities. The joint statements in recent years have listed the main threats to both countries to include al-Qaida, the Islamic State, Jaish-e Mohammad, Lashkar-e-Taiba, D-Company, and their affiliates, but the two countries' priorities within that list differ.[17] Understandably, each country still prioritizes those organizations that target it directly.[18] The U.S.'s main concerns – al-Qaida, the Islamic State, and the Taliban/Haqqanis – are not India's first priority. Conversely, Lashkar-e-Taiba and Jaish-e-Mohammed – India's main threats and all groups that receive patronage from Islamabad – are not the U.S.'s top concern. This discrepancy results in continuing divergence in the counterterrorism relationship, despite closer alignment overall.

However, it is worth noting that the U.S. has long cared more about anti-India organizations than is commonly recognized. Its concerns about these groups stemmed from their ability to provoke a conflagration between India and Pakistan. The U.S. is far from sanguine that the two countries correctly calibrate how far they can push one another without miscalculation or inadvertent escalation. The involvement of Lashkar and Jaish in the insurgency in Afghanistan, combined with the death of six Americans in the 2008 Mumbai attacks, bolstered the U.S.'s concerns about these groups. But it did not bring them on par with the top threats. There is recognition that most of the anti-India groups are strongly anti-American as well, but that they have not fully acted on that anti-U.S. intent to date. An uncomfortable reality rarely explicitly acknowledged is that one reason why these groups restrain their actions against the U.S. is because of their relationship with the Pakistani state and the need to avoid bringing additional pressure on their patron.

It is difficult to understand where the U.S.–India counterterrorism relationship is likely to go – and how Pakistan will affect it – without a brief discussion of how it arrived at the current place, particularly since 2001.[19] The relationship has experienced three critical junctures: the aftermath of 9/11, the 2008 Mumbai attacks, and Osama bin Laden's death. Each one has been a breakthrough in the U.S.–India counterterrorism relationship but has also involved setbacks.

Critical juncture 1: post-9/11

The attacks of 9/11 and the ensuing Global War on Terrorism increased the sense between the U.S. and India that there was a common interest in countering terrorism.[20] India responded to 9/11 and the U.S. invasion of Afghanistan with unprecedented offers of assistance. One former senior official argues that the resulting shared interests in countering terrorism were *the* key to establishing the basis for the strategic partnership.[21] Some early milestones following 9/11 included the October 2001 signing of a U.S.–India Mutual Legal Assistance Treaty, which provides legal privileges in terrorism-related investigations.[22] Just months later, a U.S.–India Cyber Security Forum was established to safeguard critical infrastructures from cyberattacks.[23] Though India refused to support the U.S. invasion of Iraq, progress on counterterrorism cooperation continued throughout the Bush administration. Notably, the 2005 *New Framework for the U.S.–India Defense Relationship* listed "defeating terrorism and violent religious extremism" as one of four key shared security interests and called for a bolstering of mutual defense capabilities required for pursuing that objective.[24]

While the U.S. welcomed the growth in the relationship with India after 9/11, the reality was that it needed Pakistan in much more tangible and immediate ways for its number one national security priority: countering al-Qaida and protecting the U.S. homeland.[25] Though India made generous offers of assistance, it could not provide direct assistance on that central issue. Unlike Pakistan, the U.S. did not *need* India for counterterrorism.[26] While far from a perfect relationship, Islamabad provided the required cooperation, assisting in the capture of major al-Qaida figures in the years after 9/11 and supporting actions against al-Qaida over time that helped the U.S. to significantly weaken the group.[27]

However, the attack on the Indian Parliament by Jaish-e-Mohammed in December 2001 was an early indicator of how Pakistani support for militant groups would complicate the U.S. counterterrorism effort and its counterterrorism relationship with India for years to come. In the military mobilization that followed the Parliament attack, Pakistan diverted troops from the western border with Afghanistan to the east at a critical period during which al-Qaida and the Taliban were fleeing across the Durand Line. The U.S. responded by designating Lashkar-e-Taiba and Jaish-e-Mohammed as Foreign Terrorist Organizations, something it had previously been unwilling to do. In response to U.S. pressure to cease sponsorship of militant groups, Pakistan altered the profile of its sponsorship, most notably making it more covert, but not ceasing to provide it.

The centrality of al-Qaida in the U.S.'s calculus, and by extension the relationship with Pakistan required to effectively counter it, constrained the

U.S.–India counterterrorism relationship. At the time, the U.S. saw itself as pushing Pakistan on anti-India groups, though they were not the top priority. U.S. efforts to pressure Pakistan on terrorism were constant and often involved delivering "laundry lists" of demands to Pakistan to "do more" on various terrorism issues.[28] This constant stream of demarches failed to clearly delineate the U.S. priorities, be consistent in communicating them, and look beyond what Pakistan had or had not done lately. It was not only a source of frustration in the U.S.–Pakistan relationship; it meant that the state-supported anti-India groups were not consistently and clearly raised as a priority with Pakistan. Ultimately, one official explained, "We were trying to get the Pakistani military and civilians to turn the ship and focus on security challenges internally [rather than focus externally on India], which we knew wouldn't happen overnight." He went on to say, "We were constantly going to Pakistan to push this [anti-India terrorist groups]. It was on the U.S. agenda, but we were ineffective. But there was a reality that we did not think we could push the Pakistanis too hard or be too punitive on anti-India groups while we needed cooperation on al-Qaida."[29] However, over the course of the Bush administration, the U.S. "took its eye off the ball" on anti-India groups in the face of the growing insurgency in Afghanistan, a steady stream of al-Qaida plots in the West, and a growing internal terrorist threat in Pakistan, not to mention the war in Iraq.[30]

For its part, India did not share the U.S.'s level of concern about al-Qaida and understandably resented the U.S.'s decision to provide significant aid and assistance to Pakistan. By pouring money into Pakistan, especially its military, the U.S. damaged Indian interests.[31]

There appeared to be a potential opening with the deterioration of the security situation in Pakistan as once-friendly militant groups turned on the state and new groups emerged to attack it. The subsequent tensions and in some case ruptures between the Pakistani security establishment and its militant clients left the state of those relationships uncertain – uncertainty that grew with the transition to a civilian government. The U.S. saw this as an unprecedented opportunity to see if it could persuade Pakistan to relinquish those groups. The U.S. viewed the terrorist threat that emerged in Pakistan after 2001 as the product of Islamabad's sponsorship of terrorism and tried to convince Pakistan of that, ultimately to no avail.[32] The effort has been derided by Pakistan hawks in the U.S. and India as naivety about Pakistan. Indeed, the effort ultimately failed. But at the height of the threat in Pakistan, when fears mounted that Pakistan might become a failed state, it was not a foregone conclusion that the effort was in vain.

Critical juncture 2: the 2008 Mumbai attacks

The 2008 Mumbai attacks, which came at the twilight of the Bush administration and eve of the Obama administration, helped to elevate counterterrorism cooperation with India for several reasons.[33] As will be discussed later, this event led to an increase in counterterrorism cooperation in an array of realms, such as the Counter Terrorism Cooperation Initiative. This was important because the shortfalls in the Indian response to the attack shook the U.S.'s confidence in India's capability and fueled a desire to figure out how to improve it and reorient the Indian system towards prevention rather than response.[34] In addition, the collaboration between the Federal Bureau of Investigation (FBI) and its Indian counterparts after the attack showed how productive law enforcement cooperation could be.[35] Finally, the deaths of Americans in the Mumbai attacks contributed to a shift among senior policymakers in how Lashkar-e-Taiba was viewed and led the U.S. to dedicate more resources to countering the group.[36] In the years after the Mumbai attacks, Lashkar became more involved in the insurgency in Afghanistan, which helped to solidify the policymakers' view that the group was a threat to the U.S. However, predictions that the group was poised to be the next al-Qaida proved inaccurate.[37]

While some saw the 2008 Mumbai attacks as a breakthrough, they were not as much of a breakthrough as they could or perhaps should have been.[38] Some even saw them as a setback for the relationship.[39] The Indians wanted Pakistan "delivered on a platter," and the U.S. did not do so.[40] The Indians also believed that the U.S. did not push Pakistan sufficiently on the prosecutions of those who had plotted the attack. The contradictions in the impact of the Mumbai attacks on the U.S.–India counterterrorism relationship were illustrated in David Headley. An American citizen, Headley conducted Lashkar's surveillance for the 2008 attack in Mumbai, playing a critical role in the operation. After being arrested for drug smuggling in the 1990s, Headley had been run as a source by the U.S. Drug Enforcement Agency until roughly 2001. Afterwards, he began working with Lashkar. Though two of Headley's wives reported their suspicions about him to U.S. officials, their reports were not deemed credible and Headley was able to continue his activities. He subsequently attracted U.S. scrutiny while collaborating with al-Qaida on a plot in Denmark and was arrested by the FBI in 2009.[41]

Once arrested, Headley provided unprecedented insights into Lashkar. The U.S. has debriefed detainees from a number of militant groups, but this was the first from Lashkar who had extensive access to its leadership and Pakistani intelligence.[42] His revelations about the Pakistani intelligence service's involvement in the plot went a long way in convincing U.S. officials that Pakistan had made no progress in shifting away from supporting militant groups in the intervening years since 9/11.

The U.S. failures vis-à-vis Headley are undebatable. But what stung U.S. officials were accusations from some Indian officials that the U.S. had deliberately protected Headley and knowingly failed to prevent the 2008 Mumbai attacks. The accusations revealed the depth of the Indian anger and mistrust of the U.S. resulting from the U.S. relationship with Pakistan. The U.S. had to go to significant lengths to arrange for Indian officials to interview Headley. The delay further stoked Indian anger, though the U.S. was able to arrange for him to be interviewed by Indian officials in 2010.[43]

Following the Mumbai attacks, the U.S. redoubled its efforts to ensure that any intelligence with threat implications was shared with India. However, the effort caused significant frustration on the U.S. side, as persistent leaks of that intelligence to the Indian press compromised U.S. collection.[44] There have been improvements since that time, and, as will be discussed later, the overall intelligence relationship has progressed.[45]

The result of the 2008 Mumbai attacks was not the hardline U.S. policy on Pakistan that India wanted. But the U.S. sought additional ways to weaken the anti-India groups, particularly Lashkar, that worked around Pakistan.[46] It looked for opportunities for other countries in the region, such as Nepal and Bangladesh, to help counter the threat to India, as anti-India groups sought to exploit neighboring countries' lax border security and other weaknesses to access India.[47] The U.S. also pushed countries where Lashkar raised money, particularly in the Gulf, to crack down on the group. Notably, in 2012 the U.S. pressured Saudi Arabia to hand over an Indian Lashkar operative to India, who provided further insights on Lashkar and the 2008 Mumbai attacks.[48] While some Indian and U.S. officials were not keen on this "donut" strategy, i.e. efforts that worked around Pakistan to counter anti-India groups, there was an increased effort to squeeze these organizations, with some success.[49]

Critical juncture 3: the death of Osama bin Laden

The third and final critical juncture to date was Osama bin Laden's death, which came as al-Qaida was reeling from losses from the targeted killing campaign in Pakistan's Federally Administered Tribal Areas. This event has often been misunderstood, with accusations that Pakistan deliberately sheltered bin Laden, an accusation that makes little sense from either Pakistan or al-Qaida's perspective. Rather, this was a critical juncture because, in the absence of al-Qaida's formative leader and with the group weakened overall, the U.S. grew less dependent on Pakistan for cooperation on its top priority. Moreover, in the years that followed, the U.S. reduced its presence

Striking the balance 179

in Afghanistan and shifted significant counterterrorism resources out of South Asia and back towards the Middle East to counter the Islamic State. The linch-pin in the U.S.–Pakistan counterterrorism relationship – perhaps even in the bilateral relationship as a whole – was largely removed.

In al-Qaida's place, the Afghan Taliban and Haqqani Network rose to become the biggest issue in the U.S.'s relationship with Pakistan. Instead of the highest priority being an area in which the U.S. cooperated closely with Pakistan, the main concern was now a contentious issue: Pakistani support for the Taliban. The U.S.'s inability to pressure Pakistan sufficiently to cease its cooperation with the Taliban reveals the limitations of U.S. influence; it certainly cannot persuade Pakistan to break with the anti-India groups that the Pakistani security establishment sees as even more important to its interests. However, the U.S.'s prioritization of the Taliban and recognition of the limits of its influence does not mean that the U.S. can afford a hardline approach to Pakistan. The U.S. still depends on Pakistan for its war in Afghanistan, whether that be to access air or ground lines of communication or to pressure the Taliban to come to the negotiating table. But this shift in the U.S.–Pakistan relationship brought the U.S. closer to India's view.

After repeated efforts to persuade Pakistan to abandon sponsoring terrorist groups – efforts that have spanned the three administrations since 9/11 – the U.S. seems to have finally reconciled itself to the reality that it does not have the requisite enticements or punishments to change Pakistan's calculus vis-à-vis India and militant groups which it views as assets. It was a conclusion that the U.S. did not come to easily or cheaply. While the U.S. is very unlikely to take the hardline approach advocated by India, it could and should do more to pressure Pakistan on these groups, and ensure that it does not "take its eye off the ball" again.[50]

The key issue going forward: Afghanistan

Undoubtedly, the U.S. and India share objectives in Afghanistan. As the Congressional Research Service explained, "The U.S. and India share the objective of stabilizing Afghanistan, in order to deny sanctuary for terrorist networks targeting American and Indian citizens and interests. India is currently a key partner of the U.S. in shoring up support for Afghanistan through foreign aid and long-term strategic agreements with Kabul."[51] But in practice, it continued, "concerns over Pakistani sensitivities also limited the scope and extent of U.S. and Indian cooperation regarding Afghanistan."[52]

Not even current U.S. officials have clarity about how the U.S. will proceed in Afghanistan. However, most scenarios require some continuing

U.S. dependence on Pakistan. Admittedly, the U.S. has been incoherent in its posture towards Pakistan on the Taliban, simultaneously demanding that it cut ties with the Taliban and then asking for its assistance with the group on negotiations. For the most part, the U.S. recognizes that Islamabad will not break ties, especially in the current context, yet the U.S. continues to issue that demand. Even if the U.S. opts to withdraw from Afghanistan, it will probably need some kind of assistance from Pakistan to operate counterterrorism bases, to monitor the terms of a negotiated settlement, or to exert some influence over the Taliban.[53]

The U.S. is cognizant of India's dismay about the U.S.–Taliban negotiations. Indian officials justifiably worry about U.S. plans for a withdrawal from Afghanistan, especially that it will leave a vacuum, and fret about the possibility of being cut out of any deal.[54] Indeed, the U.S.'s main demand for "counterterrorism assurances" in the failed negotiations with the Taliban this year did not account for Indian interests or include anti-India groups: another instance of the U.S. failing to prioritize Indian terrorism concerns. Moreover, India is likely to face an increased threat in the wake of a U.S. withdrawal and/or deal with the Taliban. The insurgency in Afghanistan has attracted anti-India groups, and they will likely turn more attention back to India, especially in light of the Indian government's August 2019 revocation of Article 370.[55]

Thus, the situation in Afghanistan cuts both ways.[56] A continuing U.S. presence, which India seeks, means significant continuing U.S. dependence on Pakistan. It sets a lower cut-off at how much pressure the U.S. will exert on Pakistan for its support for anti-India groups. Even when the Obama and Trump administration have opted to be tougher on Pakistan, when Afghanistan flares, they diminish that pressure.[57] But a withdrawal from Afghanistan probably will not fully alleviate U.S. dependence on Pakistan, will turn militant groups back towards Kashmir, and may leave some level of safe haven in Afghanistan.[58]

One former U.S. intelligence official summed up the situation: "the U.S.–India counterterrorism relationship will always have an asterisk to it that will reduce the opportunities we would otherwise have ... As long as we had fish to fry in Afghanistan (apparently an indeterminate period of time) the U.S. India counterterrorism relationship takes a back seat to the U.S.–Pakistan one, regardless of how frustrating, clearly counter-productive, and counter-intuitive it seems to be."[59] While the U.S. has grown clearer eyed about Pakistan, it is unlikely to break with Pakistan or develop a hostile relationship that would satisfy India. Nor are anti-India groups likely to become the U.S. priority. While they have been active in the insurgency in Afghanistan, their contribution is minor compared to the overwhelming dominance of the Afghan Taliban.

Navigating around Pakistan: cooperation

The U.S. has a significant interest in India's security for strategic reasons, not least of which is preventing attacks from Pakistan that could spur a confrontation between the two nuclear powers. In the wake of the 2008 Mumbai attacks, senior U.S. officials advocated to their Indian counterparts to adopt a posture that emphasized preventing rather than responding to attacks, a difficult shift that the U.S. undertook after 2001 and thus had some lessons learned to share.[60] The U.S. also wants India to move past viewing Pakistan as a top national security priority in the hopes that this will create more space to balance against China. Thus, it views improvements in India's capability to counter and prevent terrorism as an important objective for the strategic partnership.

However, the U.S. has found that India can bristle at offers of capacity building, seeing this as the U.S. patronizing India and treating it as a junior partner. The U.S. has had to adapt its approach to India so as to frame what it often calls capacity building as technical cooperation, sharing best practices and lessons learned, and conducting exchanges. This more respectful approach has helped to reduce Indian sensitivities about cooperation, though a number of U.S. officials privately remark that the counterterrorism relationship is not a genuine peer-to-peer relationship, at least not yet. They concede that the U.S. is far from having all the answers on counterterrorism – a fact that their Indian counterparts have sometimes pointed out to them – but also maintain that the counterterrorism relationship is asymmetric: the U.S. offers India far more than India offers the U.S., nor does India offer the U.S. the level of contribution that other peer counterterrorism partners do.[61] As one former senior official remarked, "India insists on being treated as the country it wants to become. They don't want to be a junior partner in any way but don't really behave like an equal. On counterterrorism, the Indians don't offer much, or don't have much to offer."[62] However, another current security official countered that the Indians have offered to provide the U.S. with reciprocal assistance, but the U.S. has not taken advantage of these offers.

Dialogues and exchanges

To navigate this dynamic and divergences over Pakistan, the counterterrorism relationship has been anchored by dialogues, exchanges, and technical cooperation. This includes senior-level meetings, which virtually always involve some discussion on counterterrorism, ranging from high-level forums like the 2019 formation of a 2+2 that "provide a regular structure for high-level consultation and a focal point for other bilateral dialogues to inform" to working groups with technical experts from the gamut of counterterrorism-related areas.[63] Intelligence cooperation – once a sore spot in the relationship – has improved, but largely runs on its own parallel track apart from the rest of the relationship, because of the secret and covert nature of such work. There is also an element of counterterrorism that comes under defense more broadly, often through exercises.

Dialogues between the U.S. and India have been central to efforts to institutionalize counterterrorism cooperation and increase understanding. The two countries formed the Joint Counterterrorism Working Group in 2000, one of the endeavors that helped the broader relationship to begin the recovery from the U.S. sanctions imposed on India in 1998 and that reflected the importance of counterterrorism in the bilateral relationship. Nayak described the working group as indicative of "the transformation of a previously obscure partnership into a lead element of the haltingly expanding bilateral relationship."[64] Since 2000, the Joint Counterterrorism Working Group has been a central dialogue venue for counterterrorism cooperation, meeting at the Assistant Secretary level most years and even meeting twice in some years.[65]

Other dialogues and sub-groups have subsequently emerged. Notably, in 2011, the U.S. and India held the first Homeland Security dialogue between the Department of Homeland Security (DHS) and Ministry of Home Affairs.[66] Not only was it the "first comprehensive bilateral dialogue on homeland security issues between the U.S. and India," the dialogue occurred at the secretary level, with Secretary Napolitano and Minister Chidambaram.[67] This dialogue was particularly fruitful because it met at such a senior level and linked up institutions central to the two countries' counterterrorism efforts and with limited interactions with one another.[68] This dialogue helped to establish lines of communication and break down barriers.[69] By holding the dialogue at the secretary level, it produced senior direction and generated momentum to expand cooperation.

After launching, the Homeland Security Dialogue made significant progress in developing cooperation between the two countries. By linking professionals in the same field, such as law enforcement officers, the resulting cooperation was warmer than in some other areas of the relationship. The dialogue appeared to be well on its way to shifting from a leadership-driven effort to a more institutionalized one when the leadership on the U.S. side changed. The dialogue lost momentum under Secretary Johnson, a posture that worsened under DHS's revolving leadership in the Trump administration. The dialogue has become effectively "moribund."[70] Under the Trump administration, DHS's focus has been on immigration, and this orientation

Striking the balance

extends to its international engagement. It engages most with countries with a significant impact on immigration in the U.S. rather than strategic importance overall. In DHS's engagement with India, immigration now competes with counterterrorism as the top priority. Though DHS has a sprawling mission and institutional dysfunction, this is an insufficient reason for its inattention to the relationship with India because India's Ministry of Home Affairs has similar demands and challenges.[71]

Working groups that fall under this initiative are still functioning, such as the working group on megacity policing. Working groups also discuss building capacity in cybersecurity and critical infrastructure protection, countering illicit finance, global supply chain security, and science and technology.[72]

In 2017, the two countries launched a Designations dialogue to increase cooperation on sanctions against terrorist groups and individuals, an area of frustration for India. Designations are one of the main ways that the U.S. has been willing to take punitive action against Pakistan for its support of militant groups against India. The increase in designations of Pakistani-sponsored organizations and individuals indicates how the U.S. has moved towards India in its view of Pakistan. With the designation of Hizbul Mujahidin in 2017, all of the significant Pakistani-sponsored groups are now designated by the U.S. The Hizbul Mujahidin designation in particular reflected a U.S. acknowledgment of Indian security concerns, given that the group has not targeted U.S. interests and is not interwoven with the broader jihadist networks in Afghanistan that are of concern to the U.S. The U.S. also worked with India on its legal framework, supporting India to change some of its domestic laws on designations. U.S. officials hailed this as a significant success.[73]

The two countries have increased their cooperation on designations to pressure Pakistan at the UN. After the February 2019 Pulwama attacks, the U.S. pushed China in an unusually forceful way at the UN on the listing of Jaish-e-Mohammed leader Masood Azhar. Secretary Pompeo reportedly delivered a particularly pointed message to his Chinese counterpart, drawing praise from some within the U.S. government who have long wanted the U.S. to challenge China's protection of Pakistan at the UN.[74] The U.S. and India are cooperating through other multilateral institutions, like pressuring Pakistan through the Financial Action Task Force, an effort that has contributed to Pakistan's efforts to appear as though it is taking action against militants, such as the arrest of Lashkar-e-Taiba leader Hafiz Saeed.[75]

Dialogues like the Homeland Security dialogue or Designations dialogue can seem like bureaucratic exercises, but they are "forcing events."[76] Both sides want to ensure that they have deliverables from dialogues, so they push both countries to think of how to advance the counterterrorism relationship.

Senior-level dialogues in particular produce pressure to have deliverables. Dialogues also help the two countries to build ties and learn how to best engage with one another, building what Ayres calls "habits of cooperation," including engagement between institutions unaccustomed to dealing with one another, like the U.S. DHS and India's Ministry of Home Affairs.[77] Both countries have sprawling and disparate counterterrorism apparatuses, which complicates relations. Dialogues help to ensure that different facets of counterterrorism collaborate and bring key stakeholders together.

However, some of these dialogues have been limited in their utility and frustrating to participants. One official characterized the counterterrorism dialogue as "a dialogue of the deaf" during the Bush administration. Some meetings consisted of the two sides talking past each other, with India focusing on Pakistan while the U.S. pointed to indigenous threats.[78] At times the U.S. failed to bring new intelligence or information to the table, which irritated their Indian counterparts. On the other hand, U.S. officials have felt at times that the exchanges were shallow and thus failed to produce a broader consensus or framework on how to counter terrorism.

On the technical cooperation front, the Counterterrorism Cooperation Initiative (CCI) added impetus to that line of efforts. The CCI was formally launched in 2010, in no small part motivated by the 2008 Mumbai attacks. It committed the two countries to strengthening capabilities to effectively combat terrorism. The CCI helped to elevate technical cooperation as a priority in the counterterrorism relationship and expand cooperation into new areas. It included

> promoting exchanges regarding modernization of techniques; sharing best practices on issues of mutual interest; developing investigative skills; promoting cooperation between forensic science laboratories; establishing procedures to provide mutual investigative assistance; enhancing capabilities to act against money laundering, counterfeit currency, and financing of terrorism; exchanging best practices on mass transit and rail security; increasing exchanges between Coast Guards and Navy on maritime security; exchanging experience and expertise on port and border security; and enhancing liaison and training between specialist Counter Terrorism Units including National Security Guard with their U.S. counterparts.[79]

Homeland Security

Beyond the Homeland Security dialogue, homeland security-oriented cooperation has emerged as a central, albeit underdeveloped, pillar in the counterterrorism relationship. Indeed, "collaborating to combat threats to homeland security," as some officials have characterized it, goes beyond counterterrorism but also captures the nature of much of the U.S.–India counterterrorism relationship.[80] Within homeland security cooperation, border security is an area that has received significant attention in the U.S. since 2001. Thus, the U.S. has experiences and lessons learned to share with the Indians on this issue. Border security is also a way the U.S. can help India to mitigate the threat from Pakistan without directly confronting the tensions over how to handle Pakistan. Such cooperation is more about the "nuts and bolts" of law enforcement, but it has counterterrorism benefits and is a form of technical assistance.[81]

The 2008 Mumbai attacks helped to usher in great collaboration in investigations of terrorist attacks.[82] The FBI both received unprecedented access to evidence after the 2008 attacks and provided its Indian counterparts with technical assistance.[83] Indian willingness to allow an FBI team, and the FBI's ability to provide assistance in that investigation, was a breakthrough in developing law enforcement cooperation on counterterrorism investigations.

Less often acknowledged is that the FBI's intensive role in the investigation had an effect on the U.S. perception. India has often been quick to blame the Pakistani state for acts of terrorism, and there has sometimes been little evidence provided to the U.S. to support these claims. In the 2008 Mumbai case, not only were there smoking guns demonstrating Lashkar and the Pakistani state's culpability, but the FBI's intimate involvement in the investigation meant that the U.S. had detailed evidence of this. It helped the U.S. counterterrorism apparatus to shift its perception about the degree of Pakistan's continuing support for terrorism.

Law enforcement cooperation also offers the U.S. a way to support India's effort to conduct sound investigations. U.S. law enforcement officials described their horror at the Indians' practice of quickly hosing down crime scenes and bomb sites in an effort to prevent terrorist attacks from stoking communal tensions – a goal of some terrorist groups targeting India. While this is an important consideration, it destroyed critical evidence and ways to trace bombings. The State Department's Anti-Terrorism Assistance programs subsequently provided courses on bomb-blast investigation and critical incident management.[84]

Law enforcement cooperation between the U.S. and India occurs at both the federal and local levels, which presents challenges. This is not narrowly a counterterrorism effort, but it has a counterterrorism dimension because local law enforcement is often the first responder to terrorist attacks. Indian officials have historically been wary of the U.S. federal government cooperating with state-level governments or local law enforcement. But there has been success when local law enforcement bodies cooperate with one another, such as conferences and exchange visits between cities in the U.S. and India. The 2008 Mumbai attacks highlighted to the U.S. the utility in helping India build its local law enforcement capability and spurred local law enforcement departments in the U.S. to look closely at their ability to handle such events. In particular, they created opportunities for the U.S. to help train and equip "tactical level" security personnel in India.[85]

The two countries have also made progress on information sharing. In 2016, India and the U.S. signed an agreement to exchange terrorism screening information.[86] While not a counterterrorism initiative per se, it is notable that India joined the U.S.'s Global Entry program, as this type of cooperation helps to build information sharing overall. The U.S. has Global Entry partnerships in place with few countries. Reaching agreement on these issues has rarely been easy or quick, but such outcomes break down obstacles to cooperation.[87]

Intelligence sharing

Critically for the counterterrorism relationship, intelligence sharing between the two countries has gradually improved.[88] Intelligence sharing had been a particularly weak link in the counterterrorism relationship. It is often limited between services that view one another as counter-intelligence threats. The perception among U.S. intelligence officials was that the Indian services often treated them as a counter-intelligence threat. The Indian view was not entirely unjustified, but it inhibited this important area of cooperation.[89]

The U.S. had its own reservations about intelligence sharing. Counter-intelligence concerns were a distant second to concerns that the Indian services compromised U.S. intelligence through leaks. When shared, sensitive U.S. intelligence regularly appeared in the Indian press. When such intelligence pertained to Pakistan or collection in Pakistan, this damage was particularly acute and made U.S. intelligence services reluctant to share and forced them to share carefully.

Intelligence sharing is still conceived of more narrowly than the strategic partnership label would suggest. U.S. officials, stung by accusations that they had withheld intelligence that could have helped to disrupt the Mumbai attacks, have sought to actively share threat and terrorism finance intelligence that affects India. However, sharing intelligence beyond that of direct impact to one another is still not as robust as it could be. There could be a more dynamic sharing of intelligence that would be of utility and interest to each other. The failure of the U.S.–India intelligence relationship to reach that threshold was apparent after the Islamic State attack in Sri Lanka in 2019, a plot that India had intelligence about but did not share with the U.S. Nonetheless, by all accounts, intelligence sharing has quietly improved, away from the bright lights of senior visits and joint statements.

Defense

While counterterrorism is not primarily a defense issue, there has been cooperation on that front, particularly in the training and exercises realm. In 2018, the U.S. and Indian Special Forces took part in an annual exercise in Rajasthan in which counterterrorism was one of the simulated scenarios. In 2015, U.S. Special Forces conducted an inaugural TARKASH joint combined counterterrorism training exercise with the Indian National Security Guards, the Ministry of Home Affair's leading counterterrorism force. They then held a second TARKASH exercise in 2017. In 2016, the annual *Yudh Abhyas* military exercise focused on counterinsurgency and counterterrorism scenarios. As early as 2004, U.S. army troops participated in jungle counterinsurgency exercises with Indian forces.[90] There have been counterterrorism elements in joint naval exercises, which is notable because the naval relationship has been consistently cited as a thriving area of the relationship.

India has undoubtedly improved its ability to defend itself, including preventing attacks and responding to them. The lack of a major terrorist attack outside of Kashmir since 2008 is a clear indication of improvement. It is less clear, at least to U.S. officials, how India will fare in the face of another attack on the scale of the 2006 or 2008 Mumbai attacks. But it appears that there has been improvement in India's counterterrorism capability, though how much of that can be attributed to cooperation with the U.S. is difficult, if not impossible, to assess.

Building cooperation against other threats? The Islamic State

The emergence of the Islamic State caused the U.S.'s counterterrorism focus to shift back to the Middle East. The Islamic State gained some traction in South Asia, forming its first affiliate in the region, the Islamic State in Khorasan, in 2015. However, the Islamic State's inroads into India have been limited, considering the size and circumstances of its Muslim population. A relatively small number of Indians made it to Syria to join the Islamic State. As of 2018, there were at least 100 Islamic State-related cases under investigation, and in 2019 there were more cases in Tamil Nadu, Kerala, and Kashmir.[91] Thus, while the Islamic State is a broader transnational threat, to date it has been a manageable one for India domestically.

At first glance, the threat from the Islamic State seemed to offer an opportunity for U.S. and Indian counterterrorism cooperation that would be unconstrained by differences on Pakistan. It serves as a litmus test of sorts on the two countries' ability to cooperate on counterterrorism when an issue does not involve Pakistan. There has indeed been "quiet cooperation,"[92] but India's successes against the Islamic State are about India's efforts and capability at home, not cooperation with the U.S. As one analyst in Washington argued, "India's biggest contribution has been to have the least number of Indians go to Syria to join ISIS." U.S. experts are divided about how receptive India is to cooperation with the U.S. on this issue. Some argue that the transnational dimension creates an opening for cooperation, while others see the primarily domestic nature of the threat as activating Indian reservations about cooperation with the U.S. Either way, India has prevented the Islamic State from becoming a major threat, a feat many countries have struggled to accomplish.

India did not join the global anti-Islamic State coalition, a decision that did not surprise any of the current or former U.S. officials who work extensively on India. In general, India is seen as not keen to join coalitions, such as its decision not to contribute to the U.S. war in Iraq and status as an "indirect supporter" of the Global War on Terrorism.[93] But there appeared to be an Islamic State specific calculus as well. Multiple experts argued that India did not want to draw attention from the Islamic State, or, as one former official characterized it, "put a target on its back."[94] They pointed to the number of Indians working in the Persian Gulf who could become targets, as has occurred with attacks on Indians in Iraq and Afghanistan, or who could become radicalized. One former official summed it up by saying that India "doesn't have a major problem and wants to keep it that way."[95] Consequently, India has pursued low-profile cooperation, rather than taking visible steps like joining the global coalition.

In addition, as one former official explained, "India doesn't care about scoring points with the U.S. for things like joining the anti-ISIS coalition."[96] Experienced India hands understand this as the way India operates. But this logic raises eyebrows in broader U.S. counterterrorism circles, especially given the unprecedented nature of the threat from the Islamic State and the anti-Islamic State coalition.

The threat from the Islamic State also illuminated to the U.S. the ways in which India does not factor the U.S. into its counterterrorism calculus, or, as one official explained, India's tendency to "think and look at counterterrorism in a silo-ed way."[97] On the U.S. side, there was dismay that the Indian intelligence services did not share their intelligence on the Islamic State threat to Sri Lanka. One U.S. official explained that no one thought India withheld the intelligence, rather, that it would not even occur to India to share in that way.[98] However, from the U.S. view, sharing such intelligence on terrorist threats in the region is exactly the kind of action that would help to deepen the counterterrorism relationship and that the U.S. hoped for after the years of building the counterterrorism relationship. On the India side, there was a sense of irritation that the U.S. felt "entitled" to such intelligence, and complaints that the U.S. wants more intelligence than it is willing to share.

Ultimately, rather than offering an opportunity to build the counter-terrorism relationship on an issue not involving Pakistan, there has been limited and quiet cooperation against the Islamic State. India has managed the limited threat from the Islamic State at home largely on its own. The Islamic State has not been a priority for India in the way that it is for the U.S. Once again, priorities and threat perceptions simply do not align.

Navigating other hurdles

Beyond the differences in priorities, bureaucratic and political sensitivities have hampered more robust and fluid cooperation. While dialogues are one way that the U.S. and India manage cooperation between their respective institutions, the two countries' systems do not neatly "latch up" on counterterrorism for several reasons. First, both countries' systems can be convoluted, with numerous agencies and different levels of government playing a role in counterterrorism.[99] There is hope that the reforms in India's security architecture since 2018, particularly its national security council, will mitigate this hurdle by producing counterparts that link up more naturally at that level.[100] Second, the U.S. system is far more defense heavy, with a particularly weak State Department under the Trump administration, while the State Department's counterpart, the Ministry of External Affairs, wields significant power in the Indian system. Thus, the power centers in the two systems do not match up.[101] Third, the Indian Ministry of Home Affairs is the federal lead in counterterrorism in India, while its counterpart in the U.S., the DHS, does not have a comparable leadership role. Consequently, linking up the institutions in the two systems is structurally awkward.

Beyond the mismatch of institutions, the U.S. approach to the strategic partnership, including counterterrorism, seems to inundate the Indian system – a system not well equipped or willing to respond.[102] The India's Ministry of External Affairs is universally bemoaned by U.S. officials as slow, understaffed, and difficult to work with. In addition, India does not staff its embassy in Washington to nearly the same degree as the U.S. staffs its embassy in New Delhi. The U.S. also perceives India as sensitive to requests for "extra territorial presences," like having Transportation Security administration screening at Indian airports.[103]

These bureaucratic obstacles are compounded by the "residual chill" and "lingering trust deficit" in the strategic partnership overall.[104] Some of this is about divergences around Pakistan, as discussed. But even U.S. officials acknowledge that the U.S. is quick to forget or fails to acknowledge when it has not met its partners' trust expectations. It does not see itself as an untrustworthy partner, even after egregious examples of abandoning allies, like the Kurds in Syria. Like India's preference for strategic autonomy, the U.S.'s perception of itself as a good partner is not a quality likely to change.

Conclusion

Counterterrorism is a solid pillar in the U.S.–India strategic partnership, albeit one that experiences frictions, periodic crises, morass, and differing interests. Counter-intuitively, the counterterrorism relationship could actually be harmed by overemphasis. While the U.S. can and should regenerate the homeland security cooperation, those most dissatisfied with the counterterrorism relationship more broadly are those who seek strategic changes by one or both countries that are simply not currently in their interests.

There were hopes that the U.S. and India's interests would better align once the U.S. left Afghanistan because the U.S. would be less dependent on Pakistan. But reduced dependence appears increasingly unlikely in the foreseeable future. As long as Pakistan is a gatekeeper of Afghanistan, the U.S. will avoid alienating Pakistan. For its part, India will constantly seek for the U.S. to do more on Pakistan and be dissatisfied with the U.S. approach. India justifiably fears that its counterterrorism interests will be undermined by the U.S.'s relationship with Pakistan, and the U.S. is unlikely to sufficiently reassure India to the contrary in the foreseeable future. As long as India's trust depends on the U.S. approach to Pakistan, the counterterrorism relationship will have natural limitations. Conversely, India is not likely to shift its interests to prioritize the U.S.'s primary counterterrorism concerns. Given these dynamics, steady and incremental progress is a positive and achievable expectation for both sides.

Differences do not have to equal a lack of common counterterrorism framework overall.[105] The two countries can cooperate on norms, rules, and sanctions that support a liberal international order with India as a major power – an international order that many terrorist groups seek to destroy. Steady, incremental progress is a pace that offers the two countries the ability to build "habits of cooperation" over time.[106] There is "endless scope for cooperation" in the realms of capability building and technical exchanges.[107]

The U.S.–India counterterrorism relationship may appear to fall short when compared to U.S. relations with other major powers that are democracies. But that standard is not the appropriate measure because most, if not all, of those countries are in an alliance with the U.S. Not only does India eschew the alliance relationships,[108] but the U.S. does not treat India

Striking the balance

commensurately with its treatment of those allies.[109] Instead, the U.S. needs to apply a "strategic altruism" lens that views a secure India – in particular one secure from terrorism – as the goal and accepts the asymmetry of the relationship that emerges from that objective without treating India as a junior partner.[110] It is a fine balance.

Notes

1 Embassy of India, Washington, D.C., U.S.A, "Brief on India–U.S. Relations," June 2019, www.indianembassyusa.gov.in/pages?id=4&subid=21; Bureau of South and Central Asian Affairs Department of State, "U.S. Relations With India," Bilateral Relations Fact Sheet, U.S. Relations With India, June 21, 2019, www.state.gov/u-s-relations-with-india/.
2 Interview 4 with retired senior U.S. Official who held multiple senior positions on South Asia, particularly India, September 27, 2019.
3 Sameer Lalwani and Heather Byrne, "Great Expectations: Asking Too Much of the U.S.–India Strategic Partnership," *The Washington Quarterly* 42, no. 3 (2019): 41–64, https://doi.org/10.1080/0163660X.2019.1666353; Interview 4 with retired senior U.S. Official who held multiple senior positions on South Asia, particularly India; Interview 7 with current U.S. Official specializing in South Asia, September 30, 2019; Interview 9 with Congressional staffer with expertise on South Asia, October 25, 2019; Interview 10 with former senior U.S. official, December 2016; Interview 2 with former senior U.S. Official and scholar on South Asia, October 29, 2019.
4 Interview 4 with retired senior U.S. Official who held multiple senior positions on South Asia, particularly India.
5 *Ibid.*
6 Interview 4 with retired senior U.S. Official who held multiple senior positions on South Asia, particularly India; Interview 5 with retired senior U.S. Official who held multiple senior positions on South Asia.
7 Interview 7 with retired senior U.S. Official who held multiple senior positions on South Asia; Interview 4 with retired senior U.S. Official who held multiple senior positions on South Asia, particularly India.
8 Interview 6 with scholar specializing in India foreign policy, October 11, 2019.
9 Alyssa Ayres, *Our Time Has Come: How India Is Making Its Place in the World/Alyssa Ayres. – American University* (New York, NY, United States of America: Oxford University Press, 2017).
10 Lalwani and Byrne, "Great Expectations."
11 Cara Abercrombie, "Realizing the Potential: Mature Defense Cooperation and the U.S.–India Strategic Partnership," *Asia Policy* 26, no. 1 (February 22, 2019): 119–44, https://doi.org/10.1353/asp.2019.0011; K. Alan Kronstadt and Sonia Pinto, "India–U.S. Security Relations: Current Engagement" (Congressional Research Service, 2012).

12 Interview 1 with former senior U.S. Official and expert on South Asia, October 10, 2019; Interview 3 with former senior U.S. Official with specialization in South Asia, October 22, 2019; Shanthie Mariet D'Souza, "Indo-U.S. Counter-Terrorism Cooperation: Rhetoric Versus Substance," *Strategic Analysis* 32, no. 6 (October 23, 2008): 1067–84, https://doi.org/10.1080/09700160802404562.

13 Kronstadt and Pinto, "India–U.S. Security Relations: Current Engagement."

14 Interview 6 with scholar specializing in India foreign policy; Interview 8 with current U.S. Official with expertise on South Asia and foreign policy; Interview 5 with retired U.S. Official who held senior positions on South Asia, September 26, 2019.

15 Richard Fontaine, "U.S.–India Relations: The Trump Administration's Foreign Policy Bright Spot," *War on the Rocks* (blog), January 24, 2019, https://warontherocks.com/2019/01/u-s-india-relations-the-trump-administrations-foreign-policy-bright-spot/; Interview 4 with retired senior U.S. Official who held multiple senior positions on South Asia, particularly India.

16 Interview 8 with current U.S. official with expertise on South Asia and foreign policy; Interview 3 with former senior U.S. Official with specialization in South Asia; Ayres, *Our Time Has Come*; Interview 9 with former U.S. Intelligence Official, September 17, 2019.

17 See for example "JOINT STATEMENT: The United States and India: Enduring Global Partners in the 21st Century," whitehouse.gov, June 7, 2016, https://obamawhitehouse.archives.gov/the-press-office/2016/06/07/joint-statement-united-states-and-india-enduring-global-partners-21st.

18 Interview 5 with retired U.S. Official who held senior positions on South Asia; Kronstadt and Pinto, "India–U.S. Security Relations: Current Engagement."

19 Due to space constraints, I focus on events after 2001. For an excellent examination of the U.S.–India counterterrorism discussion prior to 2001, see Polly Nayak, "Prospects for U.S. India Counterterrorism Cooperation: An American View," in *U.S.–Indian Strategic Cooperation into the 21st Century* (New York: Routledge, 2007), https://doi.org/10.4324/9780203946749-12.

20 Robert D. Blackwill and Ashley J. Tellis, "The India Dividend," *Foreign Affairs*, October 2019, www.foreignaffairs.com/articles/india/2019-08-12/india-dividend; "Joint Statement Between U.S. and India," The White House, November 2001, https://georgewbush-whitehouse.archives.gov/news/releases/2001/11/20011109-10.htm-.

21 Interview 21 with retired senior U.S. Official who held multiple senior positions on South Asia, particularly India.

22 Kronstadt and Pinto, "India–U.S. Security Relations: Current Engagement."

23 "Joint Statement Between U.S. and India."

24 Kronstadt and Pinto, "India–U.S. Security Relations: Current Engagement"; D'Souza, "Indo-U.S. Counter-Terrorism Cooperation."

25 Kronstadt and Pinto, "India–U.S. Security Relations: Current Engagement"; Interview 2 with former senior U.S. Official and scholar on South Asia.

26 Interview 3 with former senior U.S. Official with specialization in South Asia.

27 Pakistan assisted in the apprehension of high-value targets such as Khalid Sheikh Mohamed, Abu Zubaydah, and Abu Faraj al-Libi among others.
28 Interview 5 with retired U.S. Official who held senior positions on South Asia.
29 *Ibid*.
30 *Ibid*.; Polly Nayak, Michael Krepon, and Henry L. Stimson Center, *The Unfinished Crisis: U.S. Crisis Management after the 2008 Mumbai Attacks* (Washington, DC: The Henry L. Stimson Center, 2012), www.stimson.org/books-reports/the-unfinished-crisis-us-crisis-management-after-the-2008-mumbai-attack/.
31 Interview 4 with retired senior U.S. Official who held multiple senior positions on South Asia, particularly India.
32 "Snakes in Your Backyard Won't Bite Only Neighbours: Hillary to Pak," NDTV, October 21, 2011, www.ndtv.com/world-news/snakes-in-your-backyard-wont-bite-only-neighbours-hillary-to-pak-573412; Sumit Ganguly and S. Paul Kapur, "The Sorcerer's Apprentice: Islamist Militancy in South Asia," *The Washington Quarterly* 33, no. 1 (2010): 47–59.
33 Lalwani and Byrne, "Great Expectations."
34 Interview 5 with retired U.S. Official who held senior positions on South Asia.
35 Interview 4 with retired senior U.S. Official who held multiple senior positions on South Asia, particularly India; Kronstadt and Pinto, "India–U.S. Security Relations: Current Engagement"; Nayak, Krepon, and Henry L. Stimson Center, *The Unfinished Crisis*.
36 Nayak, Krepon, and Henry L. Stimson Center, *The Unfinished Crisis*.
37 Neil Padukone, "The Next Al-Qaeda?," *World Affairs*, December 11, 2011, pp. 67–72; Jeremy Kahn, "The Next Al Qaeda?," *Newsweek*, February 25, 2010, www.newsweek.com/next-alqaeda-75365; "Is Lashkar-e-Taiba the Next Al-Qaeda?," New America, www.newamerica.org/international-security/events/is-lashkar-e-taiba-the-next-alqaeda/; Peter Chalk, "Lashkar-e-Taiba's Growing International Focus and Its Links with Al Qaeda," *Jamestown*, https://jamestown.org/program/lashkar-e-taibas-growing-internationalfocus-and-its-links-with-al-qaeda/; and Ashley J Tellis, "The Menace That Is Lashkar-e-Taiba," Policy Outlook, Carnegie Endowment of International Peace, March 2012, p. 24. Tricia Bacon, "The Evolution of Pakistan's Lashkar-e-Tayyiba Terrorist Group," *Orbis* 63, no. 1 (2019): 27–43, https://doi.org/10.1016/j.orbis.2018.12.003.
38 Interview 7 with current U.S. Official specializing in South Asia.
39 Interview 1 with former senior U.S. Official and expert on South Asia.
40 Interview 5 with retired U.S. Official who held senior positions on South Asia.
41 "Interactive: David Coleman Headley's Web of Betrayal," FRONTLINE, accessed November 19, 2019, www.pbs.org/wgbh/pages/frontline/labs/i/perfect-terrorist/.
42 "United States of America *vs* Tahawwue Hussain Rana" (Chicago, Illinois: in the United States District Court for the Northern District of Illinois Eastern Division, May 2011).
43 Government of India National Investigation Agency, "Interrogation Report of David Coleman Headley," 2010.

44 Interview 5 with retired U.S. Official who held senior positions on South Asia.
45 Interview 7 with current U.S. Official specializing in South Asia; Interview 8 with current U.S. official with expertise on South Asia and foreign policy; Interview 6 with scholar specializing in India foreign policy.
46 Interview 2 with former senior U.S. Official and scholar on South Asia.
47 Nayak talks about how in the 1990s, India suspicion constrained U.S. cooperation with India's neighbors on counterterrorism. India worries about U.S. crowding it in its backyard. These concerns may not have completely dissipated but they seem to have lessened.
48 Sebastian Rotella Madani, "Militant Reaffirms Role of Pakistan in Mumbai Attacks," *Foreign Policy*, August 9, 2012, https://foreignpolicy.com/2012/08/09/militant-reaffirms-role-of-pakistan-inmumbai-attacks/; and Azmat Khan, "New Evidence of Pakistan's Role in the Mumbai Attacks?," FRONTLINE, June 28, 2012, www.pbs.org/wgbh/frontline/article/newevidence-of-pakistans-role-in-the-mumbai-attacks/.
49 Interview 2 with former senior U.S. Official and scholar on South Asia.
50 *Ibid*.
51 Kronstadt and Pinto, "India–U.S. Security Relations: Current Engagement."
52 *Ibid*.
53 Interview 8 with current U.S. official with expertise on South Asia and foreign policy; Interview 2 with former senior U.S. Official and scholar on South Asia.
54 Fontaine, "U.S.–India Relations"; Interview 7 with current U.S. Official specializing in South Asia.
55 Interview 3 with former senior U.S. Official with specialization in South Asia.
56 *Ibid*.
57 Interview 6 with scholar specializing in India foreign policy.
58 Interview 8 with current U.S. official with expertise on South Asia and foreign policy; Interview 1 with former senior U.S. Official and expert on South Asia.
59 Interview 9 with former U.S. Intelligence Official.
60 Interview 5 with retired U.S. Official who held senior positions on South Asia.
61 Kronstadt and Pinto, "India–U.S. Security Relations: Current Engagement."
62 Interview 2 with former senior U.S. Official and scholar on South Asia.
63 Alyssa Ayres, "Background Brief: Meet the U.S.–India '2+2,'" Council on Foreign Relations, accessed November 17, 2019, www.cfr.org/blog/background-brief-meet-us-india-22.
64 Nayak, "Prospects for U.S. India Counterterrorism Cooperation."
65 Bureau of Public Affairs Department Of State. The Office of Electronic Information, "U.S.–India Counterterrorism Joint Working Group," accessed November 17, 2019, https://2001–2009.state.gov/r/pa/prs/ps/2002/11922.htm; Bureau of Public Affairs Department Of State. The Office of Electronic Information, "India–U.S. 'Joint Working Group on Counter-Terrorism,'" accessed November 17, 2019, https://2001-2009.state.gov/r/pa/prs/ps/2002/7440.htm; "9/26/00: India–U.S. Statement on Joint Working Group on Counter-Terrorism," accessed November 17, 2019, https://1997–2001.state.gov/global/

terrorism/000926_india_us.html; Abercrombie, "Realizing the Potential"; D'Souza, "Indo-U.S. Counter-Terrorism Cooperation."
66 Kronstadt and Pinto, "India–U.S. Security Relations: Current Engagement."
67 www.indianembassyusa.gov.in/pdf/india_reviews/99802June%2011.pdf.
68 Interview 1 with former senior U.S. Official and expert on South Asia.
69 Interview 4 with retired senior U.S. Official who held multiple senior positions on South Asia, particularly India.
70 K. Alan Kronstadt and Shayerah Ilias Akhtar, "India–U.S. Relations: Issues for Congress" (Congressional Research Service, June 19, 2017).
71 Interview 7 with current U.S. Official specializing in South Asia.
72 "Fact Sheet: U.S.–India Counterterrorism and Homeland Security Cooperation," U.S. Embassy and Consulates in India, July 31, 2014, https://in.usembassy.gov/fact-sheet-u-s-india-counterterrorism-and-homeland-security-cooperation/.
73 Interview 7 with current U.S. Official specializing in South Asia.
74 *Ibid.*
75 Interview 6 with scholar specializing in India foreign policy.
76 Interview 7 with current U.S. Official specializing in South Asia.
77 Ayres, *Our Time Has Come.*
78 Interview 5 with retired U.S. Official who held senior positions on South Asia.
79 "U.S.–India Sign Counter Terrorism Cooperation Initiative," Indian Embassy – Washington DC, July 23, 2012, at www.indianembassy.org/prdetail1560/-india-us-sign-counter-terrorism-cooperation-initiative-).
80 Nicholas Burns, "Passage to India," *Foreign Affairs*, October 2014.
81 Interview 3 with former senior U.S. Official with specialization in South Asia.
82 Kronstadt and Akhtar, "India–U.S. Relations: Issues for Congress."
83 Nayak, Krepon, and Henry L. Stimson Center, *The Unfinished Crisis.*
84 "Fact Sheet: U.S.–India Counterterrorism and Homeland Security Cooperation."
85 Kronstadt and Pinto, "India–U.S. Security Relations: Current Engagement."
86 Bureau for Counterterrorism U.S. Department of State, "2017 Country Reports on Terrorism" (Washington, D.C), accessed November 16, 2019, www.state.gov/country-reports-on-terrorism-2/.
87 Interview 6 with scholar specializing in India foreign policy.
88 Kronstadt and Pinto, "India–U.S. Security Relations: Current Engagement."
89 *Ibid.*
90 Kronstadt and Akhtar, "India–U.S. Relations: Issues for Congress."
91 Kabir Taneja, "Uncovering the Influence of ISIS in India," Occasional Paper (New Delhi, India: Observer Research Foundation, July 2018), www.orfonline.org/research/42378-uncovering-the-influence-of-isis-in-india/.
92 Interview 7 with current U.S. Official specializing in South Asia.
93 C. Christine Fair, "The Counterterror Coalitions: Cooperation with Pakistan and India" (Santa Monica, CA: Rand Corp, 2004).
94 Interview 1 with former senior U.S. Official and expert on South Asia.
95 *Ibid.*
96 Interview 3 with former senior U.S. Official with specialization in South Asia.

97 Interview 8 with current U.S. official with expertise on South Asia and foreign policy.
98 *Ibid.*
99 Kronstadt and Akhtar, "India–U.S. Relations: Issues for Congress."
100 Interview 2 with former senior U.S. Official and scholar on South Asia.
101 Interview 1 with former senior U.S. Official and expert on South Asia.
102 Kronstadt and Akhtar, "India–U.S. Relations: Issues for Congress."
103 Interview 1 with former senior U.S. Official and expert on South Asia.
104 Abercrombie, "Realizing the Potential."
105 Interview 3 with former senior U.S. Official with specialization in South Asia.
106 Ayres, *Our Time Has Come.*
107 Interview 1 with former senior U.S. Official and expert on South Asia.
108 Ankit Panda, "Why Does India Have So Many 'Strategic Partners' and No Allies?," *The Diplomat* (blog), November 23, 2013, https://thediplomat.com/2013/11/why-does-india-have-so-many-strategic-partners-and-no-allies/.
109 Interview 9 with former U.S. Intelligence Official; Interview 8 with current U.S. official with expertise on South Asia and foreign policy.
110 Blackwill and Tellis, "The India Dividend."

10

Indo–U.S. counterterrorism cooperation: a bumpy road

Manoj Joshi

Terrorism has emerged as a major scourge of modern times. Diverse states, from the U.S. and India, to Mali and Sri Lanka, have been victims of terrorist attacks. States employ a variety of strategies in dealing with terrorism – political negotiation, diplomacy, judicial process – and employ a variety of instruments – intelligence agencies, the police or the military – to cope with the situation. Since terrorism has a cross-border domain, states also seek to construct a panoply of international law, as well as undertake bilateral and multilateral cooperation through which they can deal with terrorism. India and the U.S. may be geographically distant, but both have experienced terrorism and have come to a common understanding that cooperation in counterterrorism (CT) is in their mutual interest and in the interests of the international community. As the chapter will show, the two countries have been cooperating on CT since the 1980s. However, differing perspectives, structural constraints and varying priorities have limited its efficacy. The chapter looks at their respective individual CT strategies as well as their experience. Over the decades, the two sides have come closer in defining a common CT strategy, even if their perspectives remain somewhat different. The chapter seeks to look at the recent trends and suggest ways in which they can enhance their cooperation further.

Asymmetrical partnership

The Indo-U.S. relationship is an asymmetrical one – one is a global power with worldwide interests, the other a regional power focused more on its immediate and extended neighborhood. Likewise, while one has CT capacities that can be, and are, deployed globally, the other's emphasis has been largely in its neighborhood.

Terrorism for the U.S. has meant the activity of international groups, often backed by state sponsors, that operate globally. At various times, countries like North Korea, Cuba, Nicaragua, Libya, Syria, and Iran have been seen as "terrorist states" or state sponsors of terrorism. The U.S.'s experience has been shaped by the course of the Israel–Palestine conflict and its interests in the Middle East, which went on to get entangled in the fallout of the jihad that the U.S. sponsored against the Soviet Union.

The Indian experience has come from events in its own homeland, some arising out of the many separatist movements it has had to deal with, often, as in the case of Khalistani terrorism or the Jammu and Kashmir militancy, aided and abetted by its neighbor Pakistan. Today, under the influence of the erstwhile Global War on Terror, India classes everything from separatist militancy to deliberate attacks on unarmed civilians as terrorism. But in their own class are attacks which it confronts by proxies – Pakistani jihadi groups like the Lashkar-e-Taiba and the Jaish-e-Mohammad – on Indian military personnel and facilities in Jammu and Kashmir, which must also be classed as terrorist attacks because India and Pakistan are not in a state of war.

The Indian response at various points in time has been at five levels. First, to strengthen its domestic police and intelligence capacities. Second, to conduct military campaigns to strike at separatists. Third, to fence its borders to prevent illegal movement, especially that of weapons and personnel. Fourth, to engage various countries, including Pakistan, diplomatically to persuade them to deny funds and sanctuary to terrorists. Fifth, to use persuasion to get domestic separatists/militants to return to orthodox politics.

Given the U.S. perspective and military capacity, using the military option has often been an important element in its response. But the U.S. has also constructed an extensive CT structure involving various governmental agencies and departments, including its intelligence services. An engaging feature of the U.S. response has been its extensive use of legal instruments to check terrorism and terrorist financing in relation to both its homeland and global aspects. The economic power of the U.S., and the centrality of the U.S. dollar in the international system, have enabled the U.S. to use such tools effectively.

Institutional pillars of CT strategy

In 1996 the Secretary of State got the authority to designate an organization as a "foreign terrorist organisation" (FTO). There were three criteria for this: (1) that the organization was obviously foreign, (2) it was engaged in terrorism, and (3) the terrorist activity threatened the security of U.S. citizens or the national security of the state.[1]

The 9/11 attacks led to the Executive Order 13224 of September 23, 2001, which targeted a wider range of entities – terrorist groups, individuals, financiers, front companies which could now be designated Specially Designated Global Terrorists (SDGT) by the U.S. Department of the Treasury's Office of Foreign Assets Control.[2]

Another category of state sponsors of terrorism could also be designated so by the Secretary of State under the Export Administration Act, the Arms Control Export Control Act, and the Foreign Assistance Act. Designation here would restrict foreign assistance, institute a ban on defense exports and sales, establish controls over exports of dual-use items, and put in place financial and other restrictions.[3]

The Intelligence Reform and Terrorism Prevention Act of 2004 led the U.S. to reform and restructure many of its CT institutions and create new ones like the National Counterterrorism Center (NCTC) to provide an authoritative agency for integrating all intelligence relating to terrorism and CT.

For a long time, India has had a system of designating groups as "unlawful association" under the Unlawful Activities (Prevention) Act (UAPA) of 1967. The main purpose of this was to deny organizations the ability to collect money or hold property. People continuing to be members of such organizations, to gathering funds for them or to assist their functioning could face imprisonment and the forfeiture of their property. The Act applies only to Indian nationals or persons on ships and aircraft registered in India.

India also passed the Terrorism and Disruptive Activities (Prevention) Act in 1985 to tackle Khalistani terrorism. But its widespread misuse and the defeat of Khalistani terrorism led to it being allowed to lapse in 1995. The Prevention of Terrorism Act, passed in 2002, was triggered by the attack on Parliament House in December 2001. The misuse of the Act led to its repeal under a successor government.

Under these circumstances, the UAPA has been strengthened. It has expanded the definition of terrorist activities based on the UNSC Resolution 1373 of September 28, 2001. Following the 2008 Mumbai attack a new National Investigating Agency was empowered to investigate terrorist crimes across the country by the UAPA. In 2019 the government further amended the UAPA to investigate terror crimes in India and abroad, as well as look at cybercrime and designate an individual as a "terrorist."[4]

Somehow, India was not able to get its own NCTC going. One reason for this was inter-departmental jealousies; the other was the concerns of India's various states which are actually charged with maintaining law and order. However, a Multi-Agency Centre where various intelligence agencies are represented has been created, along with sub-centers in state capitals. This is coordinated by the Intelligence Bureau.

Among the institutional pillars must be counted the many bilateral dialogues that the two countries conduct, many under the rubric of strategic dialogue, others specifically on CT. These have graduated from the level of officials to that of the principals through the "2+2" mechanism, which now sees Indian and U.S. ministers/secretaries dealing with foreign affairs and defense meeting each other regularly.

India has no formal CT strategy. This is in contrast with the U.S., which has explicitly laid out its strategies in various documents. The National Strategy for Combating Terrorist and Other Illicit Financing 2018 was prepared by the Office of Terrorism and Financial Intelligence of the Department of Treasury flowing from the Countering America's Adversaries Through Sanctions Act. It assessed U.S. efforts to combat illicit finance and focused on the Islamic State, al-Qaida and their affiliates, Iran's Islamic Revolutionary Guard Corps, as well as networks acting to support clandestine weapons of mass destruction programs.[5]

The 2020 edition of the document charted the American success in establishing "the world's most comprehensive and effective anti-money laundering and countering the financing of terrorism regime (AML/CFT) regime." It has sought to increase transparency and close legal loopholes in business and financial practices, especially those relating to real estate and digital assets. To this end, it has sought to make the regulatory framework more effective by enhancing communications, expanding the use of data analytics and AI.[6]

In October 2018, the U.S. White House issued the latest iteration of its National Strategy for Counterterrorism. The previous document had been issued in 2011. Not surprisingly, its focus was on radical Islamist elements, the Islamic State in Syria and Iraq (ISIS) and al-Qaida, as well as Iran, as threatening U.S. interests. Though it included the Lashkar-e-Taiba, Tehrik-e-Taliban Pakistan, and the Boko Haram, who used "political and terrorist tactics to undermine local governments," it noted that they will "probably prioritise local goals." There was nothing here, really, about terror strikes on India, groups like Jaish-e-Mohammad or the militancy in Jammu and Kashmir.[7]

Early U.S. cooperation with India on terrorism

There was a paradigm shift in the relations between India and the U.S. with the arrival of the Rajiv Gandhi government in New Delhi in late 1984. Whether it was Punjab, Sri Lanka, or even Pakistan, Rajiv was not committed to his mother Indira Gandhi's policies, which had a tinge of anti-Americanism in them. He broke away from them to reach out to the U.S., which, in turn, responded positively. This did not mean that all the issues bedeviling their CT cooperation were ended, but they were certainly better aligned to cooperate in a range of areas from defense technology to terrorism.

At a broader level, in January 1986, President Reagan had approved the report of the Vice President's Task Force on Combating Terrorism.[8] As part of this process, the U.S. began to have discussions, systematic cooperation, and to provide technical training and assistance to some fifty foreign governments.

The assessment of Robert Oakley, Director of the State Department Office of Combating Terrorism, was that in South Asia international terrorism was "of less danger than internal terrorism and separatist violence." Noting that Americans were rarely a target, he referred to the Sikh militancy, to allegations of Pakistani help, and to India's aid to Tamils in Sri Lanka. In Pakistan, in his view, terrorism was "primarily international" carried out by foreign elements supporting the communist regime in Afghanistan. Oakley later served as ambassador in Pakistan.[9]

Yet, there was some activity between India and the U.S. on the issue of CT going back to the early 1980s. U.S. assisted India to evolve anti-hijack measures and then expanded this to the forensic examination of explosive devices.[10] With the improved Indo-U.S. ties, India also sought assistance from the Federal Bureau of Investigation (FBI) in the case of the assassination of retired Army Chief General A. S. Vaidya at the hands of Khalistani terrorists.[11] In the case of Daya Singh Lahoria, who had been arrested in Minneapolis and was extradited to India in January 1997, having fled India after conducting several terrorist acts, the court had recourse to a British-era extradition treaty. But later in 1997, the U.S. and India signed a fresh extradition treaty, which had a significant impact on the issue of Sikh extremists in the U.S.[12]

Though India suffered terrible terrorist attacks from Khalistani terrorists and was dealing with insurgencies in Sri Lanka and Jammu and Kashmir, the U.S. remained detached, since its interests were not affected. In its perspective, it would move only in relation to attacks and threats on U.S. nationals and the homeland.

Given the fact that terrorism in India was often a Pakistan-sponsored or -supported activity, there were limits to the extent to which the U.S. was willing to help India. Following the Soviet departure from Afghanistan, U.S. attention on the region had, in any case, waned. But important institutional ties between the U.S. and Pakistani military and intelligence services remained. As for the State Department, its primary concerns seemed to be related to non-proliferation, rather than to any aspect of terrorism. U.S. energies were also occupied in dealing with the meltdown in Russia and relations with China.

There were episodic concerns that got the U.S. back to look at the region, such as the kidnapping of six foreigners in Jammu and Kashmir and the disappearance of five of them, including an American national. The sixth, an American, managed to escape. Another issue that brought U.S. attention back to the region was the missile attacks on terrorist training camps in the wake of the al-Qaida attacks on U.S. embassies in East Africa in August 1998.

Finally, the India–Pakistan nuclear tests of May 1998 again returned American attention to the region. After a hiatus of about one year following the tests, New Delhi and Washington reached out to each other to further intensify and stabilize their relationship. This was the period in which India and the U.S. grew closer following the nuanced U.S. position in the Kargil war of the summer of 1999. A dialogue between India's External Affairs Minister and U.S. Deputy Secretary of State Strobe Talbott saw fourteen rounds of talks over two and a half years, described by former Undersecretary of State Nick Burns as "Washington's first truly sustained strategic engagement with the Indian leadership."[13]

In the aftermath of the December 1999 Indian Airlines flight 814 hijack, a Joint Working Group on Counterterrorism was established. Its first meeting was held in February 2000 in Washington, DC and the second meeting took place later in the year, in September in New Delhi. The two sides agreed to intensify cooperation, "share experience, exchange information, and coordinate approaches and action." Also, they called for a Comprehensive Convention on International Terrorism (CCIT) to be passed by the UN.[14]

Cooperation after 9/11

From the point of view of international terrorism and the U.S. approaches to terrorism itself, 9/11 is a major watershed. The attack on the U.S. homeland surprisingly brought the focus back to South Asia. Afghanistan, Pakistan, and India began to loom larger in what was called the U.S.-led Global War on Terrorism.

Growing political congruence between India and U.S. had brought about closer CT ties as well. The Joint Statement issued following Prime Minister Atal Bihari Vajpayee's visit to Washington, DC in November 2001 led off with the issue and was in marked contrast to the Joint Statement of March 2000 during the Clinton visit to India, where terrorism was mentioned, though in passing.[15]

India offered significant support for Operation Enduring Freedom in the wake of 9/11, including the offer of its air bases for the U.S. to prosecute the Afghan war. It also instituted an escort of U.S. ships passing through the Malacca Straits and the Andaman Sea. This was quite a dramatic shift from its long-standing nonaligned position.

A bumpy road

The November 2001 statement was also the first to directly connect the American and Indian terror experiences when reference was made to 9/11, along with the October 1, 2001 Jaish-e-Mohammad suicide bomber attack on the Jammu and Kashmir Legislative Assembly. Outlining the global challenge they confronted, the two leaders stressed the need for international cooperation in terms of intelligence sharing and denying terrorists safe havens. In line with this, they committed the two countries to intensifying bilateral cooperation.[16]

With the onset of the war in Afghanistan, the U.S. focus shifted back to Pakistan and, though relations with India remained good, a built-in limitation was established. India was not encouraged to participate in U.S. CT operations in Afghanistan, in deference to Pakistani sensibilities. India's contribution was, in a sense, sublimated in Indian development projects in Afghanistan, aimed at weakening the Taliban and, by extension, Pakistan. Whatever CT activity it conducted against Pakistan through Afghanistan remained outside the purview of Indo-U.S. cooperation.

The 2007 article by Nick Burns cited above[17] notes that India and the U.S. were working together to "expand the surveillance of suspect cargo vessels and real time communication" as part of their military-to-military ties. However, despite strenuous efforts, India did not join the Container Security Initiative that the U.S. had mooted as part of its efforts to protect the homeland against international terrorist threats. Relations between two countries, especially military-to-military ties, continued to advance and culminated in a major breakthrough with the Indo-U.S. Nuclear Accord in 2005.

India had also participated in training and joint exercises with the U.S. military whose subtext has been on issues dealing with terrorism. The first *Yudh Abhyas* exercise took place in Agra, involving U.S. Special Forces and their Indian counterparts. Exercise *Shatrujeet* in 2006 dealt with operating in a semi-urban terrain "to enhance interoperability at functional level and share experience of CT operations …"[18]

But the focus on CT was episodic. Subsequent versions of *Shatrujeet* did not involve any other country. As for *Yudh Abhyas*, this became the standard India–U.S. annual military exercise, but its focus varied from mountain or jungle warfare to CT. The *Yudh Abhyas* held in the U.S. in 2019 featured drills and procedures involving "counter insurgency & counter terrorist operations in an urban environment."[19]

The Mumbai attack and the Indian Mujahidin offensive

In the meantime, India was approaching its own 9/11 moment. This was the Mumbai attack of November 2008. In this case, there is clear evidence that the U.S. had the clues in the activities of Pakistani American David Coleman Headley, who provided the Lashkar attackers with a detailed picture of the targets in Mumbai. As a U.S. intelligence officer told the *New York Times*, the intelligence was there, but not put together, because the U.S. was simply not focused on India-related issues.

Many of the clues, shared by the U.S. and UK, pointed to an attack on Mumbai. The U.S. warned India of this on "multiple occasions" between June and November 2008, but the warnings were general, with no information on the timing and the method of attack. The British and the Indians had also penetrated the Lashkar's digital networks, but there was no communication between their agencies on the issue. The extent to which the British shared the information with the U.S., with which it has a special agreement, is unclear.[20]

But perhaps the biggest questions in Indian minds relate to David Coleman Headley's role. Headley was in touch with the Lashkar and Pakistan's Inter-Services Intelligence (ISI) before and after the Mumbai attacks. The U.S. National Security Agency collected some of the e-mails, but did not realise their significance till the FBI began to investigate Headley after a tip-off from the UK.

This was also the time when India suffered a series of terrorist bombings attributed to a shadowy group called the Indian Mujahidin. Though it claimed to have Indian origins and was comprised of Indian nationals, it has shadowy ties to Pakistan through its founders. Nevertheless, the Indian authorities were able to neutralize this group through arrest and detention of its personnel.

The U.S. response to the Mumbai attack was also somewhat restrained. Given the Indian response, there were no worries about the outbreak of war with Pakistan. With the information they already had, the U.S. would have had no doubts as to the perpetrators of the attack. Subsequently, the U.S. got more information about it following the arrest of David Coleman Headley. But, as Polly Nayak and Michael Krepon have noted in their study of the U.S. crisis management following the attack, the emphasis was on "de-escalating India–Pakistan tensions."[21]

In November 2010, the U.S. put Lashkar-e-Taiba leaders Azam Cheema and Abdul Rahman Makki on its SDGT list, along with the Al Rehmat Trust of the Jaish-e-Mohammad, and its leader Masood Azhar.[22] In April 2012, the U.S. announced a bounty of $10 million on Lashkar's chief, Hafiz Muhammad Saeed, for his role in the Mumbai attack.

In the aftermath of the Mumbai attack, the U.S. and India signed a Counter Terrorism Cooperation Initiative in November 2009 to strengthen all-round cooperation on CT. They also began a U.S.–India Strategic Dialogue, whose inaugural meeting took place in June 2010 in

Washington, DC with Secretary of State Hillary Clinton and External Affairs Minister S. M. Krishna serving as the co-chairs. A key theme of the meeting was advancing global security and countering terrorism. The meeting was billed as "the unprecedented and expanding India–U.S. counterterrorism partnership." Secretary Clinton reiterated full support for the process of "bringing the perpetrators of the 2008 Mumbai terrorism attack to justice."[23]

In keeping with the trend of dense engagement and cooperation, the two sides also inaugurated the India–U.S. Homeland Security Dialogue, whose first meeting was held in New Delhi in May 2011. The dialogue focused on expanding India–U.S. cooperation by focusing on agency-to-agency engagement, "including in the area of intelligence exchange, information sharing, forensics and investigation, access and sharing of data relating to terrorism, security of infrastructure, transportation and trade, conducting joint needs assessment, combating counterfeit currency, countering illicit financing and transnational crime."[24]

The Mumbai attack and the growing all-round climate of good Indo-U.S. relations led to stepped-up cooperation in CT. There has been substantial progress in intelligence sharing, information exchange, operational cooperation, and the sharing of CT equipment and technology. CT cooperation was carried out through older institutional arrangements like the India–U.S. Joint Working Group on Counter-Terrorism that was meeting annually, but it also took place at different levels between the intelligence agencies. As part of the cooperation, some 1,100 Indian security personnel were trained in the U.S. between 2009 and 2015.

In January 2015, during President Obama's visit to New Delhi, the two sides committed themselves to making the Indo-U.S. relationship "a defining counterterrorism relationship for the 21st century." Besides the al-Qaida and ISIS, the two sides also reaffirmed their commitment "to disrupt entities such as Lashkar-e-Taiba, Jaish-e-Mohammed, D-Company and the Haqqani Network."[25] One practical aspect of the visit was the signing of a Memorandum of Understanding between the U.S. Department of Treasury and the Indian Ministry of Finance to enhance cooperation against money laundering and terrorism financing.

Later that year the two countries issue a Joint Declaration on Combating Terrorism. This was done on the sidelines of the inaugural India–U.S. Strategic and Commercial Dialogue. It encapsulated all that the two sides had done, or were discussing, on the CT issue. It also reiterated their joint position on terrorism and terrorist groups and also reaffirmed their support for a UN CCIT.[26]

In 2016 there was another incremental development when the Home Ministry signed an agreement to join a global terror database maintained by the Terrorist Screening Center (TSC), a multi-agency center run by the FBI. The TSC maintains and operates the Terrorist Screening Database, which is used to develop watch lists and share unclassified information such as names, nationality, photos, fingerprints, and passport numbers of suspected terrorists.[27] Given the reservations of the Intelligence Bureau (IB) and Research and Analysis Wing, an enabling agreement was arrived only at in 2018 after discussions. The IB was designated as the nodal agency from the Indian side.[28]

The Trump administration

Initially, it appeared to India that the Trump administration's hard line of Pakistan was, at last, taking note of the support Islamabad had provided to a slew of terrorist groups who targeted India. The across-the-board cut in security aid to Pakistan in January 2018,[29] and the September 2018 cancellation of $300 million in aid that had not come under the previous cuts, seemed to conform this. The decisions were also attributed to the Trump administration's growing ties with India.[30] However, with the U.S. deciding to pull out of Afghanistan, Pakistan soon regained some traction in Washington, DC by 2019.

But the U.S. and India appear to be trying to move beyond this limitation, as was evident from the upgrading of the Indo-U.S. Strategic and Commercial Dialogue to a 2+2 format, involving their respective Foreign and Defense ministers, in September 2018. Its joint statement was notable for its strong stand against terrorism. With an eye on Pakistan, the ministers also denounced the use of terrorist proxies in the region and "called on Pakistan to ensure that territory under its control is not used to launch terrorist attacks on other countries." Further, they said that Pakistan should "bring to justice expeditiously" the perpetrators of attacks on Mumbai, Pathankot, Uri, and other cross-border attacks.[31]

Though decisions on the area of defense were the major focus of the meeting, the statement also spoke of "the expansion of bilateral counter-terrorism cooperation" and the increase in information-sharing efforts on known terrorists. They also committed to pushing their cooperation in the UN and the Financial Action Task Force (FATF). There was also reaffirmation of India's long-term demand for a UN CCIT.[32]

However, the focus of the second 2+2 dialogue that was held in Washington, DC in December 2019 shifted somewhat. In the single-page media note on the highlights of the talks issued by the U.S. there was only a perfunctory reference to terrorism.[33] A senior administration official who briefed the media noted that the meeting also discussed the issue of religious freedom, though its main agenda was more focused "on cooperation in the Indo-Pacific and military interoperability."[34]

However, the seven-page joint statement did have two paragraphs on terrorism more or less similar to the year before, and, according to the document, the U.S. "welcomed changes in Indian law that will facilitate further cooperation on terrorism designations." But there was no reference to bilateral CT cooperation or the issue of the FATF and the CCIT. Another significant development from the CT point of view was the exercise of judicial cooperation in relation to terrorism, which would be carried out by the National Judicial Academy in Bhopal and the Federal Judicial Center.[35]

During Prime Minister Modi's visit to the U.S. in June 2017, the two sides took a significant step towards enhancing cooperation by launching a new consultation mechanism of domestic and international terrorist designation listing. The first Terrorist Designation Dialogue took place in December 2017 in New Delhi. The second dialogue took place in March 2019, along with the sixteenth meeting of the India–U.S. Joint Working Group on Counter terrorism. Essentially, they are aimed at harmonizing the designation of terrorists in the two countries' respective lists.

In 2017, the U.S. took a major step in designating the Hizbul Mujahidin also as an FTO and naming its leader Syed Salahuddin as a SDGT. This was significant gesture, since, unlike the Lashkar-e-Taiba and Jaish-e-Mohammad, which comprise of Pakistanis, the Hizbul Mujahidin is a purely Kashmiri group and Salahuddin is an Indian national. The Hizbul Mujahidin and Salahuddin have been active in militancy since 1990, but his designation in 2020 suggests that the motive was either a token gesture or a signal of a longer-term shift in the U.S. position in Jammu and Kashmir. In 2018, the Milli Muslim League and Tehreek-e-Azadi, a rebranded outfit under Hafiz Saeed, and seven of its leaders were also designated SDGT.

As part of the process, the U.S. began working with India in the FATF in June 2018 to push Pakistan to block terrorist financing, on the threat of wider financial sanctions. Pakistan was placed on a grey list in October 2019 because it had not taken appropriate measures against terrorist organizations. In February 2020, the FATF gave Islamabad another five months, till June 2020, to deal with the numerous discrepancies and gaps in its handling of the FATF's demands. This process showed some promise initially, but now with Islamabad back in Washington's good books it remains to be seen where it will lead.[36]

After the Pulwama attack of February 14, 2019, the U.S. also pushed Islamabad to designate Masood Azhar as a terrorist under the UN's 1267 Committee. After China's hold on a French proposal for his listing, the U.S. circulated a draft resolution in the UN Security Council to proscribe Azhar and bypass the 1267 process.[37] Eventually, U.S. pressure persuaded China to lift its hold on the process, and Azhar was designated as a terrorist on May 1, 2019.[38]

In September 2019, the U.S. "modernized" Executive Order 13224, which had been issued in the wake of 9/11. Under the new provisions, the U.S. government got more authority to sanction leaders of terrorist organizations and those who train and support them. Further, it put financial institutions abroad on notice that they risked sanctions "if they knowingly conduct or facilitate any significant transactions on behalf of designated terrorists."[39] A significant part of this action was the decision to expand the SDGT to a slew of new leaders of old groups and, in addition, added a number of ISIS-affiliated organizations. But most significant was the designation of Iran's Islamic Revolutionary Guard Corps.[40]

In the meantime, the Modi government had also initiated a shift in India's CT strategy towards the more offensive use of the security forces and the military. One manifestation of this was the Operation All Out in Jammu and Kashmir, which sharply raised the level of violence there in the 2016–19 period. The other was the use of kinetic options, such as the so-called surgical strike of September 26, 2016 against Pakistani targets in retaliation for the attack on an Indian military base in Uri. In 2019, this was followed up with an aerial strike on a target in Balakot. Unlike previous cross-border strikes which were geographically limited to Jammu and Kashmir, the Balakot attack used the Indian Air Force for the first time in a CT role against a target in Pakistan proper.

In the case of the so-called surgical strikes, the U.S. reaction was muted, with the White House's Josh Earnest saying that Washington encouraged that both sides "continued discussions … to avoid escalation."[41] U.S. officials like Secretary of State Mike Pompeo and National Security Adviser John Bolton supported the Indian strike as a valid CT action and legitimate self-defense.[42]

Limitations on the cooperation

Though the two countries have a positive orientation towards CT cooperation, the progress in their relationship has been characterized by incrementalism, rather than any dramatic strides. In 2008, Shanthie Mariet D'Souza noted that despite the transformed U.S.–India relationship and a distinct upswing in military and political ties, the level of cooperation in CT remained somewhat disappointing.[43]

Ten years later the situation had improved but marginally. Rajeswari Pillai Rajagopalan noted in 2018 that despite "substantial diplomatic success" there had been "little real benefit" in terms of the threats

India confronted.[44] In a more recent study, Kashish Parpiani and Prithvi Iyer noted that India–U.S. CT cooperation "has seen a symbolic convergence ... [but] there have been limited tangible advances on the policy front."[45]

An official who headed an Indian intelligence agency until recently, too, told this writer that the level of cooperation was "routine" rather than substantive. This was confirmed by a Ministry of External Affairs official who said that by itself the issue of CT cooperation was not significant, but it was an important part of the overall climate of positive relations between the two countries.[46]

There are several reasons for this. Since 2001 the U.S. dependence on Pakistan for Operation Enduring Freedom has limited the cooperation that could take place. Despite the ups and downs in the U.S.–Pakistan relationship, it has never reached a point where the U.S. has been willing to join forces to deal with terrorism related activities in Pakistan that target India. For the U.S., the focus in Pakistan has been on the activities of the Taliban and the Haqqani network in the context of Afghanistan.

Another reason is the mismatch between the needs and means of India and the U.S. The U.S. CT policy, with its combination of military power, intelligence capabilities and legal instruments, is impressive and powerful but its orientation is towards American concerns, be they in the Middle East or in Afghanistan. U.S. power is not aimed at a Masood Azhar or Hafiz Saeed who exclusively target India. The U.S. may have a huge bounty on Saeed, but it has no great incentive to "take him out" as it did Osama bin Laden; that job is India's, and it lacks the capacity to do it.

Further, Azhar and Saeed collect their funds mainly from within Pakistan, plus the unknown amount they receive from Pakistan's ISI. Not much money is collected from the U.S. or Europe. The impact of U.S. sanctions on restricting financial flows to militants and terrorists from West to South Asia is not clear.

Despite major forward steps, the intelligence and security machineries in the two countries still lack a level of trust that would make for seamless cooperation. In India, at least, minus an institutionalized NCTC, there is not even seamless cooperation between its own agencies on many issues.

Perhaps the bigger problem is the lack of a common perspective as to what constitutes a security threat to each country from the point of view of CT and what their cooperation should cover. The U.S. is happy with military-to-military cooperation in what it calls the Indo-Pacific, but more or less excludes India from the western Indian Ocean and northern Arabian Sea. Likewise, the U.S. focus on al-Qaida, ISIS, and even the Afghan Taliban is not something that India shares, though India has been targeted in Afghanistan occasionally. As the October 2018 official U.S. CT strategy document reveals, there is nothing much in common between what the U.S. and India worry about when it comes to terrorism.

For the U.S., therefore, al-Qaida, ISIS, the assorted Middle-Eastern groups, and, most recently, Iran, take primacy, while for India it is those that have an immediate application in the Indian context, more often than not originating in Pakistan.

There is another reason why there is a great deal of convergence expressed in terms of statements, declarations, and structures of cooperation that the two sides have created for CT, and a lack of "tangible advances." Following the U.S. after 9/11, India classifies all attacks by separatists, terrorists, and proxy fighters as "terrorism," but there is an important difference that should not be ignored.

Terrorism is usually about attacks or armed coercion of unarmed non-combatants. Militancy, on the other hand, is about armed attacks on the security forces or symbols of the state. India has, in the past, negotiated with militants, be they in the Northeast or even in Kashmir. However, Pakistanis of the Lashkar-e-Taiba or the Jaish-e-Mohammad, who claim to fight on behalf of the Kashmiri militancy and attack both the security forces and non-combatants, ought to be classed as terrorists, since Pakistan is not in a state of war with India. So, while the U.S. is willing to sanction the Lashkar-e-Taiba or Jaish-e-Mohammad, it does not see armed militancy in Jammu and Kashmir conducted by the Kashmiris as "terrorism." This may change, of course, given the 2017 designations of the Hizbul Mujahidin and its leader as "terrorists."

There is another reality in play here. That is the sharp decline in terrorist and militant attacks in India in the present decade. The last major terrorist incidents with large-scale civilian casualties were the three coordinated blasts in Mumbai on July 13, 2011 that led to the deaths of twenty-six persons and the two blasts in Hyderabad in February 2013, killing eighteen persons. Data compiled by the South Asia Terrorism Portal show that from a peak in 2006–8, when more than 690 civilians were killed in Islamist attacks, along with twenty-nine security personnel, there have been just three non-combatants killed since 2014.[47]

Figures for casualties in the Jammu and Kashmir conflict peaked in the early 2000s, when more than 1,500 civilians and security personnel were killed in the period 2000–3. Since 2011, casualties of civilians and security personnel have fallen below 100, even dipping to 37 in 2012. They have since gone up, as the Modi government has launched an anti-militant offensive since 2016, but have remained below 200.[48]

The issue of "terrorism" has lost its salience in the U.S. ever since the Obama administration signaled its desire to terminate the Iraq and Afghanistan wars and pivot to what was subsequently termed "Indo-Pacific."

Though U.S. forces were involved in fighting ISIS, this was being done through a complex coalition that included the U.S., Russia, the Syrian government, and Iranian proxies.

It is in this context that, following the failure of its outreach to Prime Minister Nawaz Sharif in 2015, the Modi government has decided to use the issue of "terrorism" for both domestic and foreign policy reasons, primarily in dealing with Pakistan and using it as a means of electorally marginalizing Indian Muslims. In his lectures and speeches during his visits abroad, or at multilateral summits, terrorism has figured as an important element, as well as calls to isolate Islamabad. India found some congruence in the early Trump hard line of Pakistan, but now once again U.S. policy has returned to its earlier efforts to maintain a distance between the U.S. CT campaign and the India–Pakistan conflict over Kashmir.

What we are witnessing, therefore, is a symbolic process of CT cooperation, manifested by the various dialogues and working groups, aimed more at diplomatic, rather than practical, gain. The Indian government must shoulder the blame for this, as it has sought to use CT for domestic political gain, rather than as an end in itself. The U.S. administration has played along with this by vociferously supporting for India's CT campaign, backing the call for a UN CCIT designating various individuals and organizations as terrorists and terrorist organizations.

For obvious reasons, it is not possible to quantify the cooperation in terms of terrorists neutralized or terrorist conspiracies foiled. It would be interesting to see what kind of a matrix such information would reveal.

Conclusion

Even so, there is a pragmatic compulsion for U.S. and Indian to promote close CT cooperation. One way to do this is to avoid the rhetorical flourishes and move along a practical path of aligning their laws and strategies, as well as working on combined tactics. When it comes to laws, the problem lies in the two different legal systems and the asymmetry between them, in that while the U.S. can enforce third-country jurisdiction in many cases, India cannot. Currently, India depends on an upgraded version of its old Unlawful Activities Prevention Act. The U.S. has a number of laws, ranging from the omnibus Counterterrorism Act of 1995 to the Homeland Security Act of 2002 and the U.S.A PATRIOT Act amended in 2006, as well as powerful Executive Orders which focus on terrorist financing.

There is considerable room for both countries to jointly combat money laundering and drug smuggling, which are the life-blood of terrorist and militant activities. There is also a common interest in preventing their respective territories from being used by groups for money collection, sanctuary, and political mobilization. The decision to have a discussion on judicial perspectives is important and can smooth future path of CT cooperation.

As far as the Indian side sees it, the evidence from the mid-1980s suggests that Pakistan has had a major role to play in terrorist activities in India. So Pakistan deserves to join countries like the Democratic People's Republic of Korea, Iran, Sudan, and Syria as a state sponsor of terrorism and face attendant sanctions. Sanctions which will apply across the country, rather than to specific individuals and groups are likely to be more effective. This is the reason why Pakistan is so concerned over the FATF's possible black-listing, rather than with any other threat. The FATF process remains an important item in the future agenda of U.S.–India CT cooperation.

There remains the issue of looking at common threats beyond Pakistan. Over the years there have been claims of al-Qaida or the ISIS taking root in South Asia. This is something that could create a common platform for CT cooperation, but the reports have tended to be overblown. Whether it is Afghanistan or Pakistan, even al-Qaida or ISIS have a domestic rather than an international context.

The big joker in the pack is Bangladesh, where, as a recent article says, the "Islamic State ideology continues to resonate."[49] Likewise, the Easter Sunday 2019 blasts in Sri Lanka point to a wider radicalization which could bring a new wave of Islamist terrorism in South and Southeast Asia, which has seen troubling signs of ISIS activity. All these could well provide a new and more relevant context for CT cooperation which could also be incorporated in the Indo-Pacific focus of the foreign and defense policies of India and the U.S.

The outcome of the two 2+2 dialogues indicates that the Indo-Pacific and defense cooperation remain the focus areas of cooperation for the two sides. There is one key area that could enhance the level of cooperation. This is a closer linkage between the U.S. Central Command and India's military. This will not be easy, considering India's discomfort in the U.S.–Iran quarrel, and the U.S.'s hesitation in pinning down Pakistan to dismantle its state-supported terrorism structure. But this could also encourage the evolution of a common CT perspective for the region embedded in a larger strategic congruence.

Notes

1 "The 'FTO List' and Congress: Sanctioning Designated Foreign Terrorist Organisations," *CRS Report for Congress* October 21, 2003, available from https://fas.org/irp/crs/RL32120.pdf. Accessed on November 3, 2019.

2 U.S. Department of State, Office of Coordinator for Counterterrorism, Executive Order 13224 September 23, 2001 Archived Content U.S. Department of State, available from https://2009–2017.state.gov/j/ct/rls/other/des/122570.htm. Accessed on November 3, 2019.
3 U.S. Department of State, Bureau of Counterterrorism, "State Sponsors of Terrorism," U.S. Department of State, available from www.state.gov/state-sponsors-of-terrorism/. Accessed on November 12, 2019.
4 Siddharth Varadarajan, "Allowing the State to Designate Someone as a 'Terrorist' Without Trial Is Dangerous," *The Wire*, August 2, 2019, available from https://thewire.in/rights/uapa-bjp-terrorist-amit-shah-nia. Accessed on November 12, 2019.
5 [Office of Terrorism and Financial Intelligence, Department of Treasury], "National Strategy for Combating Terrorist and Other Illicit Financing 2018," available from https://home.treasury.gov/system/files/136/nationalstrategyforcombatingterroristandotherillicitfinancing.pdf. Accessed on November 12, 2019.
6 [Office of Terrorism and Financial Intelligence, Department of Treasury] "National Strategy for Combating Terrorist and Other Illicit Financing 2020," available from https://home.treasury.gov/system/files/136/National-Strategy-to-Counter-Illicit-Financev2.pdf. Accessed on November 12, 2019.
7 The White House, "National Strategy for Counterterrorism of the United States of America," October 2018, available from www.whitehouse.gov/wp-content/uploads/2018/10/NSCT.pdf. Accessed on November 19, 2019.
8 "Public report of the Vice President's Task Force on Combating Terrorism," February 1986, available from https://fas.org/irp/threat/vp-terror-1986.pdf. Accessed on October 23, 2019.
9 Robert Oakley, "International Terrorism, America and the World," *Foreign Affairs* 1986, available from www.foreignaffairs.com/articles/libya/1986-01-01/international-terrorism. Accessed on August 31, 2020.
10 Afroz Ahmad and Najish, "Before and After 9/11: Indo-U.S. Counterterrorism Cooperation," *Journal of International and Global Studies* vol 9, June 2, 2018, available from www.lindenwood.edu/files/resources/127-138-before-and-after-911.pdf. Accessed on August 22, 2019.
11 B Raman, "Agenda for Obama's Visit: Counter-Terrorism," *Indian Defence Review* October 20, 2010, available from www.indiandefencereview.com/news/agenda-for-obamas-visit-counter-terrorism/. Accessed on August 22, 2019.
12 K Alan Kronstadt and Sonia Pinto, "India U.S. Security Relations: Current Engagement," *CRS Report for Congress* November 13, 2012, available from https://fas.org/sgp/crs/row/R42823.pdf. Accessed on September 12, 2019. Subsequently, other people like Charan Jeet Singh "Cheema" in 2005, Kulbeer Singh Kulbeera in 2006, were also extradited from the U.S.
13 Nicholas Burns, "America's Strategic Opportunity with India: The New U.S.–India Partnership," *Foreign Affairs* November/December 2007, available from www.foreignaffairs.com/articles/asia/2007-11-01/americas-strategic-opportunity-india. Accessed on August 22, 2019.

14 "Indo-U.S. Statement on Joint Working Group on Counter-terrorism September 26, 2000," U.S. Department of State Archive, available from https://1997-2001.state.gov/global/terrorism/000926_india_us.html. Accessed on September 12, 2019.
15 Joint U.S.–India Statement March 21, 2000, The White House Archive, available from https://1997-2001.state.gov/global/human_rights/democracy/fs_000321_us_india.html. Accessed on August 22, 2019.
16 "Joint Statement between U.S. and India November 9, 2001," The White House Archive, available from https://georgewbush-whitehouse.archives.gov/news/releases/2001/11/20011109-10.html. Accessed on August 22, 2019.
17 See Burns "America's strategic opportunity."
18 Press Release, "Indian Army and U.S. Marines: Joint Exercise-Ex Shatrujeet," Press Information Bureau, Government of India Ministry of Defence, October 31, 2006 https://pib.gov.in/newsite/PrintRelease.aspx?relid=21633. Accessed on May 5, 2019.
19 Press Release, Ministry of Defence, "Validation and Closing Ceremony: Exercise Yudh Abhyas–2019" https://pib.gov.in/PressReleasePage.aspx?PRID=1585586. Accessed on May 5, 2020.
20 James Glanz, Sebastian Rotella and David E Sanger, "In 2008 Mumbai Attacks, Piles of Spy Data, but an Uncompleted Puzzle," *New York Times* December 21, 2014, available from www.nytimes.com/2014/12/22/world/asia/in-2008-mumbai-attacks-piles-of-spy-data-but-an-uncompleted-puzzle.html. Accessed on August 29, 2019.
21 Polly Nayak and Michael Krepon, "The Unfinished Crisis: U.S. Crisis Management after the 2008 Mumbai Attacks," *Stimson Center* February 2012, p. 28. Available on www.stimson.org/sites/default/files/file-attachments/Mumbai-Final_1_1.pdf. Accessed on August 29, 2019.
22 Press Release "Treasury Targets Pakistan Based Terrorist Organizations Lashkar-e-Tayyiba and Jaish-e-Mohammed," U.S. Department of the Treasury November 4, 2011, available from www.treasury.gov/press-center/press-releases/Pages/tg944.aspx. Accessed on May 5, 2020.
23 U.S.–India Strategic Dialogue Joint Statement June 3, 2010, Department of State, Archived Content https://2009-2017.state.gov/r/pa/prs/ps/2010/06/142645.htm. Accessed on May 2, 2020.
24 Press Release, "India–U.S. Homeland Security Dialogue Concludes: Two Sides Affirm Strategic Importance of Mutual Cooperation in Tackling Terror and Other Security Issues," Press Information Bureau, Government of India, Ministry of Home Affairs May 27, 2011, available from https://pib.gov.in/newsite/PrintRelease.aspx?relid=72365. Accessed on May 2, 2020.
25 "Joint Statement during the visit of President of U.S.A to India – 'Shared Effort and Progress for All,'" Ministry of External Affairs, Government of India, January 25, 2015, available from www.mea.gov.in/incoming-visit-detail.htm?24726/Joint+Statement+during+the+visit+of+President+of+U.S.A+to+India++++++++Shared+Effort+Progress+for+All. Accessed on May 2, 2020.
26 "U.S.–India Joint Declaration on Combatting Terrorism," Ministry of External Affairs, Government of India September 22, 2015, available from https://mea.

gov.in/bilateral-documents.htm?dtl/25836/U.S.India_Joint_Declaration_on_Combatting_Terrorism. Accessed on May 2, 2020.
27 "India, U.S. to Share Data on Terrorists," *The Hindu*, June 3, 2016 updated September 16, 2016, available from www.thehindu.com/news/national/India–U.S.-to-share-data-on-terrorists/article14380963.ece. Accessed on May 7, 2020.
28 Press Trust of India, "India–U.S. Sign Key Pact on Sharing Info on Terror," *Economic Times*, July 12, 2018, available from https://m.economictimes.com/news/defence/india-us-sign-key-pact-on-sharing-info-on-terror/articleshow/52555612.cms. Accessed on May 7, 2020.
29 Mark Landler and Gardiner Harris, "Trump, Citing Pakistan as a 'Safe Haven' for Terrorists, Freezes Aid," *New York Times* January 4, 2018, available from www.nytimes.com/2018/01/04/us/politics/trump-pakistan-aid.html. Accessed on August 7, 2019.
30 Saphora Smith and Reuters, "Trump Admin Cancels $300 M Aid to Pakistan Over Terror Record," *NBC News* September 2, 2018, available from www.nbcnews.com/news/world/trump-admin-cancels-300m-aid-pakistan-over-terror-record-n905786. Accessed on August 7, 2019.
31 "Joint Statement on the Inaugural India–U.S. 2+2 Ministerial Dialogue," September 6, 2018, Ministry of External Affairs, Government of India, available from https://mea.gov.in/bilateral-documents.htm?dtl/30358/Joint_Statement_on_the_Inaugural_IndiaU.S._2432_Ministerial_Dialogue. Accessed on August 7, 2019.
32 *Ibid*.
33 "Highlights of 2019 U.S.–India 2+2 Ministerial Dialogue, Office of the Spokesperson," December 18, 2019, available from www.state.gov/highlights-of-2019-u-s-india-22-ministerial-dialogue/. Accessed on May 2, 2020.
34 "Senior State Department Official on the U.S.–India 2+2 Ministerial Dialogue," December 18, 2019 Office of the Spokesperson, Department of State, available from www.state.gov/senior-state-department-official-on-the-u-s-india-22-ministerial-dialogue/. Accessed on May 2, 2020.
35 "Joint Statement on the Second India–U.S. 2+2 Ministerial Dialogue," Media Center, Ministry of External Affairs Government of India December 19, 2019, available from https://mea.gov.in/bilateral-documents.htm?dtl/32227/Joint+Statement+on+the+Second+IndiaU.S.+2432+Ministerial+Dialogue. Accessed on May 2, 2020.
36 Nayanima Basu, "Terror-funding Watchdog FATF Leaves Pakistan on Grey List, with a Warning," *The Print*, February 21, 2020, available from https://theprint.in/world/terror-funding-watchdog-fatf-leaves-pakistan-on-grey-list-with-a-warning/369238/. Accessed on May 2, 2020.
37 Harsh V Pant, "Forcing China's hand," *The Hindu* April 11, 2019, available from www.thehindu.com/opinion/op-ed/forcing-chinas-hand/article26799253.ece. Accessed on May 2, 2020.
38 Elizabeth Roche, "UN Ban on Masood Azhar a Victory for American Diplomacy," *Mint*, May 2, 2019, available from www.livemint.com/news/

world/un-ban-on-masood-azhar-a-victory-for-american-diplomacy-mike-pompeo-1556773650446.html. Accessed on October 12, 2019.
39 U.S. Department of State "Modernization of Executive Order 13224," Press Statement of Michael R Pompeo, Secretary of State September 10, 2019, available from www.state.gov/modernization-of-executive-order-13224/. Accessed on September 22, 2019.
40 Ibid.
41 Sanjeev Miglani and Asad Hashim, "India Says Hits Pakistan-based Militants, Escalating Tensions," Reuters September 29, 2016, available from www.reuters.com/article/us-pakistan-india-kashmir-idU.S.KCN11Z0IJ. Accessed on May 9, 2010.
42 HT correspondent "U.S. Supports IAF Strike on Jaish Camp in Pak, Mike Pompeo Tells Ajit Doval: Report," *Hindustan Times* February 28, 2019, available from www.hindustantimes.com/india-news/ajit-doval-dials-up-mike-pompeo-us-backs-india-s-decision-to-strike-jaish-camp-report/story-1p7pLWWqn3z1ltJACFavEK.html. Accessed on 31 August 2020.
43 Shanthie Mariet D'Souza (2008), "Indo-U.S. Counter-Terrorism Cooperation: Rhetoric Versus Substance," *Strategic Analysis* vol 32, no 6, pp. 1067–84, available from www.tandfonline.com/doi/abs/10.1080/09700160802404562?. Accessed on January 9, 2020.
44 Rajeswari Pillai Rajagopalan, "The Hidden Failure of U.S.–India Counterterrorism Cooperation," *The Diplomat* August 15, 2018, available from https://thediplomat.com/2018/08/the-hidden-failure-of-us-india-counterterrorism-cooperation./ Accessed on January 13, 2020.
45 Kashish Parpiani and Prithvi Iyer, "Towards an India–U.S. Consensus on Counterterrorism Cooperation," ORF Occasional Paper, No. 240 April 2020, p. 24, available from www.orfonline.org/research/towards-an-india-us-consensus-on-counterterrorism-cooperation-64261/. Accessed on May 2, 2020.
46 Personal communication with a former Intelligence chief and a senior official in the Ministry of External Affairs, December 2019.
47 South Asia Terrorism Portal, Data sheet on casualties of Islamist/Other conflicts, available from https://satp.org/datasheet-terrorist-attack/fatalities/india-islamistotherconflicts. Accessed on May 5, 2020.
48 South Asia Terrorism Portal, Data sheet on Jammu and Kashmir, available from https://satp.org/datasheet-terrorist-attack/fatalities/india-jammukashmir. Accessed on May 5, 2020.
49 Iftekharul Bashar, "Islamic State Ideology Continues to Resonate in Bangladesh," Middle East Institute September 3, 2019, available from www.mei.edu/publications/islamic-state-ideology-continues-resonate-bangladesh. Accessed on November 9 2019.

Part VI

Intelligence cooperation

11

A vision for future U.S.–India intelligence cooperation

Carol V. Evans[1]

Introduction

The focus of this chapter is to examine the geostrategic and domestic political factors shaping the future of U.S.–India intelligence cooperation and to provide a tangible roadmap for augmenting strategic and tactical-level intelligence sharing. In the following chapter, Saikat Datta provides a historical overview of the complicated, and sometimes fractured, bilateral intelligence relationship between the two countries.[2] This chapter offers a more optimistic viewpoint, highlighting potential intelligence alignment opportunities.

Continuing and emerging threats posed by China and Pakistan in the Indo-Pacific, as well as a more proactive foreign policy approach on the part of the Bharatiya Janata Party government of Narendra Modi, will provide additional impetus for the U.S. and India to expand their information- and intelligence-sharing activities. The U.S. needs to be mindful, however, of the bilateral foreign policy dynamics and Indian intelligence bureaucratic anomalies that will influence progress in intelligence collaboration afforded by these geostrategic and domestic political prospects.

Leaving aside the contemporary political dynamics between Washington and New Delhi that will continue to shape intelligence collaboration efforts, further cooperation must be based on more than temporal opportunities. Hence, it is essential to identify the overlapping, vital national security interests of the U.S. and India in the Indo-Pacific. These mutual security interests may provide an important collaborative framework from which to drive strategic and tactical intelligence-collection and -sharing efforts. As highlighted in this chapter, intelligence cooperation between the U.S. and India becomes critical in the future, and especially in the maritime domain, and its interface with the land warfare aspects on the Indian subcontinent and those geographic areas contiguous with the main sea lines of communication in the Indo-Pacific region.

A detailed plan for future U.S.–India intelligence cooperation, based on an incremental process of confidence and security building measures, is provided in the concluding section of this chapter. This approach will enable more advanced and demanding levels of bilateral intelligence collection, analysis, and dissemination than is currently utilized for primarily counterterrorism (Pakistan/Afghanistan) and traditional strategic collection efforts (Pakistan/China). In the future, U.S.–India intelligence cooperation could be augmented by the capabilities of regional allies, including the Five Eyes community and those of the Quadrilateral Security Dialogue ("Quad"), together with military and space-based intelligence platforms, networked to allow for integration across the "Ints", for timely analysis, sharing, and dissemination.[3]

The U.S., together with India and regional allies, has enormous opportunities to exploit this path forward. If approached incrementally and with sustained political support, deterrence measures – to offset Chinese hegemony in the Indo-Pacific, and Sino-Pakistani attempts to destabilize Indian interests – will be successful.

Factors affecting U.S.–India intelligence cooperation efforts

Bilateral intelligence cooperation must be viewed within the larger, evolving strategic U.S.–India relationship.[4] For intelligence- and information-sharing efforts to develop more fully, it is important to understand the various factors that may continue to influence and hamper these efforts, even as the geostrategic threats to Washington and New Delhi posed by China and the Chinese–Pakistan relationship metastasize. Indian domestic political constraints and a foreign policy legacy of nonalignment and strategic autonomy, "turf wars," and other inefficiencies within India's intelligence infrastructure are just some of the factors that will continue to shape U.S.–India intelligence cooperation. The next section provides a discussion of these key shaping factors.

Indian domestic politics and foreign policy

India clearly understands U.S. desires and expectations regarding New Delhi's greater security role in the Indo-Pacific. And while there is recognition among Indian intelligence and military circles that China is India's long-term threat, there is no consensus in the Indian political establishment at large as to whether a deeper strategic partnership with the U.S. is the best solution. Tied up in this conundrum is that India's leadership has been grappling with the fundamental issue of what should be India's future role in the international world order. The former Indian ambassador to the U.S.

and China, Dr. S. Jaishankar, neatly articulated this dilemma, "Are we content to react to events or should we be shaping them more, on occasion even driving them? Should we remain a balancing power or aspire to be a leading one?"[5] This indeterminate sense of what are India's responsibilities as a major power has often led to what Washington perceives as indecision, hesitancy, and bureaucratic foot dragging in New Delhi.

India's reluctance to assume a greater role on the world stage has its historical antecedents in its foreign policies of nonalignment and strategic autonomy which are underpinned by persistent fears regarding the loss of sovereign independence, maneuverability between its two nuclear-armed adversaries, and concerns about subordination to the U.S. So, while the U.S. has sought to draw New Delhi further into its strategic embrace through increased intelligence and defense collaboration, New Delhi has operated in a parallel rather than joint realm, "achieving the benefits of cooperation while preserving strategic autonomy."[6]

Washington's overconfidence in its strategic alignment with New Delhi ignores the deep seated anti-Americanism that runs through India's domestic and foreign policy DNA. At the core is the Indian establishment's distrust of Washington, going back decades.[7] This distrust has been particularly shaped by the U.S. relationship with Pakistan and links between the U.S. Central Intelligence Agency (CIA) and Pakistan's Inter-Service Intelligence.[8] New Delhi blames Washington for building up Pakistan's military through longstanding weapons sales, for not intervening to halt Pakistan's development of a clandestine nuclear weapons program, and for not pressuring Islamabad to cede support for Pakistani-based terrorist groups. The latter have carried out numerous attacks on Indian soil, including the 2001 assault on the Parliament of India in New Delhi, the 2008 Mumbai attack, and ongoing insurgent violence in Jammu and Kashmir. Added to this lingering distrust is the perception in New Delhi of Washington's unreliability and unpredictability, particularly under the Trump administration, as demonstrated by zigzagging approaches to crises in Iraq, Afghanistan, and Syria, and its withdrawal from the Trans Pacific Partnership, a regional trade agreement and economic centerpiece to the U.S. pivot to Asia. The Trump administration had also threatened its strategic partner with a number of insensitive and punitive economic measures, including the threat of sanctions under the Countering America's Adversaries Through Sanctions Act, should India proceed with the purchase of the Russian S-400 air defense system, and the abrupt revocation of the Generalized System of Preferences, which facilitates India's access to the U.S. market, among others.[9]

Impediments within India's intelligence establishment

Just as the September 11, 2001 terrorist attacks brought the dramatic expansion and reshaping of the intelligence community in the U.S., events in India, including the 1999 Kargil conflict and the 2008 terrorist attack on Mumbai, prompted major organizational overhauls of India's intelligence establishment.[10] In both cases, Indian government commissions highlighted failures in intelligence collection, integration, assessment, and sharing that collectively impeded the Indian security response.[11] Subsequently, new intelligence agencies were created on top of existing ones, leading to numerous, overlapping, and often competing intelligence organizations. In 1947, for example, India had only two intelligence agencies: the Intelligence Bureau (IB), then responsible for internal intelligence and security, now the primary counterterrorism agency; and Military Intelligence (MI). Today, there are more than eight additional intelligence agencies. These include: the Research and Analysis Wing (R&AW), which is the CIA equivalent; the Defence Intelligence Agency (DIA); the Multi Agency Center (MAC); the National Technical Research Organization, which is similar to the U.S. National Security Agency; the Information Management and Analysis Center (IMAC); and the National Investigation Agency (NIA).[12] In New Delhi, the National Security Council Secretariat (NSCS) and the Joint Intelligence Committee (JIC) are responsible for coordinating intelligence assessments. The JIC focuses on the immediate/near-term intelligence terrorism assessments, while the NSCS is involved in policy-oriented, predictive estimates relating to national security priorities.

The blossoming of India's intelligence establishment post Kargil and Mumbai has seen India's intelligence efforts plagued by endemic agency turf wars, duplication of collection and analysis efforts, and lack of intelligence- and information-sharing mechanisms horizontally across agencies and vertically up to the national level in New Delhi.[13] A good demonstration of these inefficiencies is evidenced with counterterrorism intelligence activities. In the border areas there are many, overlapping intelligence agencies involved in counterterrorism collection: the IB, R&AW, MI, DIA, as well as the intelligence wings of paramilitary forces and the local police. As Manoj Shrivastava succinctly notes, "These agencies are reluctant to share actionable intelligence with each other for obvious reasons of 'turf wars'."[14] Furthermore, the Indian government's almost exclusive focus on counterterrorism and counter-insurgency shapes both the intelligence and defense communities at the national level. The blurring of external and internal security as reflected in India's intelligence establishment has meant that two of the five Indian national security advisors have been former chiefs of the domestic intelligence service.

The need for enhancing intelligence assessment and centralized coordination at the national level has been pointed out by many intelligence experts.[15] One American expert, James Burch, found that the Indian intelligence community's "independent assessment capability has not been properly resourced and bureaucratic infighting greatly inhibits the ability of the executive to coordinate and direct intelligence efforts. Lastly, India's almost total lack of executive and legislative oversight severely limits accountability and the ability to reform the system."[16]

Following the Mumbai terrorist attack, one of the structural reforms that was proposed was the establishment in 2004 of a National Counter Terrorism Center (NCTC) to coordinate the multitude of intelligence agencies under a unified central organization. The proposed NCTC was modelled after its U.S. counterpart and drew from U.S. Department of Homeland Security Joint Terrorism Task Force (JTTF) mission concepts, after high-level Indian intelligence official visits to the U.S.[17] More than a decade onwards, the NCTC remains a "piece of paper," held up at the national level because of domestic political tensions regarding the power of New Delhi versus local, state autonomy.[18] The issue of center/state divide was also highlighted in a 2017 Congressional Research Service (CRS) Report on India–U.S. Relations to explain why intelligence cooperation has not moved forward as rapidly or concretely as had been anticipated. According to the CRS report, structural impediments to future intelligence cooperation remain: "Perhaps leading among these is that India's state governments are the primary domestic security actors, and there is no significantly resourced and capable national-level body with which the U.S. federal government can coordinate."[19]

As discussed by contributing authors Bacon, Joshi, and Datta in this volume, U.S.–India cooperation to date has largely coalesced around counterterrorism.[20] While understandable post-9/11 and Mumbai, this narrow and rather opportunistic focus has underestimated larger prospects for intelligence sharing across a number of strategic domains in the Indo-Pacific region. As indicated in the very first sentence in the Department of Defense's *2019 Indo-Pacific Strategy Report*, "the Indo-Pacific is the single most consequential region for America's future."[21] Thus, identifying the mutual, vital security interests of the U.S. and India in this region is the first step towards providing a framework for enlarging the bilateral intelligence relationship.

U.S. and Indian vital interests in the Indo-Pacific

Table 11.1 provides a useful schematic outline of the vital national interests that the U.S. and India share at large, and within the Indo-Pacific region specifically.

Table 11.1 The United States and India: their vital national interests in the Indo-Pacific

National security interest	United States	India
National sovereignty	X	X
Counterterrorism	X	X
Counterinsurgency	X	X
Freedom of navigation of the seas/SLOCs	X	X
Cybersecurity from attacks on: infrastructure, government institutions and political processes, theft of intellectual property	X	X
Border security	X	X
Freedom of movement of trade and goods	X	X
Protection against and elimination of: piracy; arms, drug, and human trafficking; illicit arms transfers	X	X
Protection of 200-mile economic zone (EZ) and prevention of challenges under international law	X	X
Security of energy, natural resource, agriculture/food, and industrial supply chains	X	X
Protection of defense industrial base	X	X
Fishing rights (200-mile EZ) and over-fishing	X	X
Slowing the spread of Weapons of Mass Destruction	X	X
Maintenance of balance of power in the Indo-Pacific	X	X
Maintenance of balance of power in the global economy	X	X
Security of Indian water supplies from the Himalayas[a]		X
Protection of India culture		X
Address threats posed by climate change	X	X

Note: [a] China has projects underway to dam the Brahmaputra River in Tibet that would deprive India of vital water supplies. Sahana Bose, "Chinese Dam Diplomacy on the Brahmaputra River," National Maritime Foundation, (May 8, 2013), http://maritimeindia.org/chinese-dam-diplomacy-brahamaputra-river-0.

Overarching these vital interests is the shared goal by India and the U.S. to maintain the balance of power and stability in the region, and to ensure the openness of the global economy, which relies on the freedom of navigation for the Sea Lines of Communication (SLOC) running through the Indian and Pacific Oceans. Balance of power in the military and economic spheres in this region is critically underpinned by American deterrence through its ability to project maritime power and to maintain an effective forward-deployed military presence. However, as a number of military and intelligence analysts have warned, "American military primacy in the Indo-Pacific and its capacity to uphold a favorable balance of power is increasingly uncertain."[22]

This erosion in U.S. deterrence is juxtaposed with China's rising economic and military presence in the Indo-Pacific, in ways that are demonstrably reshaping the balance of power and, with it, challenging Washington's ability to underwrite stability in the region.[23] As recognized in the U.S. 2018 *National Security Strategy*, China's goal is to obtain "Indo-Pacific regional hegemony in the near-term and displacement of the U.S. to achieve global pre-eminence in the future."[24] A brief examination of the evolving threats posed by China and the China–Pakistan axis in the narrower Indian Ocean Region (IOR) is useful, since these maritime and land-based threats will drive intelligence cooperation between India and the U.S. in the future.

China

China has justified its expanded military presence in the (IOR) on the need to secure its SLOC for its maritime trade, energy, natural resource, and supply chain requirements.[25] Indeed, the Indian Ocean is a geostrategic hub, home to the world's most critical global shipping routes and key chokepoints, such as the Suez Canal, Bab al-Mandeb, Strait of Hormuz, the Strait of Malacca, and the Cape of Good Hope. Fifty percent of the globe's seaborne trade transits the Indian Ocean annually. Approximately 80 percent of China's energy imports from the Middle East and Africa transit through the Indian Ocean and via the Strait of Malacca.

Many analysts, however, argue that the SLOC justification obfuscates the People's Republic of China's (PRC) larger objectives to undermine India's geostrategic influence in the region and to challenge U.S. naval supremacy in the Indo-Pacific. Of major concern are the increasing and expanding, "far seas", blue-water operations by Chinese Navy warships and submarines in the IOR.[26] These operations are sustained by a widening web of PRC-controlled naval logistic bases stretching from Africa to Southeast Asia.[27] Kapila articulates the Indian position forcefully, arguing that China is expanding its military presence, using a "stepped" approach characterized by:

> the implementation of "string of pearls" strategy as the opening move; followed by its active involvement in anti-piracy naval operations in the Gulf of Aden ... with a veneer of projecting China as a responsible stakeholder in international maritime security; followed by its wooing of 10 small island nations ... to gain naval footholds; and now its "Maritime Silk Road"

initiative with benign commercial development ... is nothing but a deep rooted maritime domination strategy of the South China Sea and the Indian Ocean.[28]

China's development of a "Maritime Silk Road" is part of President Xi Jinping's $1.3 trillion Belt and Road Initiative (BRI). The maritime corridor is anchored at one end of the Indian Ocean, with a newly opened People's Liberation Army Navy (PLAN) base in Djibouti on the Horn of Africa, complemented by additional, dual-use, deep-water port facilities in Kenya, Tanzania, Oman, the Seychelles, Maldives, Pakistan, Sri Lanka, Myanmar, and Thailand. All are operated and owned or under 99-year leases, often extracted for debt repayments, by the PRC government.[29] Close observers of China's force modernization and naval power projection capabilities have sounded the alarm that the PRC's deployment of ballistic missile systems in the Spratlys, "could be used in a similar fashion ... to China's emerging overseas military bases in Djibouti and Pakistan and elsewhere along the course of the BRI."[30]

China–Pakistan axis

While Chinese militarization in the Indo-Pacific continues apace, threats to India's security emanating from Pakistan, and China's support of this key proxy, also provide new opportunities for enhanced intelligence cooperation with the U.S., particularly along the borders and maritime domain. The India–Pakistan–China border and the disputed territory of Kashmir have been sites for multiple wars, conflicts, insurgencies, and ongoing cross-border terrorism incubated in Pakistan.[31] Added to these border threats is Beijing's ongoing construction of the China–Pakistan Economic Corridor (CPEC), a $46 billion BRI infrastructure project. CPEC links China's Xinjiang province to Pakistan's port of Gwadar in the Indian Ocean via an extensive network of railways, highways, and pipelines that are designed to bring critical energy and other resource supplies overland to China. The overland route is considered critical for China, since it will allow a major portion of its energy supplies to avoid the key Malacca Strait chokepoint. CPEC poses two strategic threats to India. First, to the objection of India, the corridor traverses territory which India claims (the Gilgit-Baltistan areas of the state of Jammu and Kashmir). Second, the Chinese-financed port of Gwadar is slated to become a PRC military logistics base, which would enable Chinese nuclear-attack submarines and future carrier battle groups to project PLAN force projection power into the Arabian Sea, and to contain India in its immediate backyard.[32]

Beijing has provided longstanding assistance to Pakistan's nuclear weapons and missile arsenals.[33] Beginning in 2015, Beijing has augmented Pakistan's naval capacity, including the delivery of four advanced guided-missile F-22P frigates with CM-302 supersonic anti-ship cruise missiles, and planned acquisition of eight diesel-electric submarines, Type 039 or 041 Yuan-class conventional attack submarines.[34] Pakistan's burgeoning under-sea warfare capabilities were boosted in January 2017 with the successful test of its first nuclear-capable, submarine-launched cruise missiles, called the Babur-3.[35] Together, China's naval modernization and expansion, augmented by Pakistan's naval aviation and sea- and under-sea based capabilities, provide a formidable challenge, particularly to Indian naval forces such as future Indian aircraft carriers, but also ground elements as well.[36]

With the slow and uneven pace of India's defense production programs and favoring of the Indian Army over the Navy (given the urgency of border security threats), India has little option but to rely increasingly on U.S. intelligence and military support. On the flip side, as one Indian observer of the U.S.–India military relationship opined, "The China–India military confrontation offers a unique strategic opportunity to the U.S. to position itself on the right side of 21st century Asian history."[37]

India takes action

For India, the long-feared threat of encirclement on land and by sea by China and its proxy, Pakistan, is becoming real and has galvanized the Modi government into action to attain primacy in the Indian Ocean and to serve as a "net provider of regional security" in the Indo-Pacific more broadly.[38] On the diplomatic front, the Modi government has actively pursued a number of initiatives aimed at strengthening and accelerating economic and security integration within the Indo-Pacific region in order to sure up a stable balance of power in the region and to provide an alternative to China's BRI. These mechanisms include: the "Act East" policy; Security and Growth for All in the Region; the Bay of Bengal Initiative for Multi-Sectoral Technical and Economic Cooperation; Project Mausam; and the Indian Ocean Rim Association.[39]

On the military front, India has launched an ambitious regional maritime engagement strategy designed to establish Indian naval preeminence in the Indo-Pacific and to strengthen the naval capacities of key regional partners. Encapsulated in the 2015 *Ensuring Secure Seas: Indian Maritime Security Strategy*, the Modi government is providing military assistance to the island nations of the Maldives, Seychelles, Mauritius, and Sri Lanka to develop a regional Maritime Domain Awareness (MDA) network.[40] It has also bolstered the coastal protection capabilities through the transfer of patrol vessels and maritime patrol aircraft to the Maldives, Mauritius, and the Seychelles. India is improving its maritime infrastructure capacity in the Indian Ocean by securing port access in Dum, Oman, Sabang, Indonesia, and at Assumption Island in the Seychelles.[41] Under the Maritime Capability Perspective Plan, the Indian Navy is undergoing modernization with the aim to have a 200-ship fleet by 2027, focused on power projection and sea-control missions, through continued indigenization defense production efforts and U.S. military technology, arms sales, and other Russian assistance.[42]

U.S.–India relations are at a tipping point, and one that bodes well for the future of U.S.–Indian intelligence cooperation. As discussed above, a number of factors, including a recalibration of U.S.–China military balance increasingly in Beijing's favor, encroaching encirclement of India by land and by sea from China and Pakistan, and an emboldened government in New Delhi, portend of India's determination to be a "leading" power in the Indo-Pacific, and recognition that U.S. intelligence and military assistance will be centripetal to achieving that goal. For the relationship to advance, the U.S. needs to be mindful of how it cooperates with India, for the Indo-Pacific strategy is just that, a strategy; it is not a detailed framework designed to secure the mutual vital interests that are outlined above. Moreover, the U.S. must make a deliberate move to include more "Indo" in its conception of the Indo-Pacific region as a quid pro quo for Indian assistance in East Asia.[43]

To further intelligence collaboration with India, the U.S. should disavow Pakistan and visibly support India. As one study presaged, the U.S. should "explicitly stress its national interest in preserving India's security and territorial integrity as well as its support for a strong Indian military able to deter and defeat aggression."[44] U.S. strategic and tactical intelligence support must be objective driven, with key benefits for India, especially its role as a net security provider in the region. This approach will require an incremental, focused effort by both partners – one that builds enduring trust and capacity. The current and long-term future security in the Indo-Pacific has to be underscored by the best intelligence that India, the U.S., and with regional allies, require to anticipate, plan, deter, and constantly demonstrate that collectively they will maintain international order in the region.

A vision for future strategic and defense intelligence cooperation

The literature on the U.S.–India relationship is replete with pessimistic analyses of why the strategic partnership is likely to remain stalled, and that future defense and intelligence collaboration will remain limited. The following discussion, however, provides an optimistic assessment of the many opportunities for enhanced and expanded U.S.–India cooperation. The need to secure U.S. and Indian vital mutual interests in the Indo-Pacific portends of some near-term areas that are ripe for intelligence cooperation. Looking into the future, the following section highlights a grander vision where shared intelligence collection, analysis, and dissemination efforts support real-time operations to protect India's land and maritime borders, and to provide a counterbalance to China's and Russia's growing military presence in the region.

Near-term focus on supporting Indian vital strategic interests

Indian national sovereignty and maintenance of India's free movement of goods and services across the oceans, together with protection of its land and sea borders, particularly with Pakistan and China, are preeminent strategic goals in the Indo-Pacific area of operations. Within these parameters, areas that are vital to India and require expanded U.S. intelligence support include:

- intelligence collection against piracy, drug and human trafficking, gun running, and illicit arms transfers;
- surveillance, tracking, and interception of sea- and land-based terrorist activities, including their global financing mechanisms;
- counter-intelligence operations against espionage, infiltration, propaganda, intellectual property theft, and cyber operations;
- countering the spread of weapons of mass destruction;
- defense intelligence regarding Chinese and Pakistan military modernization programs, defense sales, nuclear weapons technology cooperation etc.;
- tracking movements in Indian ports by belligerent merchant ships, major power surrogates, and flags of convenience;
- surveillance of the Indian 200-mile EZ and territorial waters, to protect fishing rights, energy, and natural resource supply chains;
- monitoring of hostile major power intrusions for intelligence collection purposes inside the Indian twelve-mile limit, port visits for agent insertion and signals intelligence/electronic intelligence (SIGINT/ELINT) collection, and transiting Indian coastal waters for intelligence collection purposes.

These are viable starting points for U.S.–India intelligence collaboration in the near term. A key takeaway from the history of U.S.–India intelligence cooperation is the necessity of creating an exchange program of diplomatic, intelligence, and military intelligence personnel to move this agenda forward. Personnel exchanges develop not just lasting relations with career intelligence specialists, they create a culture that will prevail, based on intrinsic trust and professionalism – a foundation that has yet to be deeply established at the working inter-governmental levels between the U.S. and India.

This diplomatic–intelligence–military process can enable the identification and concurrence of the key strategic intelligence sharing missions, with a complete breakdown of their tactical and operational requirements. From the American vantage point, this process would enable the U.S. intelligence community, led by the Director of National Intelligence, to assess what level and degree of data sharing are required (e.g. ELINT, SIGINT, human intelligence (HUMINT), measurement and signature intelligence (MASINT) etc.) *and can be shared* with Indian counterparts. Additionally, red-teaming, war gaming, threat assessment, and contingency planning would assist in identifying risks, resources, and mitigation strategies to enhance mission success. U.S.–Indian intelligence needs can then be focused, prioritized, and sustained by formal agreements, and executed in incremental and non-invasive ways so that possible political hurdles and public perception, within India, may be overcome.

For India, an added benefit of intelligence cooperation with the U.S. is that America brings four other key intelligence partners in the shape of the "Five Eyes", namely the United Kingdom, Canada, Australia, and New Zealand, all of whom have cooperated across the intelligence spectrum since World War II. Together, the Five Eyes have unique and hugely capable means to track developments in every domain in the Indo-Pacific region. The latter covers all the main "Ints", from classical HUMINT, SIGINT, and ELINT, to the rarefied domains of acoustic intelligence (ACINT), IMINT, and MASINT. The Five Eyes also have a legion of highly specialist intelligence collection and analysis sub-sets, dealing with nuclear weaponry, industrial research and development and production, cyber operations, deception of multiple types, and advanced cryptographic technologies.

At the more technically demanding and advanced levels of intelligence collection and analysis, a step-by-step process of confidence and security building between India and the Five Eyes can ensue. This will take time; if implemented in well-defined increments, with clearly defined operational intelligence objectives, then the U.S.–India and Five Eyes relationships will flourish into new arenas that have never been explored. Let us examine some future intelligence mission sets in more detail.

China–Pakistan border

The U.S. Army's National Ground Intelligence Center in Charlottesville, Virginia and U.S. Special Operations Command Intelligence division can work with their Indian opposite numbers to assist in border protection and counterterrorist intelligence operations. As was pointed out above, the Indian government and military have constantly complained about the lack of timely and actionable intelligence from their cumbersome and dispersed intelligence establishment. Similar complaints were levied by the U.S. military during the Gulf Wars, but intelligence has vastly improved with the deployment of joint command, control, communications, computers, intelligence, surveillance, reconnaissance, and targeting (C4ISRT) systems to each of the military services.

The Distributed Common Ground System (DCGS) is one of the U.S. military's primary C4ISRT support systems for network-centric operations. Known in the Army as DCGS-A, and DCGS-N for the Navy, it provides enhanced situational awareness, fuses national, tactical, and inter-theater sensors, and disseminates this intelligence-based data directly to the warfighter. While the Indian Navy has recognized the utility of such an intelligence platform for MDA (in large part because it has been closely following U.S. Navy enabling capabilities for network-centric warfare), the Indian Army has not had the benefit of such exposure.[45]

The American intelligence community, together with the U.S. Army, could provide technical know-how to develop a C4ISRT system designed to meet India's specific needs along the borders. A common operating picture would enable an intelligence-based, real-time "indicators and warning" system. This C4ISRT system could alert of threats pertaining to border incursions, terrorist plans and movements, and any major nuclear posture changes or actions by either China or Pakistan, or both, that might threaten Indian and U.S. interests, and stability in the region. Additionally, the U.S. could assist India, as it did during the Kargil conflict, with discreet border surveillance with deployments of, for example, Joint Stars and Rivet Joint aircraft.

Special operations

An area that has been slated for increased operational improvement is the special forces in the Indian military.[46] These forces remain limited in number and are not considered intelligence-collection assets in ways that the U.S. Special Forces operate. In this regard, U.S. Army Special Operations forces and the U.S. Navy's Sea, Air, and Land Teams (SEALs) can assist with training, data exchanges, and operational planning support with Indian forces, in concert with regular exercises and personnel exchanges in both the U.S. and India. Part of this process can include special penetration and exfiltration operations, deception, counterterrorism training, network penetration, and psychological warfare. U.S. Rangers, Green Berets, U.S. Navy SEALs, and U.S. Air Force Special Operations teams can work with Indian forces in realistic scenarios, including border-related operations. On the U.S. Navy side, the Navy Special Operations Command can begin to train emergent Indian SEAL teams, particularly in covert underwater operations, demolition, sabotage, sensor implants, SIGINT and ELINT collection, and other clandestine intelligence collection. On the land warfare side, the U.S. Army, through U.S. Special Operations Command (SOCOM), with the assistance of U.S. European Command (EUCOM) and INDOPACOM, can help create a similar special operations command, initially for Indian border protection, counterterrorism, and infiltration.

U.S. intelligence support to Indian maritime operations

As discussed earlier, India and the U.S. share vital mutual interests in maintaining a stable order in the Indo-Pacific and countering Chinese growing maritime hegemony in the region. Both Washington and New Delhi recognize that this will require support from regional allies and partners, including the Five Eyes and Quad members. As the Pentagon's *2019 Indo-Pacific Strategy Report* acknowledges, "The challenges we face in the Indo-Pacific extend beyond what any single country can address alone."[47]

For India this means developing adequate power projection in and from the seas, and sea-control capability in "blue waters" to safeguard national interests such as the SLOCs and to neutralize maritime-borne threats such as the Mumbai terrorist attack of 2008. Additionally, India has focused on an ambitious expansion of its naval and maritime operations in the Indo-Pacific. To support these missions and operations, the Indian Navy continues sizeable investments in developing a regional MDA capability, modeled after Singaporean and American maritime security concepts and inter-agency constructs.[48]

The U.S. has provided considerable operational MDA intelligence assistance with the sale to India under the Major Defense Partner initiative of eight Boeing P-8I Poseidon maritime patrol aircraft (with an additional ten to come on line) for long-range anti-submarine warfare (ASW), anti-surface warfare, and intelligence, surveillance, and reconnaissance operations in the Indian Ocean.[49] With the signing in 2018 of the bilateral Communications Compatibility and Security Agreement (COMCASA), the U.S. is in the final stages of exporting thirty weaponized Predator-B unmanned aerial vehicles (UAVs). Also known in India as Sea Guardian, these UAVs will greatly enhance India's ability to monitor key chokepoints from the Persian Gulf to the Malacca Strait.[50] Further U.S. intelligence assistance could be provided to augment India's MDA network-centricity. At the working level, the U.S. National Maritime Intelligence Center (NMIC) can support Indian naval intelligence across the various domains described above. A Joint Indian Ocean Surveillance Center can be Indian managed and staffed, with agreed U.S. NMIC and Five Eyes support and with tactical intelligence inputs provided by the Navy's very robust DCGS-N system.

In this regard, major Chinese and Russian naval movements in the Indian Ocean, Bay of Bengal, and the approaches to the Straits of Hormuz, Bab-el-Mandeb, Malacca, Sunda, and Lombok can be cooperatively monitored through combined U.S.–Indian–Five Eyes intelligence operations.[51] These operations will include real-time monitoring and tracking of surface, subsurface, and air operations by both China and Russia and rogue Chinese and Russian spy ships and those clandestine merchant ships conducting covert operations.

From these beginnings can grow more sophisticated and sensitive intelligence collection and analysis operations. For example, as indicated earlier, the acquisition by India of the Boeing P-8 Poseidon aircraft is a major, first step in long-term ASW cooperation between India, the U.S. and its two other Five Eyes allies, the UK and Australia, both of which have significant submarine and other ASW capabilities that can deploy into the Indo-Pacific area of operations. Chinese submarine operations will continue to grow in the decade 2020–30 and have already caught India off guard. In 2014 a PLAN conventional submarine docked twice in Colombo, Sri Lanka without prior warning, and in 2016, the PLAN docked a nuclear-powered submarine in the port of Karachi in Pakistan.[52] Building strong ASW relations with the U.S. Navy and regional partners is paramount. Especially for India, the threat posed by the close proximity and expanding Chinese presence at the Pakistani port of Gwadar (and possibly Karachi) for the basing, repair, and maintenance of major Chinese naval assets, including submarines, is clearly non-trivial both strategically and tactically.

India is ramping up its ASW and surveillance capabilities and the U.S. can be key in ensuring that India invests wisely. SIGINT, ELINT, and IMINT collection in the Indo-Pacific must become major Indian intelligence objectives, and Washington can assist enormously in training, infrastructure development, defense acquisition, and intelligence sharing. Upgrading India's Andaman and Nicobar island tri-service Command's relatively modest military infrastructure to allow for basing of submarines and other naval combatants, Poseidon and Indian air force fighter aircraft, is a strategic imperative. These islands dominate exit and entrance of all maritime commerce and foreign naval movement through the Malacca Strait into the South China Sea and would alter China's "Malacca dilemma" from "being a notional threat to a real one."[53] Future naval intelligence gathering and sharing between U.S. and Indian space surveillance networks will be another important conduit for monitoring and tracking Chinese and Russian maritime movements in the Indian Ocean.

Exercises

> We should be exercising together and we should be turning those [naval] exercises into coordinated operations. (Commander-in-Chief U.S. Pacific Command, Admiral Harry Harris)[54]

Naval exercises are built on intelligence assessments. The latter predicate exercise scenarios and objectives. Joint U.S.–India–Five Eyes intelligence cooperation can immediately support the ongoing annual *MALABAR* and recent *Tiger Triumph* exercises series, and could increasingly feed into what can become a regular pattern of major multilateral naval exercises, similar, for example, to the Rim of the Pacific exercise format.[55] Writing in 2019 for the *Naval Review*, retired Indian Naval Commander Ranjit Rai commented on the defense intelligence sharing and collaboration benefits of *MALABAR*:

> The series of MALABAR exercises have become a regular fixture – India is no longer non-aligned, but now advocated strategic alignments. The IN [Indian Navy] was exposed to U.S.N[avy] ... during Exercise MALABAR the Indian Navy depended on U.S. Navy's CENTRIX system for digital communications and maritime domain awareness (MDA). And much is gained through exchange of officers during such exercises.[56]

The U.S. Navy and its key allies can employ intelligence-based tabletop and full-scale maritime exercises to help prepare the Indian Navy for increasing Chinese major surface action group incursions in the Indian Ocean. Part of the countervailing naval diplomacy that India, the U.S., and their allies could embark upon is the conduct of major exercises with the UK Royal Navy and the Royal Australian Navy (RAN), in addition to the U.S Navy and Marine Corps. The UK plans to deploy the new *Queen Elizabeth* carrier battle group (that includes U.S. Marine Corps naval aviators flying the F-35 aircraft) into the region in 2021. The Royal Navy will also likely deploy Astute Class nuclear-powered attack submarines with such a battle group. Together, with deploying RAN Collins Class highly capable, non-nuclear-powered submarines and surface ships, plus Royal

New Zealand Navy frigates, this battle group, working alongside U.S. Navy nuclear-powered aircraft carriers, their escorts, plus Virginia Class nuclear-powered attack submarines, will show an enormous naval diplomatic force to counter any impressions of growing Chinese hegemony in the Indo-Pacific area of operations. In this respect, the U.S. and India, together with regional partners and allies, have enormous opportunities to exploit intelligence sharing for MDA and maritime security operations in the Indo-Pacific.

Conclusion

Chapter 12 in this volume provides an important Indian perspective and historical overview of the Indian–U.S. bilateral relationship on intelligence cooperation to date. Where progress has been made in the area of counter-terrorism, Saikat Datta spotlights the bureaucratic and mistrust factors that have led to a pattern of start-and-stop cooperation. This chapter has argued that the U.S. and Indian vital strategic interests in the Indo-Pacific region are strongly converging, which gives promise to an expanded and deepened bilateral intelligence relationship. Geostrategic challenges posed by China's demonstrable military and economic presence along India's land borders and its trade and energy routes in the Indian Ocean will place an increasing demand on India's limited intelligence resources, paving the need for enhanced intelligence cooperation not only with the U.S., but with the Five Eyes community as well.

What has been missing in the many discussions of the U.S.–India defense intelligence relationship is an analysis of *how* U.S.–Indian intelligence cooperation can be enlarged. As indicated by its title, this chapter has addressed this question directly by outlining a deliberate roadmap for incremental measures to augment strategic and tactical-level intelligence sharing between the U.S. and India. As envisioned above, the U.S.–India intelligence relationship can grow and evolve to deter and thwart any impulses and plans for Chinese regional hegemony, and Sino-Pakistani endeavors to threaten Indian interests.

Notes

1 The views expressed are those of the author and do not necessarily reflect the official policy or position of the Department of the Army, Department of Defense, or the U.S. Government.
2 See Chapter 12 in this volume.

3 The Five Eyes is a multilateral intelligence-sharing alliance created by the U.S. and the UK in 1941. The initial key technical intelligence exchange was British Enigma-derived "Ultra" data from Bletchley Park with American "Magics" data from Station Hypo in Hawaii and the Office of Naval Intelligence in Washington, DC. Under this bedrock agreement the UK brought Canada, Australia, and New Zealand, all still British Dominions in 1945, into the various highly secret intelligence-sharing agreements signed between the five nations. Because of the shared image intelligence (IMINT) sources from space and airborne systems the word "Eyes" crept into the lexicon of the five nations. See Anthony R. Wells, *Between Five Eyes: 50 Years of Intelligence Sharing* (Oxford, U.K.: Casemate Publishers, 2020). The Quadrilateral Security Dialogue was founded in 2007 as an informal strategic dialogue between the United States, Japan, Australia, and India.
4 For a seminal examination of the U.S.–India relationship see Sumit Ganguly and M. Chris Mason, *An Unnatural Partnership? The Future of U.S.–India Strategic Cooperation* (Carlisle: U.S. Army War College Press, 2019), https://publications.armywarcollege.edu/pubs/3696.pdf.
5 S. Jaishankar, "Remarks by Foreign Secretary at the release of Dr. C. Raja Menon's Book, 'Modi's World: Expanding India's Sphere of Influence'," New Delhi, July 17, 2015, http://mea.gov.in/speeches-statements.him?dtl/2549/remarks_by_Foreign_Secretary_at_the_release_of_Dr_C_Raja_Mohans_book_Modis_WorldExpanding_Indias_Sphere_of_InfluencequotJuly_17_2015.
6 For a historic overview of the role of strategic autonomy in shaping the U.S.–India relationship see Guillem Monsonis, "India's Strategic Autonomy and Rapprochement with the U.S.," *Journal of Strategic Analysis*, 34:4 (2010), www.tandfonline.com/doi/full/10.1080/09700161003802802.
7 Additionally, a tit-for-tat spy expulsion in 1997, and a 2004 spy scandal involving the defection to the United States of a senior intelligence official from India's Research and Analysis Wing – the equivalent of the CIA – also impeded the trust and relationship building that are at the heart of intelligence sharing between countries.
8 Prakash Katoch, "The Confounding Paradox of the India–U.S. Relationship," *Asia Times* (June 20, 2019), www.asiatimes.com/2019/06/opinion/the-confounding-paradox-of-the-india-us-relationship/.
9 The Trump administration has also applied pressure on New Delhi to restrict Huawei's and ZTE 5G networks in its telecommunications market – the second-largest in the world. Vinay Kaura, "U.S.–India Relations at the Crossroads: Can the Growing U.S.–India Partnership Survive 'American First'?", *The Diplomat* (June 24, 2019), https://thediplomat.com/2019/06/us-india-relations-at-the-crossroads/; and Benjamin E. Schwartz, "The Ties that Bind: From Inertia to Integration: Getting Serious about U.S.–India Defense Cooperation," *The American Interest* (June 24, 2019), www.the-american-interest.com/2019/06/24/from-inertia-to-integration-getting-serious-about-u-s-india-defense-cooperation/; and Amy Kazmin and Stephanie Findlay, "Washington Warns New Delhi over Using Huawei for 5G," *The Financial*

Times (October 3, 2019), www.ft.com/content/4181ee4e-e5de-11e9-9743-db5a370481bc.
10 Maloy Krishna Dhar observes that: "The most glaring example of total intelligence failure was the Kargil adventure by Pakistan Army. The Research and Analysis Wing, Military Intelligence and, to a lesser extent the Intelligence Bureau had miserably failed to unearth the Pakistani design and warn the policy planners. Whatever intelligence was available was not coordinated to cull out a coherent collage. The rest is history." Quoted in Manoj Shrivastava, *Re-energizing Indian Intelligence* (New Delhi: VijBooks India Pvt. Ltd, 2013), p. 5.
11 See Prem Mahadevan, *The Politics of Counterterrorism in India: Strategic Intelligence and National Security in Asia* (London: I. B. Tauris & Co., Ltd., 2012). Mahadeven is at pains to distinguish "failures of intelligence" from "failures to act on intelligence." Based on this distinction, he argues that Indian decisionmakers have frequently failed to act on long-term warnings from their intelligence agencies, despite their repeated accurate forecasts of terrorist action.
12 This overview relies heavily on Shrivastava, *Re-Energizing Indian Intelligence*. The DIA integrates intelligence collected by the three service directorates (Army, Air Force, and Navy), and serves as the principal military intelligence agency. The Agency's primary task is to track foreign troop movement in adjacent countries and to monitor terrorist groups operating both within and outside the country. The MAC is an intelligence-sharing fusion center based in New Delhi. Similar to the Fusion Centers that operate in the United States at the state level, MAC and its subsidiaries, SMACs, provide a coordination mechanism between the state police's own special intelligence branches and the other intelligence agencies. IMAC fuses radar data along India's coast and is the nodal center of the National Command Control Communications and Intelligence and the Indian Navy's National Maritime Domain Awareness system of coastal surveillance radars in Mauritius, Madagascar, Seychelles, Oman, Maldives, and Sri Lanka. NIA is the central counterterrorism law enforcement investigatory agency in India.
13 Vinay Kaura, "Too Many Spies Spoil the Broth," *Live Mint* (May 17, 2017), www.livemint.com/Opinion/cS4HVympwImh5PLi5FhNdI/Too-many-spies-spoil-the-intelligence-broth.html.
14 Shrivastava, *Re-Energizing Indian Intelligence*, p. 4.
15 Pushan Das, "The Chaos that Is Counter-Terrorism in India," *Observer Research Foundation* (November 24, 2018), www.orfonline.org/expert-speak/chaos-counter-terrorism-india-45732/.
16 James Burch, "Domestic Intelligence Agencies," *Homeland Security Affairs*, iii:2 (June 2007), p. 15, www.hsaj.org/articles/147.
17 The JTTF is a multi-jurisdictional task force managed by the Federal Bureau of Investigation, and includes other federal, state, and local law enforcement and intelligence partners, whose mission is to combat domestic and international terrorism.
18 Das, "The Chaos that Is Counter-Terrorism in India."

19 K. Alan Kronstadt, and Shayerah Ilias Akhtar, *India–U.S. Relations: Issues for Congress* (updated June 19, 2017), Congressional Research Service, https://crsreports.congress.gov/product/pdf/R/R44876/6.
20 See chapters 9, 10, and 12.
21 Department of Defense, *Indo-Pacific Strategy Report: Preparedness, Partnerships, and Promoting a Networked Region* (June 1, 2019), p. 1.
22 A 2019 study by the University of Sydney in Australia based this assessment on impacts caused by U.S. defense budget uncertainties, and an "atrophying" U.S. military force that is "not sufficiently ready, equipped or postured." Cited in Ashley Townshend and Brendan Thomas-Noone with Matilda Steward, *Averting Crisis: American Strategy, Military Spending and Collective Defense in the Indo-Pacific* (Sydney: The United States Studies Center, Sydney University, August 2019), pp. 2 and 3.
23 Michael Raska, "Strategic Competition and Future Conflicts in the Indo-Pacific Region," *Journal of Indo-Pacific Affairs* (Summer 2019), p. 84.
24 U.S. Department of Defense, "Summary of the 2018 National Defense Strategy of the United States of America," p. 2, https://dod.defense.gov/Portals/1/Documents/pubs/2018-National-Defense-Strategy-Summary.pdf.
25 Rear Admiral Zhang Hachen, Deputy Commander of the People's Liberation Army Navy's East Sea Fleet, underscored the importance of the Indian Ocean for his country: "with the expansion of the country's economic interests, the [Chinese] navy wants to protect the country's transportation routes and the safety of our major sea lanes." Cited in Qamar Fatima and Asma Jamshed, "The Political and Economic Significance of the Indian Ocean: An Analysis," *South Asian Studies*, 30:2 (July–December 2015), p. 85.
26 Since 2008 the PLAN has deployed two to three surface vessels in the AOR and in 2013 PLAN initiated patrols of its attack submarines in the Indian Ocean. Zachary Heck, "India Has Reason to Fear China's Submarines in the Indian Ocean," *The National Interest* (September 21, 2019), https://nationalinterest.org/blog/buzz/india-has-reason-fear-chinas-submarines-indian-ocean-82301.
27 The 2019 "China's National Defense in the New Era," states: "To address deficiencies in overseas operations and support it builds far seas forces, develops overseas logistical facilities and enhances capabilities in accomplishing diversified military tasks." The State Council Information Office of the People's Republic of China, "China's National Defense in the New Era," (Beijing: Foreign Languages Press Co. Ltd, 2019), p. 8. www.xinhuanet.com/english/2019-07/24/c_138253389.htm.
28 Dr. Subhash Kapila, *China–India Military Confrontation: 21st Century Perspectives* (Partridge India, 2016), p. 131.
29 See Jayanna Krupakar, "China's Naval Base(s) in the Indian Ocean – Signs of a Maritime Grand Strategy?" *Strategic Analysis*, 41:3 (2017), https://doi.org/10.1080/09700161.2017.1296622, and Michael J. Green and Andrew Shearer, "Countering China's Militarization of the Indo-Pacific," *War on the Rocks* (April 23, 2018), https://warontherocks.com/2018/04/countering-chinas-militarization-of-the-indo-pacific/.

30 Janes E. Fanell, "Asia Rising: China's Global Naval Strategy and Expanding Force Structure," *Naval War College Review*, 72:1 (2019), https://digital-commons.usnwc.edu/nwc-review/vol72/iss1/4, p. 14. See also, Michael Raska, "Strategic Competition and Future Conflicts in the Indo-Pacific Region," *Journal of Indo-Pacific Affairs* (Summer 2019), www.airuniversity.af.edu/Portals/10/JIPA/journals/Volume-02_Issue-2/06-Raska.pdf.
31 India and Pakistan have fought four wars with each other, including as recently as 1999 (Kargil). Attacks by the Pakistani-based terrorist organization Lashkar-e-Taiba in 2015 on an Indian military base in Pathankot, and another, in Uri, Kashmir, have led to a more proactive response by the Modi government, including retaliatory "surgical strikes" inside Pakistani territory by the Indian Army and the decision in 2019 to revoke Article 370, a constitutional provision that granted special status and allowed some autonomy for the Indian state of Jammu and Kashmir. See Sumit Ganguly, "Modi Crosses the Rubicon in Kashmir: New Delhi Upends the Status Quo in the Disputed Territory," *Foreign Affairs* (August 8, 2019), www.foreignaffairs.com/articles/india/2019-08-08/modi-crosses-rubicon-kashmir.
32 Peter Frankopan, *The New Silk Roads: The Present and Future of the World* (New York: Alfred A. Knopf, 2019), p. 96, and Suyash Desai, "India Should Seek 'Hawkish Balance' through Quad," *Asia Times* (October 1, 2019), www.asiatimes.com/2019/10/opinion/india-should-seek-hawkish-balance-through-quad/.
33 For an overview of Chinese nuclear technology assistance, see William Burr (ed.), "China, Pakistan, and the Bomb: The Declassified File on U.S. Policy, 1977–1997," (March 5, 2004), National Security Archive, http://nsarchive.gwu.ed/NSAEBB/NSAEBB114/. China has supplied Pakistan with M-9 and M-11 nuclear-capable missiles.
34 Iskander Rehman, "The Submarine Dimension of Sino-Indian Maritime Rivalry," in David Brewster (ed.), *India and China at Sea: Competition for Naval Dominance in the Indian Ocean* (New Delhi: Oxford University Press, 2018), p. 145.
35 Cody T. Smith, *Century of the Seas: Unlocking Indian Maritime Strategy in the 21st Century* (Monterey, CA: Naval Postgraduate School, 2017), http://hdl.handle.net/10945/56178, p. 35.
36 For a recent and detailed overview of China's naval modernization program see, Ronald O'Rourke, *China Naval Modernization: Implications for U.S. Navy Capabilities – Background and Issues for Congress* (Washington, DC: Congressional Research Service, August 30, 2019).
37 Kapila, *China–India Military Confrontation*, p. 13.
38 The role of India as a net security provider was first used by U.S. Secretary of Defense Robert Gates at the 2009 Shangri-La Dialogue as part of the original U.S. "pivot" to Asia.
39 Dhruva Jaishankar provides an excellent analysis of these initiatives in "Acting East: India in the Indo-Pacific," Impact Series (New Delhi: Brookings India, October 2019), www.brookings.edu/wp-content/uploads/2019/10/Acting-East-India-in-the-INDO-PACIFIC-without-cutmark.pdf.

40 Indian Navy, *Ensuring Secure Seas: Indian Maritime Security Strategy* (New Delhi: Ministry of Defence, 2015), www.indiannavy.nic.in/sites/default/files/Indian_Maritime_Security_Strategy_Document_25Jan16.pdf. The aim is to control four key areas: the Malacca Strait, Sunda Strait, Lombok Strait, Ombai and Wetar Straits through which Chinese navy and submarines need to transit. Darshana M. Baruah, "Expanding India's Maritime Domain Awareness in the Indian Ocean," *Asia Policy*, 22 (July 2016), p. 53, www.jstor.org/stable/24905108.

41 Vivek Mishra, "Consolidating India's Indian Ocean Strategy," *The Diplomat* (June 7, 2019), https://thediplomat.com/2019/06/consolidating-indias-indian-ocean-strategy/.

42 "Indian Navy Aiming at 200-Ship Fleet by 2027," *The Economic Times* (July 14, 2018), https://economictimes.indiatimes.com/news/defence/indian-navy-aiming-at-200-ship-fleet-by-2027/articleshow/48072917.cms.

43 Alyssa Ayres, "The U.S. Indo-Pacific Strategy Needs More Indian Ocean," Council on Foreign Relations Expert Brief (January 22, 2019), www.cfr.org/expert-brief/us-indo-pacific-strategy-needs-more-indian-ocean.

44 Robert D. Blackwill, Naresh Chandra, and Christopher Clary, "The United States and India: A Shared Strategic Future," A Joint Study Group Report, Council on Foreign Relations/Aspen Institute India (September 2011), p. 24. www.cfr.org/report/united-states-and-india-shared-strategic-future.

45 The Indian Navy uses the term Network Centric Operations, which "encompass the networking of all units, with real-time/near real-time secure exchange of operational information between sensors, decision-makers and 'shooters'." Indian Navy, *Ensuring Secure Seas*, p. 134.

46 For an overview of India's Special Forces, see Lt. Gen P. C. Katoch and Saikat Datta, *India's Special Forces: History and Future of Indian Special Forces* (New Delhi: Vij Books India, 2013). For a recent assessment of Indian special operations see Saikat Datta, "India Tries and Fails to Improve Its Special Operations Forces," *Asia Times* (May 31, 2019), www.asiatimes.com/2019/05/article/india-tries-to-improve-its-special-ops-capability/.

47 U.S. Department of Defense, *Indo-Pacific Strategy Report: Preparedness, Partnerships, and Promoting a Networked Region*, p. 16.

48 See: Ranjit B. Rai, "IMAC: Indian Navy's Eyes and Ears: Hitech Data T=Fusion Center Inaugurated," *India Strategic* (December 2014), www.indiastrategic.in/topstories3616_Indian_Navy_setting_up_Coastal_Eyes_and_Ears.htm, and Christian Bueger, "The IFC at Ten: Attending MARISX Information Sharing Exercise in Singapore," *Safe Seas* (May 18, 2019), http://bueger.info/the-ifc-at-ten-attending-the-marisx-information-sharing-exercise-in-singapore/.

49 Boeing India, "P-8I Aircraft: 21st Century Maritime Security for the Indian Navy," www.boeing.co.in/products-and-services/defense-space-and-security/boeing-defense-space-and-security-in-india, and Franz-Stefan Gady, "India Approves Procurement of 10 More P-8I Maritime Patrol Aircraft," *The Diplomat* (June 26, 2019), https://thediplomat.com/2019/06/india-approves-procurement-of-10-more-p-8i-maritime-patrol-aircraft/.

50 Rajat Pandit, "Amid Russian Arms Row, India Plans Mega Deal for U.S. Military Drones," *The Times of India* (June 16, 2019), https://timesofindia.indiatimes.com/india/amid-russia-arms-row-india-plans-mega-deal-for-us-military-drones/articleshow/69807419.cms.
51 In December 2019 China, Russia, and Iran held a four-day trilateral naval exercise codenamed *Naval Security Belt* in the Indian Ocean and Gulf of Oman. This was the first time Iran has held a joint exercise with two major world naval powers at this scale. Ben Westcott and Hamdi Alkhshali, "Russia, China and Iran hold joint naval drills in Gulf of Oman," CNN (December 27, 2019), www.cnn.com/2019/12/27/asia/china-russia-iran-military-drills-intl-hnk/index.html.
52 "China's Activities in Indian Ocean Trigger Talks on Anti-Submarine Warfare between India, U.S," *Indian Express* (May 2, 2016).
53 Shishir Upadhyaya, "Expansion of Chinese Maritime Power in the Indian Ocean: Implications for India," *Defence Studies*, 17:1 (January 8, 2017), www.tandfonline.com/loi/fdef20.
54 Dinakar Peri, "U.S. Push for Joint Patrols in Indo-Pacific Region," *The Hindu* (March 3, 2016), www.thehindu.com/todays-paper/tp-national/us-push-for-joint-patrols-in-indopacific-region/article8306481.ece.
55 This viewpoint is at odds with Chris Mason's discussion of navy exercises in which he argues that they have been of limited value in enhancing joint operability and have been undermined by India's need to maintain "strategic independence" and reluctance not to provoke China. See Chapter 1 in this volume. With the signing of the COMCASA, India and the U.S. will be on track to utilize *MALABAR* exercises for more discreet ASW operations. See Indian Defence Consultants, "How Top-Secret U.S. System Will Allow India To Track Chinese Submarines," September 6, 2018, http://indiadefence.com/how-top-secret-us-system-will-allow-india-to-track-chinese-submarines/.
56 Ranjit Rai, "The Indian Navy – An RN Pedigree, Reshaped by the Soviets and Strategised by the U.S.N," *The Naval Review* 107:4 (November 2019), p. 497.

12

Natural alliance: enhancing India–U.S. intelligence cooperation

Saikat Datta

Introduction

India and the U.S. have often highlighted the fact that they are "natural allies." The relationship has been described as "a global strategic partnership based on shared democratic values and increasing convergence of interests in bilateral, regional and global issues."[1] Following a June 2016 joint summit between Prime Minister Narendra Modi and President Barack Obama, the relationship was described as "enduring global partners in the 21st century."[2] In September 2018 India and the U.S. signed an intelligence-sharing agreement that aims to increase the current levels of cooperation.[3] These are incremental steps and similar to sharing mechanisms agreed upon in the past.[4] This ensures that bilateral cooperation in intelligence has steadily grown since 2001, when India and the U.S. jump-started their bilateral relationship in the wake of the 9/11 attacks. However, the checkered bilateral history of the two nations states otherwise. In some ways, it is a relationship of paradoxes.

This chapter examines the early years of intelligence cooperation between India and the U.S. and argues that this is an area that has seen considerable success in the past. However, due to divergent priorities and capacities, there are limitations to this cooperation. But, as argued in Chapter 11 by Carol Evans,[5] there is considerable scope to build this relationship, building on foundations that were laid in the past. The chapter will also show the limitations to such cooperation from an Indian perspective, and what could be the possible ways to overcome them.

The history of post-independence India is replete with instances of looking to the U.S. and its institutions as reference points to build its own or to shape policies to govern. However, on several occasions the end result is very different from the original point of "reference" or the "inspiration" for an institution or policy outcome in India.

Naturally, the bilateral relationship on intelligence between the two countries records a similar history of paradoxes and missed chances. While intelligence cooperation is often touted as a major area of cooperation in all official pronouncements, in reality, it has seen little growth and cooperation, barring for brief periods. This is discussed in greater detail below.

Many of India's institutions were inherited from the departing colonial British. India's intelligence apparatus is also a legacy of the British, when the Intelligence Bureau (IB) was created through a telegram sent by Her Majesty's Secretary for India to the then Viceroy, Lord Dufferin, on December 31, 1887.[6] Post-independence, the IB was the sole federal intelligence organization, undertaking domestic as well as international intelligence work. The military had its separate intelligence branches, which were largely tactical and focused on local operations.

T. G. Sanjeevi Reddy, the first Director of the IB after independence, visited the U.S. in 1949 to study the intelligence apparatus[7] and adapt his observations to India's efforts to build its intelligence capabilities. Reddy is credited with setting up a specialized desk for foreign intelligence and selected two officers who were posted to the Indian embassies in France and Germany at the rank of first secretary.[8] India's first federal home minister, Sardar Vallabhai Patel, recognized the difficulties of setting up an intelligence capability that could cater to the needs of a modern republic. "I realise how difficult it is to organise our system of intelligence and how the legacy of past prejudices against one community or another against certain types of individuals or others and the monopoly of Europeans in the branch of police service has retarded our progress," he said while addressing the All Indian conference of police chiefs on January 12, 1950.[9]

The details of Reddy's trip to the U.S. are not known publicly. However, the fact that the U.S. had already created the National Security Act in 1947 and the U.S. Congress passed the Central Intelligence Act in June 1949 must have provided fascinating insights for Reddy. There is also a view that the Office of Strategic Services, the precursor to the Central Intelligence Agency (CIA), had officers who gave tacit and overt support to the Indian independence movement during World War II.[10]

The birth of the external intelligence agencies of both countries also provides insight into their evolution as well as a comparative framework of stated aims and scope. The U.S. faced a major intelligence failure when it was unable to detect plans by the Japanese to attack Pearl Harbor on December 7, 1941. Until then, the U.S. was served by a rudimentary intelligence apparatus that contained the specialized branches of its military and Office of the Coordinator of Information set up by President Franklin D. Roosevelt in July 1941.[11]

The bilateral cooperation on intelligence between India and the U.S. would peak after the Chinese invasion that led to the Sino-Indian conflict in 1962. India's crushing defeat would lead to the beginnings of the first major reforms in the Indian intelligence structure, which would eventually lead to the birth of a dedicated external intelligence organization, the Research & Analysis Wing (R&AW). Simultaneously, the CIA's work in Tibet would also lead to the birth of India's military special operations capabilities. These two developments laid a significant foundation for bilateral cooperation that continues to have immense potential for the future.

To policymakers it was clear that the IB's Foreign Intelligence Desk was inadequate to comprehensively deal with external intelligence. In September 1968, the R&AW was carved out to build R&AW under Rameshwar Nath Kao, who had earlier headed the Foreign Intelligence Desk in the IB.

However, in terms of focus, scope and evolution, the two organizations evolved very differently. Perhaps the best example of these differences is the fact that while the CIA was born through legislative action, India's R&AW was created through an executive order. These fundamental and foundational differences would go on to create a culture, capability and structure that would impact bilateral cooperation on intelligence in many ways in the future.

From cooperation to suspicion

The Sino-Indian war fought between October and November 1962 is a landmark event in many ways for India's national security apparatus. It also shaped its foreign policy imperatives and created a new paradigm for the India–U.S. relationship, building on the premise of being "natural allies, based on shared democratic values." It was also the beginning of a substantive cooperation on intelligence.

President John F. Kennedy had just emerged from the Cuban missile crisis when he turned his attention to South Asia when China invaded India in October 1962. Two letters from India's first Prime Minister, Jawaharlal Nehru, to Kennedy reflect the urgent requirements for holding the Chinese People's Liberation Army (PLA) at bay. Much of the ill-equipped and ill-prepared Indian Army would retreat as the PLA comfortably moved into the state of Arunachal Pradesh and arrived at the gates of Assam, while also occupying vast swathes of land in the state of Jammu and Kashmir.[12] Worried by Nehru's letters, Kennedy rushed a big delegation to help the Indians and ascertain what they needed to push back the Chinese PLA.

> The composition of the American team reflected the [Ambassador Averell] Harrman mission's three goals. The third goal, which was clandestine, was to secure Indian support for the CIA's covert action operations in Tibet. The CIA component of the team was headed by Desmond Fitzgerald, chief of the

Natural alliance

Far East Division, and John Kenneth Knaus, director of the CIA Tibetan Task Force.[13]

The Americans were also using the Tibetans for reconnaissance and were prepared to set up a military presence to help India push the Chinese out. The IB was led by B. N. Mullik, who had taken over as Director of the IB. He replaced T. G. Sanjeevi Reddy in 1950. Mullik was also a close confidante of Nehru and was tasked with building cooperation with the CIA and its activities against China. He was asked to work with the CIA's ongoing support to the Tibetan resistance.[14] This cooperation also included the creation of the Special Frontier Force (SFF, also known as Establishment 22), staffed by Tibetans living in exile in India and with officers drawn from the Indian Army. This was in addition to the Tibetan resistance force that was raised and controlled by the CIA out of Mustang in Nepal. The CIA provided a clandestine air transport capability to the SFF.

> Eight C-46 aircraft and four smaller planes with their pilots were deployed to a secret Indian air base, code named Oak Tree, at Charbatia in Orissa (now Odisha), a state in the east of India. The secret air base worked with a special branch of the IB, the Aviation Research Centre.[15]

While Mullik as head of the IB wanted to use the SFF to take on the PLA in Tibet, he was also keen on short-term goals to secure India's borders. According to John Kenneth Knaus, the SFF was primarily used to carry out reconnaissance and also to place sensors in the Himalayas for detecting Chinese missile and nuclear tests.[16] The SFF received enthusiastic support from Nehru, who pushed through far more access to the Americans than ever before or after. "In 1964 the CIA was authorized $1,735,000 for the joint projects, a significant amount for covert programs. But except for the SFF patrols, the project had little success."[17]

However, the joint program did notch up a major success in predicting China's nuclear tests. Nehru agreed to give permission to the Americans to fly U-2 spying missions over China from the secret air base in Charbatia. The missions proved to be valuable to detect PLA deployments, while missions over Lop Nor in Xinjiang yielded valuable intelligence. Lop Nor was the nuclear test site for the Chinese; the U-2 missions, coupled with satellite imagery, helped the Americans to deduce that a nuclear test was imminent. According to American intelligence estimates produced on August 26, 1964 it was concluded that the Chinese were ready for a test within "two months."[18] "Clearly, the possibility of such a detonation cannot be ruled out – the test may occur during this period," it said.

As the U.S. focus moved from South Asia to Southeast Asia during President Lyndon B. Johnson's tenure, India suffered another major intelligence lapse in 1965. The "failure to predict" Pakistan's plans to infiltrate Jammu and Kashmir in 1965 by disguising their special operations troops as civilians to foment an insurgency is considered as a major intelligence lapse in India.[19] Once war was declared between India and Pakistan – the second between the two South Asian neighbors – Indian intelligence failed to gather key tactical intelligence. Indian military planners were completely clueless of the existence of an additional Pakistani armored division that could have turned the war to India's disadvantage.[20]

By this time U.S. foreign policy was also turning away from India, as President Richard Nixon's administration was coming in. As Nixon wrote in 1967, "taking the long view, we simply cannot afford to leave China forever outside the family of nations."[21] Declassified documents also show that the Nixon administration was depending heavily on Pakistan for a rapprochement with China.

Pakistan's military dictator General Yahya Khan discussed establishing "secret links" and communicating with the Chinese to establish a "form of communication."[22] The Nixon administration was already planning secret meetings with senior Chinese officials and chose Rawalpindi, the headquarters of the Pakistani Army, as one of the two options for such a possible meeting. This put the U.S. firmly on Pakistan's side and, in some ways, began to create a fairly hostile climate for India–U.S. relations.

By September 1968, India had hived off the IB's Foreign Intelligence Division to create a separate intelligence agency, the R&AW. The early officers picked to build the R&AW by its first chief, Kao, joined the organization at a time when the bilateral relationship was on a downward spiral. This would continue well into the 1980s as India's threat perception expanded to challenges posed by sub-nationalism and a rising armed insurgency in Punjab.

In many ways, B. Raman, one of the early Indian Police Service officers to be picked by Kao to join the R&AW, captures this suspicion of the U.S. within the Indian security establishment. Naturally, the intelligence community was equally vulnerable to this hostility, and, on occasion, it was also on the front lines of this conflict. India and the U.S. had moved quickly from the high of 1962–64 to a new low in a relationship dominated by suspicion and hostility.

"In 1971, one saw the beginning of joint covert action operation by the U.S. intelligence community and Pakistan's ISI [Inter-Services Intelligence] to create difficulties for India in Punjab. U.S. interest in this operation continued for little more than a decade and tapered off after the assassination of [Prime Minister] Indira Gandhi," Raman writes in his memoir. He points out that this suspicion and hostility would continue to play when Indira Gandhi returned to power in 1980. She had to dispatch Kao to the U.S. to

Natural alliance

seek assurances that the CIA would not side with separatists demanding a separate state for Sikhs, to be called Khalistan.[23]

Raman also records a meeting between Kao and the then Vice President of the U.S., George Bush, who had served as the Director of the CIA. Raman notes:

> Worried at the increasing fraternization of elements close to the Ronald Reagan administration with the Khalistani and other anti-Indian elements, Kao in his post-retirement capacity as an advisor to Indira Gandhi in the Cabinet Secretariat, visited Washington DC and met President [George H. W.] Bush ... who was the Vice President under Reagan. Kao knew Bush when the latter headed the CIA in the 1970s. He tried to remove misapprehensions about India's foreign policy in Afghanistan and expressed his concern to Bush about the "attention given to Khalistani elements" in Washington DC. This meeting led to an improvement in the atmosphere and the Khalistani elements found that they were no longer as welcome in Washington DC as they were before.[24]

The episode establishes that the relationship between the Indian and American intelligence community had broken down and they were now at odds with each other. But it also establishes that Kao did manage to forge personal relationships with American intelligence chiefs, which would lead to maintaining some contact at a bilateral level.

Raman also reveals that in 1968 Kao's first directions to his core officers were to develop their capabilities against Pakistan and China. As mentioned earlier in this section, this was a time when Pakistan was a valuable asset for the U.S. to send feelers to China for a possible rapprochement that would continue well into the 1970s. Clearly, Indian and American interests were diverging quickly.[25]

There is another incident that Raman mentions that throws light on the bilateral intelligence relationship. Raman records an episode just days before his retirement from service after twenty-seven years in the intelligence community that shows his particular animosity towards the U.S. He was asked to brief the then prime minister, Narasimha Rao, a few days before his retirement on a matter related to the Americans.

> But there is one American species, which I could never bring myself to like during the 27 years I spent in the intelligence – The officers of the U.S. State Department. My dislike for the U.S. State Department went up even further during my last days at R&AW.[26]

Raman states that he expressed his frustration after the U.S. sent a message through the Indian ambassador about the R&AW "meddling in the internal affairs of Pakistan and trying to destabilize it."

Raman's frustration was widely shared within the Indian intelligence community.[27] Raman refers to a "middle level state department official" who threatened the Indian ambassador with possible sanctions if India did not cease its "covert actions in Pakistan." This official told the Indian ambassador that the "U.S. might be constrained to act against Pakistan and India for indulging in acts of terrorism against each other."[28]

The fact that Raman was called for the briefing was also due to his position as the head of R&AW's "Special Operations"[29] desk that primarily worked on Pakistan-related work. This is a significant detail that establishes Raman's long-held suspicions of U.S. intentions in South Asia. However, Raman's frustration epitomizes the strained relationship between the Indian and American intelligence communities, both serving different political objectives. For the U.S., the war in Afghanistan had established a close and working relationship with Pakistan's ISI.[30]

The aftermath of the 1993 bomb attacks on Mumbai exacerbated these suspicions of U.S. intentions.[31] Indian investigators pieced together evidence to pin the blame on elements supported by Pakistan's ISI. Detonators recovered from blast sites indicated that some of the explosives used in the attacks had been procured by the Pakistan Army. However, when this was shared with the U.S., no action was taken and there were allegations that evidence had been "misplaced."[32]

The U.S.–India bilateral relationship also suffered from what the Indians perceived to be a forced "hyphenation" with traditional rival Pakistan. As scholars like Ashley J. Tellis have observed, the U.S. believed that its "regional policy in South Asia was defined primarily in terms of managing the security interdependence between India and Pakistan." This approach "frequently irked New Delhi even as they proved ineffective in assisting Islamabad to secure its desired political goals."[33]

Divergent priorities

The invasion of Afghanistan by the Soviet Union in December 1979 exacerbated tensions between India and the U.S. and increased the animosity between their intelligence agencies. In some ways, the U.S. intervention in Afghanistan would be a defining moment for the Indian intelligence community. The lack of trust, and hostility, between India and the U.S. that had grown under the Nixon administration would become sharper after the Soviet invasion of Afghanistan.

In many ways, the India–U.S. bilateral relationship has been held hostage by the "Pakistan factor." Despite its shared values of being a democracy, the lack of convergence on how to deal with Pakistan has been a major impediment. This prevented closer bilateral ties and building of cooperation in various sectors, including intelligence.

Indian intelligence officials feel that the cooperation between the U.S. and Pakistan and the lessons learned during the secret war in Afghanistan helped the ISI to finesse its tactics to foment an insurgency in Indian-administered Kashmir.[34] In fact, the section within the ISI known as the "Afghan Bureau" has been described as a precursor to the section that would eventually be tasked with supporting the armed insurgency in Indian-administered Kashmir. The two sections, also described as Section 21 (Afghanistan) and 24 (Kashmir) were part of the unit known as "Directorate S":[35] "Buried in this bureaucracy lay the units devoted to secret operations in support of the Taliban, Kashmiri guerrillas, and other violent radicals – Directorate S, as it was referred to by American intelligence officers and diplomats."[36]

However, part of this divergence in strategic interests is also due to the different focus areas for the two intelligence communities, as envisaged by their founders. The CIA and its predecessor, the Office of Strategic Services, were the products of a national effort to deal with and end the U.S.'s isolation and engage as World War II raged in Europe. William J. Donovan, an attorney and a World War I veteran who had toured through Europe and the Balkans in 1940–41, was convinced that the U.S. needed a "central intelligence encompassing a range of activities – collection, analysis, operations."[37]

In India, while the IB was a handover from a departing colonial British ruler, its dedicated external intelligence agency, R&AW, would emerge with a very narrow and sharp focus on two adversaries – Pakistan and China. Raman remembers that the initial briefings from Kao were sharply focused on gathering intelligence from China and the eastern and western wings of Pakistan. "In the first few months of its formation, he [Rameshwar Nath Kao] gave it two priority tasks – to strengthen its capability for the collection of intelligence about Pakistan and China and for covert action in East Pakistan."[38]

While India's foreign policy and strategic objectives have expanded beyond these two traditional adversaries, its intelligence community continues to primarily focus on South Asia[39] and engaging the big powers on matters related to its narrow strategic aims.[40] As a result, the immediate neighborhood remains its primary focus, as Indian intelligence plays a leading role in shaping and achieving foreign policy objectives in Nepal, Bangladesh and Sri Lanka. These are seen as important stations for R&AW and play, at times, a key and wide-ranging role in the neighborhood.[41]

But this narrow focus, partly driven by a lack of adequate resources and partly by what India considers its strategic "backyard,"[42] also leads to divergence in how the Indian intelligence community prioritizes information sharing with its American counterparts.

The spate of terror bombings in Sri Lanka in April 2019[43] offers a view of how India's narrow focus on its strategic backyard leads to a divergence in views on issues such as counterterrorism. India is credited with issuing an advance warning to Sri Lanka about the impending attacks.[44] The primary information came from Indian nationals from Kerala who had traveled to Afghanistan to join the Islamic State-Khorasan Province. The repatriation of several such nationals led to the discovery of nascent ISIS (Islamic State in Syria and Iraq) cells in India. The interrogation of one of these cells operating from the southern Indian state of Tamil Nadu led to early warnings about a Sri Lankan national who was also working with them. This national was later identified, suspected to be the lead bomber of Easter Sunday attacks.

However, despite a robust growth in cooperation on counterterrorism, Indian officials never shared it with their Western counterparts.[45] These seemingly insignificant differences in perception often lead to a divergence in views on intelligence assessments. While India has consistently argued that the ISI helped the ISIS-Khorasan Province and has also helped to build a relationship with Punjabi-dominated groups such as Lashkar-e-Taiba, the U.S. has seemed non-committal on these concerns.[46] However, ISIS-Khorasan Province's leaders have gone on record to claim its linkages to Pakistan's ISI on more than one occasion.[47]

In 2008, India was invited to join the global intelligence network known as "Fourteen Eyes," an extension of the Five Eyes program, which facilitates cooperation between the U.S., UK, Canada, Australia, and New Zealand.[48] However, this did not materialize, due to mutual suspicions.

The U.S. believed that any intelligence shared with India would be eventually leaked.[49] However, a series of attempts by U.S. intelligence to convert Indian intelligence officials into assets led to renewed suspicions between them. In 2004 the defection of Rabinder Singh – a joint secretary in the R&AW (a senior appointment) – with the help of the CIA proved to be a major setback to the growing relationship between the Indian and U.S. intelligence communities. Singh is believed to have been "turned" by the CIA to leak Indian intelligence secrets for several years before he was detected. As suspicion mounted within the Indian intelligence community, Singh escaped along with his family to the U.S.[50] Investigations by Indian intelligence revealed that the CIA station chief in Kathmandu, Nepal had purchased tickets for Singh and his family.[51]

The episode was reminiscent of the defection by Major R. S. Soni, a middle-level official in the R&AW, who "defected" to Canada in December 1974.[52] A few years after Rabinder Singh's defection a fresh scandal hit India's National Security Council Secretariat (NSCS). Rossane Minchew, an American diplomat serving in the U.S. Embassy in New Delhi, was accused of receiving classified information from two Indian officials. She was part of the Indo-U.S. Cybersecurity Forum, ironically set up to enhance bilateral cooperation.[53]

The Rabinder Singh and NSCS espionage episodes are attributed to the U.S. intelligence community's failure to detect India's nuclear tests in May 1998. The failure has often been cited, along with the CIA's inability to prevent 9/11, as one of the two key drivers of reforming U.S. intelligence.[54] George Tenet, the then Director of the CIA, set up a commission headed by Vice Admiral David E. Jeremiah to investigate its failure to detect India's nuclear tests.[55]

The fact that the U.S. recognized the failure to detect India's nuclear tests and took on a strategy to target Indian intelligence for possible recruits proved to be a major setback for a relationship on the mend. These cyclical episodes of cooperation and suspicion remain one of the biggest gaps in building a more robust relationship between India and the U.S. on intelligence sharing.

From 9/11 to 26/11

In September 2001, a day after commercial planes brought down the World Trade Centre, the U.S. Secret Service pulled out President George W. Bush from a meeting, citing an imminent threat to the White House by Pakistani or Pakistan-based terrorists. They attributed the warning to Indian intelligence. The threat was labeled as "credible and consistent with other intelligence that established an immediate danger. The Indian intelligence service was well wired into Pakistan."[56]

This was seen *within* the Indian intelligence community as an opportunity as well as a risk.[57] The help from India gave a fresh impetus to the bilateral relationship, still recovering from sanctions imposed by the U.S. after India's May 1998 nuclear tests. However, as many Indian analysts and diplomats have noted since, this also brought the U.S. back to Pakistan, as it launched operations against the Taliban and al-Qaida in Afghanistan.[58] The joint statement issued by then Prime Minister Atal Behari Vajpayee and President George W. Bush on November 10, 2001 emphasized the need for greater cooperation in intelligence. It described 9/11 as an event that "united as never before in the fight against terrorism."[59]

In 2002, the first major delegation of officials from the R&AW travelled to the U.S. to meet their counterparts at the CIA at Langley, as well as at the National Security Agency headquarters in Fort Meade.[60] The trip, according to members of the delegation, was the first such visit at a fairly high level to U.S. intelligence facilities. This would also pave the way for members of India's IB to interact with U.S. intelligence officials and build a mechanism to share information related to counterterrorism. While the overall relationship would be conducted by the R&AW, a mechanism was also set up for the IB to seek intelligence or surveillance material from the U.S. directly.[61] This mechanism continues to exist in 2020, and has done well since 2001.

The renewed cooperation between India and the U.S. on intelligence post-9/11 has also seen the emergence of the "China factor." There is greater synergy on sharing information on China, the PLA and the deployment of PLAN's submarines in the Indian Ocean.[62] However, the attack on Mumbai on November 26, 2008 by members of Lashkar-e-Taiba revealed the divergence in priorities between India and the U.S. on intelligence issues.

India received several intelligence inputs from August 7, 2006 indicating that Lashkar-e-Taiba was planning an attack in India by infiltrating from the western seaboard. On August 11 and November 19, 2006 two more intelligence inputs came in that not only indicated that an attack was coming but also managed to identify some of the targets that were eventually hit.[63] Both these inputs came from the U.S., but they could not be analyzed and verified in time to prevent the attack.[64]

There is considerable unhappiness within the Indian intelligence and diplomatic community[65] that the U.S. held back intelligence from India that could have prevented the attack. It is believed that a key source for much of the intelligence on 26/11 was David Coleman Headley, an American of Pakistani origin. Former Indian diplomats and intelligence officials who dealt with the case believe that the U.S. held back data as well as not sharing the fact that Headley was their "double agent." His detailed interrogation by India's National Investigation Agency in 2010 reveals the extent to which he was a part of the initial reconnaissance and planning that culminated in the final attack.[66]

The other key source of information about the 26/11 plot came from Zarrar Shah, who was a key plotter and the technology chief of Lashkar-e-Taiba. The British intelligence group, General Communication Headquarters (GCHQ), was monitoring Shah's online activities. According to documents leaked by the NSA contractor Edward Snowden, GCHQ was able to track down details of the impending attack, as well as Shah's efforts to set up VOIP (Voice over Internet Protocol) calls that would enable the Pakistani handlers to maintain communication with the attackers.[67] However, the initial official U.S. assessment of the attack did not find any official Pakistani links to them. When they did find links, Indian officials feel that the U.S. downplayed the linkages. General Michael Hayden, the then Director of the CIA, maintained that the attack could have been carried out by rogue elements in the Pakistani establishment.

Natural alliance 253

I began routinely harassing my counterpart in Pakistan, now Ahmed Shuja Pasha [the former Director General of Military Operations], on the phone, urging him to get to the bottom of the [26/11] attack [on Mumbai] and to discuss it frankly with us. We had no doubt that the attack was the work of the LeT [Lashkar-e-Taiba] and there was mounting evidence that preparation for and the direction of the attack took place from within Pakistan, where the LeT enjoyed the protection of the ISI. Pasha had come to the ISI only a few weeks earlier and had no previous intelligence experience. ISI was a heavily compartmentalized organization, so I wouldn't have been surprised if a lot of what he was now picking up was discovery learning on his part.[68]

The gains made by restarting the bilateral relationship after 9/11 had been frittered away to an extent by the lack of cooperation, perceived or otherwise.

Misaligned bureaucracies

The legacy of inheriting the intelligence apparatus of a departing colonial power has its share of challenges. While the IB adapted to the needs of a modern republic, it was unable to shed some of its colonial legacies. As a result, India's post-independence intelligence apparatus saw domination of the officers from the Indian Imperial Police, which would later evolve into the Indian Police Service (IPS). The recruiting of policemen into intelligence roles, especially at the higher echelons, led to a number of challenges for India's nascent intelligence community.

Most IPS officers would spend the early years of their careers managing large swathes of administrative units that involved a variety of law and order challenges. Intelligence would be the last priority on their minds. After a few years of service in the states, those who chose to take up intelligence as a career would apply for a deputation with the federal government either in the IB or in the R&AW after it was created in September 1968.

Both organizations also recruited directly to what would now be known as "cadre appointments." In the case of the IB, cadre officers would start at the bottom of the hierarchy and, if age permitted, retire at lower-level management positions. This ensured that IPS officers staffed and led the upper echelons from middle management onwards.

This created a problem where most of the collection of intelligence was left to the cadre recruits in the IB, while the IPS officers would dominate the analysis. When Kao was tasked with creating the R&AW, he hoped to change this and instead recruit from what he envisaged as "the open market." His vision led to the creation of the Research and Analysis Service, a dedicated intelligence cadre of officers who could be picked up outside the prescribed government rules of selection. Kao hoped that this would also give him the freedom to spot not only talent but also expertise in various disciplines that IPS officers might lack.

The result across the Indian intelligence community has not been encouraging. An assessment carried out by Kargil Review Committee (KRC) – set up to understand how the national security apparatus failed to detect Pakistani intrusions across the Line of Control, leading to the Kargil war in 1999 – provides key insights. The KRC's findings are still relevant and explain why it is difficult for these two vastly different bureaucracies in India and the U.S. to work together, let alone enhance cooperation.

"The political, bureaucratic, military and intelligence establishments appear to have developed a vested interest in the status quo. National security management recedes into the background at the time of peace and is considered too delicate to be tampered with at the time of war and proxy war," the KRC noted in one of the few comprehensive assessments of India's national security apparatus.[69]

Caught between the IPS, officers on deputation and cadre officers, India's intelligence community has never managed to evolve, unlike in the U.S. or UK, the two countries that provided templates for Indian policymakers, and has now produced systems that are inward looking and not amenable to cooperation. It struggles to build relationships with organizations like the CIA and the UK Secret Intelligence Service (MI6) that are staffed by career intelligence professionals who not only give permanence but also build a professional "intelligence culture." The KRC also noted that the process of intelligence collection, analysis and dissemination was fundamentally broken.

> There is no institutionalized mechanism for coordination or objective-oriented interaction between agencies and consumers at different levels. Similarly, there is no mechanism for tasking the agencies, monitoring their performance and reviewing their records to evaluate their quality. Nor is there any oversight of the overall functioning of the agencies.[70]

The committee also noted that, unlike the U.S., which reformed its intelligence structures after 9/11, in India, the process of intelligence dissemination and evaluation at the highest levels is broken. India transitioned from the Joint Intelligence Committee, a British legacy, to the National Security Council, borrowed from the U.S., which has not produced the desired results. The KRC recorded in its findings:

> The Committee has drawn attention to deficiencies in the present system of collection, reporting, collation and assessment of intelligence. There is no institutionalised mechanism for coordination or objective-oriented interaction between agencies and consumers at different levels. Similarly, there is

no mechanism for tasking the agencies, monitoring their performance and reviewing their records to evaluate their quality ... All major countries have a mechanism at the national and often at the lower levels to assess the intelligence inputs received from different agencies and sources.[71]

In sharp contrast, the 500-day plan for "integration and collaboration" within the various branches of the civilian and military segments of the U.S. intelligence community prepared by the office of the Director of National Intelligence throws light on the kind of measures that were taken to address the intelligence failure of 9/11. The plan focused on six areas.

1. Create a culture of collaboration.
2. Accelerate information sharing.
3. Foster collection and analytic transformation.
4. Build acquisition excellence and technology leadership.
5. Modernize business practices.
6. Clarify and align DNIs (directives from Director of National Intelligence).

Naturally, the difference in the intelligence bureaucracies, systems, tasks, resources and levels of efficacy in India and the U.S. create issues of capacity, growth and evolution that are a major impediment to enhancing bilateral cooperation.

While the primary task of liaison is left to the R&AW through a joint secretary-level officer who deals with the local "station chief" posted in New Delhi, there are periodic but carefully curated meetings between the R&AW and their U.S. counterparts. Post 9/11 the IB holds structured meetings on pre-decided agendas where information is exchanged on issues related to counterterrorism.[72]

The impact of technology has also created major gaps in India's ability to gather intelligence. The use of internet-based technologies has revolutionized how people communicate. The speed and the security that many such platforms offer for free outstripped India's ability to carry out surveillance. In 1999, the KRC had pointed out this gap.

> The U.S. has grouped all its communication and electronic intelligence efforts within a single organization, the National Security Agency (NSA). The desirability of setting up a similar organization in India with adequate resources for this extremely important and non-intrusive method of gathering technological intelligence calls for examination.[73]

Twenty years later, India has still to move the needle on acquiring technology that can keep pace with its intelligence requirements. As the gap grows and India becomes dependent on other countries for intelligence, it will not be able to establish a partnership that can grow.

The future of cooperation

The future of furthering cooperation on intelligence will rest on four key postulates.

First, the "Pakistan factor" will continue to dominate the bilateral intelligence relationship. The divergence in U.S. and Indian views on how to deal with Pakistan, though much less as compared to the years before 9/11, remains the single biggest impediment in achieving closer cooperation on intelligence. India views Pakistan as the problem, while the U.S. views Pakistan as part of any solution, peace and stability in South Asia and Afghanistan in particular. Intelligence cooperation will also be largely dominated by the political aims and objectives set by the respective governments. If there is a divergence in these objectives, then the relationship is unlikely to grow. India's focus will continue to be dominated by its two traditional adversaries, Pakistan and China. If India and the U.S. develop some common frameworks to tackle both in a de-hyphenated manner, then it will create space for the intelligence relationship to deepen. Mechanisms like the Quad will therefore see a higher degree of cooperation on China, but will remain compartmentalized from India's concerns about Pakistan.

Second, if the overall objectives align, then New Delhi and Washington will have to develop a new framework for engagement. This has to be dependent on mutual recognition and valuing of stated objectives. Recognition of the Indo-Pacific as a significant area of strategic concern can help India and the U.S. to find fresh new ground to build common strategic goals.[74] This will also enable both countries to step beyond the standard hyphenation with Pakistan that has served as a major impediment to building a deeper intelligence cooperation framework.

So far, counterterrorism has provided a better framework for intelligence cooperation than regional or global concerns in other areas. This will have to be broadened to other sectors/areas of mutual interest, while building a degree of interoperability. This could be done by creating intelligence-sharing mechanisms that are mutually beneficial. It could also be facilitated by jointly building threat assessment models for intelligence assessments and analysis. Integrating India into the Fourteen Eyes network can be a possible first step in enhancing intelligence cooperation.

Third, provided that there is an alignment on political objectives, a new framework and the areas of cooperation are broadened, India will need capacity building for new technologies and methods of intelligence collection, analysis and dissemination. There are significant gaps in India's ability to collect intelligence and these will continue to be a major hindrance in deepening intelligence cooperation. The impact of technology, and specifically the internet, has helped to improve methods to evade traditional methods of surveillance or wiretaps. Capacity building and training can form the bedrock of major intelligence cooperation between the two democracies.

Fourth, India will have to move away from its traditional recruitment and bureaucratic hierarchy and create a dedicated intelligence cadre. Not only will it create intelligence professionals who can operate in modern-day environments, but it will also give rise to centers of excellence that can serve as the training ground for future intelligence professionals who can not only deal with massive amounts of big data but also build expertise in areas beyond traditional security challenges. India and the U.S. can use capacity building in intelligence capabilities as a framework to bring about interoperability as well to enhance cooperation in intelligence.

Notes

1 Brief on India–U.S. Relations, Ministry of External Affairs, India, https://mea.gov.in/Portal/ForeignRelation/India_U.S._brief.pdf.
2 Ibid.
3 See Rajesh Roy and Nancy A. Youssef, 'U.S., India Sign Military-Intelligence Sharing Agreement,' *Wall Street Journal*, September 6, 2018 www.wsj.com/articles/u-s-india-sign-military-intelligence-sharing-agreement-1536232640.
4 See Steve Harman, 'India, U.S. to Intensify Intelligence Sharing on Terrorism,' VOA, August 30, 2016 www.voanews.com/east-asia-pacific/india-us-intensify-intelligence-sharing-terrorism.
5 See Chapter 11 in this volume.
6 See Saikat Datta, 'Created by a Telegram, IB Finds Itself Standing on Thin Legal Ground,' *Hindustan Times*, November 14, 2013, www.hindustantimes.com/india/created-by-telegram-ib-finds-itself-standing-on-thin-legal-ground/story-UFrue3ywW4P96DhvQFtadM.html.
7 Bashyam Kasturi, *Intelligence Services: Analysis, Organisation and Function* (Lancer Publishers and Distributors, 1995), pp. 28–9.
8 Ibid.
9 Ibid.
10 Richard A. Best, 'U.S. Intelligence and India's Nuclear Tests: Lessons Learned,' Congressional Research Service (August 11, 1998), pp. 3–4, www.everycrsreport.com/*files*/19980811_98–672_fab899e7514f8c944024bf5f0ff791a484f4f5b9.pdf.
11 Mark M. Lowenthal, *U.S. Intelligence: Evolution and Anatomy* (Praeger Publishers, 1984), p. 7.
12 For more on the two letters written by Nehru to Kennedy see Bruce Riedel, *JFK's Forgotten Crisis: Tibet, The CIA and the Sino Indian War* (Harper Collins, 2016).
13 *Ibid.*, p. 150.

14 *Ibid.*, p. 158.
15 *Ibid.*, p. 158.
16 Kenneth Conboy and James Morrison, *The CIA's Secret War in Tibet* (University Press of Kansas, 2002)p. 187–192.
17 Bruce Riedel, *JFK's Forgotten Crisis: Tibet, The CIA and the Sino Indian War* (Harper Collins, 2016), p. 159.
18 Special National Intelligence Estimate (August 26, 1964), https://nsarchive2.gwu.edu/nukevault/ebb488/docs/doc%2017%208-26-64%20snie.pdf.
19 Rana Banerji et al., 'A Case for Intelligence Reforms in India – IDSA Task Force Report p. 16, para. 3.
20 *Ibid.*, p. 16, para. 4.
21 See Richard Nixon, 'Asia After Viet Nam,' *Foreign Affairs*, October 1967. www.foreignaffairs.com/articles/asia/1967-10-01/asia-after-viet-nam.
22 Declassified Memorandum of Conversation (October 25, 1970), pp. 2–3, https://nsarchive2.gwu.edu/NSAEBB/NSAEBB66/ch-03.pdf.
23 B. Raman, *The Kaoboys of R&AW: Down Memory Lane* (Lancer Publications, 2007), p. 13.
24 *Ibid.*, p. 41.
25 *Ibid.*, p. 9.
26 *Ibid.*, p. 2.
27 Interview with a former senior R&AW official who worked with Raman.
28 Raman, *The Kaoboys of R&AW*, pp. 2–3.
29 Discussions of the author with B. Raman in December 2007.
30 For further reading on the U.S.–Pakistan's secret war in Afghanistan see Mohammed Yousaf and Mark Adkin, *The Bear Trap: The Defeat of a Superpower* (Casemate Publishers, 2001) and Steve Coll, *Directorate S: The C.I.A. and America's Secret Wars in Afghanistan and Pakistan, 2001–2016* (Penguin, 2018).
31 Interview with a former Intelligence Bureau official.
32 *Ibid.*
33 Ashley J. Tellis, 'The Merits of Dehyphenation: Explaining U.S. Success in Engaging India and Pakistan,' *The Washington Quarterly*, Autumn 2008, pp. 28–9.
34 Interview with a former senior R&AW official who served on the Pakistan desk.
35 Coll, *Directorate S*, p. 47.
36 *Ibid.*
37 Mark M. Lowenthal, *U.S. Intelligence: Evolution and Anatomy* (Praeger, 1984), p. 7.
38 Raman, *The Kaoboys of R&AW*, p. 9.
39 See Rana Banerji, 'South Asia Allies Essential for Indian Intelligence,' *Asia Times* (October 11, 2019), www.asiatimes.com/2018/10/article/for-indian-intelligence-south-asian-allies-have-been-essential/.
40 Interview with two former chiefs of R&AW in October and November 2019.
41 See John Chalmers and Sanjeev Miglani, 'Indian Spy's Role Alleged in Sri Lankan President's Election,' Reuters (January 18, 2015), www.reuters.com/

article/us-sri-lanka-election-india-insight/indian-spys-role-alleged-in-sri-lankan-presidents-election-defeat-idU.S.KBN0KR03020150118.
42 See: https://warontherocks.com/2018/04/when-indias-strategic-backyard-meets-chinas-strategic-periphery-the-view-from-beijing/, www.orfonline.org/research/india-marginalised-in-backyard/ and www.southasiaathudson.org/blog/2018/11/5/is-china-eroding-indias-influence-in-nepal as examples of what is considered India's "strategic backyard."
43 See www.asiatimes.com/2019/04/article/sri-lankan-pm-not-told-of-attacks-warning/?_=697714.
44 See Saikat Datta, 'Sri Lanka Failed to Heed Intel Warnings,' *Asia Times* (April 29, 2019), www.asiatimes.com/2019/04/article/sri-lanka-failed-to-heed-intel-warnings/.
45 Interview with a senior Indian intelligence official.
46 Interview with a senior Indian intelligence official.
47 See 'LeT, Afghan Taliban Follow ISI's Dictates: Militant Commander, *The Economic Times* (July 13, 2018), https://economictimes.indiatimes.com/news/defence/let-afghan-taliban-follow-isis-dictates-militant-commander/articleshow/50667466.cms. See also Saurav Sarkar, 'Afghanistan's Terror Threat Is Much Bigger Than the Taliban,' *The Diplomat* (August 22, 2019), https://thediplomat.com/2019/08/afghanistans-terror-threat-is-much-bigger-than-the-taliban/.
48 See Rana Banerji, 'India's Mixed Success with Foreign Intelligence,' *Asia Times* (October 10, 2019), www.asiatimes.com/2018/10/article/indias-mixed-success-with-foreign-intelligence-agencies/.
49 Interview with a senior Indian intelligence official.
50 See Yatish Yadav, 'Rabinder Singh, spy who defected to U.S., is no more Firstpost www.firstpost.com/india/rabinder-singh-spy-who-defected-to-us-is-no-more-double-agent-lived-his-last-years-as-a-remorseful-recluse-4688341.html. See also Rahul Tripathi, 'Rabinder in U.S., We Want Him Back: RAW in Court,' *The Indian Express* (November 2, 2006), https://web.archive.org/web/20080307091854/www.indianexpress.com/story/15865.html.
51 Yatish Yadav, 'Former Spy Reveals Secrets of Research and Analysis Wing,' *New Indian Express* (April 6, 2014), www.newindianexpress.com/nation/2014/apr/06/Former-Spy-Reveals-Secrets-of-Research-and-Analysis-Wing-594925.html.
52 See Ranjit Bhushan, 'The Vanished Spies,' *Outlook* magazine (August 2, 2004), www.outlookindia.com/magazine/story/the-vanished-spies/224695.
53 See 'Espionage Case: U.S. Diplomat Leaves India,' Rediff.com, www.rediff.com/news/2006/jul/04spy.htm. See also: www.wired.com/2006/12/spies_envy_geek_1/.
54 See Tim Weiner, 'Nuclear Anxiety: The Blunders; U.S. Blundered On Intelligence, Officials Admit,' *New York Times* (May 13, 1998), www.nytimes.com/1998/05/13/world/nuclear-anxiety-the-blunders-us-blundered-on-intelligence-officials-admit.html.
55 See 'Jeremiah News Conference,' www.cia.gov/news-information/press-releases-statements/press-release-archive-1998/jeremiah.html.

56 Bob Woodward, *Bush At War* (Pocket Books, 2003), pp. 55–6.
57 Separate interviews with two former Indian ambassadors to the U.S.
58 Interview with a former Indian ambassador to the U.S.
59 'India–U.S. Joint Statement on the Occasion of the Official Working Visit of Prime Minister to Washington DC,' (November 10, 2001), https://archivepmo.nic.in/abv/speech-details.php?nodeid=9148.
60 Interview with two former officials who were on the trip.
61 Interview with a senior Indian security official.
62 Interview with Indian security official.
63 See the report of the High Level Enquiry Committee set up by the state government of Maharashtra to investigate the 26 November 2007 attack on Mumbai by Lashkar-e-Taiba: 'Report of the High Level Enquiry Committee on 26/11,' para. 10.
64 Interview with a senior Indian intelligence official who dealt with the 26/11 post-attack analysis. See also Saikat Datta, 'Creating a Successful Intelligence and Counter Terrorism Matrix: Lessons from 26/11,' *Centre for Land Warfare Studies Journal* (Summer 2011), https://archive.claws.in/images/journals_doc/1395650530Saikat%20Datta%20%20CJ%20Summer%202011.pdf.
65 Interviews with two former R&AW officials and two former Indian ambassadors to the U.S.
66 See Saikat Datta, 'The Union Republic of Terror,' *Outlook* magazine (October 11, 2010), www.outlookindia.com/magazine/story/the-union-republic-of-terror/267300.
67 See Sebastian Rotella, 'The Hidden Intelligence Behind the Mumbai Attacks,' Propublica (April 21, 2015), www.propublica.org/article/the-hidden-intelligence-breakdowns-behind-the-mumbai-attacks.
68 Michael V. Hayden, *Playing to the Edge* (Penguin, 2016), p. 352.
69 Kargil Review Committee, *From Surprise to Reckoning: The Kargil Review Committee Report* (Sage Publications, 1999), p. 252, para. 614.1.
70 *Ibid.*, p. 255, para. 14.10.
71 *Ibid.*, p. 109, para. 6.6.
72 Interview with a senior IB official.
73 Kargil Review Committee, *From Surprise to Reckoning*, p. 252, para. 14.8.
74 See Chapter 10 in this volume.

Part VII

Defense technology cooperation

13

U.S.–India defense technology sharing and manufacturing: legacies of defense organizational processes

Frank O'Donnell

U.S.–India bilateral defense technology trade and cooperation has been a key indicator of the warming strategic partnership.[1] India has purchased an estimated $18bn of U.S. defense platforms since 2001, with at least an estimated $5.4bn of acquisitions under negotiation as of 2019.[2] Major U.S. defense firms are identifying Indian companies to partner with for co-production and transfer of leading U.S. technologies. Underlining these markers of progress is the fact that the U.S. has risen to become second only to Russia in the total volume of defense trade conducted by India.[3] This is all the more impressive, given that the U.S. had very little trade with India in the year 2000, and that the Russia–India defense partnership reaches back to the 1960s.[4]

Any indicator, however, obtains most analytic value when evaluated against an ultimate goal for the U.S.–India strategic partnership. A common theme of the chapters in this volume is that India and the U.S. harbor different visions of the ideal end-state for their strategic partnership. Detailing statistics of defense technology transfer and manufacturing agreements form useful data points, but will have limited impact if New Delhi and Washington cannot agree upon the overarching purpose of such endeavors. Indeed, a related risk is that these initiatives will themselves form a substitute for such a common vision. To this end, Tarapore has characterized the U.S.–India Defense Technology and Trade Initiative (DTTI) as being "designed to optimize the bureaucratic processes of defense relations rather than their effects."[5]

This chapter finds that the U.S. and India have indeed made impressive strides in the quantum and quality of their defense technology sharing and manufacturing cooperation. The U.S. has progressively eased its export control licensing requirements for defense trade with India, as well as launching focused initiatives such as the DTTI. Among other acquisitions, India is filling capability gaps in maritime surveillance with U.S. Poseidon P-8 maritime aircraft, seaborne power projection with Mk-45 naval guns, airborne assault abilities with Apache helicopters, artillery with M777 howitzers, and heavy airlift with C-130 and C-117 planes.[6] Moreover, New Delhi is presently considering an offer of upgraded F-16s from Lockheed Martin, with the package including partnering with the Indian firm Tata Global Systems to share defense technology, and even relocating Lockheed's global F-16 manufacturing hub to India.[7]

Furthermore, the relationship does not merely encompass such major platforms, but creates opportunities for India to improve its ground-level tactical effectiveness. An example of this is the 2019 agreement by New Delhi to purchase nearly 72,400 of the leading SIG716 assault rifles from the American arms manufacturer Sig Sauer, which will improve the individual lethality of its troops.[8]

However, the nature of this relationship is approaching a point where the absence of higher-level political agreement on the end-goals of such cooperation means that the regular interbureaucratic processes of defense technology and manufacturing cooperation are coming to play a larger role in defining the trajectory of the strategic relationship. Put differently, the high level of activity in this domain compensates for a relative paucity of political interactions.[9] In its section on India, the U.S. State Department's first public review of its Free and Open Indo-Pacific Strategy leant heavily on defense technology sales and cooperation as evidence of forward progress in the overall relationship.[10]

To obtain a deeper understanding of the nature of this relationship, academic models of bureaucratic effects on defense policy offer the greatest promise. Indeed, the routinization of many U.S. defense decisions means that bilateral logistics agreements such as the Logistics Exchange Memorandum of Agreement tend to be decided by a one-star military officer: the permanent bureaucracy, as opposed to political appointees.[11] As we will see, many of the frictions and tensions within the strategic partnership are the result of conflicting incentives written into the foundational objectives and designs of the respective U.S. and Indian defense bureaucracies.

This is to the extent that the two bureaucracies harbor different teleological expectations as to their views of an optimal end-state and progress toward this goal. The U.S. defense technology transfer system is designed to ensure that partners and allies are able to access competitive American defense technologies, with the qualifiers that they do not threaten the U.S. qualitative defense technological edge, nor lead to significant offshoring of American defense manufacturing and expertise. The idealized end-state is convergence of the partner state with U.S. foreign and defensive policy perspectives, as the growing volume of defense trade broadens the scope of diplomatic and military actions between the two states. This includes greater technical and political potential for combat interoperability.[12]

Technology sharing and manufacturing

India's bureaucratic views of the purpose of defense technology transfer are significantly different. This not only reflects the comparative contractual negotiating positions of India and the U.S., in which the former is traditionally a recipient state and the latter a provider; but also distinctive Indian concepts of the benefits and risks of defense technology transfer. A former senior Indian Ministry of Defence official has emphasized "the impact of philosophical moorings of the Indian strategic culture on defense procurement, the existing procurement system and procedures," starting his analysis with an examination of the defense procurement attitudes of Nehru.[13] Such a deep historical starting point is not controversial; as West has highlighted, "Those who make and influence policy cannot anticipate the specific issues that will arise in the administrative process, nor can they accurately predict the preferences of bureaucrats or (relatedly) the changing fortunes of different groups that might seek to shape program implementation. In response to this dilemma, *political actors choose administrative institutions that will perpetuate their interests in the future*" (emphasis added).[14] Similar imperatives account for the longevity of U.S. security cooperation structures as effective measures in support of the dual objectives of gradually incentivizing the foreign and defense policy actions of the recipient state with those of Washington, and generally ensuring greater ally/partner military cohesion through utilization of shared technology.

Nehru, in line with his foreign policy approach of nonalignment and avoiding neocolonial penetration by global powers, sought to promote indigenous Indian defense manufacturing as opposed to external military purchases.[15] Once the failures of these efforts became increasingly apparent, the approach was adjusted slightly, to permit more military technology acquisitions from abroad. However, the core conditions of avoiding neocolonial dependence on any one technology supplier remained, as did ensuring Indian licensing and domestic manufacturing of at least some of the units to be acquired. This latter condition sustained the indigenization imperative.

The incentive structure for Indian defense negotiators, acting within these bureaucratic logics, was thus to acquire the most globally advanced military technology, and to include commitments from the provider state and/or company to assist Indian indigenization by sharing defense manufacturing expertise and other assistance toward building the units in India. For India as a developing country, the negotiators were also expected to achieve this at the lowest possible price.[16] These incentive structures have not changed since then.

This chapter will firstly detail the organizational behavior model of bureaucratic effects on defense policy, and why the nature of contemporary U.S.–India defense technology sharing and manufacturing cooperation is best understood through this model. It will then explore the current status and projected trajectories of these two separate strands of the broader U.S.–India strategic partnership. The chapter argues that the "organizational essence" – the core understanding of bureaucrats of their agency's mission and image of success – is too ingrained to expect substantively more in this realm of bilateral cooperation than what is already being conducted.[17] Indeed, this organizational essence is written into the domestic law and protocols dictating the terms of U.S. security cooperation.[18] In India, it forms the only way that its defense bureaucracy has approached external technology transfer and domestic manufacturing support for decades.

Reforming such systems requires a level of political intervention on both sides that neither administration appears willing to make. In such a strategic partnership, where bureaucratic interactions play a prominent role in defining its evolution and these interactions take the form of conflictual organizational essences, the optimal approach for both capitals is to adopt a gradualist approach in developing their partnership. As such, they should seek consensus where they can, and attempt to downplay or, ideally, abandon the contrasting teleological expectations that currently bedevil the relationship.

Organizational processes and defense policy

Allison's theory of bureaucratic politics developed three models for how state bureaucratic actors could influence the foreign and defense policymaking process.[19] Model I was the rational-actor model, latterly favored by structural realists, in which the state political leadership and permanent bureaucracy act as one monolithic entity.

Model II was defined as organizational process.[20] The school recognizes the reality that political leaders can devote their directive attention and energy to only a handful of policy issues at any one time, and that the delegation of much decisionmaking responsibility to bureaucratic agencies means that the agencies themselves wield significant influence in shaping or even dictating policy outcomes.[21] Against this background, a close examination of the standard operating procedures, cultures, internal understandings of bureaucratic mission, and related vision of bureaucratic success is necessary to obtain a deeper understanding of the policy process. These collectively form its organizational *essence*.[22] More directly, it can help to explain why specific policy outcomes can often be the result of routinized outputs that are so standardized inside the agency – and linked to its own set of incentive structures regarding the agency's mission and mission success – that their broader potential policy effects might not be fully considered.[23]

A Model II organizational process example is the U.S. Air Force prescheduled intercontinental ballistic missile (ICBM) test launch from Vandenberg Air Base during the Cuban missile crisis. The routinized, scheduled launch met Air Force and Strategic Air Command objectives of ensuring the technical integrity of the force through tests. However, it took place amid other ICBMs at the base being mated with nuclear warheads in accordance with the presidential DEFCON 3 alert order. As such, it could have been interpreted by Moscow as the first salvo of a U.S. nuclear attack.[24]

This model, however, has nevertheless been theoretically underdeveloped and underutilized. It presents difficulties for scholars – already attempting to peer into the black box of policymaking – to isolate organizational essence(s) as causal or even part of a multicausal explanation for policies.[25] The model's emphasis on individual bureaucratic agency "standard operating procedures (SOPs)" as a source of policy influence creates analytic challenges, as "organizational complexity … makes it difficult to predict which SOPs will be applied in any particular instance, or what the result of multiple interacting SOPs will be … Similarly, it can be difficult to predict when policymaking will be routine and when it will be not."[26]

Model III – deemed by subsequent generations of scholars to be both the most developed and utilizable for understanding how individual state agencies can affect policy outcomes – was the "bureaucratic politics" model. This theorized that policy development was often subject to the competing interests of relevant bureaucratic stakeholders. With adequate scholarly distillation of their bureaucratic corporate interests, academics could investigate how policy decisions could be the result of internal lobbying victories for an agency or constellation of agencies; corollary defeats for those institutions with corporate interests that would be negatively affected by the policy selected; or compromises, in which the policy outcome attempted to form a minimum acceptable decision for most or all of the competing stakeholders.

The competitive expectation at the heart of this model permits scholars with an easier distillation of individual bureaucratic interests, as these are placed into relief through the policy positions they take. A recent application of a Model III approach focused upon the Indian bureaucratic competition to shape its strategic missile program during the United Progressive Alliance-II government (2009–14). It concluded that a lobbying axis of the Defence Research Development Organisation and Department of Atomic Energy formed the most influential actors in the system, against competing institutions of the Prime Minister's Office and the military.[27]

This chapter selects the Model II – organizational process – approach for its analysis of the contemporary U.S.-India defense technology sharing and manufacturing cooperation relationship. Many of these activities are conducted by the permanent defense bureaucracy of both states, which could privilege a bureaucratic politics approach. However, the nature of both its successes and dysfunctions primarily stems from the conflictual organizational essences of these two bureaucracies as they relate to each other, as opposed to domestic interbureaucratic competition in both capitals.[28] By abstracting the model from its traditional application to intragovernmental processes and applying it to intergovernmental relations, this chapter averts many of the above issues that have hitherto limited its utility in scholarship.[29] As such, it further develops the model in illuminating how it can have analytic relevance in contexts where state bureaucratic interests have an especially significant role in interstate interactions.

This chapter will now examine the state of contemporary bilateral defense technology sharing through the lens of this Model II organizational process approach, before moving to similarly consider U.S. assistance to Indian domestic defense manufacturing.

Defense technology sales

The fact that the U.S. went from being involved in virtually no defense trade and technology sharing with India in 2000 to becoming its second-largest as of 2018 is remarkable. Indeed, it suggests that the U.S. and Indian organizations responsible for negotiating and conducting such defense agreements are either more internally flexible than the "organizational essence" model might imply, or more malleable to political reform. However, this trajectory has been possible only due to the high levels of political capital invested by U.S. and Indian political leaders during the tenure of the George W. Bush administration to ensure their legislatures approved these initiatives. The Indian United Progressive Alliance-I (2004–9) government treated the legislation as a vote of confidence, and nearly fell, winning by only nineteen votes in a national legislature of 545 members.[30]

Once the key legislation was passed, however, building out the strategic partnership fell from being a regular high-priority item on the agenda of U.S. and Indian political leaders, and was instead delegated more to their foreign policy and defense bureaucracies. This is where the organizational process model becomes the most appropriate lens for understanding the nature of bilateral defense technology sharing.

The U.S. Department of Defense (DoD) and Indian Ministry of Defence (MoD) have been able to conclude Indian purchases of several U.S. platforms that represent the area of their overlapping organizational interests. These include U.S. C-130 and C-117 airlift planes, Apache combat and Chinook transport helicopters, Poseidon P-8 maritime surveillance aircraft, and M777 howitzers.³¹ In line with the MoD's organizational interests, these technologies augment India's power projection capabilities, and fill important capability gaps for which its domestic defense manufacturing base has been unable to provide. Moreover, official interactions do not explicitly or implicitly suggest that such technology transfers will be reciprocated by Indian shifts toward greater alignment of New Delhi with Washington's relevant regional and global policy priorities. Indeed, the difference with the extensive political conditions placed on U.S. military technology transfers to Pakistan is instructive.³² From the Indian perspective, the only area in which these deals could be improved is if licensing and domestic manufacturing approval was secured from Washington. However, the fact that these are the best available technologies on offer to India outweighs this consideration.

These transactions also meet several core interests of DoD organizational processes. U.S. arms sales to India create a shared military technological base that, over time, can be broadened. As it broadens, and related interbureaucratic and military-to-military interactions similarly grow in frequency and depth, New Delhi's military thinking can be expected within the DoD to gradually demonstrate closer alignment with that of Washington. The platforms on offer may be the best available to India, but still do not threaten the U.S. global qualitative military edge if proliferated. The avoidance of Indian licensing and domestic manufacturing of these technologies sustains U.S. defense manufacturing jobs and expertise, rather than offshoring it and ultimately reducing the size of the U.S. defense industrial base.

These interests also characterize major potential forthcoming U.S. arms sales to India. Deals that have been negotiated by the DoD and MoD in 2019, but which await U.S. Congressional approval, include packages of twenty-four MH-60R multi-mission helicopters, costed at $2.6bn; two 777 Large Aircraft Infrared Countermeasures Self-Protection Suites (for protection of Head-of-State aircraft), costed at $190m; and arranging C-17 ongoing technical support, costed at $670m.³³ For each proposed agreement, the DoD has certified that "there will be no adverse impact on U.S. defense readiness as a result of this proposed sale," meaning that it will not threaten the U.S. global qualitative military edge. This certification, and the technology transfer restrictions inherent in it, is written into U.S. law.³⁴ The Indian MoD obtains technologies of a sophistication not on offer from rival global defense suppliers, while averting political conditions being attached to their sale.

Moreover, each of these current proposals includes language of probable "offsets" to India as a component of the deal. As will be discussed in more detail in the following section, this represents a commitment by the U.S. defense contractor, as authorized by the DoD, to commit to either partial manufacturing of that specific technology in India, or alternative compensatory investment in the Indian defense manufacturing base. As this directly conflicts with the DoD interest of sustaining, rather than offshoring, U.S. defense manufacturing jobs and expertise, this represents one of the most difficult areas of bilateral negotiation and implementation.

There is still substantial room for technology transfer within the overlapping areas of organizational interests of both defense bureaucracies. A senior Indian Navy (IN) official has identified unmanned platforms and conventional submarines as capabilities that the service is seeking to acquire from the U.S., along with upgrades to existing IN electronic chart display and integrated bridge system technologies. Other identified capability shortfalls, such as multi-role attack helicopters, anti-submarine warfare helicopters, and maritime surveillance aircraft are being met by the proposed MH-60R contract and existing Poseidon P-8 contract.[35]

A recent U.S. official forecast, written for the purpose of promoting U.S. commercial defense exports, forecasts Indian military modernization demands for a new infantry fighting vehicle platform, "field artillery modernization (self-propelled howitzers and fire control systems), small arms and crew-served weapons, and precision guided munitions". It added "fast patrol craft" to the naval technologies specified by the IN official, and general upgrades in defense electronic systems across the Indian military. The study also highlighted "air defense systems and close-in weapon systems to provide point defense against ballistic projectiles, missiles, and other air threats" as a particular Indian need.[36]

Many of the above Indian requirements could be met by U.S. technology transfer while still retaining the U.S. qualitative military edge, and protecting and even growing the U.S. defense industrial base. However, the latter identified need – air defense and ballistic missile systems – has proved especially thorny as a proposed U.S.–India technology transfer. The reason for this is the MoD organizational process incentive of seeking the best available technology. The U.S. air and ballistic missile platform on offer serves the MoD as an example of "concerns in India that the U.S. has been offering lower-grade technologies."[37]

Missile defense technology transfer was identified as one of the first pillars of the new Bush administration approach to India, which in turn laid the foundation for the civil nuclear agreement and subsequent progressive expansion of defense trade.[38] As part of this initial outreach, U.S. officials arranged a presentation of Patriot-II (PAC-II) air and ballistic missile defense system capabilities to their Indian counterparts in 2005, in response to an original Indian expression of interest in 2002. While the more advanced Patriot-III (PAC-III) system had been developed by 2005, U.S. officials discussed only the PAC-II as a prospective technology sale to

India.[39] Indian officials, fully aware that more sophisticated technologies were available not only from the U.S. but other global suppliers, demurred from the PAC-II offer. The MoD continued work on its indigenous ballistic missile defense program, while reaching out to other potential international suppliers that would offer more modern systems.

This Indian initiative eventuated in 2015 in an agreement to instead purchase five Russian S-400 air and ballistic missile defense systems.[40] As an analyst has observed, the S-400 is a more advanced system than its nearest U.S. technological competitors:

> The S-400 surface-to-air missile defense system is a formidable capability that can strike aerial targets at ranges up to 400 km and ballistic missiles at ranges of up to 15 km. The available alternatives – PAC-3 and THAAD – do not compare in terms of capabilities. Unlike the S-400's 40N6 (400 km) interceptors, PAC-3 can only intercept aerial targets at a range of 180 km and ballistic missiles at a range of 100 km. THAAD, on the other hand, is strictly an anti-missile weapon system and cannot intercept aircraft. It would be a hard sell for the U.S. to convince India to scrap the S-400 deal or choose U.S.-supplied alternatives, which do not fit into Indian defense requirements because of their limited range (PAC-3) and inability to strike aerial targets (THAAD).[41]

Simply put, the MoD followed its organizational process imperative of seeking the best technology available. The U.S. response to this proposed Indian transaction – in which it attempts to compensate for its own organizational process imperative of maintaining its qualitative military edge as far as is possible – has been to suddenly press "New Delhi to consider acquiring several advanced, and previously unavailable, defensive systems such as the Patriot (PAC-III), complemented either by the Terminal High Altitude Area Defense (THAAD) system or the Aegis area defense system."[42] However, none of these systems still technologically compares to the S-400.[43]

Had the U.S. been willing to initially offer the PAC-III system, the current imbroglio might have been avoided. Indian officials were genuinely interested in the PAC-II offer, but largely as a potential "opening towards (acquiring) PAC-3, the latest upgraded version of the anti-missile system."[44] However, such a U.S. effort would contravene its organizational process objective of retaining its qualitative military edge. Once it looked as if this would be lost anyway with Indian acquisition of the superior S-400, the organizational process incentive structure was adjusted to make available to India the most sophisticated U.S. technologies available. This reshuffled set of the same incentives would deliver the other imperatives of supporting the U.S. defense technological base, broadening the range and depth of U.S.–Indian defense interactions, and with it the U.S. teleological expectation that such drivers would lead to greater Indian alignment with U.S. policy priorities. However, the transparent, and arguably cynical, display of these U.S. defense organizational process effects to India has even further reduced the chances of New Delhi now changing its mind on the S-400.[45]

Indeed, this teleological expectation forms another prominent contrast between U.S. and Indian defense organizational processes. India's expectation – made consistently clear in its diplomacy and defense purchases spanning decades – is that it utilizes defense purchases solely to fill capability gaps, and will seek the best technology available to it on the global market at the most cost-effective price, and ideally with domestic licensing and manufacturing rights written into the contract.[46] Foreign and security policy alignment with supplier states – even in the form of India exercising leverage over supplier states to change their own policies toward Indian preferences in return for the technology purchase – are not part of the MoD organizational process. The experiences of India rebuffing high-level Soviet military basing requests on Indian territory, at a time when most of India's military was reliant on Soviet platforms and ongoing technological assistance, underline this point.[47]

U.S. officials building this expected organizational teleological payoff into their incentive structure supporting a proposed technology transfer to India should revise this assumption. Put bluntly, if India can acquire the most sophisticated military technology and domestic licensing and manufacturing support from the U.S., it will. If it can't, then it will source these elements from elsewhere. New Delhi's foreign and security policy, regardless of the quantum and quality of U.S. military technology transfers, will continue to be made in New Delhi solely for Indian interests.

The effects of these defense organizational practices, and their amplified political effects in defining the overall relationship in a context where much of the actual regular bilateral contact is made by their defense bureaucracies, are further illuminated in the separate topic of U.S.–India defense technology co-production and support for Indian defense domestic manufacturing. This largely interbureaucratic process, absent a larger meaningful political vision with high-level political attention driving it, is characterized by the same conflicts between defense organizational essences.

Defense technology co-production and Indian domestic manufacturing

From the foregoing analysis it can be reasonably predicted that this separate path of defense technology sharing – co-production and production of U.S. technologies within India, as opposed to direct military sales – will have limited U.S. interest, given its organizational aims of protecting both the U.S. national defense industrial base and access to the technologies that form part of the U.S. global qualitative military edge. Tellingly, the major initiative to properly launch this process from the U.S. side had to be made by a high-level political decisionmaker – then-Secretary of Defense Leon Panetta – rather than being the result of a bureaucratic innovation to better deliver upon its organizational aims.[48] Put differently, political intervention had to force reform to the defense bureaucracy's organizational process.

The intention behind this reform was to create an institution within the DoD that was specifically dedicated to identifying and progressing areas of U.S.–India defense technology co-production. Named the U.S.–India Defense Technology and Trade Initiative, the institution was organized around a new, formalized interbureaucratic dialogue with senior MoD officials. Tellingly, the rationale for launching this new institution included noting that "the pace and scope of cooperation on defense technology and trade has been impeded by differing bureaucratic processes and legal requirements."[49]

Panetta's successor as Secretary of Defense, Ashton Carter, similarly politically intervened to strengthen the DTTI process. He directed the formation of an India Rapid Reaction Cell in 2015, composed of six DoD officials solely dedicated to advancing DTTI bilateral initiatives.[50] At the bilateral summit level, the U.S. DTTI delegation is led by the Undersecretary of Defense for Acquisition and Sustainment, a political appointee. However, the Indian delegation is led by the MoD Secretary for Defence Production, a career bureaucrat.[51] The Indian failure to name an appropriately empowered political appointee as head of its DTTI delegation limits the prospects of this process to overcome the organizational essences of both defense bureaucracies that hinder closer defense cooperation.

Moreover, the U.S. Undersecretary of Defense can only go so far in terms of breaking truly new ground in U.S.–India defense cooperation, as the U.S. Defense Security and Cooperation Agency is still mandated to certify that technology agreements will not threaten the U.S. qualitative defense edge. Furthermore, DoD DTTI activities are managed on a day-to-day basis by a career U.S. diplomat with experience in defense and security cooperation.[52] Despite the promise of the DTTI, therefore, organizational processes still shape the nature of defense technology transfers.

This is reflected in the progress of projects launched under the DTTI umbrella to date, starting with the jet engine technology working group. This project serves as an example of how these contrasting bureaucratic cultures and incentives can collide, and then be over-interpreted as indicative of the health of the overall strategic relationship, given the relative absence of regular political engagements. Established in 2015 as one of the work streams of the DTTI, U.S. Undersecretary of Defense for Acquisition and Sustainment Ellen Lord announced the "suspension" of this element of the DTTI in October 2019. Lord remarked that "we could not come to an understanding of what exportable technologies would be useful to the Indians and we did run into a challenge in terms of U.S. export controls."[53] While the precise technology components in dispute are not public knowledge, a former senior U.S. National Security Council and Pentagon South Asia official noted that, during his tenure, Indian negotiators "pressed hard to focus on engine 'hot sections' that involved sensitive metallurgy," and that "much (but not all) of the resistance to cooperation in that area came from U.S. companies, who struggled to find a competitive rationale for signing over decades of R&D."[54]

The U.S.'s bureaucratic objective to protect its qualitative technological supremacy within its defense technology transfer processes therefore clashed with the Indian aim to secure the most advanced technology possible. Given the initial Indian prioritization of jet engine technology transfer within the DTTI process, this outcome was reported in the Indian media as a setback for U.S.–India relations.[55] It also validated recent revisionist, pessimistic U.S. assessments of the future prospects for the U.S.–India partnership. Importantly, these accounts highlighted that India was unlikely to meet the U.S. teleological expectation that greater defense trade would organically lead to foreign and defense policy convergence with the U.S.[56]

Following the October 2019 summit, Lord remarked that the U.S. and India had nevertheless agreed to pursue seven new projects for co-development under the DTTI framework. These included, according to an authoritative account:

> ... short-term projects – to run for a period of about six months – that will focus on air-launched small unmanned aerial vehicles (UAVs), lightweight small arms technologies, and ISTAR (intelligence, surveillance, target acquisition, and reconnaissance) technologies. New medium-term projects comprise maritime domain awareness solutions and "virtual augmented reality solutions for aircraft maintenance", while longer-term projects consist of initiatives to develop smart munitions and counter-UAV technologies.[57]

While this appears promising at first sight, there is still little preventing the same conflicting organizational protocols asserting themselves within each of these new projects. The MoD will pursue its prime interest in acquiring the most sensitive U.S. technology elements of each of these projects, and ultimately look to other global suppliers if these are unavailable. The likelihood of this latter outcome is elevated by the DoD organizational interest in limiting access to these most sensitive technologies, so as to protect the U.S. qualitative military edge. Indeed, these projects are intended to revitalize the DTTI process, following the failures of its original initiatives. It should

Technology sharing and manufacturing 275

be remembered that the DTTI itself was founded to revitalize the broader U.S.–India defense technology transfer relationship, and to overcome inter-bureaucratic frictions.

This point is further highlighted in examining the DTTI projects that preceded the seven new initiatives announced by Lord in October 2019. Four "pathfinder" projects were jointly identified in 2015 for co-development. These included "Raven" small UAVs that infantry could utilize for local surveillance; reconfiguration kits for C-130J planes to expedite preparations for a shift in mission (for example, from heavy cargo to medical evacuation); a mobile multi-role power source; and NBC (nuclear, biological, chemical) protection equipment. These were joined by dedicated dialogues on aircraft carrier and jet engine technology co-production. In 2018, two new pilot-helmet digital display and biological detection systems were added as new projects.[58]

In negotiations, India demonstrated little real interest in the proposed Raven drones, instead using the discussion as a platform to push for acquisition of the more sensitive U.S. Reaper and Global Hawk drone systems. Both the Raven and C-130J reconfiguration kit initiatives were folded with a DoD acknowledgment that neither the DoD nor MoD had real interest in acquiring these systems themselves.[59] The multi-role power source and NBC protection equipment projects also fizzled out.[60]

The aircraft carrier initiative encountered the same frictions from defense organizational processes. The MoD viewed this as an opportunity to press, again, for the most sensitive U.S. technology within this broad topic – naval nuclear propulsion. As this was a non-starter from the U.S. perspective, DoD negotiators instead sought to redirect the dialogue toward other potential areas of cooperation. As a counteroffer, the U.S. proposed the sale of EMALS (Electromagnetic Aircraft Launch System) technology for future Indian aircraft carriers.[61] Given that alternative global defense suppliers such as France and Russia do not use EMALS for their carriers nor aircraft, a positive Indian decision on this offer might reduce its future fighter acquisition options to only American EMALS-capable platforms.[62] This would negatively impact its defense organizational interest in maintaining flexibility to buy the most sophisticated technology on the global market, especially when the U.S. is not offering its most advanced fighters to India.

The EMALS discussion appears to have been tabled, and the aircraft carrier dialogue now concerns the more vague themes of "learning [U.S.] carrier design and operating processes, maintenance cycles and the organization of combat operations on board the aircraft carrier."[63] Based upon the above trajectory of DTTI projects, it therefore appears that this initiative too will soon peter out. The opposing defense organizational processes of both states, fundamentally, do not support its progress.

It should be noted at this point that each of these projects has involved co-production, and their failure to reach the actual production stage has precluded the navigation by DoD and MoD of the subsequent issue of authorizing related defense manufacturing in India. The DoD organizational incentive in supporting and protecting the U.S. defense industrial base – including, crucially, its jobs and expertise – motivates against offshoring production of U.S. defense technology. However, this same end is a longstanding MoD organizational goal. Toward this objective, India's 2016 updated defense procurement rules continue to include "offsets," as first introduced in its 2005 iteration. The 2016 version specifies that a global defense contractor, concluding a technology sale to India valued at $300m or above, must invest 30 percent of the contract value in India's domestic defense manufacturing base.[64]

Moreover, a 2017 revision to these rules introduced a "strategic partnership concept," in which an international contractor bidding for an Indian defense contract must first select an Indian domestic partner company, leading to a joint bid. This directly supports the Modi administration's "Make in India" program to develop India's manufacturing base. However, it poses dilemmas for U.S. firms regarding technology transfer to India, given that sensitive information will need to be shared with the Indian partner company as part of the bid, which may in the end still turn out to be unsuccessful.[65]

The track record of offset-driven U.S. investment is not positive. Meanwhile, the ability of U.S. firms – as limited by DoD organizational process interests – to form joint partnerships with Indian counterparts that lead to actual technology delivery remains to be seen. U.S. firms have proposed offset programs and invested in India's defense sector, but have been confronted with the limited ability of India's defense base to absorb the quantum of offset investment, alongside the MoD's failure to certify that any of the offset agreements concluded since 2005 have been fulfilled. This has led to India imposing penalties on major U.S. contractors for offset non-compliance, including a $500,000 fine on Lockheed Martin. A similar fine had the effect of forcing Textron, another major U.S. contractor, entirely out of the India market for corporate financial risk reasons.[66] To avert such outcomes, the MoD is broadening the range of offset options for foreign contractors, including investing in the Indian commerical aviation sector instead.[67] It is also considering permitting investment into a dedicated Indian stock market fund as a further alternative.[68]

The signing of the bilateral Industrial Security Annex was billed by both political leaderships as a principal achievement of the "2+2" summit of U.S. and Indian foreign and defense ministers in December 2019. This agreement establishes protocols for the transfer and protection of classified

Technology sharing and manufacturing 277

technical information and sensitive materials between U.S. and Indian private sector firms.[69] On its surface, this provides firmer legal protection for the aforementioned issue of U.S. defense companies concerned with losing their valuable intellectual property to an Indian counterpart through the co-production process. However, it remains a bureaucratic process solution to an ultimately political problem and, as such, does not resolve the core challenge of differing DoD and MoD organizational processes.

Against this gloomy record, the Lockheed Martin F-21 fighter offer appears to be a remarkable breakthrough. The F-21 forms a slightly upgraded version of the F-16, and is one of the platforms that the U.S. is promoting to meet Indian Air Force next-generation fighter requirements.[70] To meet the strategic partnership criteria, Lockheed has concluded terms with Tata Advanced Systems. What is especially notable is that Lockheed is proposing to manufacture F-21s solely in India, while furthermore pledging that "Indian industry will also be integrated into the global F-16 production and sustainment ecosystem." Underlining the point, a Lockheed senior official stated that "Approval by the U.S. Government for such an important strategic move signals a significant development in U.S.–India relations."[71]

As a further commitment to Indian domestic defense manfacturing, the Lockheed–Tata partnership announced that it would move global F-16 wing production to Tamil Nadu in 2020, regardless of the outcome of the larger F-21 offer.[72] Given that the existing F-16 global production facility is located in Texas, these shifts inevitably signify offshoring of U.S. defense manufacturing jobs.[73] The extent to which this offer therefore runs against DoD organizational incentives is therefore surprising, especially after the foregoing analysis.

However, a hint at the likely fate of the F-21 offer within the MoD is included in the official Lockheed product card, which claims that the platform utilizes "technologies derived from Lockheed Martin's F-22 and F-35 – the world's only two operational 5th Generation fighters."[74] The F-21, ultimately, is not the F-22 or F-35, and not the most modern fighter that India could potentially acquire. As such, the MoD has no interest in concluding terms for the F-21 until it can determine that it is the best fighter available.[75]

U.S. support for Indian domestic defense manufacturing is therefore difficult to envision as becoming an integral part of the strategic relationship in future. It runs against core U.S. defense organizational process interests to, firstly, relocate its manufacturing facilities and technological expertise to India. Secondly, the same interests prohibit the U.S. from offering the most advanced technologies to India, in the interest of maintaining its qualitiative defense edge.

Platforms such as the F-35 are still available to U.S. NATO and other treaty allies, and thus theoretically available to India. However, such an offer is unlikely, given that India will not demonstrate the gradual convergence with American policy interests that is implicitly recognized as the reward within the DoD for sharing such sensitive technologies. In a context where many of their regular national interactions take place at the defense interbureaucratic level, the effects of the conflicting U.S. and Indian defense organizational essences threaten to define the broader strategic partnership into the third decade of the twenty-first century.

These effects naturally extend to limiting the ability of Washington and New Delhi to leverage the full potential of their strategic partnership to counter the rising shared Chinese threat. MoD organizational processes hinder the U.S. technological infusion into the Indian defense industrial base, and DoD processes preclude offering the most sophisticated U.S. defense technologies to India. The resulting Indian under-utilization of the military technological component of the U.S. strategic partnership, when the sophistication of Indian indigenous defense manufacturing continues to lag behind that of China, eases the task for Beijing in managing India as a threat on its western frontier and in the Indian Ocean.

As such, this reduces for Washington the extent to which India can strategically distract Chinese national security policymakers from their core focus on the eastern theater, encompassing Taiwan, Japan, South Korea, and U.S. forces positioned throughout that region.[76] For New Delhi, it challenges India's prospects for continuing to ensure adequate defenses against the Chinese military presence on its borders and in its regional neighborhood.[77] Absent high-level, sustained attention from political leaders in New Delhi and Washington to mitigate these risks through reforming their respective defense organizational processes, the existing processes as described above will continue to work to the benefit of China.

Conclusion

This chapter has utilized the organizational process perspective within the school of foreign policy analysis to explore the reasons for the seeming stasis in U.S.–India defense technology transfer, co-production, and support for Indian domestic production. Organizational process is difficult to employ for causal search purposes within a solely national policymaking context, due to the challenges of abstracting it as an independent variable. However, it can be valuably utilized when specific bureaucracies and their inherent essences interact with their foreign counterparts, and when these interactions form a major pillar in shaping the strategic relationship.

Consistent, high-level political attention can play an important role in dampening the negative effects of conflicting organizational essences, not least through political reform of the respective institutions themselves to reprogram their essences and internal visions of bureaucratic success. However, this has not significantly occurred in the U.S.–India strategic partnership. For bilateral defense technology cooperation to enter a qualitatively new stage, high-level intervention and sustained attention are required from both national political leaderships to bring their defense institutional essences into more deliberate alignment. As this appears unlikely at the time of writing, the bilateral transfers and projects listed above may approach the ultimate limits of their defense cooperation in these areas.

Acknowledgments

The author would like to thank Šumit Ganguly, M. Chris Mason, and Pramit Pal Chaudhuri for their valuable comments toward improving an earlier draft of this chapter. The author is also grateful to the members of the "Enhancing U.S.–India Strategic Cooperation" workshop, hosted by the U.S. Army War College Strategic Studies Institute and Indiana University at Indiana University at Bloomington, December 1–3, 2019, for their helpful feedback on a presentation based upon this chapter. Finally, the theoretical elements of this chapter were strengthened by the thoughtful comments of Jessica D. Blankshain, David A. Cooper, and Nikolas K. Gvosdev. Any errors in this chapter are those of the author alone.

Notes

1 For an invaluable recent study of this strategic partnership, see Š. Ganguly and M. C. Mason, *An unnatural partnership? The future of U.S.–India strategic cooperation* (Carlisle, PA: U.S. Army War College Press, 2019), https://publications.armywarcollege.edu/pubs/3696.pdf.

2 Cara Abercrombie, "Realizing the potential: Mature defense cooperation and the U.S.–India strategic partnership," *Asia Policy*, 14:1 (2019), 131; Dinakar Peri, "Army to sign deal for six Apache attack helicopters," *The Hindu*, December 20, 2019, www.thehindu.com/news/national/army-to-sign-deal-for-six-apache-attack-helicopters/article30361497.ece; U.S. Defense Security Cooperation Agency (DSCA), "India – MK 45 gun system," November 20, 2019, https://dsca.mil/major-arms-sales/india-mk-45-gun-system; "India – C-17 sustainment follow-on support," July 26, 2019, www.dsca.mil/major-arms-sales/india-c-17-sustainment-follow-support; "India – MH-60R multi-mission helicopters," April 2, 2019, www.dsca.mil/major-arms-sales/india-mh-60r-multi-

mission-helicopters; and "India – 777 large aircraft infrared countermeasures self-protection suite," February 6, 2019, www.dsca.mil/major-arms-sales/india-777-large-aircraft-infrared-countermeasures-self-protection-suite.

3 Jim Garamone, "U.S. officials seek to boost arms sales to India," U.S. Department of Defense, September 6, 2018, www.defense.gov/Explore/News/Article/Article/1621762/us-officials-seek-to-boost-arms-sales-to-india/.

4 N. S. Achuthan, *Soviet arms transfer policy in South Asia (1955–81): The politics of international arms transfers* (New Delhi: Lancer International, 1988), pp. 32–5.

5 A. Tarapore, "A more focused and resilient U.S.–India strategic partnership," Center for a New American Security, October 23, 2019, www.cnas.org/publications/reports/a-more-focused-and-resilient-u-s-india-strategic-partnership; U.S. Department of Defense, Office of the Undersecretary of Defense for Acquisition and Sustainment, "U.S.–India defense technology and trade initiative (DTTI)," www.acq.osd.mil/ic/DTTI.html.

6 C. Abercrombie, "Removing barriers to U.S.–India defense trade," Carnegie Endowment for International Peace, January 10, 2018, https://carnegieendowment.org/2018/01/10/removing-barriers-to-U.S.–India-defense-trade-pub-75206.

7 Lockheed terms this F-16 model the India-specific "F-21." See Lockheed Martin, "F-21 product card," 2019, www.lockheedmartin.com/content/dam/lockheed-martin/aero/documents/f21/F-21%20Product%20Card.pdf; S. Miglani, "Lockheed to begin supplying F-16 wings from Indian plant in 2020," *Reuters*, September 26, 2019, www.reuters.com/article/us-lockheed-india/lockheed-to-begin-supplying-f-16-wings-from-indian-plant-in-2020-idU.S.KBN1WB1W5; and Press Trust of India, "F-21 fighter jet will give India 'significant edge' with greater standoff capability: Lockheed," *Economic Times*, April 18, 2019, https://economictimes.indiatimes.com/news/defence/f-21-will-give-india-significant-edge-with-greater-standoff-capability-lockheed/articleshow/68921671.cms.

8 Press Trust of India, "India signs contract with U.S. firm for 72,400 assault rifles," *Economic Times*, February 12, 2019, https://economictimes.indiatimes.com/news/defence/india-signs-contract-with-us-firm-for-72400-assault-rifles/articleshow/67962476.cms.

9 Abercrombie, "Realizing the potential," 136–7.

10 U.S. State Department, *A free and open Indo-Pacific: Advancing a shared vision*, November 4, 2019, www.state.gov/wp-content/uploads/2019/11/Free-and-Open-Indo-Pacific-4Nov2019.pdf, p. 9. See also U.S. State Department, *Advancing a free and open Indo-Pacific region*, December 18, 2018, www.state.gov/advancing-a-free-and-open-indo-pacific-region/.

11 The author is aware that the State Department, and not the Department of Defense (DoD), is the lead institution for considering and deciding upon prospective Foreign Military Sales contracts. However, this chapter recognizes that there is little in the way of contemporary State–DoD daylight regarding U.S.–India defense technology transfers. Moreover, the DoD serves as the lead

interface agency with India in defense technology transfer issues, as represented by the constitutions of the national delegations for DTTI summits and ongoing negotiations. As such, this chapter will focus on the DoD and its relationship with its Indian counterpart for analytic clarity with regard to the Model II "organizational process" model. Abercrombie, "Realizing the potential," 140–1.

12 The author is grateful to David A. Cooper for the point on promoting combat interoperability. Abercrombie, "Realizing the potential," 137–40.
13 A. Cowshish, "Defence procurement in India: Challenges abound," in H. V. Pant (ed), *Routledge handbook of Indian defence policy: Themes, structures and doctrines* (Oxford: Routledge, 2015), p. 252.
14 W. F. West, "Searching for a theory of bureaucratic structure," *Journal of Public Administration Research and Theory: J-PART*, 7:4 (1997), 594.
15 Cowshish, "Defence procurement," p. 253.
16 P. R. Chari, "Indo-Soviet military cooperation: A review," *Asian Survey*, 19:3 (1979), 233, 238–40.
17 M. Halperin, with P. Clapp and A. Kanter, *Bureaucratic politics and foreign policy* (Washington, DC: Brookings Institution Press, 1974), p. 28.
18 U.S. House of Representatives, Office of the Legislative Counsel, *Foreign Assistance Act of 1961 (Public Law 87–195; Approved September 4, 1961) (As Amended Through P.L. 116–6, Enacted February 15, 2019)*, https://legcounsel.house.gov/Comps/Foreign%20Assistance%20Act%20Of%201961.pdf, p. 192; U.S. House of Representatives, Office of the Legislative Counsel, *Arms Export Control Act (Public Law 90–629) (As Amended Through P.L. 115–232, Enacted August 13, 2018)*, https://legcounsel.house.gov/Comps/Arms%20Export%20Control%20Act.pdf, p. 15.
19 G. T. Allison and P. Zelikow, *Essence of decision: Explaining the Cuban missile crisis* (Reading, MA: Longman, 2nd edn, 1999).
20 N. K. Gvosdev, J. D. Blankshain, and D. A. Cooper, *Decision-making in American foreign policy: Translating theory into practice* (New York: Cambridge University Press, 2019), p. 126.
21 *Ibid.*, pp. 145–6.
22 Halperin et al., *Bureaucratic politics*, p. 28.
23 Gvosdev et al., *Decision-making*, pp. 142–3.
24 S. D. Sagan, *The limits of safety: Organizations, accidents, and nuclear weapons* (Princeton, NJ: Princeton University Press, 1993), pp. 78–80.
25 C. M. Jones, "Bureaucratic politics and organizational process models," in R. Marlin-Bennett, M. Benson, H. D. Gould, J. B. Mattern, C. Navari, and M. Weinert (eds), *Oxford Research Encyclopedia of International Studies* (New York: Oxford University Press, 2010), https://oxfordre.com/internationalstudies/view/10.1093/acrefore/9780190846626.001.0001/acrefore-9780190846626-e-2.
26 Gvosdev et al., *Decision-making*, p. 159.
27 F. O'Donnell and H. V. Pant, "Evolution of India's Agni-V missile: Bureaucratic politics and nuclear ambiguity," *Asian Survey*, 54:3 (2014), 584–610.

28 It should be noted that a "Model III" bureaucratic politics approach would be more suitable for an earlier phase of the modern U.S.–India strategic relationship, in which the proposal for Washington and New Delhi to conclude a civil nuclear agreement was subject to robust and long-running interbureaucratic and legislative disagreements. There has yet to be a significant study of this case that applies this precise analytic model. However, Mistry's employment of two-level games, and Pant's utilization of a levels of analysis approach, indicate the strong potential for such a study. This is augmented by the quality and depth of empirical research relevant to a Model III approach in both works. See D. Mistry, "Diplomacy, domestic politics, and the U.S.–India nuclear agreement," *Asian Survey*, 46:5 (2006), 675–98; and H. V. Pant, *The U.S.–India nuclear pact: Policy, process and great power politics* (New Delhi: Oxford University Press, 2011).

29 This approach also aligns closely with the concept of "transgovernmental relations" developed by Keohane and Nye. See R. O. Keohane and J. S. Nye, "Transgovernmental relations and international organizations," *World Politics*, 27:1 (1974), 43–4. The author is grateful to David A. Cooper for this point.

30 Sunil Raman, "Cheers as Indian government wins vote," *BBC News*, July 22, 2008, http://news.bbc.co.uk/2/mobile/south_asia/7520487.stm.

31 Jon Grevatt, "U.S.–India defence trade set to reach U.S.D18 billion," *Jane's Defence Industry*, October 20, 2019, www.janes.com/article/92042/us-india-defence-trade-set-to-reach-usd18-billion.

32 For background, see U.S. Congressional Research Service, *Pakistan: U.S. foreign aid conditions, restrictions, and reporting requirements*, September 12, 2013, www.everycrsreport.com/files/20130912_R42116_b2b97c0fb192da917ab11ab1a9a86d4c4cebf767.pdf.

33 DSCA, "India – C-17 sustainment," "India – MH-60R," and "India – 777 large aircraft."

34 U.S. House of Representatives, *Arms Export Control Act*, p. 15.

35 Author e-mail communication with senior Indian Navy official, November 1, 2019. See also "MH-60R seahawk multimission naval helicopter," *Air Force Technology*, www.airforce-technology.com/projects/mh60rseahawk/.

36 U.S. Department of Commerce, International Trade Administration, "India – defense," August 5, 2019, www.export.gov/article?id=India-Defense; "Indian army's future infantry combat vehicle program grinds to a halt," *Defense Aerospace*, January 15, 2019, www.defense-aerospace.com/articles-view/release/3/199120/india%27s-future-infantry-combat-vehicle-program-grinds-to-a-halt.html.

37 Jon Grevatt, "India, U.S. look to reinvigorate trade and technology initiative," *Jane's Defence Weekly*, October 24, 2019, www.janes.com/article/92160/india-us-look-to-reinvigorate-trade-and-technology-initiative.

38 For background, see A. J. Tellis, "The evolution of U.S.–Indian ties: Missile defense in an emerging strategic relationship," *International Security*, 30:4 (2006), 113–51.

39 H. V. Pant, "India debates missile defense," *Defence Studies*, 5:2 (2005), 233–8.

40 Press Trust of India, "Issue of India's advance payment for S-400 missile system deliveries settled: Russia," *Economic Times*, August 29, 2019, https://economictimes.indiatimes.com/news/defence/issue-of-indias-advance-payment-for-s-400-missile-system-deliveries-settled-russia/articleshow/70898083.cms.

41 Sameer Ali Khan, "The United States has few good options when it comes to India's plans to purchase a Russian missile defense system," Atlantic Council, June 27, 2019, www.atlanticcouncil.org/blogs/new-atlanticist/the-united-states-has-few-good-options-when-it-comes-to-india-s-plans-to-purchase-a-russian-missile-defense-system/.

42 A. J. Tellis, "How can U.S.–India relations survive the S-400 deal?," Carnegie Endowment for International Peace, August 29, 2018, https://carnegieendowment.org/2018/08/29/how-can-U.S.–India-relations-survive-s-400-deal-pub-77131.

43 With its focus upon defense organizational processes, this chapter does not deal with the broader U.S. political response, which has been to threaten sanctions on India for defense trade with Russia under a U.S. law, the Countering America's Adversaries Through Sanctions Act (CAATSA), which was passed by Congress years after the S-400 deal was concluded in 2015. See Jon Grevatt, "U.S. delivers CAATSA warning to India," *Jane's Defence Industry*, June 3, 2019, www.janes.com/article/89008/us-delivers-caatsa-warning-to-india; and Tellis, "S-400 Deal."

44 Pant, "Missile defense," 233.

45 Press Trust of India, "India's advance payment," and Tellis, "S-400 Deal."

46 Chari, "Indo-Soviet military cooperation," 233, 238–40.

47 Central Intelligence Agency, "India's navy: Consolidating its regional predominance (Intelligence assessment)," October 1982, p. iv, www.cia.gov/library/readingroom/docs/CIA-RDP83S00854R000200020002-1.pdf; Chari, "Indo-Soviet military cooperation," 243.

48 U.S. Department of Defense, "U.S.–India defense technology and trade initiative (DTTI)."

49 *Ibid.*

50 J. Smith and A. Werman, "Assessing U.S.–India defense relations: The technological handshake," *The Diplomat*, October 6, 2016, https://thediplomat.com/2016/10/assessing-us-india-defense-relations-the-technological-handshake/; U.S. Department of Defense, "Secretary Carter's India visit highlights progress on defense technology and trade initiative," June 3, 2015, https://science.dodlive.mil/2015/06/03/secretary-carters-india-visit-highlights-progress-on-defense-technology-and-trade-initiative/.

51 U.S. Department of Defense, "Transcript: Department of Defense press briefing by Undersecretary of State for Acquisition and Sustainment Ellen M. Lord," October 18, 2019, www.defense.gov/Newsroom/Transcripts/Transcript/Article/1992962/department-of-defense-press-briefing-by-undersecretary-of-defense-for-acquisiti/; United News of India, "Centre appoints Ajay Kr as new Defence Secretary, Subhas Chandra as new Def Prod Secretary," August 21, 2019, www.uniindia.com/centre-appoints-ajay-kr-as-new-defence-secretary-subhas-chandra-as-new-def-prod-secretary/india/news/1705046.html.

52 U.S. Department of Defense, Office of the Undersecretary of Defense for Acquisition and Sustainment, International Cooperation, www.acq.osd.mil/ic/ICDirector.html. DTTI comes under the remit of the International Cooperation office, as detailed in the "Partnerships" category of this web page.
53 D. Peri, "India, U.S. cooperation on jet engines 'suspended'," *The Hindu*, October 25, 2019, www.thehindu.com/news/national/india-us-cooperation-on-jet-engines-suspended/article29787788.ece.
54 J. White, Associate Professor of Practice, School of Advanced International Studies, Johns Hopkins University, Tweet, October 24, 2019, https://twitter.com/joshuatwhite/status/1187419526331359232.
55 S. Unnithan, "India eyes United States defence tech," *India Today*, November 4, 2019, www.indiatoday.in/amp/mail-today/story/india-eyes-united-states-defence-tech-1615417-2019-11-0-; S. A. Philip, "India, U.S. 'suspend' ambitious jet engine technology plan under defence trade deal," *The Print*, October 24, 2019, https://theprint.in/defence/india-us-suspend-ambitious-jet-engine-technology-plan-under-defence-trade-deal/310965/?amp; V. Raghuvanshi, "Jet engine technology a top priority in India–U.S. talks," *Defense News*, December 10, 2015, www.indiatoday.in/amp/mail-today/story/india-eyes-united-states-defence-tech-1615417-2019-11-04.
56 R. D. Blackwill and A. J. Tellis, "The India dividend: New Delhi remains Washington's best hope in Asia," *Foreign Affairs*, 98:5 (2019), www.foreignaffairs.com/articles/india/2019-08-12/india-dividend; S. Lalwani and H. Byrne, "Great expectations: Asking too much of the U.S.–India strategic partnership," *Washington Quarterly*, 42:3 (2019), 41–64; Tarapore, "A more focused and resilient U.S.–India strategic partnership."
57 Grevatt, "India, U.S. look to reinvigorate trade and technology initiative."
58 Press Trust of India, "Defence trade and technology initiative: India, U.S. agree on 2 new 'Pathfinder' projects," *Economic Times*, July 14, 2018, https://economictimes.indiatimes.com/news/defence/defence-trade-and-technology-initiative-india-us-agree-on-2-new-pathfinder-projects/articleshow/51800651.cms?from=mdr.
59 Smith and Werman, "Assessing U.S.–India defense relations."
60 A. Shukla, "India, U.S. join hands for making warfighting gear: Drone swarms, virtual reality training aids, ultralight small arms," *Business Standard*, October 25, 2019, http://ajaishukla.blogspot.com/2019/10/india-us-join-hands-for-making.html.
61 Raghuvanshi, "Jet engine technology a top priority."
62 A. Ait, "U.S. and French fighters contend for a place aboard India's new aircraft carrier," *The Diplomat*, February 24, 2018, https://thediplomat.com/2018/02/us-and-french-fighters-contend-for-a-place-aboard-indias-new-aircraft-carrier/.
63 Shukla, "India, U.S. join hands."
64 Abercrombie, "Removing barriers."
65 *Ibid.*
66 M. Pubby, "Upset over offsets: India, U.S. to fix old problem to take ties to new heights," *Economic Times*, September 4, 2018, https://economictimes.

indiatimes.com/news/politics-and-nation/upset-over-offsets-india-us-to-fix-old-problem-to-take-ties-to-new-heights/articleshow/65664071.cms?from=mdr.
67 Abercrombie, "Removing barriers."
68 Pubby, "Upset over offsets."
69 U.S. Embassy and Consulates in India, "Joint statement on the second U.S.–India 2+2 ministerial dialogue," December 20, 2019, https://in.usembassy.gov/joint-statement-on-the-second-u-s-india-22-ministerial-dialogue/; D. Peri, "Industrial security annex opens Indian private partnerships for U.S. defence firms," *The Hindu*, December 20, 2019, www.thehindu.com/news/national/defence-ties-with-us-set-to-deepen-rajnath-singh/article30344918.ece.
70 Lockheed Martin, "F-21 product card."
71 Press Trust of India, "F-21 fighter jet will give India 'significant edge'."
72 Miglani, "Lockheed to begin supplying F-16 wings."
73 S. Miglani, "Lockheed sees potential exports of 200 F-16 jets from proposed Indian plant," *Reuters*, January 21, 2019, www.reuters.com/article/us-lock heed-india/lockheed-sees-potential-exports-of-200-f-16-jets-from-proposed-in dian-plant-idU.S.KCN1PF1CY.
74 Lockheed Martin, "F-21 product card."
75 There are other, political, issues surrounding the F-21 offer. Pakistan's air force relies upon F-16s as its main strike platform, meaning that its pilots and air defense systems will be acutely familiar with its vulnerabilities and signatures if Indian pilots are operating functionally the same platform. India may also select to simply add more French Rafale fighters to its existing order of thirty-six, given that there is a tacit understanding that France will allow India to arm Rafales with nuclear weapons. Such an understanding will not be available to India from the U.S. The Arms Export Control Act does not formally prohibit U.S. foreign sales of aircraft for nuclear delivery purposes. However, it establishes multiple certification and notification requirements to Congress – which are published, bringing significant unwelcome publicity – that can act as procedural roadblocks to such a sale. End-user certifications and related U.S. monitoring to ensure that technology sold is not employed for potential nuclear roles have become the standard means employed by the DoD and State Department in concluding terms with a state for relevant technologies. An instructive example of how the U.S. bureaucratic system is designed to place complications in the path of such transfers is provided by the testimony of a senior State Department Bureau of Political Military Affairs official before the House Armed Services Committee regarding the proposed sale of F-16s to Pakistan in 2006. The State Department official assured the Committee that "these F-16s specifically will not be sold to Pakistan to be capable of carrying a nuclear weapon," and that extensive end-user certifications and U.S. monitoring would ensure that Pakistan could not subsequently modify the F-16 for nuclear roles without alerting U.S. officials to the violation. See J. Malhotra, "India favoured Rafale also because of its 'nuclear advantage'," *The Print*, February 15, 2019, https://theprint.in/defence/india-favoured-rafale-also-because-of-its-nuclear-advantage/193103/; and U.S. House of Representatives, "Proposed sale of F-16 aircraft and weapons

systems of Pakistan: Hearing before the Committee on International Relations, House of Representatives, One Hundred Ninth Congress, Second Session," July 20, 2006, http://commdocs.house.gov/committees/intlrel/hfa28787.000/hfa28787_0f.htm, pp. 40–2.

76 O. S. Mastro, "Can India help the United States against China?," *Lawfare*, August 26, 2018, www.lawfareblog.com/can-india-help-united-states-against-china.

77 D. Kliman, I. Rehman, K. Lee, and J. Fitt, "Imbalance of power: India's military choices in an era of strategic competition with China," Center for a New American Security, Washington DC, October 23, 2019, www.cnas.org/publications/reports/imbalance-of-power; Frank O'Donnell, *Stabilizing Sino-Indian security relations: Managing the strategic rivalry after Doklam* (Beijing: Carnegie-Tsinghua Center for Global Policy, 2018), https://carnegieendowment.org/files/CP335_ODonnell_final.pdf.

14

"Make in India": a problem for bilateral defense technology cooperation

Pramit Pal Chaudhuri

Introduction

The defense policies of the Narendra Modi government are marked by attempts at structural reforms. These have meant India's pursuit of defense technology has been superseded by an overriding drive to indigenize arms production. In pursuit of indigenization, New Delhi will accept inferior technology, abandon established transfer of technology practices and demote its once all-powerful, state-owned defense firms. This puts the U.S. at a disadvantage in its attempts to expand defense technology cooperation, given its high prices and restrictive regulations. In this chapter, the evolution of the Modi government's defense reforms is outlined to show how they disadvantage the U.S. and how U.S. policy could adapt to this new Indian defense environment.

Modi and defense

The Narendra Modi government was elected in 2014 with a strong electoral mandate and a determination to differentiate itself from previous regimes by carrying out major changes to the way India is run and to lay the groundwork for a modern, unitarian Indian nation-state. While technology and the sense that it is a short cut to modernization and economic prosperity has been a leitmotif with all Indian governments, it has special resonance with Modi. He argued for technology as a means for nationwide social transformation, as one writer put it, including "unsettling the established regnum of rights and responsibilities" articulated by the Indian establishment and the constitutional order. The prime minister differed from previous governments in believing the Indian state's tight control of civil society's engagement with technology needed to be curbed.[1]

One of the government's priorities was the defense sector. Modi, in one of his first private briefings on the defense situation in early 2014, concluded that it was less a need for fresh ideas than the implementation of previous recommendations that was needed. The government also signaled that its overriding objective in the defense sector was to create the environment for an indigenous defense manufacturing sector where the private sector would have a greater role – and that it would use its mandate to succeed where previous regimes had failed.[2]

The first pronouncements of the Modi government outlined an aggressive reform agenda with four broad elements. Many of these reforms reflected a consensus, reflected in numerous committees and reports on India's defense requirements, that had emerged in New Delhi over the past nearly two decades.

One, the Indian government should promote private sector defense production even to the point of tilting the landscape against the state-owned defense enterprises. Two, the government should use defense spending, foreign defense investment and the provision of offsets to promote the manufacture of weapons in India. The Modi government made defense manufacturing one of the twenty-five elements of its Make in India program, a much-touted program to revive India's undersized manufacturing sector. It was assumed, say aides to the prime minister, that since such expenditure was controlled by the central government, defense would be among the earlier drivers for a manufacturing boom.[3]

Three, there would be an aggressive cleaning up and streamlining of the country's scandal-ridden arms procurement system, to the point that senior defense ministry personnel and senior military officers would be removed or prosecuted if found guilty of corruption. Four, there was a determination to execute a series of structural reforms in areas like budgeting to provide long-term stability to defense spending and integration of the military services to improve operational capabilities. Again, almost of all this had been recommended by earlier governments but had proved impossible to implement.[4]

This vision of creating an indigenous private sector-driven arms industry included acceptance that this would mean access to foreign technology. Within months of the 2014 election victory, the interim defence minister, Arun Jaitley, raised foreign direct investment (FDI) limits in defense to 49 percent and promised to take them to 100 percent on a case-by-case basis. Amitabh Kant, the then government bureaucrat in charge of foreign investment and later head of the government's principal economic thinktank, Niti Aayog, similarly declared that "we must look at allowing 49 percent FDI in defense through the automatic route" and be ready to take the figure beyond that after a government clearance.[5] The announcements led to speculation among defense firms from Israel and Europe that this might make it possible for them to set up assembly lines in India, but this was not evident among U.S. firms, which operated in a much more restrictive domestic environment.

Modi, in his first visit to the Defence Research and Development Organisation (DRDO) the nodal state-run agency for the design and development of armaments, publicly criticized its culture of "taking things for granted," and the head of the organization was soon removed from his post.[6] The government's desire to communicate its unhappiness with the record of its own defense firms led to major financial difficulties for the state-owned Hindustan Aeronautics Limited (HAL). It struggled at one point to even pay salaries to its staff.[7] An implicit priority was placed on indigenous production over all other reform goals, including technological superiority and fighting capacity.[8] There was also an expectation that external defense players, whether governments or firms, would have no more than a temporary role in the expansion of the private Indian defense industry, even if that role might last for a few decades.

New Delhi's assumption was that its strategic environment was benign enough that it could ignore the traditional military services' demand for the most advanced weapons systems, along with the defense bureaucracy's desire to preserve the state-owned defense companies. The Modi government saw the country's nuclear arsenal as security against any major military conflict, and that neither Pakistan nor China was interested in a conflict. It was also ambivalent about the U.S., in part because of a visa ban imposed on Modi and in part because of a broader Indian right-wing suspicion about the U.S.'s longstanding security relationship with Pakistan. The prime minister himself, as one diplomat noted at the time, had only two favorite countries, "Israel and Japan."[9]

Reform pushback

Within two years it became evident to the government that it would have to cut back the nature and extent of its reform agenda. Its various announcements resulted in widespread counter-lobbying by almost every conceivable stakeholder: right-wing ideologues, unions, retired military officers and former bureaucrats. Even the reforms' supposed beneficiary, the nascent Indian private defense industry, expressed concerns. The sitting defense bureaucracy criticized the policy internally, arguing that Modi's fervent anti-corruption program and the increased powers of official watchdogs like the comptroller auditor-general and central vigilance committee, made it difficult for them to choose a specific firm or technology.[10]

The Modi government had partly prepared for this eventuality. The choice of Manohar Parrikar, the former chief minister of Goa with no central government experience, for example, as Modi's first full-time defence minister was motivated by a desire to leverage his public reputation for integrity. The government that assumed institutional hostility to many of its reforms would manifest itself in the form of trumped-up corruption charges with an eye to paralyzing the defense system.

There were other structural issues. For example, it soon became obvious that the Indian private sector was years away from filling the shoes of the state-owned defense firms. The firms lacked deep-enough pockets, had minimal technology absorption capabilities and had no stomach for investing heavily in a sector marked by severe uncertainty in terms of contract flow and criteria for procurement. The government concluded that only five or six private Indians firms were big enough to be players in the defense sector, and even they clamored for some sort of investment protection. Subtract one or two firms which the Modi government had political problems with, and the number grew even smaller. Defense executives from the U.S. and other countries who met officials in the Prime Minister's Office and the defence ministry during this time were struck by how few Indian firms had the wherewithal to serve as partners.[11]

Accepting that it could not do without the state-owned defense firms, the government shifted its focus to reforming them internally, denying them veto power over policy, even while increasing the scope of private sector involvement. It also developed a more definitive policy on using foreign arms purchases to accelerate the process of indigenization and home-grown technology development.

Political lobbies also knocked off parts of the original reform agenda. Affiliates of the Rashtriya Swayamsevak Sangh, the Hindu revivalist social organization from which Modi's Bharatiya Janata Party derives its ideology and leadership, reacted strongly to the FDI in defense proposal, arguing that it was against the Indian right wing's belief in economic nationalism. The policy was never implemented, and the sole FDI proposal by a French naval firm was quietly buried by the government.[12]

Among the reforms dropped was a recommendation that defense research and development be handled by specialized development agencies working externally from companies. After a prolonged bureaucratic war, the government threw in the towel and declared that such research would remain internal to individual companies.

Two of the many committees set up to recommend changes to the existing defense procurement simply disappeared without a trace, thanks to determined resistance from the defence ministry's bureaucracy. The file of the Pritam Singh committee, which had recommended a special cadre of bureaucrats specializing in defense procurement and a process that would include pre-audits by the comptroller auditor-general was buried by the defense ministry. The Vinay Oberoi panel on fast-tracking capital acquisitions was announced, never held a meeting and disappeared.[13]

Legacy agreements drift

Existing defense arrangements, whose origins preceded the Modi government's election, had a mixed fate. The Modi government honored the government-to-government (G2G) purchases contracted by the previous Manmohan Singh government with the U.S. They included the purchase of Apache and Chinook helicopters, and further additions to India's military airlift capabilities such as C-17 and C-130s, P-8 Poseidon maritime surveillance aircraft and the M-777 howitzer. This reflected the regime's interest in scaling up the strategic relationship with the U.S., especially after the first summit meeting between Modi and then U.S. President Barack Obama in 2014. It also reflected a general policy to deploy U.S. military assets in two key areas. One was the Sino-Indian border: the airlift planes, helicopters and howitzers were largely designated for that front. The other was maritime domain awareness: the P-8 Poseidon and planned purchases of drones were designated for this arena. New Delhi also expected no political fallout, as all G2G deals, and especially the U.S. government variant – foreign military sales – are considered corruption proof, even by the Indian media.[14]

The only major arms deal that the Modi government scrapped was the $7.7 billion agreement to purchase 126 French Rafale fighters. The deal had been in limbo thanks to a number of corruption claims which had figured in the 2014 election campaign. The original deal was substituted with a G2G order for two squadrons of Rafales. The idea was that this would mollify France, provide for a replacement for the ageing Jaguars which served as the airborne nuclear deterrent and allow the government to jettison a politically damaged contract.

A key indicator that technology per se would be treated as secondary to indigenization, however, was the Modi government's decision to force the Indian air force to accept HAL's much-criticized Tejas I fighter aircraft. While the idea that India's indigenization goals meant that it would have to accept weapons of a quality below what it could import goes back even to the 2012 Naresh Chandra Committee on defense preparedness, the air force in particular had fought for years to limit purchases of the Tejas. Parrikar held a nine-hour meeting in April 2016 with all the stakeholders and eventually persuaded a reluctant air force to accept the planes, with the understanding that they would be replaced by an improved Tejas II.[15]

This was an important warning to overseas arms suppliers – particularly U.S. firms, as much of their competitive edge lay in the quality of their technology – that the lay of the land would be increasingly dictated by Make in India. It was also further evidence of New Delhi's assumption that protracted military conflict was unlikely with either Pakistan or China.

The government's focus on a more holistic approach to the issue of indigenization also left legacy technology agreements in limbo. The most expansive of these was the Defense Trade and Technology Initiative (DTTI) with the U.S., long held up as the flagship defense technology cooperation program between the two countries. At the time of Modi's first election, the DTTI had seventeen military technologies on offer to India, with twenty-four more on the cards. In addition, on a separate track, there were four "pathfinder" projects which had been identified by India and the U.S. for co-production of defense products based on comparatively simpler technologies.

However, almost all of these were offered through the traditional co-production channel, in which the defense state-owned enterprises were the primary partners. In many ways this traditional model of defense technology transfer to government institutions was exactly the sort of policy the Modi government was hoping to change or allow to wither on the vine. Whatever little Indian enthusiasm there was for DTTI waned when it became clear that the defence ministry's expectations regarding access to jet engine and other sensitive technologies were unrealistic.[16]

As it was, in 2016 the Indian defence ministry had a "plethora" of defense technology offers from governments and firms around the world. With New Delhi in the throes of a major defense policy shakeup, there was minimal official interest in any of these arrangements. The first four years of the Modi governments saw "an increasing number of delayed and scrapped transfer of technology projects" being reported in the defense space.[17]

Initially, the Modi government paid lip-service to the DTTI and similar defense technology offers by the U.S. and other governments. But in a few years it became evident that the government would generally ignore anything that was outside the Defence Procurement Procedure (DPP-16) paper issued in 2016 and other complementary reforms. By 2019 many of these legacy programs were being abandoned or retrofitted to be incorporated into one of the DPP-16 categories. The DTTI continues to struggle, officials admit privately, because no agency in the Indian government is taking ownership of the program.[18]

If there was any further evidence needed that the Modi government's interest in defense was about carrying out root-and-branch changes rather than amassing superior weapons, the clincher was its defense appropriations. Arguably the most right-wing government in Indian history, it nonetheless pared defense capital expenditure and redirected more funding towards military pensions. If pensions are discounted,

India's defense spending effectively fell to about 1.5 percent of GDP, the lowest since 1962.[19]

The tumult regarding the reforms, the continuing fear of scandal within the defense bureaucracy and Parrikar's increasing dislike for his job, and his ill-health, became so paralyzing that they led the Prime Minister's Office to take direct control of defense policy, with the national security advisor, Ajit Doval, placed at the helm of major defense decisions. A new body, the Defence Planning Committee, was created in April 2018 to legitimize his role as a de facto head of defense. Doval's willingness to take hard decisions made him the last word in major defense decisions, including the reform process and eventually even operational activities. After Parrikar resigned because of ill-health, successive defence ministers in the Modi government became little more than cut-outs whose primary purpose was to sell policies and use their reputation to prevent accusations of corruption.[20]

What survived

By 2016 the Modi government had reduced its defense reform agenda to a smaller but nonetheless important set of policies. This shrinkage helped to further strengthen its view that overall military superiority or weapons purchases were not an immediate priority, and it should focus on organizational reforms and private sector participation.

The most important policy signal was DPP-16, which laid out a number of clear paths by which indigenization of defense production could be pursued. Among these paths the most significant was the strategic partnership policy, which laid out a long-term plan by which Indian and foreign firms could collaborate on large defense platforms. In many ways, the Modi government saw this as the bellwether for its Make in India aspirations in the defense sector. There were other reforms, notably the introduction of the Long Term Integrated Perspective Plan (LTIPP) to introduce stability into India's normally chaotic budgetary process and the privatization of the Ordnance Board factory complex.

The DPP 2016 was the keystone in the Modi government's defense manufacturing and technology policy. The policy was notable for the degree of detail in which it laid out how it would push its reform agenda. The policy made clear priority categories in equipment purchases and levels of indigenization. It allowed for the government to provide some development costs, put forward aggressive offset requirements, offered incentives for small-to-medium enterprises to become involved and allowed for a lowest-cost plus (L1 plus) technology procurement policy.[21]

Besides the strategic partnerships policy, which is dealt with separately, there were three other key elements to DPP-16. The first was the Indigenously Designed Developed and Manufactured (IDDM) category of arms purchases, which required 60 percent indigenous content for major arms purchase and insisted that the intellectual property should be shared with an Indian firm. It was announced with great fanfare and Indian officials were especially enthusiastic about IDDM's prospects. There was "a belief among the leadership that this route will generate greater returns than technology transfers from abroad" – the traditional defense technology pathway.[22] However, it proved far too ambitious for the Indian defense manufacturing ecosystem. The percentage requirement, even when it was later adjusted to 40 percent, was too ambitious for Indian private firms. In time, said one defence ministry official, they became the strongest lobby against the IDDM. Though DPP-16 was tweaked repeatedly up to 2019, the IDDM category proved a non-starter and has existed mainly on paper.[23]

The second element was Buy Indian, and the third Buy and Make Indian. The first of these meant 100 percent Indian purchase deals and the second referred to foreign weapons systems manufactured in India. Unlike the IDDM, the second element has flourished. Buy Indian, known as Make 2 in the Indian system, has been a huge boon to Indian firms like Zen Technologies, Tonbo Imaging, Solar Explosives and other large to medium-sized companies, and it has helped India to develop private sector capabilities in sonars, missiles, grenades and other subsystems. It is widely cited by Modi government officials as evidence that they have been able to put into practice what previous governments had only been able to ideate. But it has also strengthened official ambitions regarding indigenization of manufacturing and technology development.

The LTIPP sought to end the services' tendency to generate completely unrealistic shopping lists of weapons they wanted to buy, by forcing them to tailor their wish lists to a 16-year defense expenditure perspective. The expenditure secretary of the finance ministry was an unofficial member of the early deliberations. The LTIPP focused on defense expenditure as a percentage of government budget rather than GDP and has since led to largely steady defense outlays of 15–17 percent of government expenditure. The three military services were directed to pool resources and end their tendency to duplicate equipment, reflecting the Modi government's determination to curb what one senior defense official called the services' "boys with toys" tendency to seek weapons without any thought to indigenization, cost or any parameter other than technical superiority.[24] The LTIPP should be seen in conjunction with the creation of the first tri-service Chief of Defence Staff and a Department of Military Affairs soon after the second Modi term began in 2019. This addresses the military's longstanding claim that delays in arms procurements were a consequence of political and bureaucratic dithering. The general staff would have both a budgetary timeline in hand and a direct say in purchases. The consequences of this shift, in terms of foreign weapons purchases and the indigenization drive, are at present unclear.

Ending the state-owned Ordnance Board's monopoly on the purchase of non-core equipment like uniforms was a reform that received minimal public attention. It has meant about $2.5 billion worth of contracts being shifted to the Indian private sector. The Ordnance Board was ordered to focus only on munitions production, but even there the private sector was given an entry with eight tenders for ammunition in 2016 alone. While it resolved the embarrassment of India importing even its soldiers' boots, it was a reform that succeeded because there were no issues regarding technology or intellectual property rights.[25]

Strategic partnerships

The strategic partnerships policy, a subset of the DPP-16, began to take shape in 2015 and is arguably at the forefront of the Modi government's indigenization drive. In July 2015, the Dhirender Singh committee and its follow-on, the Vasudev Aatre task force, recommended that defense acquisitions should be governed by a Indian–foreign partnership policy. Under this, Indian companies and foreign original equipment manufacturers would be required to partner to bid for and build a handful of big-ticket defense weapon systems. Even the subcontracts and offsets generated by these larger contracts would be offered to foreign and Indian co-partnerships. The choice of the partners would be left to the firms rather than the government – though it is widely expected that New Delhi would wield an unofficial veto on certain partners.

The strategic partnerships policy was inspired by the success India had experienced with two missile programs, the Brahmos cruise missile and the Barak medium-range surface-to-air missile system. They represented an evolutionary step from the production transfer of technology (PToT) model with co-development and co-production elements. In the case of the Brahmos, the design partners were the Russian firm NPO Mashinostroyenia and DRDO, with the manufacturing in India done with the involvement of a number of private firms including Godrej and L&T. In the case of the Barak, the design was done by the Israeli Aerospace Industries and the DRDO, and production was jointly carried out by the Israeli firm Rafael and the Indian state-owned firm Bharat Dynamics. Over time, with new variants of the missile, more Indian and Israeli firms became involved. In the case of the Brahmos, while the original foreign component was over 50 percent, over time it has fallen to about 20 percent. While not necessarily better than the PToT model of the traditional licensed manufacturing model, the technology passed on to the Indian partner through this model was "relatively newer."[26]

Initially the government tried to force Indian private firms to choose a specific defense system to specialize in. Instead, private firms demanded that they be allowed to bid for more than one strategic partnership category, arguing that India simply did not buy enough weapons in a single category to make it worthwhile for them to specialize to that degree. Foreign firms argued that the technology demands were simply too unrealistic, leading to the policy being reworked repeatedly over the next three years.

New Delhi, after initially considering six weapons systems, settled on four major weapons purchases to be placed under the strategic partnerships. As one defence ministry official described it, the idea would be for each contract to attract bids in which a major foreign original equipment manufacturer and a major private Indian firm would team up and then, if they won, repeat this across most of the subcontracts that would follow. The hope was that the various Indian partners would absorb know-how through "osmosis."[27] In any case it was assumed that the technology gain would be done in a manner more efficient and more sustainable than the existing transfer of technology models.

The government announced that the strategic partnerships policy would be used to procure the next set of naval helicopters, submarines, armored fighting vehicles and fighters. These represented some of the largest defense contracts India expected to tender over the next several years. Indian state-owned defense companies were deliberately kept out of the bidding process, except in the case of submarines, despite protests.

Sixfold path

At the time of writing, there are in effect six main paths by which defense procurement and, therefore, technology can pass from foreign vendors into the Indian system. The first and most ambitious is the strategic partnerships programs discussed above. Then there are the Buy Indian and Buy and Make in India programs, which are largely about transferring contracts from the Indian state-owned defense firms to the Indian private sector. The hoary licensed production system and its PToT agreements continue, largely with Russian weapons systems, but is a category viewed with disfavor by the government. It is in any case a variety of joint production that would be difficult for U.S. firms to consider if recent technology is required, because of their own domestic regulations.

Most U.S. defense firms are happiest with contracts in the fourth category, the G2G/FMS (foreign military sales) path, because it is the least complicated in terms of procurement process, technology sharing and selection of Indian partners. It is treated as corruption proof by the Indian political system. Also it plays to geopolitical relations, where the U.S. tends to score more highly than almost any other country on the Indian strategic landscape. But these are the type of contracts which New Delhi wants to move away from because they contribute the least to the government's indigenization priorities, whether in terms of technology or value-added defense production by Indian firms. Even when it comes to G2G/FMS sales the U.S. is seen by the Indian side as a difficult partner because of the attendant red tape, but U.S. firms receive high points in terms of fulfilling their contractual obligations.[28]

New Delhi sees G2G purchases through two prisms. One is the need to maintain bilateral relations for geopolitical reasons. In the first few years after the Modi government came to power in 2014, concerns about corruption, funding constraints and teething problems following from initial reform attempts meant that there had been few major arms purchases for a decade or more. India, for example, had not bought a new weapons system from Russia for several years. Most of its purchases were legacy buys going back to arms deals carried out during the Boris Yeltsin regime, with the specific goal of throwing a lifeline to the collapsing Russian arms industry. The Indian services were also increasingly put off by the poor technical specifications and expensive maintenance record of Russian equipment. The lack of deal flow began to tell on the bilateral relationship, with Moscow beginning to diverge from New Delhi in important foreign policy areas. The need to revive the relationship led the Indian system to look for a Russian weapons system that was technologically sound. This led, in turn, to the decision to buy the S-400 air defense system – also filling a niche which Frank O'Donnell in Chapter 13 writes the U.S. had proven unwilling to provide for.

The other reason for G2G deals was strategic urgency. This path allowed for fast-track purchases in which normal tendering procedures were skipped in a manner in which there could be no credible claim of corruption. In the Rafale deal the government accepted the imperative of replacing its ageing Jaguar-based aerial nuclear deterrent despite the controversy regarding the original Rafale contract. A similar plan is in place for buying Japanese US-2 seaplanes. The seaplanes have faced internal resistance because of their hefty price tag but remain in play because they are seen as a step towards encouraging the remilitarization of Japan and, as a consequence, further hemming in China.[29]

Indian firms which have won a defense deal under any of the DPP-16 categories can offer subcontracts to other vendors that have received the necessary official clearances. However, given the relatively nascent stage of the indigenous defense sector, it is more often the case that Indian firms are the bits and pieces providers. Similarly, subsystem and component makers working with Indian buyers can provide "upgrades" of existing parts. Upgrades come under much more flexible and easy contracting rules than brand-new components. While these pathways theoretically provide entry for technology, normally the transfer of know-how is not part of the agreement and the contracts are too small for either party to be interested in technology.

Finally, the Indian government has set up a defense startup program, Innovation for Defence Excellence (IDEX). The government moved senior bureaucrat Ajay Kumar from the Ministry of Information Technology into the Ministry of Defence to help develop IDEX. The program has proven quite successful, with 10 percent of the technologies created having been picked up by Indian firms. Reportedly the latest round saw that figure rise to nearly 25 percent. The DPP-2020 is likely to funnel offset funds to expand IDEX further. At present, however, there does not seem to be any role for foreign firms in the program. The contracts and deals involved are extremely small financially.[30]

Nextgen defense policies

A much more moderate defense reform agenda will be evident during the second Modi government. However, trying to plant the seeds for a future Indian defense industry capable of actual design, development and manufacturing of major weapons systems will remain the overwhelming priority. The government feels that it can contain the traditional military services' demands for the best in technology, irrespective of source or cost. Thus the continuing induction of new versions of the substandard but Indian-made Tejas fighter, including trials for its use on Indian carriers.

The Modi government still believes that any indigenization drive must put the Indian private sector, working preferably temporarily with foreign vendors, front and center. It has strongly resisted attempts by the state-owned firms to edge their way into the strategic partnerships. But it accepts that it cannot afford to do without DRDO, HAL and similar government agencies. The head of DRDO, however, was unusually modest in declaring in 2019 that he believed his agency would be able to make India self-reliant in missiles and torpedoes, radar and sonar and armaments. This is in contrast to DRDO's past record of hyperbole, claiming that it could build literally any sort of weapon required by the military, including aircraft and tanks. More striking was his pleasure at the DRDO having 1,800 private Indian firms as partners – a major shift from the days when state-owned defense firms lobbied hard to keep these firms outside the pale.[31]

The original DPP-2016 has been repeatedly tweaked. Even its latest 2019 version will be replaced in 2020 with a planned DPP-2020. The IDDM category has largely become a dead letter. However, the Make in India category 2 continues to be a success and has helped to expand the ecosystem of small and medium-sized Indian defense firms.

The government has made a determined effort to make technology available to the growing number of small and medium-sized Indian defense firms. DRDO has been ordered to provide its technology, some foreign sourced, to any private Indian firm without charge. However, budgetary constraints have meant that the original gains with the Indian private sector are being lost. With no orders coming in, many of these firms are returning to licensed production deals or simply mothballing their plants. One sector which is seen as an overall success has been artillery. Two Indian-made artillery systems have been deployed, another one – the M777 – is foreign made but has seen the transfer of the assembly line to India, and two more are under development. Again, this provision of technology is not conducive to a role for most foreign firms, and U.S. ones in particular, given their domestic regulatory environment and the cost and quality of their technology.[32]

There is a continuing priority on soft defense reforms which require minimal or zero funding. Services are being pushed to choose their priorities from their wish lists. Large-scale restructuring of the non-core defense activities is underway. For example, the ministry is shedding costly extras like golf courses and dairy sheds. The biggest reform is the creation of a Chief of Defence Staff and the eventual integration of the various commands.[33]

Future U.S. role

The Modi government is determined to maintain a close defense relationship with the U.S. for strategic reasons, especially as its relations with China remain confrontational. However, New Delhi has struggled to fit the U.S. defense sector into its Make in India priorities, despite the best efforts of both governments. There a number of reasons for this.

Several Indian defense ministry officials and military officers list the difficulties in procuring U.S. weapons systems as the primary barrier. While the technology on offer from U.S. defense firms is, most of the time, superior to anything else available, it is often prohibitively expensive. In addition, with more and more U.S. weapons systems becoming networked with the U.S.

communications, surveillance and navigation system, it runs counter to the traditional Indian method of buying a patchwork of weapons from different countries. This is less of an issue with weapons systems purchased from U.S. allies like Israel, but is a huge obstacle given the continuing purchases of Russian military equipment by India. This can work negatively in other ways: the Indian Air Force is infamously blind to the benefits of netcentric warfare and sees U.S. fighters' capabilities in this field as irrelevant to their more traditional sense of aerial warfare.[34]

An additional complaint is the legal restrictions which the U.S. places on the transfer of defense technology. This is part and parcel of a larger complaint that the U.S. beats its rivals, by a head and a shoulder, in the amount of paperwork and bureaucratic hassle accompanying its sales. Protectionist U.S. congressional mandates also make manufacturing in India difficult. The government's encouragement of arms exports has also helped Indian firms to improve their finances, though it has added a further obstacle to working with U.S. firms, who must contend with strict end-user and third-party rules at home. Foreign arms firms are now regularly asked if any of their weapons made in India can be exported by New Delhi to third countries.

The transfer of technology is seen as particularly onerous when it comes to U.S. regulations. The U.S. International Traffic in Arms Regulations (ITAR) allows the transfer of U.S. "articles and technology listed in the U.S. Munitions List to foreign persons or agencies only through an export authorization or license by the U.S. government." The limits placed on how and when such transfers can be made are arguably the tightest in the world. ITAR's restrictions mean, said one Indian study, that "there exists no scope for obtaining any technology deeper than manufacturing, i.e. PToT." It argues that ITAR "appears to be the most stringent export control regulations adopted by a major exporter anywhere in the world. European countries, Russia and Israel, all have national regulations which are apparently less stringent and therefore appear to be more attractive as sources of technology."[35]

This does not mean that defense players from other countries do not have their problems. Russian companies are reluctant to work with private firms which they perceive as unreliable. Indians see them as too close to China and declining in technological prowess.[36] Israeli firms are seen as fickle, prone to changing partners and limited in the array of weapons they can offer. French weapons are seen as exorbitantly costly.

India also needs assistance in solving its L1 (lowest-cost) problem in contracting. The L1 plus format, for example, introduced with DPP-16, never took off because no one could calculate the worth of the technology concerned in a manner that would satisfy official accounting norms. The offset policy has become a major source of contention, with bureaucrats declining to sign files for fear that they would be accused of bias in choosing partners, accepting offset offers and so on. The defense acquisition committee, for example, changed the rules to allow greater competition in the nomination of private sector partners in the strategic partnership policy over corruption accusations. The lowest-cost bidder is the bureaucracy's preferred means to avoid any controversy regarding the choice of equipment. However, lowest cost very often cuts out the U.S., potentially Japan in the future and even the Europeans for many projects.

Western contractors and Indian defense clients have come up with a number of ways to get around this requirement. For example, subsystem and component makers work with the Indian buyers to declare new equipment as upgrades rather than original material. Upgrades are not required to follow L1 guidelines. But this automatically favors legacy equipment providers and disadvantages U.S. companies, many of which are relatively new to the Indian market.

The DTTI has been drifting because the Indian side is unclear how it fits into its reform framework. The Indian government has decentralized research and development and the choosing of partnerships to individual firms, generally downgrading the role of the state-owned defense firms. The present G2G format of DTTI is a poor fit with this trend in India's defense technology policy. Somehow, the DTTI should be made more private sector and company friendly. The bouquet of technologies should be larger, suggests one Indian official, with "30 to 40 technologies" being put up for consideration so that the chances of something being picked are better.[37] The possibility of overlapping DTTI with the IDEX system could also be explored, though the micro-enterprise size of the IDEX participants will be an issue for most U.S. firms.

India believes that it has limited use for the very best U.S. technology, given that its primary strategic rivals, Pakistan and China, are still a few laps behind when it comes to know-how. The only fighting enemy, Pakistan, is increasingly not even seen as a conventional military threat. The U.S. should look to offer technologies that it is phasing out for various reasons but which could be useful to India. For example, Indian officials have been looking at the slew of counterinsurgency-related technologies and weapons systems developed by the U.S. military for its operations in Afghanistan. These may soon become redundant for U.S. forces as it slowly draws down its operations in Afghanistan but would still be useful for an Indian military that still carries out such operations on its northwest border and in the Northeast. Recently, Indian defense writers have proposed that India should consider picking up some of the Global Hawk drones being phased out by the U.S.[38]

Politically, a very large, high-profile strategic weapons program between the two countries would have the greatest impact. But this looks highly improbable, given India's determination to build its own weapons and the U.S.'s tight leash on technology and overseas manufacturing. The Indian Navy is the service furthest along the path of indigenization, making most of its hulls in dockyards mostly owned by the service.[39] The exception is submarines, but the U.S. no longer makes the conventional propulsion hulls that India needs. The Indian Air Force is expected to buy an interim fighter under the strategic partnership policy, but the sort of technology and production know-how being asked for will be difficult for U.S. firms to offer. At least India's next-generation fighter project, the advanced medium combat aircraft, is presently being designed around twin General Electric engines, but the plan is for the fighter to shift to an engine developed in collaboration with a foreign partner. France has made an offer to help India develop jet engine technology, though its credibility is still to be tested.[40]

Cooperation in areas like drones and missiles is arguably a more promising area. A comprehensive program in a variety of such vehicles, a military equivalent of the civilian nuclear deal, would help to ensure that an entire segment of India's arsenal would be umbilically linked to the U.S. for decades. Drones would be particularly useful, as all three Indian services are developing drone capabilities and the need for armed unmanned devices for counterinsurgency and counterterrorism purposes is becoming more evident. India is already a major buyer of Israeli-made drones but has yet to manufacture any sophisticated drones at home.

While they are not strictly under the rubric of technology, the U.S. should consider how it can contribute to the organizational reforms being carried out by the Indian government. The integration of the services is likely to be a difficult and protracted exercise that could do with considerable exposure to the means by which other countries like the U.S. were able to overcome the teething problems of such an exercise. The same goes for privatizing and modernizing the Ordnance Board or rationalizing the defense budget process.

U.S. will remain a key weapons provider because its geopolitical importance to India in the Indo-Pacific and elsewhere is overwhelming. Indian officials say the present contingency is to put aside $5–6 billion every few years to purchase U.S. weapons through the G2G/FMS window. While the quality and utility of the weapons will not be in question, the primary reason for selection would be geopolitical. While U.S. defense firms may be pleased, as this method of purchase is relatively easy for them to handle administratively, it is not necessarily a positive development for the strategic goals of the U.S. government and the overall development of U.S.–India strategic relations. Such deals would mean a minimal role for U.S. firms in the development of indigenous or partially indigenous Indian offensive platforms such as aircraft, ships and armor. If the Modi government's plans for a robust private defense sector are even partly successful, the country will have a multi-billion dollar corporate ecosystem with a dozen major firms. However, only a few of them will have deep relationships with a U.S. company or U.S. technology. This would be a crucial miss in an industry where path dependency on technology is measured in decades rather than years.

If the organizational reforms being implemented by the Modi government do come to fruition, the U.S. could benefit from an Indian defense structure that is more capable and amenable to working with the levels of technology which the U.S. offers and the corporate setup that exists in America. As one of the standard assessments of the Indian defense policymaking apparatus once argued, "The underlying belief is that advanced technology is a shortcut to modernization, whether military or otherwise. Military modernization is not just new technology, but new thinking about strategy and security and the ability to implement good ideas; it also includes an attempt to meet an international standard of excellence, and a willingness to adapt foreign 'best practices' to Indian circumstances." Seen at a distance, this conceptual change is exactly what the present set of defense reforms are designed to accomplish.[41]

Notes

1 Arun Mohan Sukumar, *Midnight's Machines: A Political History of Technology in India* (New Delhi, Penguin Books 2019).
2 Conversation with political aide to Prime Minister Narendra Modi in late 2014.
3 Conversation with official of the prime minister's office in early 2015.
4 'Waking the beast: India's defence reforms under Modi,' *The Diplomat* (December 16, 2016), https://thediplomat.com/2016/12/waking-the-beast-indias-defense-reforms-under-modi/.
5 'We need to open defence 100% to FDI: Amitabh Kant, DIPP Secretary,' *Economic Times* (April 21, 2014), https://m.economictimes.com/opinion/interviews/we-need-to-open-up-defence-100-pc-to-fdi-amitabh-kant-dipp-secretary/articleshow/34016966.cms.
6 'English rendering of Prime Minister Narendra Modi's address during the DRDO's awards ceremony,' Press Information Bureau, Government of India (August 20, 2014), https://pib.gov.in/newsite/PrintRelease.aspx?relid=138225.
7 Chethan Kumar, 'Broke HAL borrows Rs 1000 crores to pay salaries,' *Times of India* (January 5, 2019), https://timesofindia.indiatimes.com/india/broke-hal-borrows-1000-crore-to-pay-salaries-to-employees/articleshow/67390881.cms.

8 Ajai Shukla, 'Ministry of defence targets 70% indigenisation by 2027,' *Business Standard* (December 11, 2015), www.business-standard.com/article/economy-policy/ministry-of-defence-targets-70-indigenisation-by-2027-115121100040_1.html.
9 Conversation with military member of the national security advisory board in late 2018 and conversation with senior Indian diplomat late 2015.
10 Conversations with Indian defence ministry officials through 2015 and 2016.
11 Conversations with senior executives of four U.S. and European defense firms.
12 'FDI decision very unfortunate says RSS affiliate BMS threatens to take to street in protest,' www.firstpost.com (November 13, 2015), www.firstpost.com/politics/fdi-decision-very-unfortunate-says-rss-affiliate-bms-threatens-to-take-to-street-in-protest-2504014.html.
13 Conversations with three Indian defence ministry officials in late 2018.
14 Ajai Shukla, 'India–U.S. defence ties grow with assertive Modi govt,' *Business Standard* (January 21, 2015), www.business-standard.com/article/economy-policy/india-us-defence-ties-grow-with-assertive-modi-govt-115012100021_1.html; Sanjeev Miglani and Tommy Wilkes, 'Modi pushes obsolete made in India plane on reluctant military,' in.reuters.com (October 7, 2015), https://in.reuters.com/article/india-defence-aircraft-tejas-rafale-airf/exclusive-modi-pushes-obsolete-made-in-india-plane-on-reluctant-military-idINKCN0S10D720151007.
15 Private conversation with senior Indian defense journalist in early 2019.
16 Rajat Pandit, 'Indo-U.S. pact to develop futuristic military tech yet to deliver after 6 years,' *Times of India* (December 30, 2018), https://timesofindia.indiatimes.com/india/indo-us-pact-to-develop-futuristic-military-tech-yet-to-deliver-after-6-years/articleshow/67306050.cms; Ajai Shukla, 'U.S.–India learn from co-development fiasco, to approach DTTI differently,' *Business Standard* (October 28, 2019), www.business-standard.com/article/current-affairs/us-india-co-development-fiasco-forces-new-approach-to-dtti-119102700580_1.html.
17 Kevin Desouza, *Transfer of Defence Technology: Understanding the Nuances and Making it Work for India* (KW Publishers, 2020), p. 10, https://idsa.in/system/files/book/book_transfer-of-defence-technology_0.pdf.
18 Conversation with Indian defence ministry officials in 2018; for the text of the initial Defence Procurement Procedure 2016, Minister of Defence, Government of India, see https://mod.gov.in/sites/default/files/dppm.pdf_0.pdf.
19 Shekhar Gupta, 'Our joota hai Japani defence,' *Business Standard* (July 13, 2019), www.business-standard.com/article/opinion/shekhar-gupta-our-joota-hai-japani-defence-119071300056_1.html; Laxman Behera, 'For better arming and loading,' *Economic Times* (July 10, 2019), https://economictimes.indiatimes.com/news/defence/view-why-sitharamans-budgetary-allocation-is-unlikely-to-satisfy-defence-establishment/articleshow/70149231.cms; Ajai Shukla and Devangshu Datta, 'Defence modernization budget rises just 5% each year in real terms,' *Business Standard* (February 11, 2019), http://ajaishukla.blogspot.com/2019/02/defence-modernisation-budget-rises-just.html.
20 India-Abroad News Service, 'CDS or NSA: a bone of contention in India's strategic affairs,' *Economic Times* (August 2, 2019), https://economictimes.

indiatimes.com/news/defence/cds-or-nsa-a-bone-of-contention-in-indias-strategic-affairs/articleshow/70492578.cms.
21 Syed Mahmoud Nawaz, 'India aims to achieve defence technological sovereignty,' Press Information Bureau, Government of India (April 11, 2016), https://pib.gov.in/newsite/mbErel.aspx?relid=138758, Defence Procurement Procedure 2016, Minister of Defence, Government of India https://mod.gov.in/sites/default/files/dppm.pdf_0.pdf.
22 Desouza, *Transfer of Defence Technology*, p. xxi.
23 Conversation with member of the national security advisory board in December 2019.
24 Conversation with senior Indian defence ministry official in early 2019.
25 Laxman Behera, 'Rebuilding ordnance factories,' *Business Standard* (August 30, 2019), www.business-standard.com/article/opinion/rebuilding-ordnance-factories-119083000009_1.html.
26 Private conversation with Brahmos Aerospace officials. Desouza, *Transfer of Defence Technology*, p. 120.
27 Private conversation with defence ministry official.
28 Conversations with eight Indian defence ministry officials, senior military officers and officials of the Prime Minister's Office through 2017 and 2018.
29 Pramit Pal Chaudhuri, 'India and Japan: partners in change at home and abroad,' Ananta Aspen Centre Policy Brief No. 6, November 2016, https://anantaaspencentre.in/policy-papers/policy-brief-06-india-and-japan-partners-in-change-at-home-and-ab.
30 Manu Pubby, 'India to fund 250 defence startups over next 5 years,' *Economic Times* (November 12, 2019), https://economictimes.indiatimes.com/news/defence/india-to-fund-250-defence-startups-over-next-5-years/articleshow/72016505.cms.
31 Manu Pubby, 'In 5 years, we aim to be self-reliant in missiles, radars and armaments,' *Economic Times* (November 18, 2019), https://economictimes.indiatimes.com/news/defence/in-5-years-we-aim-to-be-self-reliant-in-missiles-radars-and-armaments-drdo-chief/articleshow/72101751.cms?from=mdr.
32 'Make in India defence sector will help realise PM's $5 trillion economy dream,' *Sunday Guardian* (December 19, 2019), www.sundayguardianlive.com/news/make-india-defence-sector-will-help-realise-pms-5-trillion-economy-dream.
33 Shaurya Gurung, 'Rajnath clears proposals to reorganize army headquarters,' *Economic Times* (August 22, 2019), https://m.economictimes.com/news/defence/rajnath-singh-clears-proposals-to-reorganise-army-headquarters/articleshow/70776839.cms; Shaurya Gurung, 'Integrated battle groups on Pak, China borders soon,' *Economic Times* (September 10, 2019), https://economictimes.indiatimes.com/news/defence/integrated-battle-groups-on-pakistan-china-borders-soon/articleshow/71057789.cms?from=mdr.
34 Abhijit Iyer-Mitra, 'F-16 never stood a chance to be in IAF fleet. Lockheed messed it up so much,' theprint.in (July 30, 2019), https://theprint.in/opinion/f-16-never-stood-a-chance-to-be-in-iaf-fleet-lockheed-martin-messed-it-up-so-much/269699/.

35 Desouza, *Transfer of Defence Technology*, p. 141.
36 *Ibid.*, p. 144.
37 Conversation with member of the national security advisory board in December 2019.
38 Conversation with member of the national security advisory board in December 2019; Ajai Shukla, 'India can save billions as U.S. to retire Global Hawk drones,' *Business Standard* (November 26, 2019), www.business-standard.com/article/current-affairs/india-can-save-billions-of-dollars-as-us-to-retire-global-hawk-drones-119112501488_1.html.
39 Ajai Shukla, 'Defence shipyards bag 85–95% warship orders without tender,' *Business Standard* (August 5, 2019), www.business-standard.com/article/economy-policy/defence-shipyards-bag-85-95-high-value-warship-orders-without-tender-119080400816_1.html.
40 Manu Pubby, 'IAF to add clause on local engines for AMCA fighters,' *Economic Times* (January 9, 2020), https://economictimes.indiatimes.com/news/defence/iaf-to-add-clause-on-local-engines-for-amca-fighters/articleshow/73162616.cms.
41 Stephen Cohen and Sunil Dasgupta, *Arming without Aiming: India's Military Modernization* (Oxford University Press, 2010), p. 145.

Index

9/11 attack 174–5, 177–9, 198–9, 202–4, 208, 210, 213n.10, 223, 242, 251–6
26/11 attack 253

Aadhaar 79
ACINT *see* acoustical intelligence
acoustical intelligence 230
Advanced Persistent Threat 81
Afghanistan 3–4, 6, 14n5, 15n.14, 112n51, 118, 123, 171, 173–80, 183, 188, 190, 201–3, 206, 209–10, 212, 220–1, 247–51, 256, 258n.30, 301
Afghan Taliban 174, 179–80, 209, 259n.47
AFRICOM *see* United States, Africa Command
Agreement Between India and Pakistan on Pre-Notification of Flight Testing of Ballistic Missiles 99
al-Qaida 174–9, 200–2, 205, 209–10, 212, 251
Andaman and Nicobar 53, 57n.39, 233
anti-piracy operations 226–7
anti-satellite 135, 139, 141–3, 146, 148n.18, 149n.25, 149n.29–30, 149n.33–4, 149n.36–7, 150n.38, 160, 167n.27, 232–3, 241n.55
anti-submarine warfare 49–50, 53, 232, 241n.52, 270
Arihant-class submarine 28, 104
arms procurement 288, 295
ASAT *see* anti-satellite
ASW *see* anti-submarine warfare
Astute Class 234
Australia 28–30, 32, 36n.19, 36.20, 42, 47–8, 52, 56n.15, 58n.37, 66, 130n.36–7, 155, 159, 161, 164, 230, 233, 236n.3, 238n.22, 250
Azhar 123, 130n.32, 183, 204, 207–9, 215n.38

Basic Exchange and Cooperation Agreement xi, 7, 48, 124, 146
Belt and Road Initiative 66, 161, 226
border security 178, 184–5, 224, 227
Brahmos 102, 295–6, 305n.26
BRI *see* Belt and Road Initiative
BRICS 42, 56n.13
  and Chinese cyberattacks 43
  and Russia 42
Burch, James 223, 237n.16
Burns, Nick 202–3
Bush, George H. W. 124, 247
Bush, George W. ix, 4–5, 65, 153, 251, 268

C4ISRT 231
CAATSA *see* Countering America's Adversaries Through Sanctions Act
Canada 156, 161, 230, 236n.3, 250
CCIT *see* Comprehensive Convention on International Terrorism
CENTCOM *see* United States, Central Command
Central Intelligence Agency 21, 105, 221–2, 236n.7, 243–7, 249–52, 254, 257n.12, 258n.16–17, 259n.55, 283n.47
CENTRIX 48, 234
Chandrayaan 153, 158, 162

Charbatia Air Base 245
China xi, 1, 5–8, 10–11, 15n.22–6,
  15.n28, 21, 29–30, 34, 38, 41–2,
  44–7, 50–5, 56n.14, 57n.19,
  57n.28, 57n.29, 58n.31–2,
  60n.66, 63–4, 66–9, 72, 75n.23,
  75n.27–8, 96–9 102, 106,
  109n.18, 110n.22–3, 110n.25,
  111n.40–1, 111n.43, 111n.47,
  111n.49, 113n.58, 113n.61,
  113n.64, 115, 118–19, 121,
  123–5, 127, 130n.32, 135, 139,
  142, 151, 157, 159–62, 165,
  171–2, 181, 183, 201, 207–8,
  215n.37, 219–21, 224–9, 231,
  233–5, 238n.26–9, 239n.30,
  239n.33, 239n.34, 239n.36,
  239n.37, 241n.51–2, 241n.55,
  244–7, 249, 252, 256, 259n.42,
  278, 286n.76–7, 289, 291–2,
  297, 299, 300–1, 305n.33
 cybersovereignty of 79
 economic espionage of 80–1, 88n.8
 hacking from 104–5, 113n.58, 60,
  65
 India's relationship with see
  China–India relations
 influence in Indo-Pacific region of
  29, 35n.2, 57n.21, 66, 225,
  227–8, 235, 238n.23, 239n.30,
  241n.54, 280n.10
 as a regional threat 64
 Tibet Military District of 101
 Type-041 submarines of 97
 Western Theatre Command of 101
 Xinjiang Military District of 101
China–India relations 1, 22, 66,
  75n.27, 111n.38 227, 238n.28,
  239n.37
China–Pakistan Economic Corridor
  226
China–Russia agreement on
  notifications of launches of
  ballistic missiles and space
  launch vehicles (2009) 100
CIA see Central Intelligence Agency
Clarifying Lawful Overseas Uses of
  Data (CLOUD) Act 72, 82–3,
  87, 90n.29, 90n.31–3
Clinton, Hillary 35, 37n.28, 205
COMCASA see Communications
  Compatibility and Security
  Agreement
Commercial Space Launch Agreement
  163–4, 167n.29–30, 167n.35,
  168n.36
Communications Compatibility and
  Security Agreement xi, 7, 48,
  146, 232
Comprehensive Convention on
  International Terrorism xi, 202,
  205–7, 211
confidence-building measures 11, 63,
  71–2
Congressional Research Service 74n.1,
  74n.5, 75n.24, 75n.27, 76n.51,
  91n.37, 165n.7, 179, 191n.11,
  195n.70, 212n.1, 213n.12, 223,
  238n.19, 239n.36, 257n.10,
  282n.32
Cope India see Exercise Cope India
Countering America's Adversaries
  Through Sanctions Act 42, 65,
  200, 221, 283n.43
counterinsurgency 187, 224, 301–2
counterterrorism vi, xi, 52, 60n.61,
  103, 127, 171–6, 181,
  186–9, 190, 194n.47,
  194n.65, 195n.71–2, 195n.84,
  195n.86, 205, 211, 213n.2–3,
  222–3, 224, 232, 235,
  237n.11–12, 250–2, 255–6,
  302
 in Afghanistan 178–9, 180, 220
 cooperation 7, 10, 12–13, 31–2,
  35n.1, 37n.23, 71, 169, 172–3,
  175, 177, 192n.19, 194n.64,
  197, 206, 213n.10, 216n.44,
  216n.45, 250
 dialogues and exchanges 181–4
 homeland security 184–6
 intelligence cooperation 13
 in Pakistan 180, 220
 post-9/11 41, 213n.10
CPEC see China–Pakistan Economic
  Corridor
CRS see Congressional Research
  Service
cryogenic engines 153, 161
CYBERCOM see United States, Cyber
  Command
cyberespionage 81
cybersecurity ix, 11, 63, 67, 68–71,
  73–4, 76n.37, 77n.59, 79–81,
  86–7, 104–7, 119–20, 125, 127,
  183, 224, 250–1

Index

cybersecurity cooperation v, 10–11, 61, 63, 73, 75n.32, 78–9

D'Souza, Shanthie Mariet 208, 216n.43
defence vi, vii, xi, 2, 5–6, 10, 15n.14, 19–23, 26–30, 35n.4, 36n.10, 36n.17, 37n.21, 45, 47–9, 51–3, 55n.4, 56n.9, 57n.22, 57n.30, 58n.32, 59n.48, 59n.53, 59n.58, 72n.59, 72n.61, 72n.64, 76n.50, 77n.52, 78, 86, 91n.43, 96–7, 101, 105–7, 108n.6, 109n.16, 109n.18, 109n.22, 111n.32, 112n.43, 113n.56, 114n.71, 114n.74, 129n.25, 138–9, 141–2, 147n.2, 147n.7, 148n.18, 150n.40, 150n.42, 150n.44, 160, 171, 181–2, 187, 189, 199–200, 222, 224, 227, 235n.1, 213n.11, 214n.18–19, 240n.40, 240n.42, 241n.53, 241n.55, 259n.47, 265, 280n.7–8, 281n.13, 281n.15, 283n.40, 283.51, 284n.55, 288, 289–90, 292–6, 298–9, 303n.4–5, 304n.8–10, 304n.13–14, 304n.17–19, 305n.20–2, 305n.24, 305n.26–8, 305n.30–3, 306n.35, 306n.39–40
  collaboration 53, 65, 221
  cooperation between India and Russia 7, 41–4, 47, 59n.5, 221, 228, 283n.40
  intelligence 222, 228–9, 234–5
  production 227, 228, 273, 288, 293, 297
  relationship between United States and India 3, 8–10, 13–14, 34–5, 35n.2, 38–44, 47, 50–5, 55n.2, 56n.5, 58n.43, 59n.54, 63, 65, 70–4, 74n.18, 76n.50, 230n.34, 175, 191n.11, 200–1, 206–8, 212, 215n.28, 221, 228–9, 232–55, 236n.9, 238n.21–4, 238m.27, 240.47, 261, 263–79, 279n.2–3, 279n.5–6, 279n.11, 282n.36–9, 283n.41, 283n.43–4, 283n.48, 283n.50–1, 284n.52, 284n.55, 284n.58–9, 285n.69, 285n.75, 286–303, 303n.4, 304n.11, 304n.15
Defence Cyber Agency 85, 91n.40

Defence Intelligence Agency 222, 237n.12
Defence Offset Policy 300–1
Defence Research and Development Organization xi, 53, 135, 146, 289, 295, 298–9, 305n.31
Defence Space Agency 147
Defence Space Research Organisation 147
Department of Atomic Energy 267
Department of Defense vii, 41, 56n.4, 59n.58, 91n.43, 104, 108n.6, 111n.32, 136, 147n.2, 147n.7, 150n.40, 150n.42, 150n.44, 235n.1, 238n.21, 239n.24, 240n.47, 268, 280n.3, 280n.5, 280n.11, 283n.48, 283n50–1, 284n.52
deterrence 51, 91n.41, 97, 103, 106, 109n.16–17, 128n.9, 220, 224–5
Director of National Intelligence 88n.8, 230, 255
disaster relief operations 24, 29, 32–4, 52
Djibouti 226
DNI *see* Director of National Intelligence
DoD *see* Department of Defense
Doklam, crisis of 2017 55, 101, 103, 110n.26, 112n.47, 113n.57, 286n.77
DRDO *see* Defence and Research Development Organisation
Dufferin, Viceroy Lord 243

Easter bombings *see* Sri Lanka Easter bombings (2019)
economic relationship 22, 38, 49–54
  between India and Russia 66
  nature of U.S.–India 66–7, 71
Electromagnetic Aircraft Launch System 275
electronic intelligence 229–30, 232–3, 255
ELINT *see* electronic intelligence
EMALS *see* Electromagnetic Aircraft Launch System
Establishment 22 245
Executive Order 13224 198, 208, 213n.2, 216n.38–9
Exercise *Cope India* 25–6, 35, 36n.10, 58n.42

Exercise *Malabar* 28–31, 32, 48, 234
Exercise *Shatrujeet* (2006) 203
Exercise *Tiger Triumph* 33, 49
Exercise *Yudh Abhyas* (2019) vii, 27, 214n.19
exports, volume of U.S.–India 67

FATF *see* Financial Action Task Force
FBI *see* Federal Bureau of Investigation
Federal Bureau of Investigation 89n.24, 201, 177, 185, 201, 204–6, 237n.17
Financial Action Task Force xi, 172, 183, 206–7, 212, 215n.36
Five Eyes Program 250
force modernization 226
foreign ownership limitations 65
Foreign Terrorist Organisations xi, 198, 207, 212n.1
Fourteen Eyes 250, 256
Framework for US–India Cyber Relationship 67, 76n.36, 76n.39, 80, 88n.7
Free and Open Indo-Pacific strategies 38, 41, 66, 70, 75n.24, 75n.27, 124, 264, 280n.10

GAGAN *see* GPS Aided GEO Augmented Navigation
Gandhi, Indira 246–7
GCHQ *see* General Communication Headquarters
General Communication Headquarters 252
Generalized System of Preferences xi, 64, 72, 221
Group of Governmental Experts (GGE) 140
GPS Aided GEO Augmented Navigation 155
Gwadar 226, 233

Hayden, General Michael 252
Headley, David Coleman 193n.41, 193n.43, 204, 252
Hizbul Mujahidin 173–4, 183, 207, 210
human intelligence 230
HUMINT *see* human intelligence
Hyderabad, terrorist attack in 2013 210

IB *see* Intelligence Bureau
ICBM *see* inter-continental ballistic missile

IMAC *see* Information Management and Analysis Center
imagery intelligence 146, 152, 245
IMINT *see* imagery intelligence
Imports, U.S–India volume of 64, 67
India Airlines flight 814 hijacking of 202
India–United States relations
  2+2 Dialogue of 2018 138, 148n.19, 148n.20, 148n.21, 150n.50, 160, 206, 212
  Counter Terrorism Cooperation Initiative of 2009 60n.60, 177, 184, 195n.79, 204
  Defense Policy Group 65
  Defense Technology and Trade Initiative 263, 273, 280n.5, 283n.48, 283n.50
  Homeland Security Dialogue of 2011 182–5, 205, 214n.24
  India–U.S.-Space Security Dialogue 12, 154, 158–9
  Indo–U.S. Joint Working Group 120, 138, 158, 166n.19
  Industrial Security Annex 54, 146, 276–7, 285n.69
  Joint Declaration on Combating Terrorism 2015 205, 214n.26
  Joint Statement of November 2001 192n.20, 202–3
  Joint Working Group on Counter-Terrorism 194n.65, 202, 205, 207, 214n.14
  Logistics Exchange Memorandum of Agreement 6, 47, 264
  military exercises viii, 10, 25, 38, 40, 43, 48–50
  Nuclear Accord 2005 203
  space cooperation between 151, 162
  Strategic Dialogue 2010 165n.1, 167n.25, 204, 214n.23
  tariffs 64–5, 72
  Terrorist Designation Dialogue of 2017 207
Indian
  Army vii, 23–4, 26–7, 46, 51, 59n.57, 85, 107, 122, 214n.18, 227, 231, 239, 245–5, 282n.36
  economy
    growth of 64
    size of 67

Ministry of Defence 40, 49, 50–2, 57n.30, 59n.48, 214n.18–19, 240n.40, 265, 268, 298, 304n.8
Mujahidin 203–4, 207, 210
Navy 28, 35, 37n.22, 44, 54–5, 231, 237n.12, 240n.40, 240n.42, 240n.45, 240n.48–9, 241n.56, 270, 282n.35, 302
  amphibious forces of 20, 37n.26
  budget of 28, 45–6
  modernization of vii, 45–6, 52, 54, 184, 228, 270
  power projection capabilities of 232–4, 237n.12
  Ocean xi, 1, 28, 45, 48, 53, 57n.28, 66, 75n.26–7, 145, 152, 209, 225–8, 232–5, 238n.25–6, 238n.29, 239n.34, 240n.40–1, 240n.43, 241n.51–3, 252, 278
Police Service 103, 246, 253–4
relations with Russia 41, 43, 55, 56n.11, 57n.22, 66, 75n.21
Space Research Organisation 120, 130n.40, 138, 143, 145–6, 148n.14, 149n.37, 150n.47, 151–8, 160–4, 165n.2, 165n.4, 165n.10, 166n. 11–12, 166n.16–17, 167n.29–30, 167n.33, 168n.41–2
indigenous defense manufacturing, Indian 278, 287–8
Indo-Pacific, the 54, 63, 66, 69–70, 75n.23, 119, 144–5, 206–7, 209, 212, 219, 220, 225, 226, 230, 232–3, 235, 238n.29, 239n.30, 256, 302
  India and 43–4, 57n.24, 57n.26, 58n.37, 219, 220, 223–4, 227–9, 233, 239n.39
  Japan and 161
  Strategy Report (2019) 41, 56n.5, 56n.7, 56n.12, 150n.44, 223, 232, 238n.21, 240n.47
  U.S. strategy for 10, 29, 41, 60n.68, 124, 164, 223–4, 225, 228–9, 238n.22–3, 240n.43
INDOPACOM see United States, Indo-Pacific Command
influence operations 11, 83–5
Information Management and Analysis Center 222, 237n.12, 240n.48

information sharing 68, 145, 186, 205–6, 220, 222, 240n.48, 249, 255
intellectual property 64, 80, 87, 88n.9, 224, 229, 277, 294–5
intelligence 4–5, 53, 72–3, 79, 82, 84, 88n.8, 90n.25, 103–4, 112n.47, 113n.56–7, 113n.59, 113n.61, 120, 125, 130n.38, 177–8, 184, 186, 188–9, 192n.16, 194n.59, 196n.109, 197–201, 203–5, 209, 213n.5–6, 216n.46, 222–3, 227, 230–5, 236n.3, 236n.7, 237n.11, 237n.13, 237n.16–17, 242–57, 439n.3–4, 257n.10–11, 258n.18–19, 258n.37, 258n.39, 259n.25–6, 259n.48–9, 259n.54, 260n.64, 260n.67, 274
  analysis of 220, 225, 234, 237n.10, 250, 254, 256, 257n.7
  collection of 69, 71, 249, 253, 220, 229–33, 237n.12, 254, 256
  cooperation vi, 10, 13, 113n.69, 182, 217, 219–20, 222–4, 226, 228–30, 235, 242–3, 256–7
Intelligence Bureau 105, 199, 206, 222, 237n.10, 243–5, 249, 251–3, 255, 257n.6, 258n.31, 260n.72
inter-continental ballistic missile 98, 111n.32, 167n.34, 267
Inter-Services Intelligence xi, 4, 204, 209, 246, 248–50, 253
IOR see Indian, Ocean Region
IPS see Indian, Police Service
Iran 3, 11, 64, 69, 197, 200, 208, 210–12, 241n.51
ISI see Inter-Services Intelligence
ISIS–Khorasan Province 250
Islamic State, the 12, 173–4, 178–9, 186–9, 200, 250
Israel-Palestine conflict, the 198
ISRO see Indian, Space Research Organisation
Iyer, Prithvi 37n.23, 209, 216n.45

Jaishankar, S. 21, 56n.17, 57n.24, 125, 221, 236n.5
Jaish-e-Mohammed 123, 173–5, 183, 198, 200, 203–5, 207, 210, 214n.22

Jammu and Kashmir 201, 207–8, 210, 216n.48, 221, 226, 239n.31, 244–6
   kidnapping of American nationals in 201
   Legislative Assembly, attack on see Jaish-e-Mohammed
   militancy in 198, 200, 210
Jet Propulsion Laboratory 154, 165n.10
JIC see Joint Intelligence Committee
Johnson, Lyndon B. 245–6
Joint Intelligence Committee 222, 254

Kao, Rameshwar Nath 244, 246–7, 249, 253–4
Kargil 222, 231, 237n.10, 239n.31
   Review Committee 254, 260n.69, 260n.73
   War (1999) 117, 202, 254
Kennedy, John F. 244
Khan, General Yahya 246
Kinetic Energy-Anti-Satellite test ban 141
Knaus, John Kenneth 245
Kudankulam reactor 81, 120, 129n.18–19, 130n.40

Lahoria, Daya Singh 201
Lazarus Group 81, 89n.16
local presence requirements, Indian 65, 72
Lockheed Martin 264, 276–7, 280n.7, 285n.70, 285n.74, 305n.34
Lop Nor 245

MAC see Multi Agency Centre of India
Make in India domestic manufacturing initiative vi, 7, 15n.21, 51, 59n.55, 276, 287–8, 292–3, 296, 299, 305n.32
Malabar see Exercise Malabar
Mangalyaan 154, 158
maritime 1, 13, 28–9, 38–9, 43–5 48–9, 52, 57n.31, 60n.67, 150n.48, 156, 219, 224–5, 229, 232–4, 239n.34, 239n.35, 241n.53, 263, 268–70, 291
   chokepoint 225–6, 233
   domain awareness xi, 135, 144–5, 161, 227, 234–5, 237n.12, 274, 291
   engagement strategy 227–8
   security 57n.19, 66, 135, 144–5, 184, 232, 235
Maritime Silk Road 225–6
Mars mission 151, 154, 158
MASINT see measurement and security intelligence
measurement and security intelligence 230
MI see military intelligence
MI6 254
military intelligence 103, 222, 229–30, 237, 257n.3
Missile Technology Control Regime xi, 153, 161
Mission Shakti 143, 149n.33, 167n.27
Modi, Narendra 7, 13, 41, 43–4, 47, 51, 56n.17, 57n.18, 57n.22, 58n.36, 127, 129n.26, 143, 149n.32, 159, 207–8, 210–11, 219, 227, 236n.5, 239n.31, 242, 276, 287–9, 290–5, 297–9, 303, 303n.2, 303n.4, 303n.6, 304n.14
MTCR see Missile Technology Control Regime
Mullik, B. N. 245
Multi Agency Centre of India 199, 222, 237
Mutual Legal Assistance Treaty 69, 82, 175

NASA see National Aeronautics and Space Administration
NASA–ISRO Synthetic Aperture Radar 154–5, 165n.10, 166n.11
National Aeronautics and Space Administration 138, 143, 149n.37, 150n.38–9, 151–5, 158, 162, 165n.10, 166n.11, 166n.21–2
National Counter Terrorism Center xi, 199 209, 223
National Cyber Coordination Centre 105
National Cyber Security Strategy 86
National Intelligence Estimate 258n.18
National Investigation Agency 60n.61, 193n.43, 222, 237, 252
National Maritime Intelligence Center 233
national security
   advisor x, 44, 104–5, 117, 120–1, 131n.44, 222, 293, 304n.9, 305n.23, 306n.36–7

National Security Act of 1947 243
National Security Agency 86, 104, 216, 222, 251, 255
National Security Council 81, 104–5, 120, 189, 254, 274
  National Security Council Secretariat 81, 105, 120, 222, 250–1
  National Security Space Strategy 136, 147n.2
National Strategy for Maritime Security 30, 51, 57n.30, 57n.32, 144–5, 150n.40, 150n.42, 227, 238n.29, 240n.40, 252n.49
national technical means xi, 98, 100, 107, 108n.4, 111n.33
National Technical Research Organization 105, 222
NCTC see National Counter Terrorism Center
Nehru, Jawaharlal x, 244
Nepal 178, 245, 249–50, 259n.42
New Delhi v, ix, x, 1, 6, 35, 38, 41–5, 47–8, 50, 53–5, 56n.8, 57n.27–8, 58n.37, 59n.47, 59n.57, 60n.67, 64, 78, 83, 97, 99–100, 105–7, 110n.25, 110n.27, 112n.49, 115–18, 120–1, 125–7, 130n.34, 130n.39, 131n.41, 131n.44, 148n.12, 151, 156, 159–62, 165n.8, 166n.23, 179n.26, 189, 195n.91, 200, 202, 205, 207, 219–23, 228, 232, 236n.5, 236n.9, 237n.10, 237n,12, 239n.31, 239n.34, 239n.39, 240n.40, 240n.46, 248, 250–1, 255–6, 263–4, 269, 271, 272, 278, 280n.4, 282n.28, 284n.56, 287–8, 291–2, 295–7, 299–300, 303n.1
New Zealand 230, 234–5, 236n.3, 250
NIA see National Investigation Agency
NIE see National Intelligence Estimate
NISAR see NASA-ISRO Synthetic Aperture Radar
Nixon, Richard Milhous 246, 258n.21
NMIC see National Maritime Intelligence Center
nonalignment 3, 9, 20–1, 24, 35, 42–3, 220–1, 265

North Korea 69, 71, 89n.20, 119–20, 125, 197–8
  hackers from 81, 89n.18
  as a regional threat 11, 64
  no first use policy 97, 107, 109n.14, 118–19, 126, 127n.2
NPU see Nuclear Non-Proliferation Treaty
NSCS see National Security Council Secretariat
NSSS see National Security Space Strategy
nuclear x, 1, 3, 5, 10–12, 38, 44, 70, 76n.46–7, 76n.49, 81, 89n.19–20, 93–101, 102–7, 108n.1–2, 108n.4, 108n.6–7, 108n.9, 109n.11, 109n.14, 109.16–19, 109n.21, 110n.27–8, 110n.30 111n.34, 111n.38–41, 112n.46, 112n.55, 113n.58, 68, 114n.71, 115–27, 127n.1–2, 128n.6, 128n.9–10, 128n.15–17, 129n.18–19, 129n.26–7, 129n.29, 130n.31, 130n.38–9, 131n.41, 131n.42, 131n.44, 138, 142–3, 152–3, 158–9, 164, 172, 181, 203, 221, 226–7, 229–31, 233–5, 239n.33, 259n.54, 267, 270, 275, 281n.24, 281n.27, 282n.28, 285n.75, 289, 291, 297, 302
  crises in South Asia v, 95
  doctrine of India 97, 109n.16, 110n.27, 115, 118, 131n.44
  doctrine of Pakistan 117, 122, 126
  escalation 109n.19, 113n.58, 115–19, 122, 126
  proliferation
    U.S. policy on 109n.16, 118, 164
  stability of South Asia v, 115
  tactical nuclear weapons xi, 11, 115–16, 122, 126
  test
    in China 245
    in India 115, 143, 153, 202, 251, 257n.10
Nuclear Non-Proliferation Treaty 95, 142–3, 159
Nuclear Security Summit 119, 128n.15, 17

Oakley, Robert 201, 213n.9
Obama, Barack Hussein 82, 242, 291

Office of Strategic Services 243, 249
OSS *see* Office of Strategic Services
Outer Space Objects Treaty 139

Pakistan 1, 3–9, 11–12, 14n.4–6,
    15n. 11, 15n.14, 15n.16 15n.17,
    34, 48, 51, 66, 70, 96–7,
    99–100, 105–6, 109n.22,
    111n.34–5, 111n.37, 115–27,
    127n.1, 128n.8–9, 129n.22,
    129n.26–7, 130n.31, 171–90,
    193n.27, 193n.37, 194n.48,
    195n.93, 198, 200–4, 206–12,
    214n.21, 215n.29–30, 215n.36,
    216n.41, 219–21, 225–33, 235,
    237n.10, 239n.31, 239n.33,
    246–54, 256, 258n.30,
    258n.33–4, 269, 282n.32,
    285n.75, 289, 292, 301,
    305n.33
  factor 248, 256
  role in terrorist activities 212
  Type-041 submarines of 97
PAROS *see* prevention of an arms race
    in outer space
Parpiani, Kashish 37n.23, 209, 216n.45
Pasha, Ahmed Shuja 253
Patel, Sardar Vallabhai 243
People's Liberation Army xi, 103–4,
    244–5, 252
  PLA Rocket Force 101
People's Liberation Army Navy xi, 226,
    233, 238n.25–6
People's Republic of China *see* China
PLA *see* People's Liberation Army
PLAN *see* People's Liberation Army
    Navy
Polar Satellite Launch Vehicle 150n.46,
    157, 162–4, 165n.4, 167n.13,
    168n.42
Poseidon P-8 aircraft 263, 268, 270
Predator-B 48, 233
prevention of an arms race in outer
    space 140–1
Project NETRA 137, 138, 149n.14
PSLV *see* Polar Satellite Launch Vehicle

Quad *see* Quadrilateral Security
    Dialogue
Quadrilateral Security Dialogue 29–30,
    36n.21, 37n.22, 54, 58n.37,
    60n.61, 66, 124, 130n.37, 220,
    232, 236n.3, 239n.32, 256

Rafale fighters 285n.75, 291
Rai, Ranjit 234, 241n.56
Rajagopalan, Rajeswari Pillai vi, x,
    37n.24, 130n.39, 151, 165n.1,
    208–9, 216n.44
Raman, B. 246, 258n.23, 258n.29
RAN *see* Royal Australian Navy
ransomware 81, 89n.17
Rao, Narasimha 247
RAW *see* Research and Analysis Wing
Reddy, T. G. Sanjeevi 243, 245
Research and Analysis Wing 103, 105,
    113n.56, 129n.20, 206, 222,
    236n.7, 237n.10, 259n.50
Roosevelt, Franklin D. 243
Royal Australian Navy 234
Royal Navy (United Kingdom) 234
Royal New Zealand Navy 234–5

S-400 missile system 2, 7, 26, 41–2,
    50, 55, 56n.10–11, 65, 74n.18,
    75n.28, 221, 271–2, 283n.40,
    283n.42–3, 283n.45, 297
Saeed, Hafiz Muhammad 204
sanctions 8, 41–2, 50, 55, 56n.9,
    56n.11, 65, 84, 153, 162,
    164–5, 182–3, 190, 200, 207–9,
    212, 221, 248, 251, 283n.43
SDGT *see* Specially Designated Global
    Terrorist
sea lines of communication 53, 219,
    224–5, 232
Secret Intelligence Service 254
Shah, Zarrar 252
Shrivastava, Manoj 222, 237n.10
SIGINT *see* signals intelligence
signals intelligence 73, 229–30, 232–3
Singh 5, 35n.4, 57n.28, 58n.38,
    59n.45, 110n.27, 129n.24,
    130n.39, 153, 158, 213n.12,
    290–1, 295
  Rabinder 250–1, 259n.50
  Rajnath 96, 109n.15, 285n.69,
    305n.33
Sino-Indian war 114n.74, 243–4
SIS *see* Secret Intelligence Service
SLBM *see* submarine-launched ballistic
    missile
SLOC *see* sea lines of communication
Small Satellite Launch Vehicle 157,
    164, 166n.16–17
Snowden, Edward 252
Sony Hack 81, 89n.16

South Asia Terrorism Portal 210, 216n.47–8
South China Sea 44, 46–7, 51, 58n.32, 66, 225–6, 234
Soviet Union, the 142, 153, 162, 198, 248,
space x, 7, 10, 12, 85, 99, 120, 125–7, 133, 135–47, 147n.1–8, 148n.9, 148n.11, 148n.13, 148n.23, 149n.24, 149n.29–31, 150n.48, 151–65, 165n.1, 165n.4, 165n.8–10, 166n.12, 166n.16, 166n.19–20, 166n.23, 167n.25–6, 167n.28–30, 167n.33, 167n.35, 168n.36–8, 168n.42, 171, 181, 192n.19, 220, 234, 236, 240n.49, 256, 292
  debris 141
  governance 140–1, 151
  presidential directive 136
  security 12, 135, 137–41, 146, 151, 153–4, 159–61, 164
  situational awareness 12, 135, 137, 159
  weapons 139, 143
SPD *see* space, presidential directive
Specially Designated Global Terrorist xi, 199, 204, 207–8
Special 301 priority watch list 64
Special Frontier Force 245
special operations 231–2, 240n.46, 244, 246, 248
Spratly Islands, the 226
Sri Lanka Easter bombings (2019) 52
SSF *see* Special Frontier Force
SSLV *see* Small Satellite Launch Vehicle
Strait
  of Hormuz 225
  of Malacca 225
STRATCOM *see* United States, Strategic Command
strategic autonomy 3, 42–3, 49, 51–2, 190, 220–1, 236n.6
Strategic Forces Command 105
string of pearls 29, 225
submarine-launched ballistic missile 95, 98, 111n.31–2
surveillance 26, 32, 60n.63, 177, 203, 229, 231–4, 237n.12, 252, 255–7, 263–4, 268–70, 274–5, 291, 300

tactical intelligence 219, 228, 233, 246
Tallinn Manual 85
Tata Global Systems 264
transparency and confidence building measures (TCBMs) 140–1
Tejas 291, 298, 304n.14
Tenet, George 251
Terminal High Altitude Area Defense 271
terrorism xi, 1, 3, 12–13, 19, 52, 60n.60–1, 120, 122–3, 125, 131n.41, 131n.43, 171–3, 176, 177, 180–1, 184, 188, 191, 192n.12, 192n.24, 194n.65, 195n.79, 195n.86, 197–207, 210–12, 213n.3, 213n.5–6, 213n.8–9, 213n.11, 214n.14, 214n.26, 216n.43–4, 216n.47, 216n.48, 222–3, 226, 237n.15, 237n.17–18, 248, 251, 257n.4, 260n.64
  definition of 199
  Indian response to 129n.6, 175, 186
  Khalistani 198–9, 201
  legal response to 186
  as Pakistani strategy 115–18, 126–7, 128n.8
  state sponsors of 176, 184–5, 212
terrorist xi, 4, 6, 8, 90n.28, 119, 123, 126, 130n.32, 174–5, 179, 188, 193n.41, 198–204, 207–12, 212n.1, 213n.4–6, 214n.22, 215n.27, 215n.29, 216n.47–8, 229, 231, 237n.11–12, 239n.31, 251
  attacks 13, 41, 117, 121–3, 171–2, 185, 187, 197, 198, 201, 222–3, 232
  1993 Mumbai attacks 248
  2008 Mumbai attacks 232
  groups 1, 4, 6, 120–3, 125, 176, 179, 183, 185, 190, 193n.37, 198, 205–6, 221
  proxies 6, 206
Terrorist Screening Center 206
THAAD *see* Terminal High Altitude Area Defense
Tibet 101, 224, 244–5, 257n.12, 258n.16–17
Tiger Triumph *see* Exercise Tiger Triumph
Tillerson, Rex 65, 74n.2
TNW *see* tactical nuclear weapons

Treaty on the Prevention of the Placement of Weapons in Outer Space, the Threat or Use of Force against Outer Space Objects 139
Trump, Donald J. 136
TSC *see* Terrorist Screening Center

U-2 spying missions 245
UAPA *see* Unlawful Activities (Prevention) Act of 1967
UAV *see* unmanned aerial vehicle
UNCD *see* UN Conference on Disarmament
UNCOPUOS *see* UN Committee for the Peaceful Uses of Outer Space
UNDC *see* UN Disarmament Commission
UNGA *see* United Nations General Assembly
United Kingdom 73, 82, 230
United Nations General Assembly 140
United States, the 36n.7, 47, 55n.3–4, 56n.6
   2016 presidential election of 84
   2017 National Security Strategy 225
   Aegis area defense system of 271
   Africa Command 44
   Air Force 25, 35, 49, 59n.47, 102, 112n.51–2, 232, 267
   Army ix, 23–4, 27, 36n.18, 48–9, 86, 187, 231–2, 236n.4, 279, 279n.1
   Central Command 44, 48, 212
   Coast Guard 24
   Cyber Command 86, 91n.44, 105
   Defense Security and Cooperation Agency of 273
   F-16 fighter of 51, 264, 277, 280n.7, 285n.72–3, 285n.75, 305n.34
   F-21 fighter of 277, 280n.7, 285n.70–1, 286n.74–5
   F-35 fighter of 26, 104, 234, 277–8
   Indo-Pacific Command 41, 35n.2
   Marine Corps 20, 25, 33, 86, 234
   National Guard 24
   National Strategy for Counterterrorism of 2018 200, 213n.7
   Navy vii, 28–30, *31*, 35, 50, 58n.44, 59n.52, 112n.51, 231, 232–5, 239n.36
      SEALs / Sea, Air, and Land Teams 231–2
   Nuclear Posture Review (2018) 95, 108n.5
   Patriot Advanced Capability-II air and missile defense system of 105
   Patriot-III air and ballistic missile defense system of 270
   Space Command 136, 147n.7
   Space Force 136
   Special Operations Command 231, 232
   State Department 56n.8, 74n.2, 76n.39, 108n.2, 111n.31, 138, 143, 162, 247, 264, 280n.10
   Strategic Command 105, 137, 138, 148n.9
United States–Russia
   Intermediate-Range Nuclear Forces Treaty 95
   New START treaty 97
Unlawful Activities (Prevention) Act of 199, 211, 213n.4
unmanned aerial vehicle 233, 274
UN Committee for the Peaceful Uses of Outer Space 140
UN Conference on Disarmament 140–1
UN Disarmament Commission 140–1

Vajpayee, Atal Bihari 38, 55n.1, 109n.15, 130n.30, 202
Virginia Class submarine 235
Visa H-1B 67

WannaCry 81, 89n.17

Xi Jinping 226

Yudh Abhyas see Exercise *Yudh Abhyas*

EU authorised representative for GPSR:
Easy Access System Europe, Mustamäe tee 50,
10621 Tallinn, Estonia
gpsr.requests@easproject.com

www.ingramcontent.com/pod-product-compliance
Lightning Source LLC
Chambersburg PA
CBHW071401300426